The Cold War Comes to Main Street

The Cold War Comes to Main Street

America in 1950

Lisle A. Rose

UNIVERSITY PRESS OF KANSAS

©1999 by the University Press of Kansas

Published by the University Press of Kansas (Lawrence, Kansas 66049),
which was organized by the Kansas Board of Regents and is operated and
funded by Emporia State University, Fort Hays State University, Kansas State
University, Pittsburg State University, the University of Kansas, and
Wichita State University

Library of Congress Cataloging in Publication Data

Rose, Lisle Abbott, 1936–

The Cold War comes to Main Street : America in 1950 / Lisle A. Rose.

p.   cm.

Includes bibliographical references and index.

ISBN 0-7006-0928-8 (cloth : alk. paper)

1. United States—History—1945–1953.   2. United States—Politics and
government—1945–1953.   3. United States—Social life and customs—
1945–1970.   4. Cold War—Social aspects—United States.
I. Title.

E813.R56   1999

973.918—dc21   98-24677

British Library Cataloguing in Publication Data is available.

Printed in the United States of America

10 9 8 7 6 5 4 3 2 1

The paper used in this publication meets the minimum requirements
of the American National Standard for Permanence of Paper for
Printed Library Materials Z39.48-1984.

In memory of Maribeth
My gentle lady with the mighty heart

Contents

❖ ❖ ❖ ❖ ❖ ❖ ❖

Acknowledgments

❖   ❖   ❖   ❖   ❖   ❖   ❖

The research for this project was conducted at the Suzzallo Library, University of Washington, Seattle, and the Harry S. Truman Library, Independence, Missouri. The staffs of both institutions are as helpful to private researchers as to professional scholars. My return to the Truman Library research room after an absence of nearly thirty years was especially pleasurable. Dennis Bilger steered me to collections that I might have overlooked. Several conversations with Elizabeth Safly on the life and times of Harry Truman and related subjects enriched my understanding of 1950 and its critical importance in shaping the country's postwar mood and policies. James Zobel of the MacArthur Memorial Archives in Norfolk, Virginia, provided me with key sources at just the right moment in the writing process.

I am deeply grateful to Michael Briggs of the University Press of Kansas, who agreed to consider the manuscript, looked at it favorably but critically, and steered it through a rigorous academic review process that improved it at many points. Richard Kirkendall's kind invitation a decade ago to write the essay on the cold war for the *Harry S. Truman Encyclopedia* rekindled my interest in assessing the impact of cold war tensions and policies on the life of Main Street America. My understanding of the dynamics of international diplomacy in the cold war era was intially shaped by David Mabon, Harriet Schwar, Louis Smith, Edward Keefer, and Nina Noring of the Historical Office, U.S. Department of State. Numerous colleagues throughout the international diplomatic community completed my education. I am especially indebted to Yuri Zurabov and Konstantin Ivanov, Soviet delegates to the COSPAS–SARSAT meetings in 1986–88, for their friendship and frankness during often grueling but ultimately rewarding negotiating sessions. I also profited immeasurably from a tragically shortened association with the late Robert E. Osgood, Dean of the Johns Hopkins School of Advanced International Studies and occasional member of the State Department's Policy Planning Staff. Bob was the embodiment of the scholar-activist, a man who was both engaged and reflective. He served the country and the academic community with unfailing grace and distinction, and he has been greatly missed. All of these professionals have contributed to whatever strengths this book may possess; none are in any way responsible for whatever errors of fact or interpretation may remain.

Finally, my wife Maribeth once again edited an entire manuscript with her usual skill and eye for grammatical absurdities and murky prose. Her sudden death as the manuscript went to press has left a void that cannot be filled.

Introduction

❖　❖　❖　❖　❖　❖　❖

Just as the first half of the twentieth century in America was characterized by general confidence and progressive reform, so the American people in the decades since midcentury have been stricken by a profound, embittered malaise. We have come to live in an age of dissent, convinced that little or nothing works right anymore, that we neither can nor should trust our neighbors, our workplace colleagues, our sources of information, or our institutions and leadership.

An elegiac tone has crept into our recollections of the time just before midcentury, a tone reminiscent of the post-1918 memories of Europeans and Englishmen about the ostensibly carefree, confident years just before the Great War. In the late seventies, journalist-historian Joseph Goulden collected a series of almost giddy reminiscences about the immediate postwar era. Unlike the disillusioned veterans of the Great War, the young men who came back from the battlefields of Europe and the Pacific in 1945 were filled with optimism. They had battled for human decency and, in the process, had unwittingly made their country the guardian and standard-bearer of Western Civilization. They were convinced that they had laid the foundations for a better world for themselves and all mankind. They were anxious to resume civilian lives, to become rich in a nation that had suddenly become prosperous beyond the wildest imaginings of a depression-era generation. Harold Russell, perhaps the most celebrated veteran of the time, summed it up for Goulden. The late forties were "a great period for our country, and you had a tremendous feeling just being alive. . . . We had problems, sure, but they didn't dominate us; we face the same things now, and we despair." Several years later, a South Dakotan confirmed to oral historian Studs Terkel that as late as 1949 "the American myth was alive. . . . Remember the '49 cars in the *National Geographic*? Postwar cars. New design, new body style. In the colored Sunday funnies there'd be ads for the new cars. We'd been driving Grandpa Herman's old prewar Chrysler. It was the only car on the block. Now everybody was getting a car. Oh, it was exciting."[1]

Whatever one's views of a particular individual or political party, there remained a basic trust in the public order, a legacy of the desperate years of the Great Depression and World War II that had brought about the New Deal and the "Roosevelt revolution." The system and the men who ran it in the early postwar era seemed to possess "a sense of the atmosphere of the American tradition. That sort of atmosphere was pervasive and a part of men's feelings for America in the [eighteen] eighties and nineties and 1900s when [President] Truman was growing up." Max Lowenthal, a civil libertarian who had become acquainted with Truman during the latter's investigations into railroad finances in the midthirties, emphasized that the tradition had its foundation in the towns and countryside of the Middle West, where both he and the president had grown up. "While there was much economic injustice at the time, there was a quality of freedom—an absence of any aspect whatever of the modern police state—that some of the younger generation today may not know of except in a limited way through their reading." Jonathan Daniels, one of Truman's first and by no means always sympathetic biographers, quoted an "old liberal" in 1946 who spoke along the same lines.

> Nothing is more important than the grasp of fundamental American principles shared by such liberals as Truman and old-time conservatives, too. I think we find it in Truman, not because he is for liberalism in economic matters, but because he senses the spirit of the American political system. . . . It is an innate part of his personality to be fair and to know what is fair, and to exercise restraint when he possesses great power, particularly the power to investigate and detect, and the power to police.[2]

Then at midcentury—long before the domestic upheavals and foreign policy crises of the sixties—the mood of breezy, can-do confidence that was a legacy of World War II, the simplistic enjoyment of ever growing prosperity, freedom, and security, the belief in the essential fairness, restraint, and accessibility of government abruptly collapsed. "I think everybody still felt good about the war in '47, '48, '49," Robert Lekachman remembered. The former army typist turned eminent economist wondered whether Truman could have committed troops to Korea in June of 1950 without formal congressional authority if there had not been "the lingering romance of the Second World War. . . . I think things began to sour and innocence end in, say, 1952 and 1953, as the Korean War dragged on."[3] Lekachman was off by only a year or two. By the end of 1950 the mood of the country had already plummeted dramatically.

The nature and intensity of the collapse went far beyond what might have been expected in a republic proud of its civility and reasonably confident of its values and its institutions. The sudden loss of confidence, hope, and direction was barely concealed by the prosperity of the Eisenhower years. By the time that Kennedy's New Frontier was cut short by an assassin's bullet, American politics was becoming savagely divided between the Right and the Left. By 1968 the estrangement of both fringes from the rapidly eroding liberal center was complete and permanent. Extremists on both sides expressed their politics through rage, violence, and ultimately outright terrorism. The Weathermen of the late sixties were replicated by such right-wing paramilitary organizations as the Minutemen, the Paul Revere Yeomen, and the Counter-Insurgency Council, who live on today in the various militia groups that dot the countryside from Florida to Michigan to the Pacific Northwest. Diana Oughton, Cathy Wilkerson, and Kathy Boudin have now been joined by Tim McVeigh. What went wrong half a century ago, and how did it happen?

No explanation based on human reason alone will suffice. We must go bottom fishing in the frequently troubled waters of American politics, seeking out those fantasies—and fantasizers—that have so often exercised enormous influence on the political culture. As historian Robert Kelley wrote two decades ago, the wars and mass hysterias through which twentieth-century man has had to pass "have given us a far more complex view of human nature. Entire regions of feeling and passion hitherto ignored have been opened to us. We now understand that the energies which release themselves in public life are emotional as well as rational, cultural and ideological as well as economic and pragmatic."[4]

But before confronting those passions and their sinister effect on mid- and late-twentieth-century American life, it is necessary to correct some long-held impressions about recent world and national history. According to conventional wisdom, a cluster of early postwar tensions and crises over Eastern Europe, Berlin, the Dardanelles, northern Iran (Azerbaijan), and to a much lesser extent northeastern Asia and Japan ushered in what Walter Lippmann in 1947 dubbed the cold war.[5] Thereafter another set of crises— the division of Germany and Allied access to Berlin; Soviet threats to Greece and Turkey; the communist coup in Czechoslovakia; the economic, political, and military reconstruction of Europe (including the formation of NATO); the "fall" of China to an agrarian brand of communism; and Soviet acquisition of nuclear weapons—completed the rigid division of the international community into communist and "free" camps, which were defined, as the nuclear arms race proceeded, by a balance of terror based on mutual assured destruction. Only later would bipolarity be challenged by the rise of the Third World, led initially by India and Egypt.

This is a familiar story reflected in and buttressed by an extensive scholarly literature. But if we listen carefully to what the American people of 1949 and 1950 are telling us, it obviously requires substantial modification. When one compares what the national press was saying and reporting during Christmas week 1949 with what it said and reported a year later, it is clear that the enormous change in the American temperament, generally assumed to have taken place at the outset of the cold war in 1946–47, actually occurred several years later.

If one believes contemporary polls, the cold war emerged slowly in the American consciousness. As early as the late spring of 1946, a substantial majority of Americans had come to disapprove of Soviet foreign policy, and 58 percent of those queried believed that the Kremlin desired to dominate the globe. But even in a world of nuclear weapons such conclusions did not translate into immediate anxieties. In January of 1947, only 22 percent of those asked believed that a U.S. city would be A-bombed within the next decade. By the autumn of that year, the mood had turned more somber after the collapse of several foreign ministers' conferences and enunciation of the Truman Doctrine and the Marshall Plan. A slim majority of those queried (48 percent versus 42 percent) believed that the United States would fight another war within a decade. But in light of subsequent events, the question was poorly worded, because it did not specify whether such a war would be a major or a minor conflict—a world war or, as in Korea, a "police action." By July 1948, with the recent communist coup in Czechoslovakia fresh in public memory and the crisis in Berlin building toward Soviet closure of access to the city and the initiation of an Allied airlift, 67 percent of those queried believed the nation would be engaged in a war within ten years; 24 percent disagreed. But by August 1949, the mood had calmed again. Half of those queried thought another war might come within twenty-five years, but nearly the same percentage disagreed. Moreover, the attitude of college-educated persons was more optimistic than that of high-school or grade-school graduates. Only 45 percent of college-educated people polled believed another war was "likely"; 49 percent said no. Those with a high-school education were basically split (49 percent versus 42 percent) on the question. Only those with a grade-school education were overwhelmingly convinced that the nation would have to fight a war some time in the next quarter century.[6] Moreover, Americans were confident that they could and should be firm with the Soviets. In a poll conducted just three days after Truman's astounding 1948 victory over Dewey, 73 percent of Republicans and 70 percent of Democrats agreed that the United States was "too . . . soft in its policy toward Russia."[7]

The public temperament at the end of 1949, although far from buoyant, thus remained cautiously optimistic. The warm recollections of later years, seen through the golden haze of nostalgia, really did reflect the era. Soviet Communism was a grave menace; no one doubted or denied it. Some Americans were obsessed by it. But no American boys were being sent into battle against communist armies, Western Europe was slowly gaining sufficient strength to oppose whatever political-military pressures Stalin might exert against it, and the implications of China's fall to communism were not yet clear (indeed, it was uncertain whether Mao and his cohorts were really communists in the strict sense of the term). The United States seemed comfortably ahead of the Soviets in nuclear weapons, and as for Commies at home, well, there certainly were or had been some in the labor movement, a few in government, and maybe a lot in Hollywood, though the studios by 1948–49 were issuing a flood of anticommunist films. By and large the often strident, melodramatic hunt for ostensible Red moles remained on the fringes of national life, although the Hiss case attracted widespread notice because it promised to either make or break the issue. The early postwar crises with the Kremlin, however portentous they were to presidents, diplomats, soldiers, senators, a handful of media czars, and especially to writers and intellectuals (who had been fiercely debating the merits and demerits of Marxism for a generation), remained rather distant abstractions to most Americans. While his GI sons (and a few GI daughters) were finishing their postwar college degrees, John Q. Public was reluctantly continuing to pay his taxes to rebuild Europe and even Japan, was diligently reading the newspapers to keep up on world events that a decade and a half before he or many of his fellow citizens would have assiduously ignored, and was worrying vaguely about what "the Russians" were doing in Europe and elsewhere. But the country was prosperous (though for how long scarred veterans of the depression decade were unwilling to say), the traditional sense of relative safety, of an era of free security, remained unchallenged.

One year later the United States had become another country. The wealthiest business executive, the modest white-collar worker, the commonest farmer, and the most unskilled laborer shared an obsessive fear of communist subversion. They were terrified that the Soviet Union, through its sleepless moles, had raced far ahead in the quest for the thermonuclear doomsday device; above all they were sickened by the shameful rout and killing of their boys by communist boys on a distant Asian battlefield. More than security fled American life in the tumultuous midcentury year. Hope, trust, and the last tendrils of wartime unity also were gone, to be replaced by anger, suspicion, division, and a dogged rather than sanguine determination to protect the republic somehow in some way regardless of the cost. The five-year confrontation between Washington and Moscow was no longer a mere cold war over the future of Germany and Eastern Europe. The new, much warmer global contest between the communist and noncommunist worlds, arising from Korea and the bomb, was more dangerous and stressful than we have let ourselves remember.

The thermonuclear weapon and the conflict in Asia served as dramatic bookends to the emergence of McCarthyism: what one contemporary defined as a blend of " 'the big lie,' of the furtive informer, of the character assassin, of inquisition, eavesdropping, smear and distrust."[8] By the end of 1950, McCarthy and his small but strident band of political and religious zealots had established a tone, a temper, a habit of thought, an expectation of impending calamity, and an assumption of outright treason within our public institutions that has shaped and debilitated national life to the present.

When I was a kid sailor in the navy in the midfifties, there was an evil-tempered boatswain's mate on my first ship who habitually and colorfully damned the service. One day I mustered the courage to ask him why he hadn't left after his first enlistment if he hated it so. "Truman's Year," he replied sourly. "I was about to get out when Korea came, and Harry kept us all in an extra twelve months to fight the Commies. By the time they were ready to let me go, I'd been in so long I decided to stay for twenty and then find snug harbor." It took me many years to realize that at midcentury all Americans were condemned to Truman's year and that they have yet to find snug harbor.

1

Liberals

❖ ❖ ❖ ❖ ❖ ❖ ❖ ❖ ❖ ❖ ❖ ❖ ❖ ❖ ❖

On the last day of 1949, media king Henry Luce plucked Mr. Junius Shaw of St. Louis, Missouri, out of obscurity and proclaimed him the typical American of the first half of the twentieth century, a man to whom typical things had happened. Shaw had come into the world a few seconds after midnight on January 1, 1901. He had gotten married at about the same age (twenty-one) as everyone else in his generation. During Prohibition he had been blind drunk on bathtub gin, suffering a case of lockjaw, which he cured when, on advice from a friend, he sucked on four aspirin tablets washed down with sips of the hottest water he could find. Like millions of others in the early thirties, Shaw had lost his job, divorced, and gone broke. He made a comeback in 1935, starting out as a $30-a-week-plus-commission salesman with the Gates Rubber Company. His sales boomed during World War II, and he promptly resigned from Gates to start his own auto parts store. He bought a car in 1946 and by 1949 did $160,000 worth of business each year and lived in an upscale St. Louis suburb in a house with "every modern luxury including television."[1]

According to the *Life* writer who profiled Shaw's career, it was difficult to hear the man tell his story without experiencing an eerie feeling that not one American was talking but millions. Shaw and the country had plunged from the heights of early twentieth-century prosperity to the depths of personal and collective despair, then had pulled themselves up again to whip a crippling economic depression, win a world war, and enjoy a steadily enriching if increasingly uneasy peace. Shaw was thus a social prototype: He was like a familiar face that constantly reappeared in a crowd; he was Mr. Mainstream.

❖   ❖   ❖

As midcentury approached, it seemed to many that Shaw and his fellow citizens owed much if not all of their good fortune to the new political order
called liberalism. The United States had been founded on the principle that
men were often corrupt and that government was inherently so. The Founding Fathers had framed the Constitution so that it would prevent any major
political action that was not acceptable to most of the citizenry. The psychological contract that Washington, Jefferson, and Madison had concluded
had endured for nearly 150 years. The American people revered their
national institutions and those like Jackson, Lincoln, and Teddy Roosevelt
who protected and promoted them. But they had little patience or respect
for the average, run-of-the-mill politician or civil servant.

The Great Depression changed all that. The middle class was both hum-
bled and frightened by economic disaster, and Franklin Roosevelt and his
bureaucrats were able to institute a new psychological contract. Government was no longer the enemy of the people, it *was* the people. Roosevelt
convinced a basically conservative country that unprecedented hard times
demanded practical and continual reform based on a sense of national community. He used a formerly limited federal government possessed of limited funds to put Americans back to work, guarantee their farms and a
minimum wage for their labors, and provide public electrical power for
their homes and money for their old age. Washington created an unprecedented balance between capital and labor, built model cities and huge dams,
restored ravaged landscapes, soaked the rich with heavy taxes, and seemed
blithely unconcerned about the social and political costs of it all. Roosevelt
and his hot-eyed reformers told the "little people" again and again that the
country and the federal government were theirs, and the people responded
with enthusiasm and even adoration. New Dealers argued that public welfare was a right during hard times and collective bargaining was a right at
all times. They denounced "government by organized money" and the arrogant "economic royalists" who fought every effort at broad-scale economic
recovery.

Roosevelt's closest confidant, Harry Hopkins, defined modern American
liberalism most clearly and forcefully in off-the-cuff remarks at his alma
mater, Grinnell College, in 1939. He had been in public service for nearly
thirty years, Hopkins told the students and faculty, and he had seen government both succeed and fail. The lesson that he had learned was that

when the people ignored or condemned government, the selfish interests—privately owned public utilities, the railroads, industrial barons, the Wall Street crowd—came in and took over.

> This government is ours whether it be local, county, State, or Federal. It doesn't belong to anybody but the people of America. Don't treat it as an impersonal thing; don't treat it as something to sneer at; treat it as something that belongs to you. I don't care how much you criticize it, or to what Party you belong, just remember that this government belongs to you, and needs you, and it is going to take brains and skill to run it in the future.

There was no way, Hopkins said, for the United States to continue as a viable political system with millions unemployed or mired in poverty. "It just can't be done. We have got to find a way of living in America in which every person in it shares in the national income, in such a way, that poverty in America is abolished." After years of serving the comfortable classes, the government in Washington had become a caring government. "I have lived to see the time when the Government of the United States worries about how much a farmer gets for his corn, wheat, or cotton. I have lived to see the time when a farmer gets a check signed by the Treasurer of the United States for doing something. I see old people getting pensions; see unemployed people getting checks from the United States Government; college students getting checks signed by the United States Government."[2]

World War II and its aftermath expanded American liberalism from an impulse for domestic reform to an international movement of reconstruction and, in the process, brought the Democratic Party directly into conflict with the Communist Party for control of the shattered postwar world. By Christmas week 1949, pundits and professors surveying the national and international scenes found much to applaud.

"World War II was, in some ways, *our* finest hour," historian Allan Nevins proclaimed. The war made the United States indisputably the last, best hope of democratic mankind. The country regained the sense of social adventure, of constant renewal, of confident response to great challenge that had marked its birth and development but had been lost in the early years of the Great Depression. Never was the bold, pragmatic experimentalism of the nation more dramatically decisive than during the long, terrible months between Pearl Harbor and Hiroshima, when American industrial production triumphed over Nazi and Japanese barbarism and brought a rebirth of prosperity at home.³ In the four and a half years after V-J Day, industrial production was directed not only toward global reconstruction but also to the satisfaction of long-suppressed civilian needs. The United States prospered as no country ever had. Two million farm families in southern Appalachia continued to live anonymously in shocking squalor "not surpassed in any country west of Turkey." Slum dwellers and probably a majority of the black population lived badly and had few prospects for advancement. Those few whose salaries or pensions doomed them to permanently fixed incomes experienced anxiety for the future. "Elsewhere, there was little hardship." Visible America was wealthier than it had ever been, and private enterprise had recovered much of the respect and prestige it had lost during the thirties.⁴

Somehow, out of the twin ordeals of depression and war, the American people had transformed their nineteenth-century pioneering spirit of physical adventure and expansion into a twentieth-century social, economic, and political miracle. Between 1900 and 1949, real wages more than doubled, and the work week was reduced from fifty-eight to forty hours. Nearly every family owned an automobile, a radio, and a telephone, products that in Teddy Roosevelt's day had been scarcely conceived or were the playthings of the very rich. The divided turn-of-the-century nation, whose smug ruling elite was preoccupied with China trade and the suppression of a minor rebellion in the far-off Philippines, had become a global dynamo whose restorative reach extended into remote Asian villages and into every neighborhood of every Western European city. Americans had become mature and worldly wise, Nevins maintained. They were too smart to depend for either personal comfort or personal redemption on any single authority, whether big business or big government. They were neither optimistic nor pessimistic; they knew only "the chilling, neutral, almost emotionless sense of awful responsibility and its ruthless compulsion." How could people worry about the possibility of another depression when they were busy helping to finance, feed, and arm the democratic world? All the average American knew was that there simply could not be another depression. The country and the world could not endure it or its inevitable aftermath: World War III.⁵

After seventeen years of nearly uninterrupted power, liberals had developed a formula for national progress and welfare. Full employment was essential to steadily rising living standards at home and abroad, and only federal laws and regulations could guarantee it. Better health, housing, and education all relied on a booming, productive economy. But "to burden private enterprise with the responsibility for maintaining full employment is to destroy private enterprise." When the Morgans, Carnegies, Rockefellers, and other captains of industry (or robber barons) had been left alone with that responsibility, the result had been "peaks of inflation and . . . pits of depression." Thus, "to deny democratic government the responsibility" for managing the economy "is to destroy democracy. We need the dynamic force of competitive enterprise to raise productivity. We need the dynamic force of government to expand purchasing power, to raise standards of welfare, and to develop our resources." Government and enterprise had to work together. Business would produce the goods. Washington, through spending and welfare policies, would provide the mass purchasing power required to buy those goods.[6]

It all seemed to work. Those who lived through the late forties would always recall them with the warm glow of nostalgia. These were years when developer William J. Levitt and a host of imitators across the country first put young America into cheap but serviceable and well-made housing. Using a government home loan or a mortgage guarantee, a youngster who had grown up in fetid urban tenements and teeming city streets and expected to die there suddenly found himself the owner of a patch of suburban green with a touch of blue sky above. An entire generation took snapshots of young mom and dad with a small child standing proudly in front of their "starter home" and their first car, peering into the future with hope. In less than half a decade, Washington, together with Levitt and his colleagues, transformed a country of urban renters into a nation of suburban property owners. Here was the liberal formula working at its best.

These were also the years when an exciting new toy called television first began to invade the American living room. On Christmas Eve 1949, AT&T completed a $12-million network of thirty-one relay stations between New York and Chicago. Soon the three million people who had bought sets the previous year would have another channel to watch, although cumbersome coaxial cables continued to limit decent reception to the immediate environs of the big eastern and middle western cities. Out in the heartland and throughout most of the South and West, people still listened to rather than watched the news, the soap operas, and the football games. Business corporations spent their advertising dollars accordingly. The Hotpoint Corporation lavishly advertised its Radio Holiday Hour from five to six o'clock on Christmas evening. Jack Benny, Dorothy McGuire, Charles Boyer, Gregory Peck, Gene Kelly, Rosalind Russell, and Henry Fonda would star in a brief dramatization of George S. Kaufman and Moss Hart's comedy, "The Man Who Came to Dinner." Hotpoint boasted that the program would showcase the most brilliant group of stage, screen, and radio stars ever assembled.

While radio provided Americans with the audio dimension of their lives, great urban newspapers, newspaper chains, and weekly news and feature magazines provided the visual dimension. The print media were dominated by a remarkable group of barons—Luce, William Randolph Hearst, Col. Robert McCormick, Roy Howard, and others—who did and wrote as they pleased, stamping their prejudices on the daily and weekly editions of their publications and on the lives of their often fervently loyal readers. There was a peculiar inbreeding among the more conservative, wealthy, and successful publishers. McCormick, whose *Chicago Tribune* had the second highest daily circulation in the country, was a cousin of Capt. Joseph Medill Patterson, whose *New York Daily News* claimed first place, and of Eleanor (Cissy) Patterson, who in the early war years had bought the *Washington Times-Herald,* partly to have something to do, partly to make a splash in Washington society, but mainly to vent her spleen against Franklin Roosevelt and the New Deal.

Luce came closest to dominating and shaping the national dialogue and perspective. With his mass circulation news and business weeklies, *Life, Time,* and *Fortune,* and his often hokey newsreel, *The March of Time,* Luce had been the country's preeminent tutor in public affairs since at least the midthirties. Other aggressive media moguls had their own constituencies. The well-read, well-hated, and generally moderate members of America's eastern political establishment, both Democrats and Republicans, relied on Arthur Hays Sulzberger's *New York Times* and the *Washington Post.* McCormick's *Tribune* led numerous other publications, such as the *Omaha World-Herald,* much of the southern press, and magazines like the *Reader's Digest* in espousing a frequently rabid opposition to every thought, policy, bill, and bureaucrat in Washington. J. Edgar Hoover and the FBI, however, were a singular exception. Hoover's muscular anticommunism and drive for personal control over internal security matters brought him into frequent conflict with the liberal establishment in and beyond the nation's capital and made him the darling of the conservative press, which was convinced that everyone in Washington was a "Communist stooge." Hoover often leaked files and rumors to such archconservative, hyperpatriotic columnists and national radio personalities as Walter Winchell, Fulton Lewis, Jr., and George Sokolsky and such leading journalists as the Chicago *Tribune*'s Walter Trohan and Frederic Woltman and Tony Smith of Roy Howard's Scripps-Howard chain.[7] Weekly magazines like the *Saturday Evening Post* and *Colliers* made their own generally conservative influence felt. *Newsweek* had long before joined *Time* as a reputable weekly journal of ongoing public commentary.

Hollywood made its own contributions. Studio films continued to dominate the entertainment industry, and on most days movie theaters in cities and towns across the country still showed double features along with a newsreel. The lasting popularity of war films suggested that the nation was still trying to work its way out of its recent and prolonged experience with separation, anguish, and death. In a review of the best pictures of 1949, well-known critic Bosley Crowther emphasized that serious subjects were portrayed on American screens. Four selections were about "members of the Negro race," and a common theme was the tension of light-skinned blacks trying to pass as whites in Caucasian communities and their constant fears of eventual discovery. The most popular of these films, *Pinky*, starred a young white actress, Jeanne Crain. Crowther observed that the recent spasm of anticommunist movies had subsided once the House Committee on Un-American Activities had at least temporarily suspended its hunt for Reds in the world movie capital. Certainly J. Edgar Hoover had become discouraged. At the height of the anticommunist cinema blitz in 1948, he had directed the FBI to cooperate closely with Twentieth Century Fox in producing *The Street with No Name*. But Hoover had been displeased with the result; he had not been able to control the final product and it had not been anticommunist enough, nor had the Bureau been given sufficient credit in leading the fight against the Red menace. When Assistant Director Louis Nichols pressed Hoover to assist MGM in making an anticommunist movie in 1949, the FBI Director refused.[8]

All but a handful of Americans still journeyed by train, bus, or automobile, and while the war and postwar crises were slowly knitting the country together, it still remained largely what it had always been, a nation of distinctive sections and regions. Except for the wealthy and adventurous few willing to risk transcontinental travel in small, noisy, vibrating, propeller-driven "airliners," New York and Los Angeles were still at least three days apart. Sex remained in the bedroom or between the pages of serious if shocking books by sober sociologists like Alfred Kinsey.[9]

All in all, early postwar life seemed easy and manageable compared to the dreary years of the thirties or the endlessly exciting but always sad days of the war. This was especially true for the war's twelve million young veterans. One ex-marine remembered "exquisite years of easy laughter and lovers' vows, whose promises lingered like the fragrance of incense burning in little golden vessels on the altars of the heart. To be young and uncrippled was to be unbelievably lucky; to marry was to give of oneself, an exchange of gifts that multiplied in joy."[10] College and university campuses were filled with hundreds of thousands of former warriors impatiently grinding out degrees under the GI Bill, living with their young families in Quonset huts or, if unmarried, stacked like cordwood with fellow veterans in makeshift living accommodations. Beyond the campuses, the country's great business corporations waited to welcome these young men and their wives to lives of middle-class ease inconceivable only a few years before. Not many young people looked forward to becoming conformist organization men, but depression, war, and incessant postwar crises had made them leery of risk. *Fortune* magazine discovered that the June 1949 college graduating classes were "taking no chances." Only 2 percent of the graduates planned to build businesses themselves. "The men of Forty-nine everywhere seem haunted by the fear of a recession. . . . 'I know AT&T might not be very exciting,' explains one senior, 'but there'll always be an AT&T.' "[11]

Not only had liberalism rescued the country from want, it was also busily restoring a world recently shattered by its own follies. Throughout 1949, the global outlook seemed to warrant a cautious optimism. If real peace was still far away, so apparently was the probability of another major war. When James Forrestal, the nation's first secretary of defense and a dedicated cold warrior, committed suicide in May because of chronic overwork and anxiety, he was mourned as a man driven by unrealistic demons and fantasies that had led him to "overestimate . . . the military needs for this Nation. In this respect he succumbed partly to military badgering for all that the traffic would bear, partly to an obsession that the Cold War was the prelude to a shooting war. This obsession became an *idée fixe* as time went by."[12]

In October, after the Russian atomic explosion and with the fall of China to communism imminent, Britain's influential weekly, the *Economist*, observed that "the likelihood of an immediate Soviet threat to peace is remote." In its Christmas issue, the *New York Times* reported "a more optimistic outlook than at Christmas 1948" in "both the Communist and non-

Communist spheres," adding that "the consensus in world capitals was that a general war was unlikely in the foreseeable future." George Gallup's poll for the *Washington Post* a week later was especially striking. Gallup concluded that "at this half-way point in the twentieth century, the majority of Americans appear confident of winning the 'battle of ideas' with Russia. They believe that by the time the present century is over, most nations of the world will have democratic forms of government, not communistic or socialistic." Only those with a college education tended to think that socialism, not democracy or communism, was the wave of the future. Gallup also found that most Americans believed that by the end of the century trains and planes would be run on atomic power; a cure for cancer would have been found; religion would have become more, not less important; and the power of stronger labor unions, along with steady technological progress, would have guaranteed everyone a thirty-hour work week.[13]

The unfolding of the cold war had forced Washington and the nation to embrace two fundamental postulates: first, that communism was a worldwide movement and threat directed squarely at the United States and its handful of Western allies by a few men in the Kremlin; second, that Soviet conventional military strength was so overpowering that the war-weakened West could never successfully confront the Russians on nonnuclear terms. "The USSR desires to achieve eventual control of both the European-Mediterranean area and the Far East," the CIA concluded in a top secret report of September 1949. When large parts of China had begun to fall to the communists the previous spring, the authors of another CIA report had stated that "it is the intention of the Soviet Union to advance toward its goal of eventual world domination by adding to the Soviet orbit the enormous territory and population of China, and by employing China to facilitate Soviet expansion into other Far Eastern areas."[14]

Because the Kremlin seemed to possess such overwhelming conventional military power, Washington concluded that a Soviet lunge toward the Rhine and the Channel could only be restrained by the threat of atomic bombing raids against Moscow, Leningrad, Kiev, and other Soviet urban, communication, and military centers. Only so long as the United States maintained a clear predominance in nuclear weapons would the world be safe from outright communist aggression.

Even Soviet possession of the bomb did not initially shake public optimism. The United States was so far ahead in research, development, and application of nuclear warfare that there seemed little cause for concern.

Protected by America's atomic shield, Europe was slowly, painfully rising from the ashes of war. In London that Christmas of 1949, Englishmen enjoyed a better season than the year before despite continual shortages, disheartening trade statistics, and the recent devaluation of the pound, undertaken at Washington's insistence. As in other European cities, the scars of war marred nearly every street in the city center and the dock area to the south. Still-ruined buildings and empty lots remained as mementos of Hermann Göring's bombing blitz of 1940–41 and the V-1 and V-2 rocket attacks of 1944. Britons of all classes, exhausted by the war, were dispirited by the even harsher privations and deadly squalor of a barren peace marked by a steady decline in overseas trade and the dramatic divestitures of empire. But Christmas trees were gayer and more numerous than in the four previous postwar years, and the city lights were brighter than at any time since the final prewar Christmas of 1938. Under Clement Attlee's Labor government, workers and farmers toiled doggedly to raise production, increase exports, and grow more food so that Britain would acquire sufficient dollars to be a major force again in a world market now dominated by Wall Street, Pittsburgh, and the farmlands of Illinois and Kansas.

Across the Channel, the French remembered with a shudder the previous holiday season with its rationing, climbing prices, and war scares during the Berlin airlift. Christmas 1949 was better. The Berlin crisis was over and so was rationing at last. Although inflation continued to plague the economy and wages were very low, the French had begun to enjoy a modest abundance. Children hoped for a merrier Christmas; their parents wished for a happier New Year. French intellectuals, unlike their sullen and depressed British colleagues, were ebullient and stimulated by challenging new ideas that had germinated during the bitter years of defeat and occupation. But vital signs remained disquieting. The inexpressible weariness of the war years, followed by the liberation with its charges and countercharges of collaboration with Nazism or surrender to communism, had left French politics drained and extraordinarily apathetic. On occasion communist organizers could not even bring their hundreds of thousands of supporters into the streets to demonstrate. General elections would undoubtedly be held in 1950, but at best they would solve nothing; at worst they would exacerbate historic and bitter differences in French society among Right, Left, and center, each of which was internally divided. From his Paris listening post, a *New York Times* reporter concluded that on the eve of midcentury the French wanted fun and enjoyment, not serious political activity.[15]

Down in Italy, the people seemed in a lighter mood. They were apparently more confident of themselves and their country than at any time since 1940. Roman shops overflowed with every variety of goods, and most people, especially those at the middle-income level, had more money in their pockets than the year before. Over in Belgrade, the tense mood of 1948, when Marshal Tito had broken with Stalin, had lifted. People grumbled about high prices and the scarcity of goods, but they no longer felt isolated. If the Red Army attempted to recapture Yugoslavia, the West in general and the United States, in particular, would surely intervene.

Berliners continued to struggle through hard times. The "city" around them remained largely miles and miles of dust and rubble on the north German plain nearly five years after the end of the war. Life was still grim. Berlin was no longer Germany's capital, and most people thought it probably never would be again; it had become instead a symbol of unnerving, unending East-West tensions. The year before, Berliners had huddled around stoves in frigid, drafty basements and bombed-out flats listening to the incessant roar of U.S. and British transport planes bringing essential supplies into the Soviet-blockaded city. Few men and women had seen any reason for hope. But the Germans were industrious if not optimistic. When Stalin lifted his blockade in August 1949, the western portion of the ancient city along the Spree slowly began to reemerge with Marshall Plan aid. The black market stalls around the Brandenburg Gate flourished. (In this pre-Wall era, they were freely accessible to both East and West Berliners and to Soviet and American occupation troops.) Hundreds of thousands of Russian soldiers, tanks, and warplanes still surrounded the American, British, and French sectors, but West Berliners were rebuilding bomb-shattered shops and reconstructing shell-torn apartment buildings. People dared to hope that the future might bring some measure of peace under American protection.

The hope was not as foolish as it might have been in earlier years. Partly as a result of ancient ethnic tugs but more especially because of recent shared experiences and sacrifices of war, many Americans were changing their minds about what had popularly been called (often derisively) the Old World. Despite its frustrating and apparently eternal rivalries and hatreds, Europe on the eve of midcentury seemed to be a place worth cherishing, worth defending, worth knowing, worth visiting.

Five years and a month after the Allied landings at Normandy, *Newsweek* magazine devoted its cover story to the new, peaceful American assault on

France. The newcomers were not soldiers but tourists, 160,000 strong, "the largest invasion since D-Day"; indeed, the biggest group of Americans to come to the Continent since 1930. Among the crowds of Yanks were a few descendants of those bumptious and naive young nineteenth-century nouveaux riches from Boston, Pittsburgh, and New York whose parents had more or less pushed them into making the grand tour of the Continent in search of culture and a titled mate. There was also undoubtedly a handful of expatriate artists and writers who yearned to emulate Hemingway, Dos Passos, Fitzgerald, and other disaffected members of an earlier veteran generation. But *Newsweek* reported that most of those who walked off the big transatlantic steamers at Le Havre or the few four-engine Pan Am "Clippers" at Orly after an exhausting twenty-hour flight from New York, Gander, and Shannon were middle-class tourists plus the usual teachers and students. They had paid large sums to cross the ocean. The days when one could spend a summer in Europe for a few hundred dollars, including travel fare, were long gone. A good cabin on one of the handful of postwar steamers cost nearly one thousand dollars; round-trip tickets on the Pan Am Clipper cost a minimum of $630.[16]

The noisy Americans, whose casual clothes and airs both antagonized and captivated the French, showed no inclination to visit recent battlefields. They wanted to see the usual attractions: Westminster Abbey in London, Notre Dame and the bright cafes and naughty theaters in Paris. With all its lingering shortages and devastations, Europe lured the adventurous, and more and more Americans agreed with their president and his secretary of state that the Continent had become, along with Japan, Formosa (Taiwan), and the Philippines half a world away, America's new defense line of freedom.

Nineteen forty-nine was a major turning point in postwar European history. Lucius Clay, military governor of the American zone in Germany, departed, to be replaced by a civilian high commissioner, John J. McCloy. McCloy had been the personal choice of Secretary of State Dean Acheson, an old friend. Acheson had been instrumental in transforming the 1948 Brussels Pact, Europe's first faint effort to defend itself against the Soviet military threat, into a North Atlantic Treaty Organization of limited strength but unlimited possibility. Washington left McCloy alone to rule West Germany as he saw fit, and the New York investment banker promptly began to work on two interrelated objectives. First, he insisted on treating the Germans decently and immediately gave them substantial powers of self-rule.

Second, he worked to overcome ancient national hatreds on the Continent. If Europeans could be induced to acknowledge common interests and needs and to work for common objectives, they could construct an economically sound political community as a permanent buffer against the Soviet Union.

Germany was the key. It had to be democratically reconstructed before any kind of unified Europe could be created. Germany was also essential to short-term American cold war policy. Its airfields provided the staging areas needed for any atomic blitz of Soviet cities by the short-range B-29 bombers, which still constituted America's strategic striking force (the huge, eight-motor, long-range B-36s were just coming into production; the jet-engine B-52 was still three years away). McCloy worked closely with Chancellor Konrad Adenauer to resurrect West Germany and with French statesman Jean Monnet, an old friend and law client, to break down historical enmities among the nations of the West. Monnet also dreamed of a United States of Europe, and in the spring of 1950, he and McCloy would collaborate to create the European Coal and Steel Community, which pooled the mining resources of previously bitter enemies France and Germany. McCloy hoped that the Community would be the first step (or perhaps second after NATO) toward a European integration that eventually would allow the United States to withdraw completely from Continental affairs. In fact, the opposite was true. The United States was becoming increasingly involved in European politics and economics. It was clear not only that Europe's reconstruction hinged on collaboration, not competition, but that American influence, if not American power, would be instrumental in that process.[17]

Across the Pacific in their own ruined cities, the Japanese were also determinedly optimistic. The Tokyo housewife going about her New Year's shopping, baby snuggled securely on her back, had more yen concealed in her multilayered winter kimono than she had possessed the year before. During 1949, General Douglas MacArthur's occupation force had relaxed many social and economic controls and granted greater political autonomy. Foreign trade had begun to increase. There was cautious talk of a larger food ration by the spring of 1950 as Japan began to accumulate the dollars needed to buy instead of beg for vital foodstuffs from the United States and Europe. MacArthur's planners had kept inflation rigidly in check, although prices remained high and money was still tight. The necessities of life were available for all in this defeated, ravaged nation, and there were also a few luxuries for a handful of Japanese who could already afford them.

All eyes remained fixed on Moscow as the half-century mark neared. The Russian people had just concluded an enormous, jubilant celebration of Joseph Stalin's seventieth birthday, and, although communists were not particularly interested in the almighty (years later Soviet Cosmonaut Yuri Gagarin would claim after man's first space flight that he had looked for God but had not found him), Western observers were encouraged when "Grandfather Frost" appeared on Moscow streets at Christmas to pass out toys and wish everyone season's greetings. The Kremlin reported steady progress in rebuilding a nation that had been devastated by four years of the cruelest and most bitter war fought primarily inside its boundaries. Diplomatically and militarily Stalin and his people could point to several resounding successes during 1949, including the establishment of the German Democratic Republic and similar "peoples' democracies" throughout the captive states of Eastern Europe, the establishment of communist rule throughout China, and, of course, the "Soviet atomic achievement."

There was no evidence that Stalin was about to fling the Red Army against Western Europe, nor did Soviet detonation of a nuclear device immediately emasculate Western power or escalate world tensions. A month after Truman announced the Soviet detonation, the CIA concluded that "for the moment, the military security position of the US has undergone no instantaneous and fundamental modification. If it was valid previously to point to an exclusive possession of an atomic technology as a significant item on the US side, it is still valid to point to a superior US stockpile as a signficant item."[18] The American public perceived the Soviet triumph as simply one more burden to be borne. Some liberals were actually pleased with the Soviet achievement, arguing that U.S. proposals for international control of atomic energy had failed utterly. Now that Washington's monopoly was broken, creative new efforts could be undertaken.

Despite the apparent calm and optimism, however, deep currents of fear, dissent, and skepticism flowed beneath the surface of American life. Millions had never become reconciled to the folklore and folkways of liberalism with its focus on the problems of urban-industrial democracy, its lukewarm but unmistakable commitment to civil rights, and its relish for global politics. Many had begun to convince themselves that liberalism was simply a variant of the international communist conspiracy that Fair Deal

Washington was ostensibly opposing with diplomacy, expensive foreign aid, loans, investments, and the atomic monopoly. As the cold war clarified and intensified after 1946 and the areas of conflict between East and West steadily broadened, there developed in the United States an impulsive, often absurd obsession with communism.

2

The Red Menace

❖ ❖ ❖ ❖ ❖ ❖ ❖ ❖ ❖ ❖ ❖ ❖ ❖ ❖ ❖ ❖

In his Christmas Day 1949 column, Arthur Krock of the *New York Times* marveled at Communist Russia's new power and influence over the American mind. In 1900, czarist Russia had held "infinitesimal" interest for the government and people of the United States. Now Washington based every policy, act, and thought on what the Kremlin response might be and analyzed every social, economic, and military development in Europe, Asia, Latin America, and even Africa for its relationship to the cold war. The very streets, country lanes, offices, and factories of the United States and its exterior possessions were closely watched by a large, vigorous group of vigilantes for traces of Soviet espionage. The American people, Krock concluded, had become exquisitely, constantly aware of communism anywhere and everywhere. Countless polls, editorials, and man-in-the-street interviews supported his observation, and there seemed no end to the torment. Arnold Toynbee, the foremost public scholar of the time, predicted at the beginning of 1950 that the cold war would continue until at least the close of the century. The tensions and anxieties that had beset the world since 1946 would harass the children of 1950 and their children for decades.[1]

One great truth had dominated public thinking since the end of the war. The United States had lost the peace that its sons had fought so gallantly to win. Although a handful of optimists clung to the belief that Stalin possessed some decent, exploitable instincts and that the Soviet Union could be induced to behave responsibly in the world, Roosevelt and Truman were widely condemned for having foolishly trusted the Russian Communist leadership during the crucial months of the wartime alliance. Since V-J Day gullible leftists had inevitably been betrayed by the communist tyrant, and it served them right. "If there are in Russia people well-intentioned toward peace," wrote liberal historian Henry Steele Commager on the first day of 1950, "we see no prospect of their influence prevailing."[2]

Critics of a later generation, steeped in the bitterness of Vietnam and the seductive simplicities of Marxist analysis, would place blame for this attitude on the arrogance and economic aggression of those American statesmen who were determined to "contain" and "roll back" international communism in order to make the world safe for a capitalistic imperium. Midcentury Americans viewed the situation much differently. Their world had begun exactly a decade before with Adolf Hitler's sudden, devastating defeat of the West. In two weeks, Nazi armies, flooding across France and the Low Countries, crippled if not destroyed four hundred years of painfully accumulated civilization. For fifty months, Paris and her sister cities on the Continent lay shrouded in Nazi rule, while the United States was dragged into the war by the shocking Japanese ambush-massacre at Pearl Harbor, which no amount of prior American folly or miscalculation could justify. The Bataan Death March, the Nazi death camps, and horrendous German and Japanese medical "experiments" confirmed popular beliefs that World War II was a struggle against naked barbarism.

The cost of eventually defeating Hitler and his Japanese ally had been nearly incalculable, and the brief moment of triumph was immediately followed by an age of disillusion as the wartime Soviet ally transformed itself into as menacing and ferocious an opponent as Nazi Germany.

It would be another four decades before the judgment of midcentury Americans was vindicated. The gradual opening of the Soviet archives at the end of the century revealed that Stalin and his henchmen were as sinister and threatening as the worst 1950 Red-baiter could imagine. Stalin was a man of incredible malevolence and reckless malice. His colleague, Foreign Minister Vyacheslav Molotov, was, if possible, even worse. Perusing Molotov's autobiography, a scholar wrote in 1992, was like engaging "in a one-on-one conversation with a major figure in a gigantic criminal organization." Molotov was not a man of normal human emotions but a bloodless operator steeped "in the stupefying cynical amorality that characterized the Communist Party of the Soviet Union."[3]

Stalin believed explicitly in the power of war to advance the cause of total-itarian communism. He understood the ghastly effects of nuclear energy (whose secrets began flowing in from Los Alamos as early as 1943) but did not care as long as he ultimately possessed enough of it to wage another world war. His power seemed absolute, and he reveled in it. Yugoslav Communist Milovan Djilas later wrote of a wartime visit to the Kremlin:

> An ungainly dwarf of a man passed through gilded and marbled impe-rial halls, and a path opened before him, radiant, admiring glances fol-lowed him, while the ears of courtiers strained to catch his every word. . . . His country was in ruins, hungry, exhausted. But his armies and marshals, heavy with fat and medals and drunk with vodka and vic-tory, had already trampled half of Europe under foot, and he was con-vinced they would trample over the other half in the next round. He knew that he was one of the cruelest, most despotic personalities in human history. But this did not worry him one bit, for he was con-vinced that he was executing the judgment of history. His conscience was troubled by nothing.

During a state banquet, Djilas saw Stalin rise, hitch up his pants, and cry out "almost in a transport, 'The war shall soon be over. We shall recover in fifteen or twenty years, and then we'll have another go at it.'" By midcen-tury Stalin was busily planning a third world war, which he confidently believed Russia would win if it occurred at a time and place of his own choosing. He told Molotov that "the First World War tore one country away from capitalist slavery. The Second World War created the socialist system, and the Third World War will finish imperialism forever."[4]

Molotov's dominant emotion was hatred of imperialist "right deviation-ists," who included not only Truman and Churchill but later Nikita Khrushchev and Leonid Brezhnev. Molotov was so immersed in Stalinism that he promptly divorced his wife when the great man asked him to (Mrs. Molotov, it should be noted, concurred for the good of the party). He sup-ported Stalin's belief that the Soviet state had to expand everywhere. The two men dreamed of grabbing Libya and Iran and expropriating some of the Greek shoreline to give to the Bulgarians. In his wilder moments, Stalin even thought of regaining Alaska. Molotov's hatred of Truman was bottomless, undoubtedly reflecting his master's own spite. Molotov concurred with such bitter American critics as Westbrook Pegler that the man from Missouri was a "thin-lipped . . . hater, a bad man in any fight. Malicious and unforgiving and not above offering you his hand to yank you off balance and work you over with a chair leg, pool cue, or something out of his pocket."[5]

An atomic bomb perhaps. Mao Zedong might dismiss the bomb as inconsequential in the unfolding of history. Stalin knew better. Not only were his scientists working on nuclear weapons as early as 1943, but in 1948 physicists were brought into the Moscow laboratories to begin research on a thermonuclear device. The Soviet leaders prosecuted the cold war as intensively as their worst enemies in the West feared. "But what does 'cold war' mean?" Molotov asked rhetorically. Then he answered:

> Tense relations. They [the West] were responsible . . . [perhaps because] we were on the offensive. They were of course bitter about us, but we had to consolidate our conquests. Create our own, socialist Germany. . . . Czechoslovakia, Poland, Hungary, Yugoslavia—they were feeble, we had to restore order everywhere. Squeeze out capitalist regimes. That's the "cold war." Of course, you have to know when to stop. In this regard I think Stalin observed strict limits.[6]

Midcentury Americans disagreed. Communism was on the march everywhere, and to many citizens the most important reason was the weak and vacillating foreign policy of Franklin Roosevelt and Harry Truman. At Yalta a dying Roosevelt had virtually given Eastern Europe to Stalin and had pressured Chiang Kai-shek into a concessionary treaty with Moscow that enabled Mao's communist hordes to assume a commanding position in postwar China. Truman had compounded the folly by not urging Dwight Eisenhower and his armies to roll on toward Berlin and Prague while Germany collapsed. When the Red Army spread over Eastern Europe, nightly gunfire again echoed along ancient city streets, political opponents of communism disappeared, and coalition governments were subverted to ruthless one-party rule backed by Stalin's bayonets and tanks. Aleksandr Solzhenitsyn had not yet labeled the Soviet Union's great cluster of interrogation centers, prisons, and slave labor camps the "Gulag Archipelago," but early postwar Americans knew that such places existed, and they described them with a more generic, geographically correct term: Siberia.

Were the follies and miscalculations of the Roosevelt and Truman administration the result of error or of design? Did communist moles exist within the inner circles of democratic government and society, twisting free-world programs and policies to meet the needs of their Kremlin masters? The issue had infected the American psyche like a stubborn, low-grade fever since the early thirties. Only a month after Roosevelt's first inaugural, the Rotary Club president in Muncie, Indiana, charged that Americans refused to realize they were living in a "red fog. . . . We are getting pretty close to Communism right now in Washington. We have known, out-and-out liberals in the government. The farm program they are putting through is nothing but the Russian system." Professors and propagandists were as much to blame as politicians. Muncie opinion makers claimed that more than 170 organizations were spreading communist propaganda across the country, while the nation's colleges, universities, and high schools were filled with radicalism dispensed by such subversive groups as the League for Industrial Democracy. A local youth leader complained that "our college boys are bringing back radicalism. . . . The head of our Y.M.C.A. is scared to death of it and tells the boys they can't talk radicalism in the building, but you ought to hear the fellows talking around the 'Y' soda fountain."[7]

Deep currents of anticommunist hysteria built steadily beneath the surface of American politics in the New Deal years. Several sensational books attracted mild public attention in the midthirties, especially Elizabeth Dilling's potboiler, *The Red Network: A "Who's Who" and Handbook of Radicalism for Patriots,* which listed roughly five hundred organizations and thirteen hundred individuals supposedly implicated in a communist plot to take over America. Among those identified as subversives were such eminent conservatives as William E. Borah and Chiang Kai-shek, along with New Dealers Felix Frankfurter and Eleanor Roosevelt and curmudgeon H. L. Mencken. The *National Republic,* a monthly magazine founded in Washington, D.C., in 1925 to expose all forms of alien radicalism that were ostensibly destroying "the American way of life," strenuously promoted such lesser known works as *The Red Hand in the Professor's Glove* and *Crucifying Christ in the Colleges.*[8]

In midwinter 1936, the surge of anxiety reached the national level. "The United States alone in the world is the universal target of all brands of Communism organized in the different foreign sections [of the Comintern], because of the presence in this country of 6,000,000 to 7,000,000 counted aliens and their dependents," Raymond G. Carroll wrote in that bible of middle-brow opinion, the *Saturday Evening Post.* Could American institutions resist the infection? Carroll was skeptical. He quoted but did not identify the dynamic young director of the Federal Bureau of Investigation, J. Edgar Hoover, who complained that his agents could not investigate radical activities because they lacked the necessary legal justification. As so often happened in America when formal institutions and the law were unwilling or unable to confront what many citizens regarded as a crisis, bold individuals appeared to take command. Such a person was Make Mills, Russian-born head of the "radical detail" of the Chicago Police Department. Carroll approvingly wrote of Mills's incredible card file of known radicals and his encyclopedic knowledge of the activities of "Communist diplomatic, commercial and propaganda organizations in the United States." Mills claimed to have seventy-five thousand current names on his list of alien subversives; one-third were active communists, "of whom 40% are foreigners of many races." It would help if these conspirators were deported, but Mills complained that Americans were "more lukewarm in their patriotism than the people of any other nation. They let themselves be led along by the theorists, instead of being alert to the danger of the sudden changes these theorists advocate."[9]

Carroll's article was suffused with subliminal themes that reflected much of the emerging paranoid style in 1930s politics: the fear of the "alien" with his "foreign" ideas; the admiration for the lone ranger willing to confront a crisis when formal authority is either timid or powerless; the gathering of meticulous details about subversion in huge filing systems, reflecting the care, vigilance, and above all, intelligence of their creators; the incessant worry about possibly not being patriotic enough, not being aware enough; and especially the normal human fear of being taken in by the smooth-talking stranger, of being "duped" and therefore laughed at for listening to sinister "theorists."

By 1938 America had become part of the global battleground between communism and Nazi Germany. Stalin's plea for a "popular front" against Nazism had enlisted the conscious or starry-eyed collaboration of thousands of influential educators, social workers, clergymen, youth leaders, novelists, racial spokesmen, writers, Hollywood stars and directors, trade union officials, and "men and women of abnormal wealth."[10] Joseph Goebbels's propagandists and Fritz Kuhn's German-American Bund struggled to match the communist campaign, and when the FBI arrested a German alien on spy charges and Bundists subsequently rioted with American Legionnaires in New York City, a previously obscure, rabidly reactionary Democratic congressman from Texas, Martin Dies, demanded the creation of a new legislative committee to investigate foreign propaganda in the United States. In May, the House adopted Dies's Resolution 282, which established a Committee to Investigate Un-American Activities. Thus was born that famous—or infamous—institution, the House Committee on Un-American Activities, popularly but erroneously known as HUAC.

From its inception, HUAC was virulently anti-New Deal.[11] Dies had proudly styled himself "President of the House Demagogues' Club," and his hatred of Franklin Roosevelt was notorious. Dies was a right-wing populist champion of both Main Street's small businessmen and the independent farmers who patronized them. He and they despised centralization and bigness wherever it was found.

The legislation authorizing HUAC was vague: The committee was to investigate "subversive and un-American propaganda" activities that attacked "the principle of the form of government as guaranteed by the Constitution." But what constituted "un-American" activities? Were they unpatriotic, unpopular, unconventional, undesirable, unapproved ideas? If so, who should determine their unsuitability? What kind of propaganda or behavior was "subversive"? Presumably any idea, argument, or organization that assaulted the "principle of the form of government as guaranteed by the Constitution." But what *principle* had the Constitution guaranteed? The document had originally legalized slavery, restricted the franchise to white males and the election of U.S. senators to state legislatures, and had been silent regarding a national income tax. Would those who now supported women's suffrage, the popular election of senators, equal rights for blacks, and the national income tax be branded "un-American"? These would not be frivolous questions in light of the sweeping mandate that Dies had secured for his committee. In later years, a former chief counsel to HUAC, Ernie Adamson, publicly castigated a liberal veterans' group and conservative columnist Drew Pearson for equating the United States with democracy.[12]

It soon became clear that "un-Americanism" and "subversion"—"disloyalty" in other words—would be what Martin Dies and his like-minded committee colleagues from both parties would determine them to be. Dies had a clear if crude idea of the forces menacing America. "If democratic government assumes the responsibility for abolishing all poverty and unemployment," he wrote in 1940, "it is simply preparing the way for dictatorship." Full employment was a "Trojan Horse," because government would have to control all individuals to achieve it. The Trojan horse was, in fact, communism in disguise. Fascism's fifth columns as well as communism's organizations "can never be properly dealt with so long as we retain in the government service . . . hundreds of Left-wingers and radicals who do not believe in our system of private enterprise."[13]

The committee was an immediate sensation. It clashed with prominent New Dealers in the Justice Department and investigated controversial labor unions, especially the CIO, and labor leaders such as West Coast radical Harry Bridges, along with such suspected radical groups as the Federal Theater Project. Despite the anguished warnings of liberal reporters and New Deal bureaucrats that it represented a fundamental threat to American liberties (it did), HUAC largely killed itself through excess and buffoonery. The committee soon went to Hollywood, where its investigators charged that prominent film stars—including Clark Gable, Robert Taylor, James Cagney, and even eight-year-old Shirley Temple—were dupes or stooges of the Kremlin. "No one, I hope, is going to claim that any of these persons is a Communist," HUAC research assistant J. B. Matthews pontificated. "The unfortunate fact, however, [is] that most of them unwittingly serve, albeit in [a] slight way, the purposes of the Communist Party." Interior Secretary Harold Ickes, a crusty old veteran of many political and bureaucratic wars, promptly snorted in a public address that HUAC had "gone into Hollywood and there discovered a great red plot. They found dangerous radicals there, led by little Shirley Temple. Imagine the great committee raiding her nursery and seizing her dolls as evidence."[14]

The committee was nearly laughed out of existence, and for nearly a decade it remained, in Hollywood writer-director John Huston's felicitous phrase, "a little-recognized back-street operation"[15] exploiting dubious or questionable leads and providing a sensational forum for a series of shady characters with uncertain or sleazy motives, including labor spies, professional informers, and vigilantes for "100 per cent Americanism." In 1945, it narrowly escaped legislative extinction.

While HUAC was relegated to the fringes of American life, it continued to give comfort to those who remained convinced that the New Deal was selling out the country. The committee's initial activities generated two pieces of restrictive legislation, the Hatch and Smith Acts of 1939 and 1940, respectively. The Hatch Act prohibited any political activity by federal workers, and subsequent amendments during the war years, along with various executive orders, permitted abrupt dismissal of any federal employee found to be a member of any organization that pledged to overthrow the government by force. The Smith Act not only demanded government registration of all aliens; it also specified that Americans could not "knowingly or willfully advocate, abet, advise, or teach the duty, necessity, desirability or propriety of overthrowing or destroying any government in the United States by force or violence." Both pieces of legislation incorporated "the idea that guilt could be established through mere imputation of belief" and gave credulous or unscrupulous politicians and bureaucrats enormous powers of harassment and coercion. As three million aliens reported to local post offices for registration and fingerprinting during the tense summer of 1940, while war raged in Europe, the *New York Times* dryly observed that if the vague, sweeping strictures of the Smith Act were enforced against any written or spoken word that might cause insubordination, disloyalty, or mutiny among members of the armed services, several speakers at the recent Republican National Convention could be convicted.[16]

A year later, as the nation edged closer to war, Eugene Lyons, an embittered former communist, published a long book titled *The Red Decade: The Stalinist Penetration of America,* which forever after became the standard textbook for dedicated anticommunists. Lyons charged that throughout the thirties thousands of supposedly sophisticated American artists, intellectuals, writers, and political figures gladly allowed themselves to be taken in and shamelessly exploited by Stalinist agents demanding a popular front against fascism. The book contained endless lists of "dupes," a "horde of part-time pseudo-rebels," who possessed "neither courage *nor* convictions, but only a muddy emotionalism and a mental fog which made them an easy prey for the arbiters of a political racket." But these gullible fools comprised only the outer ring of an "incredible revolution" in American thought and taste, which Stalin's Comintern was directing at every stage through "transmission belts" of "official resident agents of the Moscow hierarchy" and "the solid ring of Communist Party members, the mass of them acknowledging their allegiance," while "an effective minority" concealed both their names and affiliations to better subvert the nation.[17]

But no writer, publicist, vigilante, or demagogue could match the enormous popularity and influence, however brief, of John Roy Carlson, whose sensational 1943 book, *Under Cover: My Four Years in the Nazi Underworld of America,* captured the almost hysterical mood of a nation fighting a global war. Carlson, whose real name was Arthur Derounian, had been an obscure New York journalist until one day in 1938, when he stumbled across a virulently anti-Semitic leaflet in a Manhattan subway train. Curious, he traced the leaflet's imprint to a seedy little group that called itself the American National-Socialist party. Derounian was both appalled and intrigued by the group and its obsession with purging America of all Jewish influences ("Take Roosevelt, he's a Jew. The Cabinet, the Supreme Court, the Post Office—they're all Jewish").[18] He immediately decided to do what he could to expose the Nazi ring or rings that sought to destroy American democracy. Five years later, he emerged to tell his story under a solid American pseudonym.

The entire country was entranced by a tale that simply rehashed the semi-Fascist propaganda and activities that had sprung up around the popular radio priest, Father Charles Coughlin, in the late thirties and identified other anti-Semitic, pro-Nazi antiwar clubs, groups, and organizations that were remnants of the German-American Bund or William Dudley Pelley's Silvershirts and therefore were well known to the FBI. The several hundred men and women whom Carlson repeatedly named as self-conscious tools of a Nazi conspiracy were pathetic creatures: frustrated housewives, failed professional people, bitter blacks who believed that Fascist racism would rescue them from further degradation, angry urban laborers posing as intellectuals, and religious bigots. Their "activities" ranged from support of Elizabeth Dilling's virulent anticommunist crusade to "disruptions" of the war effort through hoarding, from financial support of small radio networks equating Nazism with Christianity to the drafting and dissemination of savage defeatist leaflets.

What gave *Under Cover* a sense of drama and immediacy were Carlson's cloak-and-dagger writing style, his repeated assertions that these silly "subversives" actually constituted a menace to the national security because they had gone "underground" and that he, Carlson, had risked reputation, tranquility, even life itself, by going into the "Nazi underworld" after them to expose their nefarious schemes.[19] In fact, these Fascist crackpots were neither subtle nor threatening. Carlson did not "penetrate" their inner councils; he walked into them off the street after obtaining complete addresses from their leaflets, and he was accepted as an ally after a remarkably brief period of ritualized suspicion. While wandering from coast to coast thereafter to ferret out these demons, Carlson was never denied entrance to a meeting or permission to interview. His subjects were pitifully trusting and eager to talk, proselytize, rant and rave, and mouth the same tired clichés of spite and malice over and over again with no questions asked.

Carlson never uncovered a single Nazi paramilitary organization that could threaten the nation with armed insurrection; he apparently never met anyone who carried a weapon. All he found were people spewing venom but eschewing violence (except on one occasion when some Nazi types advocated stirring up racial problems in black neighborhoods by throwing rocks through windows at night). Terrible domestic violence occurred in America during the war years: the Detroit race riots and the Los Angeles "zoot suit" rampages took place while *Under Cover* was racing to the top of the best-seller lists. But these vicious disturbances did not reflect Nazi activities in the country so much as a Fascist mentality among several thousand citizens who were otherwise wholeheartedly supporting the war effort.

But *Under Cover* became an immediate and incredible success. It went through eleven major printings between June and October of 1943. Dust jacket encomiums were lyrical. The most popular literary critic of the time, Clifton Fadiman, called it a "tremendously fascinating personal adventure story" and claimed that it was "the first completely documented account of the enemy within. . . . If enough of us read [the book] perhaps we can avert a civil war which American Fascists, with the help of Axis agents, are deliberately preparing." The *New York Times* added: "This book is of sensational importance to every man and woman who hopes for victory. . . . Of the hundreds of persons he exposes, most are still free and carrying on their dirty work. Those who neglected to take them seriously enough in Europe are dead, in concentration camps, in hiding or in exile." The *New York Herald-Tribune* argued that Carlson's exposé was a salutary warning: "Remember that Adolph [*sic*] Hitler (the crackpot paper hanger) started in a small way, too. . . . It seems wise at least to raise your head and listen, and perhaps go down to investigate when some one [*sic*] tells you that there is a wolf in your cellar." And the *Book-of-the-Month-Club-News* hailed Carlson for "single-handedly" doing "more to expose un-American activities than the entire Dies Committee."[20]

The real target of *Under Cover*, like *The Red Decade*, the HUAC hearings, and the Smith Act, was not the threat that tireless, effective subversives posed to national security. It was the folly and gullibility of a people—and their government—who would not realize that they were under grave threat from those traditions they cherished most: free speech, the right of assembly, and the freedom to listen to anyone they wished and to think as they pleased. Carlson, like Lyons, Dies, and Smith, ritualistically championed the right of all Americans to hold and disseminate a wide range of opinions and ideas—but within decided limits. "The Kremlin's right to carry on conspiracies for the expunging of your liberties and mine—for subordinating American independence to Stalin's whims or needs—is in no way guaranteed by the Bill of Rights," Lyons had asserted, adding: "Despite the outcries of muddled liberals under shrewd Muscovite cheerleaders, Stalin's prerogative of placing a candidate for President of the United States on our ballot is not exactly an 'inalienable right.'" He concluded with the observation that would become the staple of radical right-wing thinking in coming years: "I submit that the right to survival is the first law for democracies as for any other society." Carlson concurred. "In the course of my investigations," he wrote, "I found that many otherwise fine Americans were propagating the lies and the 'party line' originally advanced by Hitler's agents and doing it sincerely in what they believed to be good Americanism."[21]

By 1944 the poison of mistrust, hatred, and smear—the notion of "the enemy within," of the "wolf in your cellar"—was well established. Not even presidential candidates were immune. As his scant hopes for the White House visibly faded that year, Thomas Dewey blurted out that "the Communists are seizing control of the New Deal . . . to control the Government of the United States."[22] When the cold war emerged unmistakably in late 1946 and early 1947, Truman instinctively expanded the dimensions of the Hatch and Smith Acts, instituting a formal federal employee loyalty program complete with thorough "security checks" on each worker, whatever his job. The program was complemented by a long list of real and ostensible subversive organizations compiled by Attorney General J. Howard McGrath, a rabid anticommunist, from such readily available sources as FBI and HUAC files and Lyons's book.[23] Great metropolitan dailies and local newspapers from one end of the country to the other were again filled with screaming headlines about communist subversion in or on the periphery of the national capital, and professional communist hunters were again making a good living from "Espionage Fever" and the "Myth of the Vital Secret."[24] During the next three years, Congress, the Catholic church, the publishing industry, and the news media made anticommunism a cottage industry.[25]

In 1948, a Senate Internal Affairs subcommittee released a report with the chilling title *Interlocking Subversion in Government Departments*. Relying on recent testimony by an obscure government clerk named Elizabeth Bentley, the authors of the report claimed that communists had penetrated New Deal economic recovery and war-making agencies. HUAC issued a flood of pamphlets dealing with the Red menace, including "100 Things You Should Know about Communism in" religion, education, labor, and the government. Congress published official reports such as *Soviet Espionage within the U.S. Government, One Hundred Years of Communism, Communism in the Near East, 500 Leading Communists,* and *Communism in Action: A Documented Study and Analysis of Communism in Action in the Soviet Union.*

The Justice Department and the FBI mounted their own barrage of anti-communist literature despite Truman's obvious distaste for Red-baiting. The U.S. Chamber of Commerce issued booklets titled *Communism in Government*, *Communism in the Labor Movement*, *Communist Infiltration in the United States*, and *Community Action for Anti-Communism*. The national radio networks featured dozens of programs about Soviet spies and communist intrigue. Nazi and Japanese villains in children's comic books were replaced with Russian and later Chinese Communist infiltrators and saboteurs.

Anticommunist and anti-Soviet literature glutted the nation's bookstores. It seemed that every diplomat, politician, military man, refugee from behind the Iron Curtain, Red Army deserter, communist renegade, social democrat, Trotskyite, socialist, and "anti-Communist liberal" had something to say or a story to tell about the evils of communism. Publishers signed them up and produced their work with relish, knowing a hot topic when they saw one. Between 1947 and 1950, people in Manhattan, San Francisco, and the heartland could choose among the following titles:

One Who Survived
I Chose Freedom
The Great Globe Itself
The Red Plotters
The Soviet Spies
American Communism
This Is My Story
The Struggle behind the Iron Curtain
Communism and the Conscience of the West
Last Chance in China
False Christ of Communism and the Social Gospel
Why They Behave Like Russians
Stalin and German Communism
American Capitalism vs. Russian Communism
I'll Never Go Back
Why I Escaped
Iron Curtain

The great weekly magazines followed suit. A full-page advertisement in the *New York Herald-Tribune* introduced a forthcoming serial in *Colliers* by Gen. Frank Howley with the headline: "Russians Are Colossal Liars, Swindlers!" Howley's article, titled "My 4-Year War with the Reds," told his "own story of Soviet arrogance, deceit and gangsterism, murder and rape." Another serial in the same magazine was promoted with a full-page ad in the *Herald-Tribune*, headed "How Moscow Wrecked an American Home."

Among the many anticommunist articles that Americans could read in 1947–48 were:

"How Communists Get That Way," *Catholic World*
"How the Russians Spied on Their Allies," *Saturday Evening Post*
"Turn the Light on Communism," *Colliers*
"Labor and the Communists," *Current History*
"Trained to Raise Hell in America: International Lenin School in Moscow,"
   Nation's Business
"Let's Make It a Professional Red Hunt," *Business Week*
"Commie Citizens," *Newsweek*
"Communists Penetrate Wall Street," *Commercial and Financial Chronicle*
"Why I Broke with the Communists," *Harpers Magazine*
"Is America Immune to the Communist Plague?" *Saturday Evening Post*
"Reds Are after Your Child," *American Magazine*
"Capture of the Innocent," *Colliers*
"Destruction of Science in the USSR," *Saturday Evening Post*

The Roman Catholic church had, of course, virulently opposed the Soviet Union from the beginning. The Catholic Information Society issued dozens of pamphlets on communism with such titles as *Communism Means Slavery*, *Communism and Fascism: Two of a Kind*, *Justice by Assassination*, and *The Enemy in our Schools*. Priests routinely condemned communism and the Soviet Union from radio and pulpit and at public meetings.

In 1947, HUAC had again traveled to Hollywood. The film colony persisted in viewing the Committee as nothing more than "a shabby and backstreet operation, specializing in anti-Semitic and racial insinuations. . . Respectable Congressmen avoided it."[26] Now in a series of spectacular hearings, HUAC used FBI files and the allegations of such key Bureau informers as Ronald Reagan and Adolf Menjou to expose a handful of communists, mostly screenwriters. Ten men were jailed by the Committee for contempt. More than a dozen people committed suicide. Despite scanty evidence linking the movie capital with communism, the studios panicked. Hundreds of writers (Dalton Trumbo, John Howard Lawson, Ring Lardner, Jr.), prominent actors (including Larry Parks and later John Garfield and Anne Revere), producers, directors, electricians, wardrobe and makeup specialists, and the like were blacklisted. A handful of other stars, including Spencer Tracy and Katharine Hepburn, just missed having their careers destroyed. The studios also quickly produced and distributed a series of usually low-budget and sensational anticommunist films that ranged from the mildly interesting to the completely inane. Between mid-1947 and 1949 the American public could see such movies as *I Married a Communist, The Red Menace, The Conspirator, Guilty of Treason,* and *The Red Danube.*[27]

Ambitious politicians swiftly exploited this steadily building anticommunist hysteria. For a time, federal bureaucrats seemed immune thanks to Truman's internal security program, so employees of city and state governments, schools, and universities became the chief targets of anticommunist zealots. By 1948, scarcely any local official, clerk, janitor, garbage collector, schoolteacher, or college professor anywhere in the country could escape a security check, a loyalty oath, and the nagging fear that a professional informer might report him or her to this or that legislative investigating committee. Harvard's president, James Bryant Conant, acknowledged the existence of "thoughtful and troubled citizen[s]" who wondered whether their universities were "being used as centers for fifth column activities."[28]

In fact, public schools and government education bureaus were scrambling frantically in exactly the opposite direction. The U.S. Office of Education began promoting a "Zeal for Democracy" program, which was designed to counter twenty years of popular disillusionment over international affairs and to "promote and strengthen democratic thinking and practice, just as the schools of totalitarian states have so effectively promoted the ideals of their respective cultures." The inevitable conference of experts from elementary, high school, and university faculties and administrations gathered in Washington in the early spring of 1948 and made the inevitable recommendations, including the introduction of study units "showing how undemocratic forces endeavor to infiltrate American institutions and organizations." The conference also urged that 1948 commencement programs emphasize bolstering American democracy and, in a rather strange contrast to the study units on subversion, recommended that American schools strengthen "basic loyalty to, and trust of, fellow citizens to an extent that the courage, vitality and unity of American democracy will grow and endure, and withstand all attempts to divide our people."[29]

Although public schoolteachers were always suspect, it was the nation's professors who became the focus of Red-hunting. The professoriat had been prominently associated with the New and Fair Deals both as government "Brain Trusters" in the thirties and as enthusiastic supporters of generous labor and civil rights legislation and civil liberties throughout the Roosevelt and Truman years. Many professors had also supported Henry Wallace's far-left Progressive party campaign in 1948 either through conviction or as a lark. To humorless Red-hunters, this was a serious matter.

In June 1949, HUAC wrote to eighty-one colleges and high schools, demanding lists of textbooks used in literature, economics, government, history, social science, and geography classes, and the same year the University of California at Berkeley and the University of Washington in Seattle became bitterly divided over the issue of faculty loyalty. Berkeley's regents demanded that all professors sign a loyalty oath. The scholars replied heatedly that they should not be singled out as potential subversives. The regents felt differently, and within a year twenty-six Berkeley professors were "ejected," thirty-seven resigned in outrage, and the curriculum lost fifty-five courses. Reaction was prompt. More than twelve hundred university and college teachers from more than forty institutions wrote the regents in protest during the academic year 1949–50, and the oath was rescinded. Eighteen prominent scholars publicly proclaimed that they were "fighting for the principle that loyalty in America is to be judged by the substance of men's lives and actions," and they deplored the reduction of teachers to second-class citizens.[30] Although the Berkeley regents grudgingly recanted, the school had suffered a serious blow to its integrity and reputation.

Both college professors and secondary-school teachers began to fear informers, and soon many tailored their lectures and course work to conform to rigid standards of "Americanism." In June 1949, the National Education Association (NEA) and the American Association of School Administrators (AASA) issued a fifty-four-page booklet on educational policies and practices, in which they stated flatly that schools should not employ members of the Communist Party of the United States as teachers because they embraced "doctrines and discipline completely inconsistent with the principle of freedom on which American education depends." But NEA and AASA also deplored the "careless, incorrect, unjust use" of such words as "red" and "communist" to attack teachers and others who were not actually communists but merely had different views than their accusers. An Indiana University report written a few months later indicated that teachers not surprisingly suffered from "fear and insecurity" partly because of "repressive and restrictive rules and regulations" along with "expressions of critical attitudes by school patrons" and "pressures for conformance to community mores and traditions."[31]

Freedom of thought and even scientific inquiry was stifled. In November 1949, an unknown bard at one of the California colleges sent the *American Civil Liberties News* a sardonic parody of Gilbert and Sullivan titled "Ode to Hysteria: University Division," which reflected as much despair as humor:

> I am the very model of a member of the faculty,
> Because I'm simply overcome with sentiments of loyalty.
> I daily think of reasons why I'm glad to be American,
> And thank the Lord I've always been a registered Republican.
>
> The thoughts I think are only thoughts approved by my community.
> I pledge allegiance to the flag at every opportunity.
> I haven't had a thing to do with Communist conspirators,
> And neither have my relatives, descendants, or progenitors.[32]

The public was inundated with names and institutions symbolic of internal subversion: *Amerasia*, the Institute of Pacific Relations, Bentley, Philip Jaffe, Harry Dexter White, John Service, and Judith Coplon. Americans from Scarsdale to Sacramento could be pardoned for concluding that the nation was in terrible and immediate peril. The hand that rocked the cradle might be Red; the Wall Street broker or financial adviser might be a communist sympathizer; that third- or ninth-grade teacher who talked a lot about politics and social justice could be a dupe or even a parlor pink; that pleasant neighbor down the street might be a conscientious tool of the international communist conspiracy.

At midcentury, anticommunism remained a powerful but diffuse popular impulse that, if handled with sufficient finesse or ruthlessness, was potentially capable of exploitation by amoral politicians on either side of the ideological spectrum. But its intrinsic appeal was to the opponents of the liberal establishment, those who believed that the big government political culture created by FDR and perpetuated by Truman had destroyed the American Way of Life and had delivered the country into the hands of alien collectivists and planners determined to destroy the twin pillars of national might and righteousness: capitalism and God-fearing evangelical Protestantism. These people were overwhelmingly concentrated in the Republican Party, whose dominant conservative wing seethed with resentment over its displacement from the center of national power.

3

Conservatives

❖ ❖ ❖ ❖ ❖ ❖ ❖ ❖ ❖ ❖ ❖ ❖ ❖ ❖ ❖

At midcentury the Democratic and Republican parties were both split internally along sectional lines. The Democrats, united in an internationalist foreign policy, divided north and south over domestic reform. Almost any socially or economically progressive program quickly collided with white supremacy, and Truman's commitment to civil rights in and after 1948 further alienated the solid South. The east-west Republican split between corporate and village America was in some ways even more profound and visceral.

❖ ❖ ❖

Corporate America, the sophisticated eastern wing of the Republican Party, was loosely organized around "the Wall Street crowd" and its financial and industrial allies in the eastern and midwestern cities. Progressive Republicans had long recognized that in an increasingly complex, interrelated industrial world some expansion of government power and services was essential to preserve basic individual freedoms, protect the national interest, and promote corporate welfare. During the war, Roosevelt had been able to recruit New York Republican lawyers and bankers like Henry Stimson, John McCloy, Robert A. Lovett, and Robert Patterson. These men had subsequently served Truman devotedly and effectively. Some midwestern industrialists, notably Paul Hoffman of Detroit, later joined the Fair Deal to help revive Western Europe with Marshall Plan aid. Other eastern Republicans, like Wendell Willkie (Indiana-born but Wall Street bred) and New

York Governor Thomas E. Dewey, had ritualistically opposed the New and Fair Deals during their failed presidential campaigns in the forties but had made it clear that if they won, they would not dismantle big government but would reshape it to be more responsive to the needs of free enterprise.

Such apostasies were anathema in small-town and rural America, that dense cluster of small and medium-sized communities that stretched across the nation's heartland from rural New England through western Pennsylvania to the treeless plains beyond Minneapolis, Omaha, and Kansas City. This was Norman Rockwell country, embracing the small-town, Christmas-card culture that Booth Tarkington, Hamlin Garland, and Sinclair Lewis had made famous.

Long before midcentury, sociologists had put labels—Yankee City, Plainville, and Middletown—on these communities, which seemed to embody most clearly the traditional American way of life. They were as much states of mind as they were places, and no one who ever lived there quite forgot the daily sense of smug, stultifying righteousness, the outbreaks of intolerance and repression in response to rebellious ways, new thoughts, or novel perspectives.[1]

The experience of hometown America was undecipherable to those who grew up in the noisy, teeming, frantic cities of the East and Middle West. Although life on Main Street was often incredibly constricted, it was also secure, stable, satisfying, even oddly romantic in its stolidity of purpose, ordinariness, and warm predictability. For all the grotesqueries that Sherwood Anderson claimed for it, Winesburg, Ohio, and ten thousand communities like it were places of endlessly comfortable days and years of buying, selling, gossiping, and courting amid endless meals, malts, cups of coffee, and speculation about crops, rain, seasons, business, and people. If the best of our literature celebrates the escape from hometown's cloying embrace into the world of freedom and experience, Main Street nonetheless forms the basis of all our nostalgia.

In each of America's Middletowns and Plainvilles a gentry of local landowners, shopkeepers, bankers, lawyers, and professional people controlled affairs and developed a common culture of status and power that ruled the American mind virtually unchallenged until the upheavals of the 1930s. Sociologists recognized as early as the depression era that the concept of social differentiation as an index of community values and aspirations had become entrenched in American thought.[2] The communities themselves became critical components of national life from the 1870s to the

1950s not only intrinsically but because they also served and therefore deeply influenced rural America. The shopkeeper and the farmer, the banker and the cattleman, tended to form instinctive cultural alliances against all "outside" forces whether they were labor unions, "big business," or "those fools down in Washington." The Yankee Cities, Plainvilles, and Middletowns provided the essential support for the coalition of northern Republicans and conservative southern and border-state Democrats who ran the country from the sectional Compromise of 1877 to the onset of the Great Depression.

Plainville and Middletown elites ruled as much by arbitration as by the exercise of economic power, imposing on their communities an unmatched "ferocity of blue-nose attitudes" regarding manners, morals, and conduct, especially in race relations. As late as the depression era, people in a Plainville community in the southern Middle West would not accept a new-comer until they had satisfied themselves about "his business, how honest he is, and what his morals are." And those morals had better be Republican and "churchly," or the poor devil would not remain in the community for long. In the larger Middletowns, the mores and prejudices of the country club set and the Rotary Club defined the boundaries of permissive public behavior. Such attitudes were not the artifacts of a New England Puritanism carried west with the covered wagons but instead reflected the spirit of vig-orous southern and western frontier religion, a legacy of early nineteenth-century Baptist and Methodist circuit riders and the great camp revival meetings. The revivalist spirit was egalitarian and anti-intellectual, but above all it was fundamentalist in the strictest sense of the term. Plainville and Middletown were obsessed with rigid adherence to stark truths and outraged by those who refused to conform to them.[3] It was a foolish person indeed who desired community acceptance but failed to pull down the blinds whenever he wanted a midday drink.

And it was a foolish shopkeeper, banker, clerk, physician, or lawyer who denied or contested the intimate interrelationship between religion and busi-ness. The Protestant ethic was the overriding concept embraced by all the denizens of Middletown and Plainville, the one social value that had sur-vived intact during the geographic and emotional move west. When a per-ceptive reporter observed in early 1950 that Nebraska Senator Kenneth Wherry had developed "a profound, almost religious, feeling of approval for those able to make important money by their own efforts," he was identify-ing the essence of the Protestant ethic. So was evangelical anticommunist

Billy James Hargis, an Oklahoman who proclaimed reverence for the "down-to-earth, honest-to-God individual who believes in the pre-millennial coming of the Lord, the security of the believer, the efficacy of the Blood of Christ, Americanism, and free enterprise."[4]

Americans were the inheritors and preeminent practitioners of "a specifically bourgeois economic" conception that had emerged in early modern Europe and traveled to the New World in numerous Puritan bosoms. From its inception, Protestantism encouraged the belief that business was meant to be as much a spiritual odyssey and justification—a calling—as it was a grubby materialistic pursuit. Decent success in commerce, navigation, or market agriculture was a sign of God's blessing and approval and therefore a powerful indicator, if not a guarantor, of eternal salvation. Any Middletown businessman could agree with R. H. Tawney's definition of protestantized capitalism as "a creed which transformed the acquisition of wealth from a drudgery or a temptation into a moral duty." "With the consciousness of standing in the fullness of God's grace and being visibly blessed by Him," Max Weber wrote, "the bourgeois business man, as long as he remained within the bounds of formal correctness, as long as his moral conduct was spotless and the use to which he put his wealth was not objectionable, could follow his pecuniary interests as he would and feel that he was fulfilling a duty in doing so."[5]

As Michael Paul Rogin has observed, conservative ideologies are complicated. The American experience and especially the rise of industrialism added new layers of occasionally ironic conviction to the Protestant ethic. Social Darwinism, grounded in a purely secular, materialistic view of evolution and human nature, legitimized the ruthless, relentlessly competitive corporate industrial order of the late nineteenth century as one "in which only the unfit had not survived."[6] Courts and corporations consequently employed the doctrines of "natural law" and "rugged individualism" to protect business enterprise and prevent any regulatory efforts by the state.

Such ideas conflicted with the Protestant emphasis on morally responsible and prudent business success and the corollary belief in salvation through good works. Something was needed to reestablish the traditional link between American capitalism and religion, and Andrew Carnegie supplied it. This quintessential late nineteenth-century captain of industry (or robber baron, depending on one's perspective and prejudices) developed the "gospel of wealth" to justify the huge Gilded Age fortunes being accumulated and lavishly displayed.

The truly Christian businessman, Carnegie asserted, should become a steward of the wealth he had made, doling out hard-earned dollars to such worthy social causes as libraries, symphony orchestras, charities to aid the poor, and, of course, the churches. Carnegie practiced what he preached with such ostentation that political commentator Finley Peter Dunne was moved to observe that every time Carnegie gave away a dime it sounded like a waiter falling downstairs with a tray of dishes.[7]

Devotion to rigid religious and social dogmas brought Main Street into a natural but always tenuous alliance with Wall Street. The undeniable tensions between hometown gentry and the great financial and industrial barons of the East were greatly eased by the shared view, so pungently expressed by Calvin Coolidge, Yankee City's most famous product, that the business of America was business. Thus, businessmen, wherever and whoever they were, were obviously the best Americans. Plainville, Middletown, and Manhattan cherished common beliefs that the country had been built on the rock-solid base of individualism, on the personal efforts and honest toil of pious, Protestant, native-born, white males who practiced initiative, sobriety, and thrift, nurtured and protected their families, developed their agricultural or commercial enterprises, enriched their communities (and churches) thereby, and led exemplary lives of God-fearing righteousness. By the 1920s, a few corporations even began experimenting timidly with their own social welfare systems based on modest pensions and accident insurance.[8]

Like Horatio Alger, the best of these Protestant businessmen had captured the majority of the wealth and power in their villages and towns, and they were expected to shape the growth and define the mores of their communities accordingly. Banker Jones and Judge Smith, gazing eastward from their Main Street offices, and farmer Brown, looking over his coffee cup in the Plainville cafe, could fantasize without greatly stretching the truth that the Morgans and Rockefellers had simply gone a bit further, enjoyed a few privileges or better luck, and so had been able to dominate the nation's business as Jones, Smith, and Brown dominated the commerce and labor of their own communities. The moral superiority of commerce, either in agriculture or trade, and of those who pursued it was perhaps the most powerful myth in American history. Comfortable and secure within their religious-economic society, Main Street and Wall Street knew that the American world belonged to them. Sophisticated Wall Street might look abroad; Main Street was seldom induced to do so.

❖ ❖ ❖

In the decades between Appomattox and the Great Depression, Republican Wall Street and Republican Main Street had developed an image of themselves and their role in shaping national life that was part truth, part conceit, and wholly self-congratulatory. They maintained that the Grand Old Party had created industrial America and thus all its wealth and power. It was Abe Lincoln's Homestead Act that had opened up the dry farmlands of the middle border and the lush agricultural valleys of California, Oregon, and Washington to mass settlement. It was Lincoln's immigration legislation that had brought in millions of European peasants and unskilled laborers to fill in the fifteen hundred miles between the Mississippi and the West Coast and to man the huge industrial plants that soon dominated the late nineteenth-century skylines and economies of Pittsburgh, Birmingham, Cleveland, Detroit, and Chicago. It was Lincoln's tariff that had kept cheaper and better foreign manufactured goods out of the United States until the great American industrial machine was operational. And it was later Republican railroad legislation that had created lines of transportation and communication across the rolling woodlands, prairies, plains, and mountains of the continent, tying local agricultural and industrial systems into one mighty economy. If outright chicanery and corruption became part of the process, if gigantic frauds were practiced and huge, controlling business monopolies formed, these were small prices to pay for making America by 1918 the mightiest nation and the wealthiest economy on earth. At the end of World War I, the United States was the world's major creditor nation, and it would remain so even during the worst of the Great Depression.

From 1860 to 1932 the Republicans won fourteen presidential elections, the Democrats just four. During those seventy-two years, only Grover Cleveland and Woodrow Wilson occupied the White House as representatives of the party of Jefferson and Jackson. America was a Republican country and a business civilization. Periodically something would go wrong with the economy or society, and the other chaps would be allowed to run things for a few years. But they inevitably displayed a chronic incompetence, and as business America again pulled things together, the Republicans would return to the White House and all would be well. That was the beauty of the two-party system as self-satisfied Republicans saw it. The country was given occasional and salutary glimpses of the inherent worthlessness of a Democratic party based, as a campaign slogan of the 1880s put it, on "Rum, Romanism, and Rebellion." It was the "democrat party" that enlisted and corrupted ignorant, foolish immigrants in eastern cities with booze and free baskets of food and coal; it was the democrat party that gave a home to hundreds of thousands of illiterate, semiskilled Irish, Italians, Poles, and Jews whose true loyalty was not to their adopted land but to the papacy in distant Rome or to "international Zionism"; it was the democrat party that had permitted the Union to collapse; it was the Republican party that had saved it.

Republicans fondly, if somewhat inaccurately, recalled their days of glory, when gentlemen pursued a politics of high morality and debated and carefully resolved questions about the national purpose and direction. In Republican eyes there was no intrinsic conflict between the interests of the moneyed class and the welfare of the country. The nation's incredible growth in material well-being had been based on the single-minded pursuit of the dollar by superior individuals. Politics was not meant to be an avenue for social progress, betterment, and change but a simple extension of commerce and property, a means of protecting what the moneyed class had gained by hard work or fraud. The turn-of-the-century Progressive movement of enlightened businessmen and the lawyers and politicians who served them had reformed the few undeniable, acknowledged injustices that had emerged from the nation's headlong rush into industrial organization. Unconscionable exploitation of female and child labor was eased although not ended, egregiously unsafe workplaces were cleaned up somewhat, and Congress reluctantly allowed the inspection and grading of previously uninspected processed foods. At the same time, representatives of the new industrial order manned the new regulatory agencies (most notably the Federal Trade Commission), which were intended to oversee the transition from illegal or extralegal combinations in restraint of trade ("trusts") to chartered institutions ("corporations") designed to promote "economy, efficiency, and better relations in business."[9] These reforms had been accomplished without recourse to dangerous social experiments or impassioned appeals to or against the "little people."

But a dangerous fundamentalism crept into grass roots Republican politics in the twenties in reaction to postwar disillusion, nativistic fears of an increasingly heterogeneous population, the Bolshevik revolution, and a growing challenge to churchly morality from Hollywood and Vienna. In 1925, Walter Steele brought out the first issue of the *National Republic,* a monthly journal unabashedly devoted to "fundamental Americanism." The publication survived for the next thirty years as the most influential forum for ultraconservative thought. Although Steele wrote and published in Washington, D.C., his perspectives and prejudices came straight from Middletown and Plainville. Each issue proclaimed his creed, which would give character, form, and essence not only to McCarthyism but to the radical Right of the sixties and beyond.[10]

Steele and the *National Republic* stood foursquare for "vigorous, unimpaired American nationality," for "the protection of the family, religion, individual freedom and representative government from the assaults of alien and subversive forces." Steele championed "restriction of immigration, an alien registration law to promote enforcement, and expulsion of all aliens illegally in the country and such alien agitators as are unworthy of American citizenship." He demanded "diplomatic and commercial nonintercourse with Soviet Russia or any nation committed to the policy of overthrow of the American government." He promised readers that he would fight incessantly and ardently against "socialism, communism, internationalism, ultra-pacifism and all other forms of Old World despotism" including "atheism, liberainism [sic], and all other social and political subversion." There would be no room in his America for "international alliances and entanglements" or for "Government in business and Government ownership and operation."[11]

The shopkeepers, bankers, and lawyers of the heartland heeded Steele and other political fundamentalists and embraced a blindly patriotic cult of "true Americanism" and a strident evangelicalism that first expressed itself in the famous Scopes "Monkey Trial." The Ku Klux Klan reached its peak of power in Indiana in 1924 as Middletown, Plainville, and Yankee City joined much of the rest of the country in applauding those professors and writers who warned that Anglo-Saxon and Teutonic peoples were being engulfed by the more fertile colored races all around the world and that liberal social democracy was giving off "a distinctly sour, bolshevistic odor." Looking east toward the Democratic-controlled cities of Boston, Philadelphia, and especially New York, Main Street shuddered at the corruption and radicalism that seemed to flourish there. "On the one side," said Representative Jasper Tincher, Republican of Kansas, "is beer, bolshevism, unassimilating settlements and perhaps many flags—on the other side is constitutional government; one flag, stars and stripes."[12]

Then came the Great Depression, which Republicans at first believed was just another cyclical problem period in the national experience, another annoying dip on the upward spiraling chart of commercial progress. The other chaps again took power, but at least Franklin Roosevelt was a gentleman who could be expected to respect and protect private property, that is, the economic and business interests that had made America what it was. Roosevelt quickly disabused his opponents of that belief. He might have come from the ranks of the wealthy and privileged, but his sympathies were squarely with the common man.

Roosevelt and his colleagues replaced the Progressive ideal of simple moral politics practiced by and for the comfortable classes with a complex system that was neither philosophic nor ideological but attitudinal. The New Deal was grounded in an idealization of the people, acknowledgment of the legitimacy of demand politics by competing interest groups, and the value of mass organization, management, and both physical (the Tennessee Valley Authority, Grand Coulee Dam) and social engineering. To horrified Republicans, prudence and restraint in national affairs gave way to unlimited experimentation, confrontation, regulation, and punishment. The New and Fair Deals constituted not only a threat to basic American values but also a personal crisis in self-respect. Franklin Roosevelt became "the root cause behind every war, famine, unpaid bill, and thankless nigger that ever threatened the common good."[13]

Republican Main Street was more deeply bruised by the depression than was any other part of the nation, and it quickly focused on the source of its anguish. Returning to Muncie, Indiana, in 1935, sociologists Robert and Helen Lynd discovered that the depression had "sharpened the harsh edge of human meanness." A growing divisiveness, an in-group favoritism, and a coldness to everyone else belied the tradition of open midwestern friendliness. Middletown's business class wanted "to be let alone to run its own business" and bitterly resented federal intrusiveness, which was equated with radicalism and communism.

In 1936, the GOP countered the New Deal with a careful Kansan and watched Alf Landon suffer a crushing defeat. Conservatives were incensed but rationalized the setback by arguing that after all, Cleveland and Wilson had each served two terms, so Landon's defeat was explicable if barely tolerable. By 1940 Europe was embroiled in another war, and conservative Republicans reluctantly deferred to the moderate eastern wing, which brought in Willkie to try to keep Roosevelt from winning an unprecedented third term. The move failed, and the venomously hated Hyde Park squire returned to Washington for another four years. So Republicans blamed

FDR's 1940 victory on Adolf Hitler and Benito Mussolini. Roosevelt's fourth term was rationalized, too: One could not change horses in the middle of a stream or expect a nation to change its leader (no matter how disliked) in the middle of a world war—not even for a solid, respectable Republican crime fighter like Tom Dewey.

The war made conservatives even more furious and frustrated. They became convinced that FDR was trying to use the latest national emergency to keep himself and his liberal party in power forever by crushing the forces of free enterprise. Roosevelt had been reluctant to impose sweeping wartime controls, but by mid-1942 he concluded that he had no choice. "Compulsion began replacing voluntarism, and the Office of Price Administration [OPA] pushed its way further and further into areas of American life where no government agency had ever pushed before."[14]

Conservatives promptly concluded that the New Deal intended to destroy American business. Wherry and Senator Robert A. Taft of Ohio promptly initiated "a campaign of abuse and insult," accusing OPA and its director, Leon Henderson, of being "derelicts from the war" and "leeches on the body politic." Businessmen large and small were ready to exploit the war effort for a huge profit and, as Taft said, "No goddamned bureaucrats are going to deny it to them."[15]

But, of course, the bureaucrats did, and FDR struck back at his tormentors. In his 1944 State of the Union Address, he proposed a greatly expanded postwar New Deal, which would guarantee nothing less than economic and social security for all Americans. Aiming directly at Taft and his followers, Roosevelt concluded: "If history were to repeat itself and we were to return to the so-called 'normalcy' of the 1920's—then it is certain that even though we shall have conquered our enemies on the battlefields abroad, we shall have yielded to the spirit of fascism here at home."[16]

Then suddenly FDR was gone, to be replaced by a little-known but cocky party hack. Harry Truman, the noisy bantam from Missouri, dared not only to continue but to expand Roosevelt's "socialistic" New Deal under a "Fair Deal" rubric. Frustrated Republicans, both moderate and conservative, had had enough, and in the 1946 off-year elections they asked the country if it agreed. It did. Winston Churchill had been thrown out of power by English voters even before the gunfire stopped in the Pacific. Truman should have expected a similar response from an American people as fed up with blood, sweat, tears, and crusades as were their British cousins. But with a blunt insensitivity the new president unveiled his sweeping Fair Deal reform package to Congress and the country just hours after the war's formal end. Polls indicated that only one in three Americans supported him. The abrupt onset of a cold war with the former Soviet ally and Truman's bumbling efforts to reconvert the economy from war to peace suddenly made American liberalism seem irrelevant, exhausted, and incompetent.

The congressional elections of 1946 were not just a stinging rebuke to Truman and the Fair Deal; they brought to Washington a new group of Republicans such as Dick Nixon of California, Jim Kem of Missouri, Bourke Hickenlooper of Iowa, and Joe McCarthy of Wisconsin: ruthless, combative men who gladly took the sour rumors and charges of communism in Washington out of California and midwestern country clubs and Rotary clubs and made them the center of their campaign appeals and promises. Republican National Chairman B. Carroll Reece claimed that "the choice which confronts America this year is between Communism and Republicanism." Kem claimed that Truman was "soft on Communism," and Charles Kersten of Wisconsin ran on the slogan "Put Kersten in Congress and Keep Communism Out." In Nebraska, Senator Hugh Butler told audiences that "if the New Deal is still in control of Congress after the election, it will owe that control to the Communist Party in this country."[17]

Apparently the country had at last discarded its depression-era infatuation with leveling political reform and social engineering. Republican stalwarts, organizers, and followers literally rubbed their hands in anticipation of finally returning to the White House with Dewey in 1948. With his fussy little mustache and fussy little ways, Dewey was not what conservative America really wanted; Taft had long been Main Street's man, and many, in fact, harbored a yearning for a real, true-blue conservative like Taft's Ohio senatorial colleague, John Bricker, or Wherry or Bill Jenner of Indiana. But Dewey would do.

And then the dream of a sound, Republican America, built up over eighty years, collapsed. After again nominating a gentleman, the Republicans watched him get beaten to a pulp by a slugger. In a strident, abusive, effective campaign, Truman convinced the voters to keep both him and his party in power. The Republicans emerged from the humiliating ordeal spoiling for a fight. "I don't care how the thing is explained," Taft said shortly after the 1948 debacle. "It defies all common sense to send that roughneck ward politician back to the White House."[18]

An entire way of life seemed to be slipping away from Main Street. Conservative mythology, Cornell Professor Clinton Rossiter wrote in the spring of 1950, idealized a golden age of small government, free business, equal opportunity, sound money, low or no taxes, empty bars, full churches, kindly managers, devoted workers, and security for all who did an honest day's work. But modern forces had been so immense, so unrelenting, that many conservatives had concluded in despair that soon there would be no nation for them to imagine or to live in, no common myth around which to organize aspirations and meaning. The republic seemed to be trembling on its foundations, and ahead loomed the "the monstrous figure of the Triumphant State, whether Welfare or Marxist seems hardly to matter."[19]

Conservatism was in desperate trouble, Rossiter continued, because, although its adherents deeply feared for the future of the natural competitive order and for economic individualism, they had no real ideas and no real leadership. Conservatives were basically interested in making money; they were not interested in intellectual pursuits, theorizing, public philosophy, or public service. Their often brilliant liberal opponents were both thinkers and doers, and so they had taken over public policy. Rossiter, who would spend his life attempting to define an attractive American conservatism, begged his *Fortune* readers to study the ideas of Edmund Burke and other great conservatives of an earlier age and to consider disinterested public service as a kind of noblesse oblige. He also urged his fellow conservatives to admit their antidemocratic bias and to work to get the country to recognize the perils of unbridled democracy.

Rossiter was far better at description and prescription than mobilization. His conservative readers heard him but did nothing but seethe and hate. Where intellectual conservatism would repeatedly fail, an angry, reactive, fundamentalist conservatism would succeed. Conservatives found it far more comfortable to indulge in liberal-bashing and Red-baiting than to bestir themselves to formulate a coherent, attractive ideology.

There were many strains to midcentury Republican anger, but none was stronger than the contempt that conservatives held for certain high officials in the Truman administration. To fundamentalist conservatives, the New and Fair Deals had not only attracted campus crackpots, woolly-headed do-gooders, labor agitators, socialists, and "pinkos" but also snotty eastern "gentlemen" who should have better understood their true interests and responsibilities. Corporate attorney Dean Acheson, financier W. Averell Harriman, and businessman Lewis Strauss had joined Lovett, McCloy, and others in guiding or influencing postwar American foreign and national security policy with the help of a small but brilliant corps of diplomats including George Kennan, Charles E. ("Chip") Bohlen, Paul Nitze, and Dean Rusk.

The group was closely inbred. Acheson (secretary of state), Harriman (the wartime ambassador to Moscow who had succeeded Paul Hoffman as coordinator for European economic recovery), McCloy (U.S. high commissioner for Germany), and Lovett (who had succeeded Acheson as undersecretary of state and was now a frequent consultant on foreign policy) had known each other since Groton and had studied and played together at Harvard or Yale. Groton had emphasized the ideal of disinterested public service, and the Ivy League had provided the needed connections for launching successful public careers. Throughout their lives, the four kept track of one another, helping each other out when necessary and recommending each other for important jobs in and out of government. Although they occasionally held widely differing views of American interests, they remained firm friends and allies. Above all, they trusted one another's character, judgment, and integrity. When Truman contemplated appointing Harriman as, in effect, the first national security adviser, he asked Acheson if there would be any trouble. Truman reminded his secretary of state that Harriman had badly wanted the job that Acheson now held. There would certainly be gossip that Harriman was being primed to take Acheson's place. "Long knives," Truman said, "would be sharpened to fulfill that prophecy." No, it was all right, Acheson replied. Of course, he and Harriman were and had been rivals. But he had known Averell for forty-five years; he was a man of honor, there would be no trouble. And there was none.[20]

As their time in government lengthened and their stature grew, Acheson, Harriman, Lovett, and McCloy, along with Kennan and Bohlen, became known informally as the "wise men." Most, although not all, displayed their breeding and status ostentatiously. Honestly respectful of the "little people" who did their jobs competently and cheerfully (Acheson enjoyed talking about baseball with construction workers), they despised mediocrity. They viewed themselves as statesmen, as men of politics but not politicians. They expressed impatience and contempt toward those congressmen and senators who tried to disguise thoughtless criticism as honest Republican partisanship. They succeeded more than they failed, but their failures, especially in China, made them anathemas to the fundamentalist conservative wing of the GOP. Acheson's infuriating condescension to opponents, his ostensibly crude humor ("I learned everything I know at my mother's knee—and other low joints"), combined with elegant clothes (elegantly worn) and a guard's mustache, were condemned as examples of everything that Main Street believed was absolutely wrong with American life. Hugh Butler summed up the fundamentalist conservative hatred of Acheson perfectly: "I look at that fellow, I watch his smart-aleck manner and his British clothes and that New Dealism in everything he says and does, and I want to shout, 'Get out! Get out! You stand for everything that has been wrong in the United States for years!' "[21]

Not only was Acheson in with the wrong crowd; he kept preaching the wrong message. To men like Taft, Wherry, Jenner, Kem, and Hickenlooper, World War II had been fought "matter-of-factly, for the simple purpose of ending it. The chief war aim was to get home; and, since the quickest way to do that was to beat the enemy, everyone was in favor of beating him" and then returning to a 1920s-style way of life.[22] But from his high position in the Truman State Department, Acheson repeatedly told the American people after 1945 that the rush of history, over which no one had control, had forced the United States to end its disengagement from Europe's interminable, intractable troubles. Isolationism had been one of the most appealing legacies of the Republican era; it could no longer be sustained. The United States had paid an inevitable price for becoming the world's most powerful—and untouched—nation. Americans had exchanged comfort for inquietude, security for danger, and they could not turn back. The Russians with their enormous Red Army were a terrible, insistent problem that would not go away. Nor would the Chinese Communists, who by the end of 1949 had gained complete control of the Chinese mainland and had sent Chiang and his handful of supporters scuttling into exile on the island of Formosa. On New Year's Day 1950, the *Washington Post* recalled Acheson's observation that tension and conflict were endemic in international affairs; they could not be considered a kind of headache that could be cured by taking the right pill or powder. There was no panacea, and it was time for thoughtful men and women to realize that international relations were like the average person's existence: One had to deal with them the same way one dealt with making a living, as a problem to be met and solved anew every day.

Humiliated and baffled Republicans did not want to hear such talk. There was something deeply wrong with the country that no amount of preaching from a wealthy, condescending Fair Deal liberal could cure. The moderate Republican eastern wing had had its chance to redeem party fortunes under Willkie and Dewey and had failed miserably. As midcentury approached, elder statesmen and rank-and-file members searched frantically for a new messiah and yearned for indisputable evidence that might somehow link the Democratic party with genuine radicalism and the New Deal with outright treason. In 1949, two men battled for the soul of the GOP, although they scarcely knew each other.

Arthur Hendrick Vandenberg had been a U.S. senator from Michigan since 1928, when he was appointed to serve out the unexpired term of a man who had died in office. In his first dozen years on the Hill, Vandenberg had been a competent, unremarkable lawmaker, a tepid aspirant to presidential nomination, an avowed isolationist (he preferred the term *insulationist*), and a moderate anti-New Dealer. The events of December 7, 1941, transformed him into a national figure, some would say a national icon. He understood immediately that the attack on Pearl Harbor had irrevocably thrust the United States into the middle of world affairs. From that day forward, Vandenberg became an architect and undeviating champion of bipartisan foreign policy, and he enlisted a small but firm and influential faction of enlightened congressional Republicans. He supported FDR's insistence on a United Nations organization that would bind every member of the international community in a web of collective security. He subsequently supported the Truman Doctrine and the Marshall Plan of 1947 and the formation of NATO in 1949, all of which were designed to contain Soviet expansion in Europe.

Vandenberg was a generous man. He began a 1940 Gridiron Club speech by reminding his listeners that he did not approve of most of the New Deal, that he and Roosevelt had often quarreled over national policy. Then he turned to FDR and praised him for his gallant spirit. Roosevelt had made America *"social minded.* And it was high-time this phenomenon should come to pass because our best defense of democracy—in a sodden, saddened world of dictators—is to make democracy consciously and intimately advantageous to our whole people."[23]

Truman and Vandenberg became good friends, and their mutual esteem derived largely from similar experiences and shared values. If Truman had experienced a somewhat difficult youth, Vandenberg's was even grimmer. The business panic of 1893 had destroyed the harness-making establishment that Vandenberg's father had run for years with a modest profit. Nine-year-old Arthur promptly got a job hauling freight in a pushcart to help bolster the family's suddenly ruined finances. Soon he had several boys working for him, and he continued at various jobs until graduation from high school. He drove himself into a state of collapse that permanently damaged his health, and he discovered after a year of prelaw studies at Ann Arbor that he simply could not work and go to school at the same time. He became a cub reporter on the Grand Rapids *Herald*, whose owner, William Alden Smith, was so impressed with his talents that he promoted the twenty-two-year-old to editor of the almost bankrupt newspaper. Half a lifetime later, Vandenberg entered the Senate as a respected, moderately prosperous southern Michigan newspaperman.

Vandenberg's pursuit of bipartisanship in foreign policy was no political ploy. It resulted from a real and sophisticated appreciation of the dangerous world around him, an appreciation that his more deeply conservative and alienated colleagues in the Republican party could not or would not share. In a Lincoln Day speech in Detroit in February 1949, less than two months before NATO came into being, Vandenberg told his listeners that it would be a sad hour for the nation if its people ever deserted the fundamental concept that partisan politics ended at the water's edge. Recent attempts by ill-natured Democrats to reduce the Republican representation on the Senate Foreign Relations Committee were deplorable. But these "raids" should not be used as a pretext to abandon the quest for a united voice when America demanded peace with honor in the world.[24] Seven months later, Vandenberg proudly summed up the results and significance of four years of bipartisanship in an address before the Overseas Writers Club in Washington. The basic pattern was clear. The Senate had ratified by overwhelming margins the UN Charter, the Inter-American Rio Pact, the initial Marshall Plan, and Vandenberg's own resolution demanding more effective financial and political strength for these commitments. It had approved the NATO treaty by 82 to 13, and the previous week the Joint Senate Committee on Foreign Relations and Armed Services had voted 22 to 3 in favor of an arms bill to implement NATO.

There was "a powerful consistency" in these votes, which reflected a general and deep conviction throughout the "free world" that men of decency and character had to work together for a collective peace free from the threat of war or the corruption of appeasement. These votes reflected America's "disposition to render every rational, economic aid within our prudent power," not to buy friends or dispense charity but "as a matter of intelligent self-interest" for building a sound, interdependent world.[25]

Vandenberg was no fool. From the beginning, he had set decided limits on bipartisanship. It could go no further than the administration's UN and European policies. The Michigan senator always believed that "Palestine" (Israel) and especially China policy were fair game for Republican assaults, and this thinking allowed him to maintain tenuous relationships with the conservative Senate Republican power brokers: Taft, Bricker, Wherry, Jenner, Kem, and Hickenlooper.

But in August 1949, Vandenberg's health suddenly began to fail badly. He spent progressively less time on the Senate floor and in committee hearings. His speech before the Overseas Writers Club was his last public address. He made a final, brief appearance on the Hill in May 1950 and returned to Michigan, where he died early the next year. His faction had already begun to crumble under pressure from the party's conservative wing, and his departure marked the end of an era. A Gallup poll in the spring of 1950 revealed that only 26 percent of those queried understood what bipartisan foreign policy meant.[26] If the hated liberals of the Democratic party were to be overthrown, it would have to be through confrontation, not kindness.

Republicans searched desperately for someone who could find and focus the issue or issues that would bring the party back to respectability and eventual power. The handful of true patricians, wealthy and self-confident practitioners of disinterested public service such as Leverett Saltonstall and young Henry Cabot Lodge of Massachusetts or youthful Nelson Rockefeller of New York, were too far removed from the main currents of American politics to be effective. The field was open to the remainder of the Republican old guard led by Taft. But it was a much younger and even more driven and impatient man, Richard Milhous Nixon, who showed the old guard how to effectively go for liberalism's jugular, how to browbeat and humiliate arrogant Democrats in a no-holds-barred effort to move the country back to traditional Republicanism.

Since childhood Nixon had been a daring risk taker. His loud, verbally abusive father taught the boy and his brothers to think big, to "succeed."

According to one biographer, there was "noise and violence in the Nixon home," as mother Hannah tried to keep peace between Frank Nixon and his boys.[27] As Richard grew toward adulthood, pictures of him became almost frightening. Some showed a tight, closed face with heavy, angry eyes and a pursed mouth, as if the youngster were perpetually stifling a scream. Others revealed a sullen boy, stiff and awkward.[28] Young Nixon became a bit of a prig and began to exhibit two other striking sides to his character: an enormous capacity for grievance and self-pity and a growing inability to trust. Although Frank Nixon always had a job and a paycheck throughout Dick's childhood and youth in the twenties, the growing boy concluded that he and his family were poor and that polite society condescended to them. Whereas real hardship had broadened and deepened Vandenberg's innate decency, imagined hardship accustomed Nixon to react to life's inevitable setbacks with a bitter sourness. Years later, his special Watergate counsel, John Dean, said that Nixon was one of the strangest and meanest men he had ever known. Dean expressed amazement at the eulogies given at Nixon's grave site and said he was "flabbergasted" that Democratic president Bill Clinton could speak so reverently of Nixon. "Every time I dealt with him," Dean recalled of Nixon during the Watergate days, "there seemed to be a very mean streak I found I was dealing with. . . . This is a man who, for some reason, needed to control his entire world."[29]

Nixon harbored and honed grievances throughout his youth, but at Whittier College he successfully suppressed them behind the mask of the polished politician. His senior yearbook in 1934 lauded Nixon for being "always progressive" and "liberal" and having "led us through the year with flying colors."[30] At Duke Law School, however, he became known as an antisocial grind. It may never be known what drove the young man other than grievance, ambition, and perhaps considerable fear. But when he came out of the navy in early 1946 and was invited to appear before a "Committee of 100" eastern Los Angeles small businessmen, bankers, and ranchers who were seeking a war veteran to run on the Republican ticket against ultraliberal Jerry Voorhis, the thirty-three-year-old Nixon eagerly grabbed the opportunity.

Ill at ease in one-on-one situations or in small groups, Nixon by sheer willpower was able to overcome his almost crippling shyness before large gatherings. He told the committee exactly what it longed to hear. America's vets did not want to live on a government dole or handout. They wanted to find respectable jobs in private industry or start their own small businesses;

above all, they wanted to be accepted for what they could produce, not just what they could consume. When Nixon concluded his brief, trenchant remarks, Roy Day, head of the committee, remarked that he was their man: He was eminently "salable merchandise."[31] The alienated young lawyer had finally found the home he had been seeking among the polite circles in his district, and with a new sense of pride and purpose he went out to do battle.

Nixon developed a great contempt for Voorhis during the subsequent campaign. The man did not seem to know how to fight; he was a liberal wimp. Nixon's masters, desperate for victory after more than a decade of what they perceived as assaults against the American way of life and an outright wartime alliance with communism, believed that all means to end liberal rule were legitimate. Over the years liberals had proved to be little different from and little better than communists. Anxious conservatives ignored or dismissed the virulent hatred of Voorhis by dedicated communists because of his 1940 legislation requiring them to register and his subsequent attacks against Stalin's control of eastern Europe. To Roy Day and his colleagues, Voorhis was a communist just like many liberals in America. Out in the Middle West, another obscure veteran, Joe McCarthy, was making the same charges against Robert La Follette, Jr., in the Wisconsin senatorial campaign. Nixon and McCarthy repeated the communist theme so vigorously and often that Voorhis and La Follette became confused and unfocused. Both were defeated.

When Nixon entered Congress in January 1947, he shrewdly reshaped his anticommunist impulse into an ostensibly more respectable and rational commitment. A closet internationalist, he supported the Marshall Plan because, he argued, its agricultural provisions would open new markets for southern California vegetable and fruit growers. Appointed to the House Labor Committee, he supported the Taft-Hartley Bill, which reconfirmed labor gains during the New Deal while placing curbs on strikes. According to Nixon, he was also asked to join HUAC, because House Republican speaker Joe Martin thought the committee, which had become almost a joke, needed a young lawyer "to smarten it up."[32]

Nixon quickly but carefully began to dominate the committee, realizing that it could be a marvelous forum for someone of intelligence who could move the communist subversion issue from buffoonery to legitimacy. He carefully distanced himself from the more shrill and outrageous charges that HUAC leveled at the Hollywood film community in 1947. At the same time, he began to control the committee selectively on issues he believed could be won and in 1948 sponsored with South Dakota's Karl Mundt a bill that would expose and deal with the Communist Party as a menace to the American way. The Mundt-Nixon bill passed in the House as a result of Nixon's shrewd management. Although it did not have any chance of passing in the Senate, it was debated publicly and heatedly by Harold Stassen and Dewey, the two leading contenders for the Republican nomination that year. Nixon suddenly had a reputation as a comer.

In floor debate, the young congressman had insisted that Mundt-Nixon was no police-state bill, but of course it was. He added that it would pose no threat to sincere and honest liberals and progressives, but, of course, it did. The bill's requirements for registration of all Communist Party members was perhaps not exceptional given its premise that the nation was in the grip of communist subversives. Nor was denial of passports to party members. But publication of the sources of all printed and broadcast materials issued by communist front organizations and the creation of a Subversive Activities Control Board to determine which organizations were or were not communist fronts clearly extended the police powers of all federal and state authorities well beyond constitutional bounds. Moreover, the sloppy but appealing anticommunist impulse behind Mundt-Nixon encouraged other right-wingers to consider even further extensions of the coercive powers of governments and courts.

In the late spring of 1949, Bourke Hickenlooper, a thin-faced, middle-aged fundamentalist conservative with tightly slicked-down hair and the sour look of a perpetually constipated small-town banker, began the first of twenty-three Senate hearings designed to ferret out fraud, mismanagement, and, above all, communist elements in the Atomic Energy Commission, which was headed by David Lilienthal. America had maintained its atomic monopoly, and apprehensive Republicans were determined that it would not be lost. The Senate sessions, which were almost invariably silly, trivial, and interminable, left Lilienthal deeply discouraged and fatigued. "I even used the word 'despair' one day, and this is an emotion that under no circumstances should a human being permit himself."[33]

Hickenlooper and his reactionary colleagues scored only one point off the AEC chairman, forcing Lilienthal to admit that a student granted an AEC fellowship had turned out to be a "professed Communist." Lilienthal then had to agree that henceforth students desiring to work at the commission would have to be investigated regarding their affiliations and beliefs.[34]

Aside from that early victory, Hickenlooper's efforts to discredit the AEC were an unmitigated disaster. Lilienthal and his colleagues scored point after point against the uninformed senator and his staff. To unearth real fraud, mismanagement, or subversion required a somewhat sophisticated knowledge of atomic technology and production, which Hickenlooper and his people simply did not possess. When the senator charged that the AEC had lost precious amounts of uranium, commission scientists easily demonstrated that the uranium had simply disappeared in a conversion process during weapons making. When Hickenlooper asserted that Lilienthal had hired men of doubtful loyalty without sufficient security checks and had allowed flagrant cost overruns, changes in blueprints, and other administrative improvisations, the AEC chairman readily justified his actions as by-products of essential ventures into uncharted areas in order to hasten nuclear developments in both weapon technology and civilian applications. Nuclear scientists jeered that the senator was just another midwestern boob with no understanding—and no desire to understand—the sophisticated workings and underpinnings of advanced technology.

The scientists charged that Hickenlooper's greatest crime (and one shared by many of his fellow Republicans) was adherence to an absurd, destructive cult of secrecy. Since Hiroshima, "Congress and a large section of the press and radio [had] set themselves up as 'watchdogs' of the Great Atomic Secret," the editors of the *Bulletin of the Atomic Scientists* wrote scornfully at the end of 1949. These critics had claimed that the great secret was endangered "by the internationalist leanings and leftist sympathies of Mr. Lilienthal and the scientists in the AEC installations." Hickenlooper's bumbling, embarrassing hearings had shown that they were wrong. The "diehards in Congress and the press," who "have maintained that we have had not too much but too little secrecy" in atomic affairs needed to realize that "this kind of talk has lost its effect on the American mind; that the cult of the Great Atomic Secret has now collapsed." Openness in research and communication was essential to scientific progress. The atomic scientists trusted that all idiotic beliefs in "salvation through secrecy" had now been discredited forever.[35]

The Republicans retreated in confusion and frustration. But time and events were not necessarily against them. Hickenlooper had friends as well as enemies in the atomic community, including Edward Teller. An impatient forty-one-year-old nuclear researcher from Budapest, Teller had worked at Los Alamos during the war and firmly believed in the communist menace abroad if not at home. All atomic scientists knew that with or without help from spies the Soviets would stumble across the secret of the bomb within a few years if not months. Teller, who had been working on the theory of a hydrogen bomb for more than half a decade, bet an acquaintance in 1949 that if the United States did not begin unlocking the secrets of a thermonuclear weapon immediately, the man would be under arrest in a Soviet United States within five years.

Little more than a month after Hickenlooper completed his hearings, the African-American forewoman of a New York jury announced that she and her colleagues had found eleven of the leading members of the Communist Party of the United States (CPUSA) guilty of conspiring "knowingly and willfully to advocate and teach the duty and necessity of overthrowing and destroying the Government of the United States by force and violence."[36] Liberals were appalled not only by the decision but by the instructions Judge Harold Medina had given the jurors. He had told them that it was absurd to demand proof that the CPUSA constituted a clear and present danger to the government of the United States; if it was established that a secret, Kremlin-inspired conspiracy existed in the form of the CPUSA, then indisputable danger was indeed present. Constitutional lawyers and observers at home and abroad immediately observed that Medina's instructions, if upheld by a higher court, would substitute the principle of guilt by association for that of clear and present danger (itself a vague concept), which had been written into the 1940 Smith Act.

The conviction of the "Communist eleven" by a jury of twelve average Americans revealed how deeply fears of a Red menace had penetrated society. After years of apparently futile alarms and excursions, the issue of communist subversion of American liberalism finally seemed about to become a central element in the national dialogue. All hinged on the outcome of one case. By the end of 1949 much of the country was expectantly waiting for the conclusion of the sensational jury trial of Alger Hiss. Nixon, using his position on HUAC, had orchestrated the whole affair. If Hiss were found innocent, Nixon's fledgling career as a Red-hunter, and indeed the entire anticommunist impulse in America, might be destroyed. But if Hiss were found guilty, opportunities for a comprehensive anticommunist crusade would be limitless.

The Hiss case possessed every possible element in a spy story turned courtroom drama: scruffy accuser versus established, elegant socialite and diplomat; communist spies burrowing deep into the American government; breathless revelations by one side on the brink of ridicule and defeat; and a daring young defender of the public interest fighting for truth and his political life.

When Whittaker Chambers, an avowed former communist, went before HUAC in August 1948 and charged that Hiss had been a member of Chambers's own communist cell in the late thirties, his tale seemed preposterous. Hiss had a long, distinguished record in the New Deal–Fair Deal foreign policy establishment, had served an important role in the creation of the United Nations, and was currently president of the Carnegie Endowment for International Peace. Chambers, on the other hand, was a nonentity. Son of a failed commercial artist, he had left home at an early age to indulge in adolescent wanderlust, which led to many jobs "with some questionable episodes." He later talked his way into Columbia University but was expelled because of "blasphemous" behavior. Chambers then allegedly made a suicide pact with a brother, who went through with it alone. Rushing off to Europe in the mid-1920s, the unstable young man concluded that the old civilization was doomed and that communism was the only solution. He joined the CPUSA and was briefly editor of the party's *Daily Worker* in the early thirties. Then his bosses ordered him to go under cover and to devote himself to the Russian spy ring that was already flourishing in the United States. Not long after, he claimed, he met equally dedicated communists Alger and Priscilla Hiss. But by mid-1938, Stalin's great terror in Russia had disillusioned him. He left the party, ultimately managed to get on the editorial board of *Time* magazine (he was proficient in several languages and widely self-educated), and tried with little success to inform the FBI about the activities of Soviet moles in America.[37]

When Hiss vigorously and eloquently denied even knowing Chambers and Truman called the whole affair a "red herring," HUAC members were both embarrassed and frightened. Only Richard Nixon grasped the possible truth of Chambers's allegations and insisted on pressing the case. At that point Hiss began to panic.[38]

Nixon took Chambers's detailed recollections of the Hisses' home life and behavior to amazed and discomfited reporters and officials familiar with the couple (including Wall Street lawyer and Republican foreign policy expert John Foster Dulles), who told him that, incredibly, Chambers could not be lying. Hiss then demanded a confrontation with Chambers in a Manhattan hotel room filled with reporters, cameramen, and HUAC members. Yes, Hiss reluctantly admitted, "Chambers" might be a George Crosley, whom Hiss vaguely remembered from years before. As cameras flashed, Hiss looked into "Mr. Crosley's" mouth to see whether this man with the skillfully reconstructed dentures was the Crosley he remembered with noticeably bad teeth. Hiss concluded that he was the same individual.

Having conceded that much, Hiss then compounded his folly. When Chambers subsequently stated on a nationwide radio program that "Alger Hiss was, and still may be, a Communist," Hiss sued for libel.[39] Once again Truman charged Republicans with dragging a red herring across the 1948 presidential campaign trail in a desperate effort to avoid confronting the serious issues that faced the country. Once again timid HUAC members wondered if they had gone too far.

But Chambers countered masterfully. He now charged that in 1937 and 1938 Hiss had passed to him for transmission to the Russian spy ring secret State Department documents that Hiss had copied on an old Woodstock typewriter. The charge was sensational, for now Hiss was being accused not merely of unpopular affiliation but of outright treason. Chambers promptly took stunned HUAC members to a walled-up dumbwaiter shaft in a Brooklyn house and then to a pumpkin patch on his own Maryland farm, where he produced the State Department documents (some on microfilm) that he claimed Hiss had passed to him. Several of the documents had marginalia in Hiss's handwriting. Even Hiss's strongest defenders were shaken by the revelation. The incriminating records were turned over to the Justice Department along with Chambers's testimony. Attention swiftly focused on the typewriter that had been used to copy the documents in question, and by the end of 1948 the FBI had found the Woodstock through incredible legwork and luck. Hiss was indicted.

"Is America Safe for Spies?" *Newsweek* asked. For years the often abused and just as often abusing HUAC had been condemned for witch-hunting. But now it had suddenly found a smoking gun. "Undisputable evidence" revealed "that thoroughly trusted State Department employees in 1938 had actually been supplying a Communist spy ring with documents of the highest secrecy." If Hiss and other alleged diplomatic traitors were not brought to trial, Washington would be guilty of incompetence in protecting the national interest; if Chambers was ruined by his courageous identification of such a traitor, the government would be slamming the door on all future communist confessors.[40]

As midcentury arrived, perceptive critics sensed that the country might be drifting into crisis. Washington correspondents reported that to whatever extent the capital reflected the mood of the nation it seemed safe to say that the United States was healthy (the death rate had declined substantially during the previous twelve months), increasingly wealthy, and comfortably self-assured. But a writer for the *New York Times* noted that there was "a peculiarly bracing and expectant quality in the Washington climate; the year 1950 promises to be a tumultuous one politically."[41] As Americans raised their glasses in toasts to the new year, they could not imagine the awful events that were about to overwhelm them. Their ordeal would begin with the abrupt reappearance of a specter thought banished weeks before.

4

The Bomb

❖ ❖ ❖ ❖ ❖ ❖ ❖ ❖ ❖ ❖ ❖ ❖ ❖ ❖ ❖

When Harry Truman announced on September 23, 1949, that there had been an "atomic explosion" in the Soviet Union, Americans reacted with studied indifference or bravado. The administration's "official orchestra" for once played in tune, emphasizing that there was no reason for panic because the Soviet achievement had long been foreseen and would not unduly disturb the course of international politics.[1] The day after Truman's announcement, *Washington Post* reporters questioned a random sample of people on the corner of 13th and F Streets and concluded that men and women thought the Soviet achievement was important but not catastrophic news.[2] Perhaps now the two powers could do some serious bargaining to end the cold war. Scientists and the president had been saying for years that the bomb could not be kept a secret forever; they were right. The news was not encouraging, but of the more than twenty persons interviewed, only one expressed outright fear and only one other thought that Russian possession of the bomb meant war.

Out in Seattle, a *Times* headline about public reaction to the news read: "Russ Got the Bomb? So Wot? How'd the Bums [Brooklyn Dodgers] Do Today?" The story indicated that those interviewed on Manhattan streets were either resigned or apathetic. The bomb, like a terrible natural disaster in another part of the country, was something they could do nothing about. The article treated international relations like a college football game in which "the race for A-bombs between the cold war champions of the West and East pitted the United States and the U.S.S.R. in a contest" for the future of civilization. "With growing realization that this country was not caught napping, [Washington] today began to share the calm with which President Truman disclosed that America's monopoly had been shattered." Two days later, the *Times* editorialized that the Soviet achievement was "inevitable" and that the question of war or peace depended entirely on Stalin.[3]

In Chicago, the *Tribune*'s Washington correspondent, Walter Trohan, said that congressmen were urging the people to avoid hysteria. Cold war tensions were neither increased nor decreased by the Soviet bomb. *Tribune* editorial writers took the same position. The bomb, horrible as it was, was not infinitely destructive. If only the Truman administration would stop shoveling money to ingrate nations abroad so that they could buy obsolete conventional weapons, the United States could devise a civilian defense against the new Soviet threat.[4]

Senate Majority Leader Scott Lucas of Illinois insisted that Soviet possession of the bomb did not change the fundamental pattern of world power. The United States, he added, still had a four-year lead in the research and development of nuclear weapons, and its superior scientists and technicians would maintain that lead. Walter Bedell Smith, Eisenhower's wartime chief of staff and future head of the CIA, insisted that the United States was ten years ahead of the crude ruffians in the Kremlin.[5]

Bernard Brodie, the country's leading nuclear "scholar," was also undisturbed by an event "so thoroughly expected and previously discussed." Obviously Soviet science was not as backward as many in the West had believed. But the West had given away many of its nuclear secrets in the publicly issued Smyth report of 1946, in which the United States had revealed the three best methods (although not the specific processes) for obtaining Uranium-235. The "phenomenal complexity of the [American] bomb mechanism itself" was largely due to the development of safeguards for human life and capital equipment, which the Soviets (like the Japanese in World War II) could and probably did ignore because of their lesser interest in protecting individuals from harm. In addition, the United States had dedicated only about 10 percent of its wartime scientific and capital investment to the Manhattan Project, which had developed and built the bomb. "The Russians may have organized a much greater concentration of their much lesser resources on their A-bomb project."[6]

Foreign correspondents reported from their listening posts in London, Paris, and Tokyo that the Soviet nuclear achievement had generated scarcely a ripple of public concern. British newsstands were still full of papers hours after the announcement, a sharp contrast to several weeks before, when devaluation of the pound had emptied kiosks minutes after the news hit the streets. Six months later, the eminent French sociologist, Raymond Aaron, recalled that Frenchmen and Europeans generally reacted with bored indifference because they realized that the world would be a terrifying place for decades. Announcement of the Soviet bomb "was all that was needed for everybody to return to his daily business even more resolved than before to look the other way—and not at the horizon, now covered with new and more threatening clouds."[7] The consensus in Western Europe and Japan was that world leadership had passed to the United States; it was America's problem to defend the free world, and the Yanks were still far ahead in the nuclear race.

But two mutually exclusive groups in the United States—the atomic scientists and the anticommunist crusaders—reacted immediately and strongly to the Soviet bomb. In later years the myth would grow and solidify that America's atomic scientists, obsessed with guilt over developing the atomic bomb and then seeing amoral bureaucrats and statesmen take its use out of their hands, fought vigorously to prevent the spread of nuclear weapons. Only a few evil schemers in their midst, like Teller, insisted on building even bigger bombs and gigantic stockpiles while humbling the gentle, humane nuclear science community epitomized by J. Robert Oppenheimer.

In fact, the nuclear science community was deeply and bitterly divided from the beginning over the best response to the Soviet bomb. Chairman Lilienthal, who later argued for restraint, issued a statement on behalf of himself and the AEC. The United States had to do everything necessary to "establish unquestioned and unmistakable leadership" in the coming atomic armaments race between East and West. "We believe as one man, and the President, our immediate superior, believes that we should let nothing stand in the way of arming this country atomically in such a way as to erect a great deterrent to aggression in the world."[8]

Five leading scientists at the Metallurgical Laboratory of the University of Chicago, where the first sustained nuclear reaction had taken place in 1942, released a statement on October 1, sharply disputing Bedell Smith's smug assertion that the Soviets would always be ten years behind in the atomic arms race. "We . . . are aware of the problems involved in the large-scale production of atomic bombs," Harold Urey, Leo Szilard, and three others wrote. Smith's statement had "no basis in fact."[9]

Frederick Seitz of the University of Illinois warned that knowledgeable scientists had realized the Soviets would get the bomb soon rather than later. Many "quarters in American life" took refuge in an ostrichlike belief that the Russians would be unable to solve the problem of mass production of nuclear arms. This was a "vain and dangerous hope." By devoting just one-tenth of their present industrial outlay to bomb production, the Soviets could match the current American effort. Seitz argued that the Soviets would begin stockpiling nuclear weapons soon and quickly. Only a return to the feverish pace and "dynamic state" of the Manhattan Project years would ensure that the United States could remain somewhat ahead of Russia.[10]

Eugene Rabinowitch, also of Illinois, reminded his colleagues that they were devoted to a calm, rational lifestyle. Creating panic among the public should never be their intent. He then argued that although Americans should not expect atomic bombs to begin falling on their heads within the next year or two, they had good reason "to be deeply alarmed and to be prepared for grave decisions." Not only was the national leadership in atomic offense threatened; "we are even more in danger of falling behind the Soviet Union in our capacity for *defense*." The only hope was some sort of international control of atomic energy. Otherwise there was an "inexorable trend leading to atomic war."[11]

Szilard in a long essay took the nuclear science community over the brink into foreign-policy making. The only way to save the world was to get Stalin and his Kremlin colleagues to agree to international control of atomic energy. To achieve that goal, the United States had to convince the admittedly thuggish Soviet leadership that it had nothing to fear from the West. The United States would have to abandon NATO and neutralize Western Europe while maintaining mutual defense treaties with individual nations. Only by making it in Stalin's interest to reduce development of atomic arms could the peace be preserved. What was required, Szilard said, was a shift in American policy from containment of Soviet expansion to development of contentment in the Kremlin.[12]

More than any other atomic scientist, Nobel Prize winner Urey, the discoverer of the hydrogen isotope deuterium, shaped debate and perspectives on future policy. Urey was not only alarmed but deeply embittered about recent events. Progress in atomic research had steadily deteriorated in the United States during the four years since Hiroshima. The best men had left Los Alamos and the other government laboratories and had returned to university work, totally disgusted by the stupid insistence of Congress and the

American people on keeping an atomic secret that was actually no secret at all. When these disaffected intellectuals tried to tell legislators and citizens the "disagreeable truths" about the folly of maintaining atomic secrecy, "we have even been accused of wishing to give up our progress because we are impractical dreamers or plain traitors." Every person in a responsible position in atomic research "is hampered or even paralyzed in his work if he must permanently be on guard to defend himself against ridiculous accusations of real or imaginary violations of petty security regulations or against charges of having Communistic leanings." Many of the best nuclear scientists yearned to go back to government research, and their talents were being sorely missed. It was of "the utmost importance" to acknowledge the damage that reliance on secrecy had done to the AEC. Effective international control of nuclear weapons could not be obtained if the United States lost its edge in atomic research and development. But that edge would be irretrievably lost if its scientists continued to be harassed by ignorant bureaucrats and reactionary congressmen.[13]

Urey, Szilard, and others immediately concluded that the Soviet bomb rendered Western Europe indefensible. The Continent "from here on is at the mercy of Russia," Urey declared. He and his colleagues agreed that if there were to be an atomic war it would be at least a ten-year struggle. Because of its enormous distances and concealed war industries, the Soviet Union, when compared with the open United States, would not require nearly as many nuclear weapons to attain practical parity with the West. Moreover, "Russia is at least abreast of the United States in development of long-range rockets—potential carriers of atomic warheads." Within hours after publication of Urey's comments, Allied and German sources in Frankfurt stated that "Russia has virtually ringed western Europe with super-secret V-2 rocket launching bases . . . aimed at strategic points in western Europe from the English Channel to the Adriatic." Soon the Soviets would be able to "blanket" the entire continent with nuclear-tipped missiles in the event of an "East-West war." Several days later, a Czech army newspaper boasted that the "Soviet Union's camp now has the crushing upper hand" in world affairs.[14]

The Kremlin reacted shrewdly to Truman's announcement. A Moscow press release reminded the world rather contemptuously of Foreign Minister Molotov's 1947 assertion that Russia had the know-how to make a bomb (a point that was promptly and hotly disputed by both Senator Brien McMahon of Connecticut and Urey). Andrey Vyshinsky, Soviet ambassador to the United Nations, arrived in New York the last week in September, calling for the five great powers on the Security Council to form a global peace pact that would ban all nuclear weapons and initiate a "rigid system of international control." But the Soviets were unwilling to comply with Western demands for on-site inspection of nuclear facilities and collection of all nuclear weapons at a single site under UN jurisdiction.[15]

The most recent Soviet–United States clash had occurred at Lake Success on September 8, when America's UN representative John Hickerson observed that a Soviet proposal for international control of atomic weapons "implied that nations should continue to own, operate and manage dangerous facilities. . . . To permit nations to own dangerous quantities of nuclear fuel ipso facto permits them to own atomic weapons." His Soviet counterpart, Semyon Tsarapkin, a striking, hatchet-faced man with a bristling crew cut, had replied that U.S. insistence that no nation possess significant amounts of nuclear fuel and facilities was a "fantastic, unreal and absurd idea." Such fuel and facilities had to be located somewhere on the earth; they could not be placed on the moon. But every bit of land on earth was under sovereign national jurisdiction. Where were you going to put such materials and fuels? "If analyzed to its logical conclusion, this whole [U.S.] concept was a blind alley."[16]

When questioned by the United States and its allies about how a five-power peace pact might effectively control atomic materials and weapons development, Vyshinsky left no illusions about his government's real view of international affairs. According to one account, his speech before the General Assembly "did not differ one jot from a score of previous harangues in which the imperialism and the warmongering of the west were compared with the peaceful intentions of Russia." British Foreign Minister Ernest Bevin delivered a somber rejoinder, repeating "the whole record of Russia's troublemaking since the end of the war." Hopes that the Vyshinsky mission would help lessen cold war tensions were dashed.[17]

Almost immediately after Truman's announcement, anticommunist vigilantes were on the radio and in front of press briefings to call for exactly what Urey and his colleagues most feared: another investigation of the internal subversion of America's scientific community. Senator Hickenlooper announced that now, more than ever, the Senate had to listen to his charges that "security in our atomic programme has been treated with indifference."[18]

Representative Harold Velde, a forty-year-old Republican from Abraham Lincoln's district in Illinois, a former FBI agent, and one of HUAC's most vocal members, claimed that the Soviets had undoubtedly gained three to five years in bomb production because since 1933 the American government, "from the White House down," had assumed an official attitude of great tolerance and even sympathy toward the views of communists and "fellow travelers." The inevitable result was an infiltration of the federal establishment "by a network of spies." Velde urged that Congress investigate the government's "entire security setup" and determine the reasons for its "disgraceful record." It was time to throw out of office "those incompetents who regard their political lives as more important than our national security."[19]

Democratic Senator Herbert R. O'Connor of Maryland went on the air to demand laws that would "stop Reds from coming to America" under the protection of diplomatic immunity and status. "The ring leaders of the Communist apparatus in this country are coming in by the hundreds" and were "'the brains and guiding force of subversive activity,'" the "'generals of the Communist fifth column.'"[20]

Tragically for the country, the anticommunist zealots were on the right track. They, rather than a bumbling and defensive administration, took the initiative in trying to ferret out the extent of treason in the West's wartime nuclear program.[21] That treason had first been exposed in 1946 after the defection late the previous year by Igor Gouzenko, a code clerk in the Soviet embassy at Ottawa. Gouzenko identified Alan Nunn May, a British physicist at the wartime Cavendish Laboratory who later went to work in Montreal, as the one who had provided the Soviets with some information on the heavy water project on which he was working. It is now known that Nunn May also gave his Soviet contact microscopic amounts of precious uranium 235 and 233, which were in drastically short supply in Russia. Obviously the Soviets had conducted some successful nuclear espionage. But even the most suspicious midcentury anticommunist vigilante could not guess the dimensions of the Soviet penetration. Only the opening of Moscow archives near the end of the century would begin to reveal the true story.

As David Holloway has demonstrated, the Soviet atomic and later thermonuclear achievements owed as much to plain, dumb luck, the openness of the Western political and scientific systems, and, above all, the intuitive and rational capabilities of key Russian scientists as they did to treason. In

1940, for instance, young Bill Laurence, the science writer for the *New York Times*, guessed from a flurry of recent activity in Germany and the United States that active work was beginning on the construction of atomic bombs. He wrote a front page article on the subject that was noticed by George Vernadsky, a young Russian emigré and professor of history at Yale. Vernadsky sent a copy of Laurence's article to his father, a well-regarded Soviet physicist who promply alerted his scientific establishment, which mobilized Russian work in the field. Five years later, just days after the atomic raids against Japan, the U.S. government published the Smyth Report, which, although it omitted sensitive details about the American program such as the implosion process, nonetheless provided the Soviets "with an overall picture of what the United States had done."

Serious Soviet nuclear espionage, which began in September 1941, was essential to Stalin's quest for a workable bomb. The resident Soviet KGB agent in London, Anatolii Gorskii, began transmitting critical baseline information on Britain's work on nuclear energy, which at that time was the most advanced in the world. Gorskii's source was undoubtedly John Cairncross, the notorious "fifth man" of the Cambridge University group of traitors who had coalesced in the thirties around Anthony Blount. Cairncross had become private secretary to Lord Hankey, who as chairman of the War Cabinet's Scientific Advisory Committee was privy to all information on Britain's wartime nuclear work.

Isolated as the Soviet Union was by late 1941, Stalin had to have brilliant scientists who could understand and imaginatively apply the data that were gradually seeping in from the outside world. Fortunately for Soviet security, he possessed two of the world's best physicists, Igor Khurchatov and Iulii Khariton. On April 12, 1943, the State Defense Committee of the Soviet Union issued a decree initiating a nuclear project, and by that autumn Khurchatov, Khariton, and their subordinates were ready to start. But from the beginning the project seemed doomed because of a lack of critical uranium 235. Programmatic paralysis was avoided only when crucial information was supplied by moles working within the Anglo-American project, who put the Russians onto the possibility of developing a plutonium bomb, then supplied all the critical information on how to build it. The chief mole and essential contributor was a mild-mannered, bespectacled little British scientist and bachelor who had fled Nazi Germany. His name was Klaus Fuchs, and while he was busily transmitting nuclear secrets to the Soviets, he was much appreciated by the wives of Los Alamos as a reliable baby-sitter.[22]

Veterans of the Soviet program have emphasized that although the espionage information was critical, it would have been useless without the capability and hard work of an isolated Russian scientific community, which could not count on the constant flow of ideas and criticisms to advance and enrich its work, as was the case in the West. Years later, Khariton would emphasize that despite the "good haul of atomic secrets in 1945, the obtained materials 'still required an enormous amount of work on a great scale by our physicists'" before they could be used. Moreover, Stalin was becoming obsessed by the notion that somehow the purity of Soviet science had to be maintained if its unique genius was to be fully expressed. He loved crackpots like the geneticist Trofim Lysenko, who sought to enfold Russian biology and physics in the cloak of scientific Marxism, and he told Kurchatov in early 1946 not to spare resources, but to conduct his work "broadly, on the Russian scale."[23] By the late summer of 1949, Kurchatov and his staff had completed their mission; Stalin awarded them all medals, while the West, in delayed shock, started to quake.

Within days of the Soviet atomic blast, voices from the mainstream began to support the alarmists, and gradually Americans realized that the Soviet bomb was indeed a major turning point in the brief postwar period. *Newsweek* devoted the first eight pages of its October 3 issue to the Soviet achievement. Stalin was on its cover, and under his portrait were the words: "The man who has the bomb." *Newsweek* writers claimed that "the public felt Sunday-supplement creeps chase up and down its back." The "average man's reaction to President Truman's atom-bomb announcement," *Newsweek* concluded, was probably best summed up by Urey: "There's only one thing worse than one nation having the atomic bomb—that's two nations having it."[24] By mid-November, the Soviet bomb was being described as "this new Pearl Harbor," and academic pundits were in full cry.[25] Hans J. Morgenthau, a leading political scientist, wrote that Soviet acquisition of the bomb was of transcendent importance. "In comparison with it, all the great issues of the post-war period fade into insignificance. . . . it overshadows even the passing of China into the Soviet camp."[26]

As the counterattack against complacency grew and spread, impatient members of the atomic community schemed to take the nuclear arms race to a higher, ultimately unlimited dimension. On October 5 two University of California scientists, chemist Wendell Latimer and physicist Ernest O. Lawrence, had lunch in the charming, wooden faculty club set in a leafy Berkeley glade. The conversation quickly turned to the Russian bomb. If the Soviets could build an atomic weapon, they might also be working on a "super" (i.e., thermonuclear) bomb, a frightening prospect. The two men agreed that it was essential that the United States develop the super first, and after lunch they went up to the Radiation Laboratory in the hills overlooking the campus and quickly enlisted the enthusiastic support of another prominent physicist and Manhattan Project alumnus, Luis Alvarez. All three men were going to a scientific conference in Washington in several days. All had developed contacts in Congress as a result of their work on the Manhattan Project. It was time to get going on a "super" project.

The theoretical basis for developing a thermonuclear bomb had been discovered in 1927, when two young European physicists, Fritz Houtermans and Geoffrey Atkinson, had hypothesized that solar energy could be recreated on earth by fusing lightweight atoms. Within several years, it was clear to scientists that fusion of certain hydrogen isotopes, such as deuterium or tritium, would set off a thermonuclear reaction. "Once the [fusion] reaction was initiated, it could be sustained, theoretically, simply by adding more heavy hydrogen," liberating enormous amounts of energy and producing explosions of potentially unlimited size. In July 1942, a "theoretical group" of nuclear scientists at Berkeley reported to the fledgling Manhattan Project that an "atomic" bomb deriving its force from nuclear fission (the splitting of heavy elements uranium and plutonium) was limited by the process itself. But there were no such constraints on a fusion weapon that would derive its force from the coalescence of nuclei of light elements at the other end of the atomic table (i.e., hydrogen and its isotope deuterium). This "breathtaking" possibility had been largely ignored during the Manhattan Project because the United States wanted to win the race for a usable atomic weapon.[27]

Teller quickly became obsessed with the many problems involved in developing a hydrogen bomb. By February 1944, he and a small group of colleagues at Los Alamos had concluded that one of the chief obstacles was the incredibly high ignition temperature of liquid deuterium. It might be possible, however, to "wrap" an atomic bomb inside a hydrogen weapon to provide the necessary heat. A top secret 1949 AEC report stated "that a fission [i.e., atomic] bomb could be used as a 'match' to ignite the deuterium just as a fuse is used to ignite a charge of powder. As in the latter case, the size of the explosion would be limited only by the amount of deuterium present."[28] But finding an efficient means of doing this would require years of constant research and analysis. A hydrogen bomb of sufficiently greater yield than an atomic weapon might be as big as a railroad freight car or larger; no existing or conceivable delivery system could carry it. The cost of such a bomb would be prohibitive in any case. And it would require an atomic weapon as a starter, and during World War II no such weapons existed. Nonetheless, Teller and his small clique spent nearly all their time at Los Alamos working on the super. Oppenheimer and the other scientists became impatient, then disgusted, with Teller's obsession. He was not doing the work he had come to do. If he really wanted to develop a thermonuclear bomb, he should be helping to achieve an atomic bomb, which was its essential component. But Teller pressed on, and Oppenheimer was afraid to fire him for both security and professional reasons. No one could doubt the Hungarian's brilliance.

In 1946, with the atomic bomb now a fact, distinguished Austrian physicist Hans Thirring publicly described the theory of a hydrogen bomb, based on "a kind of 'ignition' mechanism," in a chapter of his book *Die Geschichte der Atombombe* [The Story of the Atomic Bomb].[29] From then on, no reputable scientist anywhere in the world could deny at least the hypothetical feasibility of a hydrogen bomb whose power and intensity could approach that of the sun. The only limit on such a weapon would be size. Somehow scientists would have to compress such a monster into a reasonably sized and cost-effective container. By the summer of 1945, Teller had become a zealot for the super bomb, dividing the world into those on his side and those who remained skeptical of the feasibility or merit of building a thermonuclear weapon.[30] He resigned from Los Alamos and took a position at the University of Chicago. He traveled frequently to Washington, where he assiduously cultivated congressmen and bureaucrats. He became a frequent guest at the home of Atomic Energy Commissioner Lewis Strauss and a good friend of Hickenlooper, who was attracted to the scientist's sincere, uncompromising anticommunism. He courted Senator McMahon, chairman of the Joint Congressional Committee on Atomic Energy, and was soon appointed to the air force's Scientific Advisory Panel, ultimately becoming its chairman. He spoke tirelessly about the importance of thermonuclear fusion work.

Teller was visiting Los Alamos when Latimer, Lawrence, and Alvarez dropped by on their way to the Washington conference to speak with scientists about the need to move ahead on a super bomb. Teller was delighted and spent hours with his Berkeley colleagues. Eventually he decided that he, too, had to go to Washington and inform his congressional and bureaucratic network of the need to rush ahead on thermonuclear research.

Strauss had already reached the same conclusion. On September 30, he summoned his secretary and dramatically told her that she was about to take down one of the most important letters in her career. Strauss's missive to his fellow atomic energy commissioners stated that increased production of fissionable materials and weapons as a logical response to the Soviet bomb was not enough. "It seems to me that the time has now come for a quantum jump in our planning . . . that is to say, that we should now make an intensive effort to get ahead with the super." By "intensive effort" he meant, if necessary, a commitment as large as the Manhattan Project. It was the only way to stay in front of the Soviets. Strauss read his memorandum to the Atomic Energy Commissioners on October 5 and concluded by asking Lilienthal to convene the AEC's General Advisory Committee (GAC) as soon as possible to consider the project. Lilienthal promptly asked Oppenheimer, GAC chairman, to begin rounding up his eight colleagues, who were scattered around the United States and Europe. A meeting was finally set for Washington at the end of October.[31]

Long before then, Teller, Alvarez, and Lawrence were in Washington, where they bombarded Oppenheimer, Congress, and the Pentagon with appeals for a commitment to the super. Alvarez tackled Oppenheimer and several other colleagues from his wartime days at Los Alamos and was shocked and dismayed when "Oppie" said that America should not build the super. All evidence indicated that the Soviet A-bomb was a purely "imitative" effort, Oppenheimer explained. The United States could stay ahead of the Russians in the atomic field for years, and the Kremlin could live with it. But if the United States went forward with a super, the Soviets would have to do likewise. Oppenheimer apparently did not mention specifically what was in everyone's mind: The atomic bomb, horrible as it was, was not really the ultimate weapon.

Alvarez, Teller, and the others challenged Oppenheimer. How could the United States be sure that the Soviet nuclear program was modest and imitative? For those who believed that the communists intended to use any means to rule the world (a point that Soviet leaders themselves frequently boasted), it seemed criminal to assume that the Russians would not try to surpass the "capitalist oppressor." Indeed, the more some alarmists considered the situation, the more possible it became that the Soviets might not pause to stock atomic bombs, but simply proceed directly to the testing and production of the super. If the Soviets got the super first, they would dominate the United States and the world. When Alvarez was asked for details on how the Soviets might race ahead of the United States in the quest for the super, he replied that if you needed details, you did not understand the situation.[32]

Teller and Lawrence besieged Congress with their messages. Teller first approached McMahon, who agreed to arrange a luncheon meeting with key senators and representatives. The Hungarian, with his foreign accent, incisive gestures, and fervent anticommunism, seemed the perfect, patriotic academic. Over steak and salad, he reiterated his message, and the congressmen agreed that the super should be studied immediately. McMahon established a special four-man subcommittee of his Joint Congressional Committee on Atomic Energy, headed by Representative Chet Holifield of California, and sent it around town and out to the western laboratories to study the issue.

Teller and Lawrence then went to the Pentagon, where they discussed the super with the air force. It was a propitious moment to do so, for those who opposed total reliance on nuclear retaliation to contain Soviet expansion had just been routed.

When military planners had first approached the question of employing the atomic bomb against Russia in the autumn of 1946, they had come to some disturbing conclusions. There was no way to guarantee that an atomic blitz might prevent the Red Army from seizing Western Europe. "The Russian transportation system, identified as 'the most vital cog in the war machine of the U.S.S.R.,' was too widespread to be vulnerable to attack. Bombing major industries such as steel, aircraft, and electric power would take too long to become effective. Only the Russian petroleum industry, vital to troop mobility, was considered possibly vulnerable to an air offensive, using either conventional or atomic weapons."[33] Such a conclusion delighted the navy, which was fighting desperately to keep the Army Air Force (soon to be redesignated the U.S. Air Force) from not only obtaining control over all military air forces (and perhaps the aircraft carrier fleet as well) but from subordinating all future military operations to strategic bombing.[34] Consistent cuts in the military budget, however, along with the persistent unwillingness of Congress and the country to support partial mobilization during the several European crises of late 1947 and early 1948, forced the Pentagon to consider the bomb its first line of both offense and defense. In December

1947, the Joint Chiefs of Staff (JCS) asked for and obtained a sharply accelerated timetable of atomic production that would yield four hundred bombs by January 1, 1953. Joint Emergency War Plan "Halfmoon," approved the following May, called for the destruction of the Soviet will to resist by "a powerful air offensive designed to exploit the destructive and psychological power of atomic weapons against the vital elements of the Soviet war making capacity."[35]

A year later, however, in May of 1949, an ad hoc JCS committee, appointed by Defense Secretary James Forrestal to continue studying the impact of atomic weaponry on modern war, concluded that a planned attack on seventy Soviet cities in fulfillment of "Halfmoon" would not "per se, bring about capitulation, destroy the roots of Communism, or critically weaken the power of Soviet leadership to dominate the people." Quite the opposite. The committee chairman, Lt. Gen. Hubert Harmon, stated that for most Russians an atomic blitz would "validate Soviet propaganda against foreign powers, stimulate resentment against the United States, . . . and increase their will to fight."[36]

Nonetheless the Harmon committee did not suggest a dramatic reversal of atomic policy; it was too late for that. The previous year, the JCS had estimated that an annual defense budget of $21 to $23 billion would be required to maintain a military foothold in Europe in the face of Soviet aggression and to carry out naval operations in all or part of the Mediterranean. The increasingly desperate military chiefs claimed that even a compromise budget of just under $17 billion might do the job. But Congress, fretting over the specter of inflation, gave the Pentagon only $14.4 billion, and subsequent budgets were slashed even further by both the White House and the Hill.[37] Under the circumstances, Harmon and his colleagues had no choice but to support the atomic policy despite their reservations.

By the time Harmon submitted his report, Forrestal was already on his way out as defense secretary; his successor, Louis A. Johnson, was an ardent champion of the air force and the bomb. Johnson managed to keep the Harmon report from the president throughout the subsequent debate over thermonuclear weaponry, knowing that Truman had finally become convinced that an atomic blitz of the Soviet Union was the only way to achieve victory in World War III. On April 6, 1949, the president had finally conceded that international control of the atomic bomb was a lost cause and publicly stated for the first time since 1945 that he might use it again.[38] The JCS, meanwhile, had responded to the Harmon report not by reconsidering atomic strategy but by solidifying it. If the Soviet Union could not be coerced or obliterated by the proposed four-hundred-bomb stockpile, the solution was not to seek an alternative means of warfare but rather to expand dramatically the size of the stockpile, including the development of "tactical" nuclear weapons to use on Western European battlefields while Soviet cities were being vaporized far to the east. An increased stockpile, of course, would require a dramatic growth in the number of "delivery systems." Air Force Secretary Stuart Symington was already drafting a report to Johnson urging that the service's long-cherished and long-frustrated dream of seventy wings not only be realized but exceeded to confront the new Soviet atomic menace adequately.[39]

Teller and Lawrence thus encountered a positive atmosphere when they walked into the Pentagon with their super bomb proposal. At first concerned that a super project would mean fewer materials for atomic bombs, the airmen, led by Chief of Staff Hoyt Vandenberg, quickly capitulated when they realized the super's awesome potential. Vandenberg then set about convincing the rest of the Pentagon, including his always skeptical and embittered colleagues in the navy.

Alvarez and Lawrence next went directly to Lilienthal to push for AEC support. They were as distressed and puzzled by Lilienthal's reaction as Alvarez had earlier been by Oppenheimer's opposition. After a long exposition on the super's power, feasibility, and necessity, the two scientists sat dumbfounded as Lilienthal abruptly turned his back on them and silently gazed out the window. A quintessential liberal, Lilienthal had always been ambivalent about the atom. He recognized that the bomb was a brutal reality that no one could avoid, but he was deeply disturbed that America's "defense" policy since 1945 had relied exclusively on atomic weapons for any war with the Soviets. In a guarded diary entry the previous summer, he had suggested that throughout the late forties the country's "operating reserve" of A-bombs was much lower than the public (and the Soviets) believed. He criticized Eisenhower for suggesting in a series of *Look* magazine articles the previous year that an atomic war would be over in seventy-two hours.[40]

A longtime booster and administrator of public power (he had been the first head of the Tennessee Valley Authority and had written a widely read defense of the agency), Lilienthal believed that atomic energy could be peacefully and safely exploited to literally light up the world. He was thus not averse to Truman's policy of limited sharing of atomic information with the British and Canadians, who, after all, had been vigorous and effective wartime partners in the Manhattan Project. This stance had gotten him into trouble with Hickenlooper and other Republicans on Capitol Hill (including Arthur Vandenberg), who insisted that the United States should maintain its monopoly not only to safeguard the national security but also to play atomic diplomacy if and where needed. Now the Soviet bomb and prospects for a super had suddenly disrupted Lilienthal's emphasis on atomic restraint.

Clearly hoping to prevent the super project, Lilienthal had supported the Joint Chiefs' proposal for a dramatic expansion ("a whopping big one") of the atomic program ("more and better bombs") in the wake of the Soviet atomic test. On October 10, a special committee of the National Security Council (NSC) agreed, concluding "that the proposed acceleration of the atomic energy program is necessary in the interests of national security." But that same day Truman decided against sending an AEC supplemental appropriation to the Hill. Admiral Sidney Souers, the president's national security adviser, told Lilienthal that the timing seemed wrong.[41]

Several days before the GAC was scheduled to meet, McMahon asked Alvarez and Lawrence to go to Capitol Hill to bolster Teller's earlier arguments on the need for moving forward on the super project. The two scientists told McMahon that Stalin might well be giving top priority to a thermonuclear bomb even as they spoke. Soviet scientist Peter Kapitsa was a leading authority on the physical properties of light elements, including deuterium. Thus, it was logical to assume that with the atomic "match" now in their possession, the Soviets could perfect a fusion weapon in a short time, possibly before the Americans could.

While the scientists were steadily pressuring key senators and military people, Lewis Strauss received confirmation of shocking news from his FBI contact. Several weeks before, Charles Bates, the bureau's liaison with the Atomic Energy Commission, asked commission security people to investigate the activities of an obscure, German-born, British scientist named Klaus Fuchs, who had worked at both Los Alamos and Oak Ridge during the war. On October 19, Strauss met for an hour with FBI Director J. Edgar Hoover and apparently received most of the bad news: Fuchs was a Soviet spy. Not only had he undoubtedly given the Russians invaluable information on the development of the atomic bomb, he had also carried out theoretical studies on aspects of a thermonuclear device before departing Los Alamos for Britain in 1946. Because American scientists had not developed any really new ideas on the "super" since then, it was entirely possible that the Soviets were as much as three years ahead of the United States in thermonuclear weapons development. Although he apparently kept the information about Fuchs's activities from everyone else (possibly at Hoover's request), "from this time on, then, Strauss saw the super as a way to establish equality in the arms race, not escalation."[42]

The GAC met at AEC headquarters on Constitution Avenue over a cloudy Washington weekend at the end of October 1949. Everyone realized the vital importance of the session. On Saturday morning, Oppenheimer took his place at one end of a long table. He had just written to fellow GAC member and Harvard president James Conant, reporting that Lawrence and Teller, "two experienced promoters," had been urging an immediate super project. "I am not sure the miserable thing will work," Oppenheimer wrote, "nor that it can be gotten to a target except by oxcart. . . . What does worry me is that" the project "appears to have caught the imagination both of the Congressional and of the military people, as the answer to the problem posed by the Russian advance. It would be folly to oppose the exploration of this weapon. We have always known it had to be done, though it appears singularly proof against any form of experimental approach."[43]

Now Conant was sitting near Oppenheimer, who looked gray, "almost translucent."[44] George Kennan, newly appointed counselor of the Department of State, was present. So was Joint Chiefs Chairman Omar Bradley, who, in Lilienthal's words, was "very G.A.R.ish" and spoke with "countryman's accents." Bradley represented the Pentagon along with several members of the Military Liaison Committee to the AEC and Gen. Lauris Norstad, chairman of the interservice Weapons Systems Evaluation Group. Hans Bethe of Cornell and Enrico Fermi of Columbia were there for the general scientific community. Most of the AEC commissioners were also present.

The GAC and its distinguished guests first agreed that the Russian bomb had "changed the situation drastically, and that the talk about our having anticipated everything and following the same program we had before is the bunk." It would take Europe years to rearm sufficiently to stop a conventional Soviet military thrust toward the Channel. Would the United States launch an atomic blitz against the Russians if they attacked the West, knowing now that there would certainly be retaliatory strikes against London and New York? Everyone agreed it was "a close question . . . meaning, [they] guessed, that we wouldn't."

Convinced that the Soviet weapon had created an atomic stalemate, which practically gave the initiative in world affairs to the Red Army, members of the GAC found their "eyes light[ing] up" when a hydrogen bomb was first mentioned. But no one could deny that there were formidable questions to be answered and obstacles to be overcome. On October 17, the JCS had sent a memorandum to Lilienthal, requesting more information on a fusion bomb and asking why the AEC had not already sought funds to develop such a weapon. But now, twelve days later, Bradley suddenly reversed course, expressing skepticism about claims that the super was actually the ultimate weapon; he believed that its only real worth was psychological. Fermi said the odds for developing a deliverable weapon (i.e., one small enough to fit into the largest bomber then in the planning stage) were little better than even. Norstad later told Lilienthal that stepping up production of atomic weapons was no answer; the Pentagon had been studying the question every six months for years and had been unable to determine the extent to which atomic weapons could decisively affect the course of a world war.

The afternoon session was confined to members of the GAC and the atomic energy commissioners. Discussion quickly focused on the super. Conant was flatly against it. So was fellow GAC member Hartley Rowe, who observed that the United States had already built one Frankenstein. Oppenheimer was cautious but seemed to Lilienthal to be "inclined that way." Oliver Buckley of Bell Labs voiced a different opinion, one already expressed by Alvarez: There was no real moral question between an atomic and a hydrogen bomb, between "x and y times x." Since both were awful weapons, why stop at an A-bomb when the other fellow might get the ultimate weapon first? Conant disagreed. There were shades of morality, after all, and a hydrogen bomb was a substantial, indeed potentially unlimited advancement over a fission weapon. Isidor Rabi of Columbia sided with Buckley. The decision to proceed with an H-bomb was inevitable; the only question was who would be willing to agree to it.

Fermi sought a middle ground. The GAC and AEC should recommend exploring the feasibility of a thermonuclear weapon without suggesting that the United States proceed with its construction. Lilienthal jumped in, denying any inevitability to political decisions. Strauss added that the decision would not be made by the country in a popular referendum but by the narrow decision-making community around the president. That might be,

Conant replied, but whether the decision would "stick" depended on how the nation viewed the moral issue. If the determination to proceed was made, could it be declassified, or would it always remain a secret? What would be the effect on secrecy if the United States did make and success-fully test an H-bomb? What would the public think if it then discovered that Washington had made this awful weapon without telling the country? Lilienthal replied rather weakly that the president would announce any decision to go ahead with the super "if he wished to." Privately Lilienthal doubted that Truman would do so. For if the White House announced that the United States was initiating research and development of a super, "then the arms race fat would be in the fire." Truman was more likely to say: "Well, move along but don't say anything about it." Lilienthal kept such thoughts to himself, tacitly supporting Conant, while committee member Cyril Smith strongly supported the Harvard president and Strauss remained openly dubious. Conant apparently had the last word: "This whole discus-sion makes me feel I was seeing the same film, and a punk one, for the sec-ond time."

The group spent Sunday drafting a GAC report, and when Oppenheimer polled his colleagues, he was surprised to discover unanimity. Everyone had assumed that at least five of the eight attending GAC members (the ninth, Glenn Seaborg, could not return from Europe in time) supported beginning work on the super immediately. But when the crunch came, all advised against it. Oppenheimer told his colleagues that he was delighted, adding that if the decision had gone the other way, he would have resigned.

The report, signed by six of the eight commissioners headed by Conant, Rowe, and Oppenheimer, was as confusing as it was emphatic.[45] It stated "that the extreme dangers to mankind inherent in the proposal" to build a hydrogen bomb "wholly outweigh any military advantage that could come from this development." The GAC emphasized that the hydrogen bomb *was* the ultimate weapon. "If super bombs will work at all, there is no inherent limit in the destructive power that may be attained with them." Ther-monuclear weapons were capable of devastating a huge area, causing untold civilian casualties, and perhaps covering the entire globe with a cloud of fatal radioactivity. It was "by no means certain" that super weapons could ever be produced and by no means certain that the Soviets could pro-duce one "within a decade."

Thus far the report was straightforward and rational. But then the GAC abandoned logic. Even if the Soviets did develop a super, a similar American weapon would not deter them. This was probably an accurate assessment. But the committee then concluded that the American stockpile of atomic bombs would be as effective against the Soviet Union as would be a Soviet thermonuclear attack against the United States. The logical absurdity of assuming that a mass of limited weapons would be as destructive or as great a deterrence as a few unlimited weapons apparently escaped Oppenheimer, Conant, and the others.

"We believe," the GAC report concluded unambiguously, that "a super bomb should never be produced. Mankind would be far better off not to have a demonstration of the feasibility of such a weapon until the present climate of world opinion changes." The United States had a unique opportunity, the GAC report concluded, to demonstrate by example a restraint on total war.

Fermi and Rabi submitted a minority report, in which they agreed that a hydrogen bomb "goes far beyond any military objective and enters the range of very great natural catastrophes.[46] By its very nature it cannot be confined to a military objective but becomes a weapon which in practical effect is almost one of genocide." Such a weapon could never be justified on ethical grounds, and its use, even once, "would leave unresolved enmities for generations." No desirable peace could ever come from such "an inhuman application of force." But the two differed from their colleagues on the crucial issue of disclosure. Instead of suppressing the fact that a super was at least theoretically possible, Truman should tell the world that the United States thought it was ethically wrong to initiate a thermonuclear development program and that it would invite the international community to join in a solemn pledge not to instigate such an undertaking. The president should also state that if a nation (i.e., the Soviets) did, in violation of all moral principles and common sense, develop an H-bomb, it was "highly probable that an advanced stage of development . . . could be detected by available physical means" and that the United States might then retaliate with its existing stockpile of atomic bombs.

But it was too late for anyone to stop the momentum for a super bomb. As the GAC completed its report that last Sunday evening in October, Lilienthal wrote in his journal that reports from Los Alamos and Berkeley "are rather awful. . . . Scientists who can only be described as drooling with the prospect and 'bloodthirsty'" were bombarding McMahon's congressional subcommittee with demands to proceed with the super. Lawrence (who had returned to California) was "quite bad," telling Holifield and the others that there was no time to lose, "nothing to think over," and that the country faced a major crisis that necessitated a revival of the wartime spirit of the Manhattan Project. "The ground is laid," Lilienthal concluded glumly, "for the Joint Committee members to come back and demand that we plunge ahead and think about it, if at all, on vacation or something."[47]

Worn down by nineteen years of government service, including administering two highly controversial agencies (the Tennessee Valley Authority and the AEC), Lilienthal had already decided to resign. But he was determined to go down fighting. A super project could only be stopped if the statement of renunciation was linked directly to national policies and purposes. Only Acheson or Truman had the authority to proclaim such policies. Therefore, Lilienthal devoted the remainder of his time and energies to enlisting Acheson in a crusade to stop the super. Author Richard Rhodes has stated that Acheson was first informed about the GAC proceedings by Lilienthal on November 1, but Kennan had surely briefed the secretary about the general outlines of the GAC discussions by the time Lilienthal called. Nonetheless, the chairman gave the secretary a complete account of the GAC meetings, and the more Acheson heard, the gloomier he became. By the time Lilienthal finished, Acheson had turned gray. What a depressing world it was, he sighed.[48] But Acheson, as well as others in government, was receiving constant pressure from the large and vociferous pro-super lobby, including some of Lilienthal's colleagues.

With the GAC report in hand, Strauss told his fellow commissioners that the AEC should make its own recommendations to the president after further consultations with the State Department and the Pentagon. By this time, Strauss had a hammer in hand, and he knew it; while the GAC was meeting over the last weekend in October, all of the Atomic Energy Commissioners had been told of Klaus Fuchs and his frightening treason. Strauss's earlier suspicions of Oppenheimer's loyalty had been quickened by the GAC report, and he hoped to present to Truman a comprehensive paper setting forth the diplomatic and military aspects of the issue along with the AEC's views on the feasibility and cost of a super.[49] Lilienthal and the others balked; despite his hopes of enlisting Acheson, Lilienthal believed that the AEC would have a stronger voice in the decision-making process if it submitted its report without consulting either the State or Defense Departments.

Strauss was upset when he discovered that he was the only one who wanted to proceed "urgently" with development of a hydrogen bomb. Despite Fuchs, the other four commissioners had been deeply impressed with the arguments set forth in the GAC report. So was Strauss, but as he wrote to Truman on November 25, the overriding consideration in any international crisis was the need for the United States to be "as completely armed as any possible enemy." Therefore, renunciation of any potential weapon system that an enemy might develop was utter folly.[50] Soon one other commission member, Gordon Dean, a law partner of McMahon, supported Strauss's position.

The AEC was so confused and upset by the issue that it decided not to send Truman one consensual agency report but five individual positions preceded by a joint statement. Strauss and Dean urged that the United States develop the super as quickly as possible and then use it as a diplomatic bargaining chip, "a hypodermic in the realm of international cooperation," to try to persuade the Soviets to accept control over all nuclear weapons. "To announce that we will not undertake such a development is to grant to the USSR a potential monopoly in this field," which would dishearten both the American people and their allies abroad. Dean and Strauss did not shrink from the ultimate possibility of thermonuclear warfare. If "we should find ourselves some day in a war with Russia, the [hydrogen bomb] must be regarded as a reprisal weapon which might be a decisive weapon." Lilienthal was firmly against such thermonuclear development or diplomacy. The goals of the United States were to remain strong and to work for world peace. A hydrogen bomb would not advance the first objective and would destroy the second. "This country is the possessor of a substantial and growing stockpile of atomic weapons, and a large military arm with which to deliver those weapons if need be." There was no reason to proceed further. Sumner Pike, a Wall Street New Dealer, and Henry D. Smyth, professor of physics at Princeton, wanted to see whether the United Nations could pressure the Kremlin into accepting an international control agreement by threatening the specter of an H-bomb before it was built. The military advantage to the United States of supers was doubtful even if the Soviets did not develop them. A decision not to build the super "is a gesture of good faith and optimism."[51]

In their joint statement, the commissioners told Truman that only he could make the decision on the super. The bomb currently contemplated would be one hundred to one thousand times more powerful than the weapon that had leveled Hiroshima and left behind a horrible and long-standing legacy of radioactive poisoning. Also, unlike the fission bomb, the power of a single hydrogen bomb could be increased indefinitely by adding a relatively cheap explosive. Deuterium was "plentiful and reasonably inexpensive." Moreover, there was a "better than even chance" that a thermonuclear bomb could be made to work, although there was "no certainty of success." The minimum development period would most likely be three years, and "probably" nothing short of making a bomb and giving it a definitive test would prove whether thermonuclear weapons were feasible. In a passage that must have broken Lilienthal's heart, the commissioners agreed that unlike atomic energy, thermonuclear power had no known civilian applications. It was purely a dead-end weapon system. The bottom line was inescapable: The Soviets were "familiar with the ideas" about thermonuclear energy and probably could develop a bomb as quickly as the United States. Thus, by late 1952, the world would stand on the brink of self-destruction unless there was a miraculous change in global affairs.[52]

In conclusion, the commissioners posed three basic questions. First, could the decision on a super be used as leverage to pry the Soviets into a reasonable position on international control of nuclear energy? Second, how would development of an H-bomb affect U.S. relations with the European allies, Japan, and the rest of the world? Third, would possession of a super actually strengthen America's global position? With this report the AEC practically removed itself from any further participation in the thermonuclear decision-making process. Lilienthal had not been able to impose discipline on his fellow commissioners, and Truman would not forget it.

The Holifield subcommittee had returned to Washington in early November and had begun working on a report of its own, urging an immediate crash program to develop the super. The twenty-page report was written by the executive director of the Joint Committee staff, William Borden, a former World War II bomber pilot who retained many close ties with the air force and was adamantly opposed to and horrified by the GAC report. His conclusion was simple: If the H-bomb was the ultimate terror weapon that the scientific community said it was (the only point of consensus among scientists), then the United States had to possess it to avoid having its national security compromised perhaps irretrievably. McMahon and Holifield took the report to Truman personally, spending forty-five minutes discussing it with the president. Truman promised to consider the findings seriously.

McMahon had also been deeply angered by the GAC's conclusions. "I read this report," he told Teller, "and it just makes me sick."[53] He, too, began sending Truman numerous messages about the super. In a long, eloquent letter from Los Angeles dated November 21, McMahon laid out for the president all the pro-super arguments.[54] After observing that he was in the midst of a nationwide round of secret conferences on the super that had taken him from Washington to Los Alamos, the Argonne National Laboratory outside Chicago, and the Hanford nuclear power plant in Washington State, McMahon stated that "those who oppose an all-out 'crash' effort on the super impress me as being so horrified at the path down which the world is traveling that they have lost contact with common sense and reality."

Of course, the weapon was terrible, McMahon continued, but Lilienthal, Oppenheimer, and the others were arguing out of both sides of their mouths, on the one hand stating that the super would accomplish no more than existing atomic bombs but on the other hand denying that it should be developed. If the super actually represented a new dimension of destructive power—and it did—"then its military role would seem to be decisive."

McMahon then proceeded to describe a thermonuclear war scenario. Any attacker who dropped half a dozen supers on the enemy's largest industrial areas "would free the hundreds of fission bombs otherwise needed to do the same job for other purposes." Why, there was no limit to what these comparatively puny atomic bombs could accomplish in terms of destroying air and land bases and smaller industrial targets. The attacking power could compress into just a few hours or at most a few days several times the total punishment inflicted on Germany and Japan during the entire four years of U.S. involvement in World War II. Even better, such a one-two thermonuclear-atomic blitz would so devastate the enemy's military infrastructure that he could never retaliate effectively. Of course, twenty-five or one hundred or two hundred atomic bombs might equal one hydrogen bomb, but to stress that point was "to overlook the shock and demoralization, psychological and otherwise, that [would] follow from concentrating an offensive within the shortest possible space of time."

Moreover, a thermonuclear bomb would solve the admittedly messy problem of accuracy. During the last war, the army air corps had engaged in daylight "precision" bombing of targets in Nazi Germany and Japan instead of employing the RAF's policy of "area" bombing at night. The United States expected to suffer and did suffer appalling losses. Only slowly and with grudging reluctance did strategists realize that precision bombing of well-defended enemy installations from twenty-five or thirty thousand feet was impossible with the instruments and weapons available in 1943 and 1944. The U.S. Strategic Bombing Survey of 1945 had confirmed this gloomy assessment. Aerial bombing did not become significantly influential until Curtis LeMay sent his B-29s roaring over Japan nightly at five thousand feet to torch enemy cities indiscriminately with incendiary missiles.

McMahon admitted to Truman the somber truths about aerial warfare that continued to exist as late as 1949. Even an A-bomb would have to detonate a mile or even less than a half-mile from the target to be effective. The advantage of a thermonuclear weapon was that a bombardier could drop it even ten miles away from the immediate target area and still be sure that the blast would "serve the purpose intended." Delivery of such an awesome weapon would be a problem, but that could be overcome. Although only Moscow and Leningrad, comprising 120 and 110 square miles, respectively, were potential targets for a super, the Soviets were urbanizing and rearming rapidly. There was no telling how soon other cities might be candidates for a thermonuclear blitz, and besides, it was important to make sure that basic enemy factories and industries were really destroyed.

"The contention is made," McMahon added, "that a war involving the super would leave behind such chaos and vengefulness as to create a worse situation, with a darker outlook for lasting peace, than the one existing at present." Perhaps this was true, but perhaps not. If there were no precluding tactical reasons, the inhabitants of Soviet cities could be warned that they were about to be attacked with a thermonuclear bomb and that they had to "either evacuate or suffer the consequences." If the warning were heeded, bomb damage would be confined to physical facilities. Moreover, the disruption to the enemy's war effort caused by mass evacuations would itself be an advantage, "hamper[ing] the enemy's war effort more seriously even than mass casualties." But the basic question was what would happen if enemy supers were aimed at New York, Chicago, Los Angeles, and Washington? Would the United States have supers available to retaliate or, in the best case scenario, to "throttle the attack at its source"?

McMahon could see "no moral dividing line . . . between a big [thermonuclear] explosion which causes heavy damage and many smaller [atomic] explosions causing equal or still greater damage." Where was the ethical distinction among the RAF's 1943 firebomb raids against Hamburg, which killed 135,000 people, U.S. raids against Tokyo in 1945, which killed 85,000 people, and Hiroshima, where 65,000 perished?

McMahon's primary consideration was simple: "Our first duty consists in doing what is necessary to win." The United States possessed neither the manpower nor the resources for garrisoning the Eurasian landmass either to prevent war or safeguard peace. "The only choice left open is heavy reliance upon strategic air power" despite America's own "immense vulnerability" to nuclear weapons. "The super should end all debate as to whether or not strategic air power could win a war. Without American victory—which supers alone might render feasible—there would be no post-war existence for our country, much less post-war problems."

Other arguments against the super could be quickly dismissed, McMahon continued. He had been assured that radioactivity from hydrogen bombs probably would not be any greater than from fission bombs and might even be less if effective casing materials were used. Questions of the bomb's feasibility were red herrings designed to dampen legitimate feelings of urgency.

McMahon then made a startling assertion: The AEC weapons program formulated in 1948 "envisaged achievement of a super by about 1958. No one in authority protested against the program; no one argued that problems affecting the super should be left unexplored." Now that the Soviets had gotten the A-bomb, "giving us a compelling reason to speed up the rate" of thermonuclear research and development, a new school of "anti-super counsellors" [sic] had suddenly appeared to reverse earlier logic. McMahon intimated that perhaps some sinister motive was behind the calls for restraint by Lilienthal, Conant, and especially Oppenheimer.

McMahon concluded his letter by stating that the moral arguments against the super were nonsensical. Of course, the United States should and would give up the quest for an H-bomb as soon as the entire international community could agree on a "just and enforceable" system of controls. Yes, "Western civilization may well crumble whether we win or lose" a thermonuclear war. And yes, U.S. cities would be far more vulnerable to a super than would Russian urban areas. "My thesis, however, is that if we let Russia get the super first, catastrophe becomes all but certain—whereas if we get it first, there exists a chance of saving ourselves."

So far the debate over the super had been restricted to the highest echelons of government and had been conducted secretly. But on November 1 Senator

Edwin C. Johnson of Colorado revealed the story during a New York television panel discussion devoted to the question: "Is there too much secrecy in our atomic program?" Johnson had been arguing vigorously with liberal scientists who condemned the cult of concealment that still dominated federal laboratories and exchanges. The trouble with atomic scientists, the senator insisted, was that they had a "yen" to tell all they knew. Johnson was asked whether it would not be all right now to ease security restrictions since the Soviets, by whatever means, had obtained the bomb.

"I'm glad you asked that question," Johnson replied heatedly, "because here's the thing that is top secret." While his fellow panelists sat appalled, the senator proceeded to tell the entire story of the U.S.-Soviet nuclear rivalry, including the current status of thermonuclear research:

> Our scientists from the time that the bombs were detonated at Hiroshima and Nagasaki have been trying to make what is known as the super-bomb.
>
> They've been devoting their time to two things: one, to make a super-bomb, and the other, to find some way of detonating a bomb before the fellow that wants to drop it can detonate. And we—we've made considerable progress in that direction.
>
> Now, there's no question at all the Russians have a bomb more or less similar to the bomb that we dropped at Nagasaki, a plutonium bomb.
>
> Our scientists are certain that they have that bomb, but it's not a better bomb than dropped at Nagasaki.
>
> Now, our scientists already have created a bomb that has six times the effectiveness of the bomb that was dropped at Nagasaki and they're not satisfied at all; they want one that has a thousand times the effect of that terrible bomb that was dropped at Nagasaki that snuffed out the lives of 50,000 people just like that.
>
> And . . . that's the big secret that the scientists in America are so anxious to divulge to the whole scientific world.[55]

For the next week, AEC officials held their breath and hoped no one had noticed. In those days, New York television broadcasts did not extend much beyond the immediate metropolitan area. Maybe the senator's outburst would be ignored or forgotten. But on November 10, the *Washington Post* published a brief editorial comment on Johnson's statement and eight days later included Johnson's statement in a feature article by Alfred Friendly, who speculated on the existence or possibility of a super.

In the State Department, Kennan promptly drafted a memorandum for Acheson to use if he was questioned. It was impossible to put the genie back in the bottle. Whether or not the United States should develop a thermonuclear weapon, Kennan wrote, was a dilemma of "tremendous proportions." There were powerful arguments on both sides. To arrive at a rational decision, policymakers would have to answer a number of basic questions: Would use of an H-bomb menace the existence of civilization? Would the weapon be a deterrent to war? If the Soviets got the super, would U.S. possession impede Kremlin attempts to intimidate the world community? Would development of the H-bomb make its use a foregone conclusion in war? Would it actually enhance U.S. military capabilities? Would production of such a weapon significantly drain America's social and economic energies? Should a U.S. determination to proceed be dictated by what the Russians did?[56]

Acheson had already told Truman that the decision about the super was an important, complex issue with broad domestic and international ramifications and should not be hurriedly resolved. Then Acheson asked Kennan and his policy planners to work on a State Department position paper and have it ready shortly before Thanksgiving. Others were plucking the president's sleeve on the super issue. On November 18, the same day that Kennan completed his State Department memorandum, Truman's naval aide, Capt. Robert Dennison, wrote the president a memorandum in which he noted that the AEC report was so confused and diffuse that it "does not provide sufficient information to establish a basis for resolution of" the super bomb issue. The super was obviously the "absolute weapon," and the prospect of its development had generated an "urgent need for the effective elimination of weapons of mass destruction from national arsenals." At the same time, the prospect of a U.S. hydrogen bomb meant that "we now have a most potent and perhaps critical tool to assist in our negotiations for world peace." Effective thermonuclear diplomacy had to be carefully and fully developed, and therefore Dennison urged Truman to appoint a "sub-committee of the [National] Security Council" comprising Acheson, Johnson, and Lilienthal. The next day the president directed Admiral Souers to appoint the three men special national security advisers to help him determine "whether and in what manner the US should undertake the development and possible production of 'super' atomic weapons."[57]

Five days later, on November 23, the Joint Chiefs sent a memorandum to Secretary Johnson that virtually settled the issue. "Possession of a thermonuclear weapon by the USSR without such a possession by the United States would be intolerable." It was necessary to determine the feasibility of a thermonuclear explosion and its characteristics in order to plan U.S. defense, prepare for retaliation, and direct research.[58] Bradley promptly forwarded a copy of the memorandum to Truman. Two days later, Strauss wrote his letter to the president, arguing that unilateral renunciation of the super by the United States could have incalculable consequences. In an enclosed memo, Strauss admitted that both the atomic and hydrogen bombs were hideous weapons.[59] But all wars were horrible, and until they could be eliminated the United States could not abandon development of any potentially winning weapon. If the United States followed a policy of renunciation, the Kremlin would not believe it, and if the United States later reversed that policy, Stalin and his colleagues might interpret the decision as an implicit declaration of war. That same day, November 25, Truman summoned McMahon and Attorney General J. Howard McGrath to the White House and demanded that they prevent any unauthorized disclosures of nuclear secrets.

As was customary, Acheson, Lilienthal, and Johnson promptly established a working group of subordinates to draft position papers on the super and to develop a consensual recommendation for their superiors. The State Department representatives were Paul Nitze, arms specialist on the Policy Planning Staff; R. Gordon Arneson, the department's science adviser; and Adrian Fisher, State's legal adviser. Kennan was excluded. According to Arneson, he, Acheson, Fisher, and Nitze, State's "four principals," were all united in the belief that proceeding with a super bomb was inevitable. "We all were of a mind that there really wasn't any choice. Acheson, I think, showed more flexibility than any of us. He talked to Dr. Conant at length; he talked to Oppenheimer at length; he talked to Lilienthal at length. They were all opposed, and he was not persuaded. He did try. I don't see how we could say we're not going to do this thing, that we will put it in a bushel basket somewhere; because if we didn't do it, certainly the Russians would, the British would, maybe even Pakistan, certainly the French."[60]

Between Thanksgiving and Christmas, the diplomats, soldiers, and bureaucrats began to confront the issue, and it became immediately clear that the national military establishment, not just the Joint Chiefs, now favored development of the bomb without delay. On December 16, Defense Department representatives circulated a memorandum at the beginning of a meeting in Souers's office.[61] Within several years, the United States could probably build a super roughly thirty times more powerful than the Hiroshima atomic bomb. There were no known restraints on Soviet capabilities to match this effort. Repeating the earlier JCS statement to Truman that unilateral Russian possession of hydrogen bombs would be intolerable, the memorandum explained why.

A Soviet monopoly of the super would allow the Kremlin to understand the real capabilities of thermonuclear warfare, "its positive effects." Soviet announcement that it had the thermonuclear bomb and the United States did not would almost certainly demoralize the American public, the peoples of Western Europe, and Asian allies. At the same time, a Russian super would give the Soviet leaders, peoples, and their captive satellite populations in Eastern Europe a "tremendous psychological boost," which might create both overconfidence and truculence, leading to miscalculation and world war. If world war broke out, Soviet monopoly of the super, along with the Eastern bloc's superiority in conventional military power, would almost guarantee a communist victory.

If the United States developed the super and the Soviets did not, possession of such a powerful weapon would ensure the obliteration of nearly all Soviet war-making potential, including the airfields from which the Soviets might try to launch an atomic counterattack. Even simple possession without use would disrupt Soviet military calculations and capabilities, which were based on applying superior massed forces against Western defenses in Europe.

What if both the United States and the Soviet Union got the super? The Pentagon did not flinch from the inevitable implication: Each side would be tempted to mount a preemptive strike. Because such a prospect was anathema to American values and morality, the Pentagon couched its conclusion in elliptical bureaucratese: "The advantage of the surprise attack could become as significant as to make the option of the initiative, in its relation to a clear definition of an overt act, more meaningful." It was imperative to begin vigorously investigating techniques for optimal dispersal of U.S. atomic and thermonuclear weapons and delivery systems "in order to achieve an adequate degree of invulnerability of the retaliatory attack force."

Above all, it was essential to test conclusively the feasibility or infeasibility of thermonuclear weapons and their "characteristics." Only in this way could future U.S. defense needs be determined. There undoubtedly were numerous "possible" social, psychological, and moral objections to such action, the Defense Department officials concluded, but national survival overrode all of them. Because the super was at least potentially the ultimate, unlimited weapon, premature disclosure of U.S. studies of its feasibility would severely damage the national interest. Work on the super had to remain the most closely guarded secret in the U.S. government; the public should not know what its leaders were doing in this critical area of national security.

The AEC did not respond officially to the Pentagon memorandum, and the State Department's initial reaction was brief and tepid. Acheson had asked Kennan and the Policy Planning Staff to develop an agency position, but Kennan was an invariably slow worker who produced cumbersome, wordy results, so Acheson had Kennan's deputy, Paul Nitze, draft a brief working memorandum, which Nitze completed three days after the meeting in Souers's office.[62]

Nitze distinguished between the cold war, which he claimed was essentially political, ideological, and economic, and the military confrontation between East and West. He argued that the most immediate security risks confronting the free world were from the cold war, not from the prospect of a "hot" conflict. An abrupt U.S. emphasis on the possible use of weapons of mass destruction against the Soviet enemy would be "detrimental to the position of the U.S. in the cold war." But Nitze and his agency could not evade reality. More was to be feared, Nitze admitted, from Soviet possession of a super than was to be gained by U.S. ownership of such a frightening weapon. The conclusion was obvious. The United States would have to test the feasibility of a hydrogen bomb and should undertake an accelerated program to do so, but it did not have to begin development of thermonuclear weapons "at this time."

Acheson, Lilienthal, and Louis Johnson were scheduled to meet on December 22 to review the work of their subordinates and, if the working group had moved far enough along, to advise the president formally. Meanwhile, the super issue had finally exploded into public consciousness after the *Post* published Senator Johnson's indiscrete remarks. In early December, nationally syndicated columnists Stewart and Joseph Alsop had written that "a 1,000-power atomic bomb is more than a simple possibility." Its unimaginable explosive power would be derived "from the nuclear fission [*sic*] of hydrogen, the lowest of the elements in the electron table, instead of uranium, at the top. The theory of how to make it is already understood and generally accepted." Although actual development would require an effort duplicating if not exceeding the wartime Manhattan Project, "the job is actually farther along than was the job of making the Hiroshima bomb when the Manhattan [Project] was established." The two bombs dropped on Japan had obliterated an area of two to four square miles. A hydrogen bomb could utterly wipe out an area of sixty to one hundred square miles.[63]

In preparation for his meeting with Johnson and Lilienthal on the twenty-second, Acheson saw Johnson alone the day before. He showed the defense secretary a paper that he had prepared and then had had revised by Kennan, Nitze, and others, but he did not give it to Johnson. Acheson stated in this memorandum that it was wrong to continue insisting on international control of atomic energy while secretly pushing ahead with thermonuclear research. Focusing entirely on the issue of the atom, Acheson urged that the Pentagon devote most of its energies to determining the exact role that atomic weapons might play in a future war.[64]

Acheson probably had been influenced by the devastating comments of Rear Adm. R. A. Ofstie, who was the navy's representative on the AEC's Military Liaison Committee and a stout defender of his service. The navy was already having trouble justifying continuation of its aircraft carrier fleet in an age of atomic warfare because the fission bombs were still so big that they could barely be delivered by the largest carrier-borne aircraft. Thus, the navy was skeptical about the feasibility of atomic, to say nothing of thermonuclear, warfare, and Ofstie had made some telling points in recent testimony before Congress. Just how did the United States propose to use atomic weapons in defense of Western Europe, the admiral had asked. Would the United States bomb wide areas of the Continent that might become occupied by the Red Army during an East-West conflict? Would U.S. bombs obliterate Berlin, Paris, Prague, Hannover, or Lyons in order to destroy large concentrations of Soviet troops and matériel? "Are we to atomize or otherwise destroy such urban and industrial areas, where friendly peoples outnumber the invaders in a ratio of perhaps fifty or one hundred to one?" Other navy spokesmen made the same point. "The Navy's case against the bomb boiled down to two points," a knowledgeable Washington correspondent wrote at the end of 1949: "(a) strategic bombings with atomic weapons are militarily ineffective; and (b) atomic bombing on the scale contemplated [in current Pentagon planning] is immoral and does not serve U.S. political aims and policies."[65]

Apparently Acheson was hoping to derail the Pentagon's super express by exploiting the deep and bitter internal divisions within the national military establishment. "Which are the most immediate dangers to our security?" he wrote in the memorandum he showed Johnson. "Those involved in the cold war or those involved in military aggression?" After several pages of protracted argument, he finally concluded: "The point . . . is not to disregard the dangers of military aggression, but to devise policy to give priority to what comes first."

Such an argument was largely irrelevant to military men, who were responsible not for defining the national interest and security but for defending them. The Soviets had achieved the threshold of atomic parity; now another ultimate weapon system seemed within their grasp. That was enough for the Pentagon and its impatient and unsophisticated secretary, Louis Johnson. To expend precious days and energy in a game of intellectual hairsplitting over whether the Soviet menace was military or economic was idiotic. Lilienthal's inclination just to ignore the entire super issue was even more infuriating.

The December 22 meeting of the three Special Committee members was thus a disaster, in Acheson's words a "head-on confrontation" between Johnson and Lilienthal that "produced nothing either new or helpful to the President."[66] Lilienthal tried to link the super decision to ongoing efforts to achieve international control of atomic energy. Going ahead with the hydrogen bomb could kill any hopes of suppressing nuclear weapons. Nonsense, Johnson replied; control of atomic energy had nothing to do with the issue of proceeding with the super unless the Soviets suddenly reversed policy and agreed to the U.S. position on control. Lilienthal insisted on taking the high moral ground. This was not just a decision on any weapons system; the "purpose and course of mankind [was] wrapped up in this." No one was willing to admit that the hydrogen bomb was anything more than another military gadget, and that had been the trouble with the debate from the beginning. One simply could not talk about the super "without relation to men's objectives and philosophy." According to Acheson, Lilienthal also argued rather inconsistently that deflecting critically scarce supplies of fissionable material to experiments on the hydrogen bomb would disrupt the accelerated schedule of atomic bomb production that he was trying to establish.

Johnson bluntly rejected all Lilienthal's arguments and "said some slighting things about not getting philosophy mixed in here." The AEC chairman was deeply chagrined, and in his journal that night he referred to Johnson sarcastically as the "Strong Man," "Man of Heroic Mould," and "Big Boy." He added petulantly that Bradley and other Pentagon officials who accompanied Johnson were "more schoolmasterish-looking even than usual in civilian dress."

Johnson concluded by stating that the Pentagon's chief scientific adviser on nuclear matters, Karl T. Compton, had written a letter urging development of the super, "as if," Lilienthal bitterly noted, "to settle all question about where 'the scientists' stand, as if [the] only question is [the] squeamishness of some." Lilienthal ended his diary entry sadly: "It's now clear that sponsors [of the H-bomb] are scientists and military establishment, active and ardent." Acheson decided that after such a protracted display of rancor, "perseverance was necessary but not through meetings." He agreed to be a go-between, shuttling among his colleagues and trying to find some common ground.

State's own slowly evolving position paper proved to be no help at all. Amplifying Oppenheimer's most idealistic position, Kennan and his colleagues argued that before beginning research and development of a super, the United States should make one more strenuous effort to compress the atomic genie into the bottle of international control under United Nations auspices. As an inducement for Soviet cooperation, the United States should renounce first use of atomic weapons. Unless Moscow chose to mount an atomic blitz, Washington should rely on conventional arms for deterring future Soviet aggression. Kennan added that, until the question of policy was resolved, no work should proceed on the super bomb program. "A main aspect of his argument was his assessment that the Soviet Union placed chief reliance on nonmilitary means: subversion, political action, economic pressure, terror, etc., to gain control over other peoples. He doubted the Soviet Union would deliberately initiate atomic warfare and thought the Soviet Union would not proceed with a thermonuclear weapons program if we did not. He urged we strengthen our nonmilitary means of countering Soviet power moves." Strenuous opposition to Kennan's paper quickly emerged in the State Department itself. Arneson wrote Acheson on December 29 that Kennan's approach was based primarily on "a fundamentally incorrect assumption," that prohibition of atomic weapons and meaningful international control of atomic energy could be achieved

without a basic change in Soviet attitudes and intentions, and, in fact, in the Soviet system itself. The history of the debates and discussions on international control in and outside the U.N. have revealed that the Soviet Union not only refuses to accept those elements which are necessary for effective control, but, far more important, it refuses to accept any system which would require it to cooperate with the rest of the world in the maintenance of peace.[67]

Kennan finally completed a seventy-nine-page memorandum on the international control of atomic energy on January 20, 1950. He tried to weave the issues of thermonuclear weapons, national security planning, and international control into the document, but it was simply too long and abstruse to serve as an effective advocacy tool. The State Department's idealists, like those in the AEC, had effectively placed themselves beyond the decision-making process through confusion, ignorance, and considerable incompetence.[68]

Between Christmas and New Year's, Omar Bradley showed Acheson a sixty-seven-page memorandum on the super bomb, which the secretary thought "'beautifully rendered'" the entire issue. "But when I got through," he later told Lilienthal, he discovered that the document "didn't clear things up at all." Acheson was determined that the Joint Chiefs, if not the secretary of defense, begin thinking of military policy in terms the State Department (and the AEC) considered palatable. Acheson's basic question to Bradley and the other soldiers was simple: "'If we keep saying we want the [nuclear] control policy when we don't, we are perhaps fooling others, but we shouldn't commit a fraud upon ourselves.'" What kind of policy on nuclear weapons did the military really want?[69]

Bradley had his own questions and problems. In a meeting in his Pentagon office on New Year's Eve, he told Lilienthal frankly that "all we have right now, but all, is [our A-bomb stockpile]. Without that we are helpless to aid our friends and must, if they are overrun, try to hold our foes off from home base." The United States would never again be able to "normandize," that is, to invade Europe as it had in 1944. If the Russians attacked the West but were somehow thrown back, it would take France, Germany, Britain, and the smaller countries of the Continent at least ten to fifteen years to rebuild to the point where they were at midcentury. Even then Europe might not survive. If Soviet forces in 1945 had remained on the far side of the Pripet Marshes in Eastern Europe, they might now be hobbled by long, vulnerable supply lines. But World War II had brought the Red Army to the center of the Continent; their supply dumps were less than one hundred miles from their jumping-off points for an invasion of the West.[70]

The problem was, Bradley continued, that if World War III were truly a long way off, the United States could afford to keep a small military establishment and dabble with an international system of nuclear weapons control that was less than perfect. But American military policy was now made in Moscow. Stalin and his handful of fellow totalitarians knew what they wanted to do; the United States had no idea what was in their minds.

This was the frightening world of early 1950, less than five years after the most extensive and devastating war the planet had ever endured. Who could know when the next, infinitely more terrible conflict might erupt? The people might not be aware of the ticking clock, but those charged with their defense were. When Truman had announced the Soviet bomb explosion back in September, the doomsday clock that adorned the front page of every issue of the *Bulletin of the Atomic Scientists* had jumped from eight minutes to three minutes before midnight. Lilienthal showed his growing despair when he asked Bradley what would happen if the United States, as a symbolic gesture toward dreadful reality, abruptly dropped its campaign for international control of atomic weapons. Bradley demonstrated his pessimism by replying that it might be worth thinking about.[71]

Throughout the first weeks of 1950, the press and public slowly awoke to the possibilities of a new, even more terrifying nuclear weapon. On January 2, the Alsops devoted another lengthy column to the issue. "None of those now arguing the [super bomb] problem doubts for a moment that this hideous weapon will be built eventually." The question was whether to direct the AEC to do the job immediately (within two to four years) or hold off for a while. The Alsops added that Truman, Conant, and Vannevar Bush, the president's science adviser, had first addressed the question of building a hydrogen bomb in late 1945 but had concluded that, because of the magnitude of the task and America's atomic monopoly, no decision needed to be made. Now the "hell bomb," as some had already labeled the super, was being debated once again.[72]

On January 19, Souers phoned Acheson to say that the president was aware of the rising interest in a possible hydrogen bomb and that he had just received a lengthy document from Johnson at the Pentagon, "which to him made a lot of sense and he was inclined to think that [building the super] was what we should do."[73] In this January 13 memorandum the Joint Chiefs stated that although a "crash program" to develop a super was not required at present, "the determination of the technical feasibility of a thermonuclear explosion" was "a matter of top priority."[74] At the same time, studies of "ordnance problems" and of a suitable delivery system (i.e., an advanced, high-performance bombing plane) should be begun concurrently with thermonuclear research.

The military chiefs argued that the Soviets would not be deterred from thermonuclear research by a unilateral U.S. pledge of restraint or disinterest. In modern warfare, offense totally dominated defense; therefore, a hydrogen bomb was an essential defensive as well as an offensive weapon because of its deterrent value. "Possession of the super bomb would most certainly increase the United States' retaliatory power and total military strength." An H-bomb would be hideously expensive, costing perhaps $100 million to $200 million for research and development, but the United States could afford a "normal super bomb development program" without gutting other essential defense production, including improvement and expansion of the atomic arsenal. Of course, some questions could not be answered: whether a suitable and cost-effective delivery system for the super could be built and whether the super really would permit wholesale destruction of Soviet industrial and military complexes with only a few bombs.

Bradley and his colleagues rejected using the first hydrogen bomb as a demonstration of the super's terrible power. Any possible moral or psychological advantages would be compromised by the intelligence that Soviet observers could obtain about the bomb. They also disputed the suggestion that hydrogen bombs would somehow elevate warfare to a transcendent plane of destruction that would jeopardize civilization if not humanity. The U.S. military would never use the super bomb as a terror weapon, as a means of genocide. The Chiefs "do not intend to destroy large cities per se; rather, only to attack such targets as are necessary in war in order to impose the national objectives of the United States upon an enemy." Whether the imposition of national will could in practice be kept distinct from terror bombing, the Joint Chiefs did not say. The recent world war did not provide encouraging precedents.

The JCS concluded with a ritual bow to the advocates of international control, but they "strongly reaffirm[ed] their opinion" that research on thermonuclear reactions should be continued at least until the United Nations reached an agreement for international control of atomic energy that was satisfactory to the United States. The Chiefs added that they had "serious objections" to any unilateral U.S. decision to deprive the military of the results of thermonuclear research. The United States should not abandon its strenuous efforts to bring the Soviets into a system of international nuclear control, but the Pentagon wanted the final say on whether to develop thermonuclear weapons.

By the last week in January, the news of an impending decision on the hydrogen bomb was all over the national press, radio, and Capitol Hill. Urey and Bernard Baruch, author of the stillborn 1946 plan for international control of nuclear weapons, were advocating an immediate commitment to develop and build a super. Urey was especially strident, insinuating that perhaps something sinister (a "curious prejudice") had restrained the Truman administration from going ahead with a super in 1945. Urey stated that if the United States did not embark immediately on a super project, the Soviets would soon be able to exert thermonuclear blackmail on the entire world.[75]

Urey and Baruch had substantial support on the Hill. Tom Connally of Texas, chairman of the Senate Foreign Relations Committee, stated that America had to have the super. "We want to preserve the peace of the world and the hydrogen bomb will serve that cause just as the atomic bomb has done." Senator Harry F. Byrd of Virginia, a longtime power in the upper chamber and a constant advocate of economy in government, insisted that the United States needed "a plentiful supply" of super bombs. Congressmen John Kee (Democrat, West Virginia), chairman of the House Armed Services Committee, Carl Vinson (Democrat, Georgia), and Carl Durham (Democrat, North Carolina) of the House Atomic Energy Committee joined the chorus.[76]

Lewis Strauss was known to be working behind the scenes with fellow Atomic Energy Commissioner Gordon Dean to round up Republican patronage. The Pentagon provided congressional crusaders with muted assistance. In a speech at Rensselaer Polytechnic Institute in New York, Bradley stated that scientists should not be restrained from following their instincts and civilian and military authorities should not be restricted in appropriately applying whatever discoveries the scientific community made.[77]

Public and press reaction to the crusade for a super was mixed. Henry Luce's editorial writers observed that "with the sure instinct of self-sustainment, 20th Century man refuses to be overwhelmed by himself." Frightful news had become commonplace, and "what man has wrought, man learns to bear." Thus, the American people received news of the hell bomb and its unthinkable destructive power "with notable calm." The "idea of refusing to make the H-bomb," Luce's people wrote confidently, was "suicidal nonsense, a foolish relic of the period when the U.S. thought it had an atomic monopoly." What Truman needed to do now was to make a public overture to Stalin "'to find a sure basis for world peace.'" If such a gesture failed, as it probably would, it would be "'time to stop deceiving ourselves'" that everything in the world was fine and hopeful.[78]

Those on the other side of the argument were in despair. Initial thermonuclear research had demonstrated that humanity now could literally make a small star. That star would be in the form of a packaged weapon, a hydrogen bomb, which symbolized how far the world had fallen from Christian grace. "Man has become a god—a god without moral responsibility," the editors of *Christian Century* mourned. "He is a devil-god who wills evil not good—the sort of moral monstrosity the divine action on Calvary was enacted to redeem."[79]

Truman could not wait much longer for Acheson, Johnson, and Lilienthal to make their recommendations. The White House and State Department were already sitting on a horrible secret that could not long be kept, and so on the last day of January the NSC Special Committee met again to discuss a draft report to the president. For nearly two hours, the three men and their advisers sat in Room 216 at the ornate "Old State Building" across the small alleyway from the White House, arguing and debating. As they glanced up from time to time they saw "a lovely winter's day" framed "through the windows on the 17th Street side" of the building. Lilienthal, in his last week as AEC chairman, fought valiantly but fruitlessly for patience amid the mounting excitement. There was a weakness at the center of American policy, he said, that needed to be addressed with careful analysis before reaching any decision on the super. The nation's overriding reliance on weapons of mass destruction to contain the Soviet Union—of having, as Bradley candidly admitted, "virtually nothing else but the atomic bomb" to counter a possible Soviet thrust into Western Europe— was sterile and potentially counterproductive. Proceeding with a crash program to test the feasibility of thermonuclear weapons would exacerbate the problem, not resolve it. A decision to develop the super would tend to hide the lack of any U.S. policy other than atomic-thermonuclear brinkmanship. If Moscow called Washington's nuclear bluff, either Europe would fall to communism through default or it would be utterly destroyed in a nuclear war designed to "save" it.[80]

Lilienthal's colleagues were not impressed. Acheson said he agreed with everything the AEC chairman said, but that did not resolve the problem that a super could someday be built. At that point everyone's patience was exhausted. Johnson suggested that he, Acheson, and Lilienthal take the draft report to the White House and let Truman decide the issue. The Committee adjourned at 12:30 P.M. The members—"lost in thought"—walked to the White House.[81] The three men were admitted to the Oval Office shortly after, for a meeting that lasted just seven minutes.

The draft report that the Special Committee handed Truman was a masterpiece of balance that implicitly or explicitly acknowledged and incorporated much of what Lilienthal was trying to convey.[82] A super could probably be built, but "an all-out effort" would "seriously impair the efficiency and output of the fission bomb program," and nobody wanted that. All evidence indicated that the Soviets wanted to win a cold war, not wage a hot one. Development of a super by the United States could have a devastating effect on Russian opinion and would undoubtedly stimulate the Soviets to accelerate their own super program. The Soviets would eventually build a super, so it was imperative to work toward effective international control of "the entire field of atomic energy."

The evidence and speculation generated three specific recommendations. The AEC and Pentagon together should press ahead to determine the feasibility of a thermonuclear bomb and the necessary ordnance and delivery systems to make it an effective weapon. The president should publicly announce this decision and then impose rigid censorship on government laboratories and industrial plants regarding progress made. The State Department and the Pentagon should reexamine the entire range of U.S. foreign and defense policies in light of Soviet possession of the A-bomb and possible development of a thermonuclear weapon.

Truman accepted the report and its recommendations without question. Turning to the disheartened Lilienthal, the president said he had always believed and still did that America should never again use nuclear weapons. The whole purpose of U.S. foreign and military policy was peace, not war. But the Soviet A-bomb left him with no choice. The United States had to make the super "because of the way the Russians were behaving"; it had "no other course."[83] Lilienthal then asked for and received permission to state his "reservations" one last time, but he was constrained by both his position and his intentions. Truman had become impatient with those who tried to frame nuclear policies in even implicitly moral tones. Already Oppenheimer had permanently lost favor with the president by stating at an Oval Office meeting that he felt like he had "blood on his hands" because of Hiroshima. After Oppenheimer had departed, Truman had blown up.

"Don't you bring that fellow around here again," he told Acheson. "All he did was make the bomb. I'm the guy who fired it off."[84]

Eloquent as he might be, Lilienthal was a lame duck who had no influence. Soon after he began to state his views, Truman cut him off. The United States could have had as much policy reexamination of the super as it wanted, he said, if Senator Johnson had not shot off his mouth. But he had. "Since that time there has been so much talk in the Congress and everywhere and people are so excited" that there really was no alternative but to go ahead and at least determine the feasibility of thermonuclear weapons, "and that was what he was going to do."[85] Later that afternoon, the White House Press Office released a brief 127-word statement: The United States would soon begin studying the feasibility of a hydrogen bomb.

Truman had a good reason for fearing public opinion about the super. He and Acheson had been informally told about Fuchs weeks earlier. On January 27, the counselor of the British embassy, Sir Derek Hoyar-Millar, made the matter official, appearing at the State Department with an official message. British investigators, following up on tips from their American cousins in the Atomic Energy Commission, had concluded their debriefing of Fuchs, and there was no question that he had been a Soviet spy for at least a dozen years. It was all most regrettable, of course, but there it was. Fuchs would be formally arraigned in a London courtroom within several days.

The story broke in the U.S. press on February 4, 1950, and the country was never the same again. The screaming headline in the *Washington Post* said it all: "Hydrogen Bomb Secret Feared Given Russians; British Seize German-Born Scientist on FBI Tip; His Confession Is Reported; Implications Grave. Prisoner, While on Atom Project Here, Had Access to Virtually All Developments; Hoover's Agents Tracing 'Other Ramifications.'" The source of the news was the Senate Appropriations Subcommittee, which had been routinely listening to J. Edgar Hoover's testimony on the need for added funds to combat the Red menace in America. Fuchs was a once-in-a-lifetime gift to the FBI director. Unnamed senators told the press that Fuchs had also apparently passed data on the "super-secret" hydrogen bomb to the Soviet Union.

Suddenly the horror of the "hell bomb" was transformed from a theoretical future possibility to an immediate probability. As Senator McMahon put it, the Soviets soon would possess "'chunks of the sun' . . . to incinerate 50 million Americans in a matter of minutes."[86] Did the Soviets already have a super? Would they get it before the United States? If Fuchs had given his communist masters the key to thermonuclear weapons, would not the Kremlin develop suitable delivery systems before the United States even if it did not yet have a bomb? The press did nothing to dampen the hysteria. Neither did many nuclear scientists.

The *Washington Post* stated that it had obtained confidential information indicating that "during his three-year association with atomic research in this country, Fuchs had access to virtually every development and every process, no matter how secret, in the atomic field."[87] Moreover, he had attended a 1946 meeting devoted exclusively to expounding the theoretical pathways to thermonuclear weaponry, although "much has happened since 1946," when the hell bomb was only an interesting sidelight of atomic research. But Eric Long of the University of Chicago, who had worked with Fuchs on the atomic bomb, estimated that Fuchs's knowledge of thermonuclear theory could have advanced Russian hydrogen bomb production by as much as a year. Conservative Senator Styles Bridges (Republican, New Hampshire) described Hoover's testimony as "one of the most shocking things I ever listened to."[88]

On February 5, there was worse news. Senator McMahon had hailed Gen. Leslie Groves, military head of the Manhattan Project, before the Joint Committee on Atomic Energy. According to press stories, Groves had stated flatly that Fuchs had given data on the hydrogen bomb to the Soviets.[89]

The small nuclear science community was devastated by the revelations about Fuchs and sought to purge its guilt over his undeniable treason by demanding either that the super be built immediately or that it not be built at all. Curiously, each side sought to buttress its argument by emphasizing the horrible, limitless destructive power of the hydrogen bomb. Both Fred Seitz and Harold Urey proclaimed that because of Fuchs and a shocking lack of progress in American nuclear weapons since 1945, the Soviets were well ahead in developing the super.[90] The *Bulletin of the Atomic Scientists* took note of Fuchs's treason but emphasized that only two of the hundreds of atomic scientists had given in to the temptation of committing treason for ideological satisfaction. The editors also observed sullenly that of course the case would provide ammunition for those sensationalists in the Hearst press and HUAC who demanded tighter secrecy in the nuclear weapons program. The public had to be clearly informed that the Soviets had gotten the atomic bomb not because of Fuchs (and earlier discovered spying activities of Alan Nunn May) but because they had fine scientists of their own.

Hans Bethe led a group of "top-ranking scientists" who urged the Truman administration to declare publicly that the United States would not be the first to use thermonuclear weapons. Bethe and his colleagues began a six-week crusade to acquaint the public with the practical meaning of a hell bomb. Their most sensational effort was on February 26, when Bethe, Szilard, and Seitz appeared on NBC Radio's weekly University of Chicago Round Table program.[91]

The atomic bomb, they said, was not the ultimate weapon it had first seemed. Nations and societies could survive even a rain of atomic missiles, but the hydrogen bomb projected nuclear warfare into the realm of the truly unthinkable. Bethe told the radio audience that the range of blast destruction from a super would be one hundred times the area destroyed by an atom bomb. (Both the *Bulletin of the Atomic Scientists* and *Life* provided graphic maps to make the point.[92]) A Hiroshima-type nuclear weapon would destroy midtown Manhattan, whereas a thermonuclear blast one thousand times greater would obliterate an area running roughly from south Yonkers through the entire Bronx, across Long Island Sound to Great Neck, then around to northern New Jersey. All of Brooklyn, Queens, Manhattan, Jersey City, and most of Newark, Paterson, Yonkers, and the Bronx would be wiped out. But that was not the worst effect. Seitz emphasized that 30 percent of the casualties at Hiroshima were flash-burn victims. The radius of flash burns from a Hiroshima-type bomb would roughly equal that of the blast area, Seitz maintained. But a hell bomb would produce much more flash than blast. People would be severely burned in an area including the entire lower third of Long Island, all of metropolitan New York City, southern Connecticut, most of northern New Jersey, and south to the Sandy Hook area. Of course, the flash would ignite huge fires throughout this region and perhaps in a larger area. Although the scientists did not say so, their remarks clearly indicated that four thermonuclear bombs (one each for Boston, the New York area, Philadelphia, and Baltimore-Washington-northern Virginia) would destroy the entire Boston-Washington corridor.

Szilard insisted that the only defense would be evacuation of the great urban-industrial centers of the eastern and Great Lakes regions. Pittsburgh would have to be dismantled and moved to the plains of central Kansas. Thirty to perhaps fifty million Americans, along with their entire industrial and social infrastructures, would have to be uprooted. Seeing a fat lob when it came to him, panel moderator Harrison Brown smashed the ball back to Szilard. Industrialists would never stand for such a disruption of their production and markets, he said. Szilard spiked the ball right back: Brown was right; defense against the super would require government controls "much stricter than we ever had during wartime. It would not be a New Deal but a Super, Super New Deal."[93]

But this was inconvenience, although on a grand scale. Szilard had something more in mind, and Bethe obligingly provided him with an opportunity to say it by mentioning the long-term effects of atmospheric radioactivity from a thermonuclear blast. The question had first been raised in the AEC report of the previous November 9. A month later, on December 7, Acting AEC Chairman Sumner T. Pike, had written the president that "several independent calculations" had been made and scientists had "concluded that this danger is not serious. Very conservative assumptions indicate that about 500 such [thermonuclear] bombs could be exploded before the danger point would be reached. More reasonable assumptions lead to a figure of 50,000 bombs."[94]

But three months later, set up by Bethe's question, Szilard argued that atmospheric radiation on a global scale was entirely possible from a single bomb. It was "very easy to rig an H-bomb, on purpose," so that it could become a true doomsday weapon. A scientist would merely have to explode a bomb containing fifty tons of neutrons anywhere on earth and permit all the neutrons released in the blast to be absorbed by another radioactive element within the bomb casing, whose lifetime could be five years. Once this neutron-laden radioactive element was released in the blast, it would be carried all around the earth by the global wind systems, gradually settling as lethal dust in every part of the planet. In time, the earth would become as lifeless if not as cold as the moon. This was the real meaning of the hell bomb.[95]

Within weeks, nuclear scientists spread Szilard's doomsday scenario throughout the nation in books and magazines. Professor Harrison Brown, a nuclear chemist at the University of Chicago, wrote that a string of thermonuclear bombs could be set off on a north-south line in the Pacific approximately one thousand miles west of California and "the radioactive dust would reach California in about a day, and New York in four or five days, killing most life as it traverses the continent." Western powers exploding a similar line of hydrogen bombs about the longitude of Prague could destroy all life within a strip fifteen hundred miles wide extending from Leningrad to Odessa and from Prague to the Urals.[96]

Would even godless communists dare to threaten humanity with extinction? Szilard insisted that they might try if they finally seemed to be beaten after a ten-year atomic war. If the United States found itself in the same position, it too might be tempted to trigger a doomsday device. Of course, the scientists argued, it might be difficult to predict wind patterns precisely enough to kill absolutely everyone and everything on earth in five years. In that case, nuclear scientists would have to use one of several elements whose lifetimes were not five years but twenty or fifty. That would not be difficult.

Surely such a bomb should never be built, but Bethe and his colleagues gloomily concluded otherwise. Because a super seemed feasible, the Soviet Union would certainly attempt to build an arsenal of thermonuclear weapons. Truman had made the right decision on January 31. The United States had to immediately begin research into if not development of a super bomb.

Lilienthal was infuriated with this line of reasoning, and three days later, on March 1, he gave a New York Town Hall speech specifically aimed at the round table participants. He scathingly condemned "oracles of annihilation" for spreading senseless panic—a feeling of "hopelessness and helplessness"—as they predicted the end of the world through atomic and hydrogen bombs. This "new cult of doom" did nothing to advance international trust or rational appraisal of national security needs. The suggestion of evacuating thirty million or more souls from the big eastern cities was "highly intellectual nonsense. . . . This can't be done, and everyone knows it can't be done, so why scare the daylights out of every one?" What was needed to confront the admittedly ghastly new world of thermonuclear power was understanding, courage, and faith.[97]

Szilard promptly replied in a March 4 letter to the *New York Herald Tribune*. He, Bethe, Seitz, and other concerned nuclear scientists were not trying to frighten people but to educate them. Lilienthal had not disputed what was said at the round table, only the way in which it was said. Well, too bad; facts were facts. Thermonuclear weapons would wreak hideous destruction, and Szilard emphasized again the potential doomsday nature of a hydrogen bomb deliberately designed to spread radioactivity around the globe.[98]

Eight days later, Eleanor Roosevelt presided over the first of a series of televised "teas" in which genteel guests were to debate calmly and carefully the issues of the day. "Naturally," Mrs. Roosevelt said in her distinctively high, quavery but somehow firm voice, "there can be only one subject we can deal with—and that must be the hydrogen bomb and the future of the atomic energy program and its direct effect upon our future lives." Lilienthal was there; so were Bethe, McMahon, and Oppenheimer. The men were obviously tense and stiff in front of this new medium with its intrusive cameras. Bethe read a statement asking that Truman pledge no first use of nuclear weapons. Lilienthal looked unhappy as he sat rigidly with his left hand jammed into a pocket. McMahon seemed bored. Oppenheimer was intense as always. The decision to make or not to make a hydrogen bomb, he said, was rooted in complex technological considerations but touched the foundations of human morality. "It is a grave danger for us that these decisions are taken on the basis of facts held secret." As *Life* concluded, "the soul-searchers" found no answers.[99]

The fight between Lilienthal and the scientists was actually more illusory than real. All were horrified by the thermonuclear specter, and the scientists were more deeply divided than Lilienthal seemed willing to admit. The question of building the bomb had nothing to do with its feasibility or destructive force; it had everything to do with individual scientists' impressions of the Soviet Union. Thus, Seitz emphasized the "impossibility of compromise between the two ideals" of democracy and communism. Because the underlying ideals of the West and the Soviet Union were so diametrically opposed, Seitz told his colleagues in the American Physical Society that February, "I do not believe that any genuinely broad compromise is possible. . . . We may compromise on minor issues, such as German reparations or currency," but communism simply could not embrace Western concepts of freedom and the open society without falling apart.[100]

Bethe expressed a different view. Writing in the April issue of *Scientific American,* he echoed Lilienthal's earlier anguish over the super, asking how "can we who have always insisted on morality and human decency between nations as well as inside our own country, introduce this weapon of total annihilation into the world?" Of course, the communists denied all the human values that Americans cherished; of course, the United States had to do everything possible to prevent the Soviet Union from dominating the world. But a thermonuclear war would destroy American society, civilization, and values. If the Soviets did get a super and the United States did not, would Americans supinely surrender as Urey had insisted? No. They could and would resist. Atomic bombs could do enough damage to remain a credible deterrent. If the United States had to initiate a super program, Bethe pleaded again for the Truman administration to make a no-first-strike pledge. Bethe's colleague, Robert Bacher, agreed. Writing in the same journal the next month, Bacher argued that precisely because the super was such an immense weapon, it had no practical military value. He derided those who would further frighten "laymen . . . pumped full of hysteria by Red scares, aggravated by political mud-slinging."[101]

Bacher's appraisal of public opinion was precise. Gone now was the fragile optimism of Christmas week, the hope that somehow the cold war with Russia could be kept within manageable bounds. A week after Truman's announcement and four days after the Fuchs story broke, Gallup pollsters discovered that 70 percent of those queried had heard of the super. Of the 49 percent who gave arguments for or against the "manufacture of the hydrogen bomb," 77 percent said the United States should build the super and 17 percent said it should not. When Gallup's people asked a follow-up question—Should the United States try to work out an agreement with the Soviets on international control before trying to make a hell bomb?—48 percent responded "yes" and 45 percent said "no." A month later, when Fuchs's betrayal was well known, 68 percent said that Washington should try for an international agreement on nuclear control with the Kremlin before building a super and 23 percent said it should not.[102]

Several days after the news appeared about Fuchs, an interviewer in Denver asked a man what he thought of the atomic bomb now. "I just feel better when I don't think about it," the man replied uneasily. The editors of *Life* commented that this typical response from John Q. Public did not reflect a head-in-the-sand attitude but a feeling of resignation: "It did seem to be pretty useless to worry about something that, like tomorrow's sunrise, was entirely out of his hands." But, the editors continued gloomily, "for anybody who read the papers or listened to the radio or couldn't afford a desert island, it was getting harder all the time not to worry and to avoid thinking about it."[103]

In the weeks after Truman's announcement and Fuchs's arrest, *Newsweek* observed that the super was casting a "darkening shadow over the nation. . . . While there was still no evidence of panic or even discouragement, there was evidence aplenty of serious thought . . . that humanity, in its rush for material progress, had devised the means of its own obliteration."[104]

On February 24, David Sarnoff, president of the powerful Radio Corporation of America (RCA) called on Louis Johnson at the Pentagon. The public was "now very much worried over our relations with Russia and the possibility of a world-destroying war because the public has learned that Russia has already exploded an A-bomb or an H-bomb," Sarnoff told the defense secretary. Sarnoff had come to plead for the creation of a high-level government commission or board to study the nation's defenses and the prospect of reviving international control of nuclear and thermonuclear energy. When told that Truman was in the process of establishing such a committee, Sarnoff responded with relief.[105]

There was a brief surge of opinion in favor of a summit meeting between Truman and Stalin to work out a deal to curb the headlong thermonuclear arms race, but, on February 22, the president flatly told the American people that there would be no summit. Nor would the United States ever consider a preemptive nuclear strike to destroy Soviet thermonuclear installations before Russia could develop its own hell bomb.[106]

As politicians and scientists filled the nation's airways with arguments over how far the United States should go in building a super, Henry Luce threw the full weight of his opinion-making journals into the debate. "This is the age of obliteration," *Life* editorialized at the end of February. Formal war between possessors of nuclear (i.e., atomic *and* hydrogen) weapons would mean complete destruction of society and civilization as mid-twentieth-century men and women conceived them. Obviously, avoiding war had to be a major task of statesmanship. But "opposed to" this apparently overriding necessity was "the elemental fact of 1950: The enemy of the free world is implacably determined to destroy the free world. . . . There can be no compromise and no agreement with Soviet Communism" because the communists simply twisted and tortured whatever agreements they were willing to make to further their own goal: the destruction of free-world capitalism.[107]

Never had Soviet power and prestige been so ascendant. Possessed of nuclear power, the Kremlin could subject the free world to an "atomic ambush" at any time. The newly emboldened Reds were on the march everywhere. In Moscow, Stalin and Mao watched as their foreign ministers signed a treaty binding the world's two largest countries "in [a] Red tie." During a "riot by Reds" at the Mediterranean port of Nice, dockside shipments were dumped as a protest against sending arms to the French expeditionary force that was battling communist guerrillas in Indochina. In Berlin, five thousand "Reds," barred from the French sector, rallied in the communist zone during a concerted Soviet drive to get the Western allies out of the city.[108]

At home "urgent demands for 'one more talk with Stalin'" were being heard "on every hand," yet such appeals only fed, however "unwittingly," the Soviet propaganda machine, which consistently tried to instill in Western minds a sense of guilty responsibility for creating the current "war situation." The task of Western statesmanship was to remain armed and strong and to wait for the first cracks in the Soviet facade of invincible and threatening power.[109]

How great was the Soviet threat? Luce had put his cartographers to work, and *Life* presented a superbly drawn map of the upper northern hemisphere with the North Pole at the center, showing how Soviet bombers from Murmansk and northern Siberia could easily fly over Greenland and Alaska, respectively to saturate New York, Washington, Chicago, Kansas City, Salt Lake City, and the West Coast with nuclear weapons. Soviet war production and manpower were far superior to those of the United States and its Western allies, and even now Stalin might be preparing "a quick knockout" blow, although knowledgeable military officials still believed that World War III would not come before 1952.[110]

Gallup's pollsters continued to track the super story closely. By mid-March, 85 percent of those questioned had heard of the hydrogen bomb. Of those, 49 percent believed the Soviets already possessed it; only 21 percent thought the Soviets did not have the bomb. A large number, 68 percent, believed the Soviets would use a hydrogen weapon against the United States; only 9 percent said no. It was not surprising that 69 percent of all persons questioned stated that the United States should try to make such a bomb, while only 14 percent urged restraint. Because of the Soviet A-bomb, the fall of China to the communists, and domestic industrial discord, Truman's popularity was plummeting. The previous summer 57 percent of those queried had approved of the president's job performance; by October, the figure had fallen to 51 percent. By January 1950, the president's approval rating stood at 45 percent.[111]

With the public, much of Congress, and many nuclear scientists urging total commitment to the super and with his popularity precipitately declining, Truman was easy prey for the Pentagon. *Newsweek* had observed in mid-February that the world had entered the "Hydrogen Age," and the "ugly truth" was that the president had no choice except to proceed with the super. If he refused to do so, the Soviets would "unquestionably" assume that they had received "an invitation to aggression."[112] Louis Johnson wrote Truman on the twenty-fourth, reminding him of a recent conversation (apparently lost to record) in which the two men had agreed that the Soviets were making rapid progress toward development of a super. "In view of the extremely serious, in fact almost literally limitless, implications to our national security," Johnson had ordered the Joint Chiefs to consider the super issue again. "They are [now] of the opinion, with which I fully concur," that the United

States had to begin an "all-out program" of hydrogen bomb development. Truman promptly passed the letter to the members of the Special Committee of the NSC for action, and two weeks later, on March 9, 1950, the committee told the president that it agreed fully with the JCS recommendation.[113] The next day Truman formally announced that the United States had now gone beyond a simple commitment to study the feasibility of a hydrogen bomb; it would make every effort to uncover the thermonuclear secret and build an arsenal of hydrogen weapons. Within five months the national security establishment developed a new production schedule of fissionable materials that would "nearly double those attainable under presently authorized programs" so that by July 1, 1956, "an even greater rate of" nuclear and thermonuclear arms production could be attained.[114]

Even before the president announced his H-bomb decision, millions of his countrymen envisioned a future of ashes. The men and women of Junius Shaw's generation had been born into a smug world of peace and material progress only to be pitched into the middle of two cataclysmic global wars that had hideously killed millions and had wrecked the international community. They also confronted frightening and illimitable hatreds and appetites; some had been overcome, but the Communist Moloch remained. Now they were being told that a perverted science was about to produce a weapon that would destroy humanity and every memory that it had ever existed. Here was nihilism with a vengeance.

In the remote apple country of Washington State, the editor of a weekly newspaper wrote that there could be no reasoning or compromise with the insane men in the Kremlin. "Neither can negotiations be successfully carried on with a mad government. . . . That is why the dark clouds hanging over the world will doubtless become darker. A storm is brewing, a catastrophic collision of man's own making such as can end only in chaos. It will be every people for itself. Civilization will come through badly battered, or it will perish. The survivor will be the government which kills the most people and does so first."[115]

To a minority of Americans, such thinking was horrifying. Now, with the Soviets and Americans locked in a rough parity of nuclear power, was the time to try to achieve a bargain on international control. "The problems of atomic politics cannot be solved by atomic bombs," the *New Republic* editorialized. Truman's decision was based on an incredible presumption of American righteousness and superiority, for in promoting their own security, the people of the United States would be forfeiting the security of the rest of humanity. "We are not the keepers of the world's conscience; the arbiter of its morals; the helmsman of its course; the judge of its errors. We hold no monopoly of its resources, of its wisdom or its weapons. We are not alone in seeking security and peace. We have no unique genius for prescribing the methods by which these ends can be promoted." Then came enunciation of the ultraliberal dream, the ultraliberal fallacy: "To the extent that Soviet Communism is willing to compromise, is anxious to avoid war, and is subject to internal change, our unwillingness to search out these qualities and our incitement of an atomic-armaments race become a crime against humanity."[116]

But the Soviet Union had no wish to compromise, no ability to change. Stalin was anxious to avoid war only until he could wage it on his own terms and with his own superior weapon systems. No one in the West at midcentury could predict that Soviet officials would one day make the remarkable journey toward openness and responsibility that they did under Mikhail Gorbachev. Waiting with less effective weapons for such a journey to begin would have sacrificed the security of every person in the North Atlantic community. The United States was caught in a tragic paradox for which it was not exclusively responsible. Insatiable curiosity and wartime imperatives had led to Alamogordo and Hiroshima; the genie of nuclear power had been forever released. Now Washington would threaten destruction of the human race in order to save it.

The emotional and psychological price was shattering. "For the people of the earth," wrote national correspondent William S. White in early February, the discovery of atomic power "and now the urgent progress toward the infinitely more destructive hydrogen bomb" had "thrust into the ordinary way of life a clutching mass fear of death not even fully understood." For the first time (but not the last) White wrote of the nation's "grim laboratories" and "dim corridors" of power "where lay the essential secrets" of a world gone mad with its own omnipotence and hatreds.[117]

Who had created this world? Professional anticommunists and Red-baiters like Hickenlooper and Velde, along with HUAC and its many supporters, were sure they knew. The smart-alecky science professors with their fancy degrees and the smooth-talking bureaucrats who stood behind them were responsible. They had finally—all of them—gotten their comeuppance during the Fuchs case. Never again would they be able to deceive truly vigilant Americans. The longhairs and the Lilienthals had laughed at those who had tried to tame the AEC in the interests of both efficiency and security. They had condemned the FBI and certain senators and congressmen for trying to maintain the nuclear secret; they had scorned as hysterical fools advocating a cult of secrecy those patriotic Americans who worried about communist infiltration of the atomic program. And look what had happened. One of the longhairs' own had proved to be a traitor. His egregious betrayal had placed not only the United States but all of the world in immediate, permanent, and mortal jeopardy. That was what the intellectuals, with their outrageous demands for openness in scientific research, and the bureaucrats, with their snide condescension toward the people's representatives, had done to the cause of freedom.

The horror would mount in the following weeks as the British government finally allowed FBI agents to interrogate Fuchs secretly. The FBI quickly discovered that Fuchs had given his information to an American contact, Harry Gold. Gold, in turn, had been part of a wartime Soviet spy ring that included U.S. Army Corporal David Greenglass, who had also passed on nuclear secrets from his humble wartime position at Los Alamos, and Ethel and Julius Rosenberg, who had funneled the information they received from Gold and Greenglass directly to their Soviet contacts, Semyon Semyonov and Anatolii Yakovlev. When the news broke about the secret interrogation of Fuchs on June 2 without any reports of what Fuchs had actually said, the press had a field day, proclaiming, "ONE HUNDRED RED SPIES NAMED BY FUCHS."[118]

Newsweek, noted for neither right-wing proclivities nor excessive emotionalism, reacted to Fuchs's treason with both fear and loathing:

This, then, was the Communist Man, a man who could betray the country that had given him refuge, freedom, and fame; betray his closest friends; betray his sacred oath. This mild-mannered little man named Dr. Klaus Emil Julius Fuchs, called himself a "controlled schizophrenic" and his fanatical belief in Communism had turned him into a living Dr. Jekyll and Mr. Hyde. . . .

Fuchs did not stand alone, for behind him—in France, Germany, Poland, Russia, Hungary, China, everywhere, even in the United States—were tens of millions of equally fanatical and dedicated Communists, equally determined to destroy the democratic world.

Two weeks later, while condemning Truman for continuing to follow an obviously failed foreign policy, *Newsweek* observed that the just-concluded trial of Alger Hiss had "uncovered Russian pipelines into the State Department."[119]

Nixon had finally unmasked Hiss as a smooth-talking Judas. But, professional anticommunists asked, how many more Fuchses and Hisses were lurking in the shadows of national life? How many other men blessed with big minds and even bigger egos were springing from the world's most privileged circles only to swindle, deceive, and double-cross their trusting fellow citizens for the sake of an international conspiracy against property, freedom, and God himself? No one could define the exact dimensions of a communist conspiracy that seemed to be slowly but inexorably subverting American democracy. Suddenly a new champion appeared who would try. In the process, he would take the anticommunist crusade to heights—or depths—that not even Nixon had imagined.

5

McCarthyism

❖ ❖ ❖ ❖ ❖ ❖ ❖ ❖ ❖ ❖ ❖ ❖ ❖ ❖ ❖ ❖

On January 21, 1950, as British agents closed in on Klaus Fuchs, jury fore-woman Ada Condell stood up in a tension-filled federal courtroom in New York City and pronounced Alger Hiss guilty of perjury. When the verdict was announced, a slight gasp arose from the spectators. Hiss leaned forward slightly, then slumped back. His wife, Priscilla, remained motionless, her eyes glazed and unfocused, as they had been throughout the trial. Only her constantly throbbing neck muscles indicated her state of mind. Four days later, Hiss was sentenced to five years' imprisonment. A case that had con-sumed seventeen months and seventeen days of investigation during two trials and had generated raging arguments in courtrooms, bars, homes, and offices across the nation was finally resolved. Hiss had lied about being both a communist and a traitor.

Liberals were heartsick; conservatives were ecstatic. Within hours, Dean Acheson, with a brightly flushed face, told the press that he would not turn his back on his friend Hiss. Others might do so in good conscience; that was up to them. But he would not because the standards of those who had brought Hiss down were lower than any act of treason that Hiss might have committed. This was the meaning of Acheson's reference to Matthew 25:34: "Inasmuch as ye have done it unto one of the least of these my brethren, ye have done it unto me." From now on there would be open war between the Fair Deal secretary of state from Harvard and the "yelping pack" of Red-hunters in and out of Congress.[1]

Richard Nixon promptly told reporters that the secretary's comments were disgusting. Then he amplified his response on ABC radio. The Truman administration had deliberately kept the Hiss case from the American people (implying that the pattern being followed in the hydrogen bomb decision had been carried over into the issue of internal subversion). "I don't wish to be mysterious," Nixon added. "All I can tell you at this moment is that I believe President Truman will have further reason to regret his red herring remarks." Did that mean the Hiss case was not over despite the verdict? No, it was not, Nixon replied. As Whittaker Chambers had said repeatedly, this was not a fight between two individuals. It was a struggle over the principle of allowing or not allowing known communists to join and sabotage the U.S. government. Nixon went on: "I have information—which I intend to place before the House next week—which will show this conspiracy would have come to light long since had there not been a definite, determined and deliberate effort on the part of certain high officials in two administrations to keep the public from knowing the facts." As for Acheson's defense of Hiss: "My advice to Secretary Acheson would be that he ought to be more careful about giving his friendship . . . to our enemies."[2]

Senate Republicans joined Nixon in a chorus of condemnation.[3] Acheson, while assistant secretary of state, had personally cleared Hiss. William Knowland of California, chairman of the Appropriations Committee, threatened to hold back the annual State Department appropriations bill until Acheson provided complete information on Hiss's career and his access to key documents and policymakers. Joseph McCarthy, an obscure junior senator from Wisconsin, "stormed, 'I think the American people ought to begin to wonder what's going on.'"

House Republicans were even more vociferous. Karl Mundt interrupted a floor speech to describe the endorsement of Hiss as "something that 'could have been issued only by poor, befuddled Dean Acheson.'" Several days later, Mundt portrayed Truman as a blundering leftist and called for "vigilante action to combat Communism, through . . . grass-roots committees in every American town." How many other communists was Acheson coddling? How ethical was his support of a man found guilty of lying about treason? What did such support signify for the future of U.S. foreign policy?

Conservative southern Democrats were as infuriated as the Republicans. Rural Dixie did not cotton to traitors, particularly those from the Ivy League. Several days after his press conference, Acheson made a routine appearance before the House Foreign Affairs Committee, where he received a tongue-lashing from Maury Maverick. "I'm not going to be polite," the Texas congressman began. "I'm tired of hearing about you and Harvard and Yale and that you're witty. I've never heard you say anything funny." Acheson laughed weakly and said he could not help it if he had gone to Yale. Maverick cut him off. If old Harold Ickes, the curmudgeon New Dealer, "got caught in a whore house at 3 A.M. killing a woman, a lot of people would bail him out. But not you, you've got no friends."

On February 2, Nixon, as he had promised, delivered an hour and a half speech on the House floor, "meticulously" assailing Truman for not bringing to public attention the communist "conspiracy" within his administration. Although the president and others could only speculate on the source of much of Nixon's information, it came in fact from J. Edgar Hoover, who had been providing the crusading young California representative with information from FBI files for at least fourteen months. Brazenly quoting at one point from an unattributed November 1945 file on Harry Dexter White, Nixon charged that Truman had known for years that both Chambers and Elizabeth Bentley had fingered White, a prominent Treasury Department official, as a communist, but the president had done nothing. "'Traitors in the high councils of our own government have made sure that the deck is stacked on the Soviet side of the diplomatic tables,' Nixon cried. 'The odds are 5 to 3 against us.' "

Long before the end of the Hiss case, conservatives had turned it into yet another referendum on the "Americanism" of the New and Fair Deals. But the verdict did more than indict the "Roosevelt revolution" one more time. It changed the entire direction of American politics. Both liberals and conservatives believed that the Democratic party had become the agent of mass empowerment, the natural home of the nation's "little people" in their ongoing struggle against those comfortable classes who inhabited and ran the Republican party. But Chambers had come from the "masses" to be championed by Republican Red-hunters, and he had now disgraced a New Deal aristocrat who had been born and raised with a silver spoon in his mouth. The Hiss case seemed to prove that the New Deal was an alien, rogue movement imposed on the country during a time of crisis by a little group of wealthy, radical elitists, and that it had been exposed by one of the little people it was supposed to assist. An English observer wrote that the whole affair satisfied the goals of congressional investigators: to discredit Roosevelt and the New Deal and to undermine Truman's policies. "Moreover, it cannot be considered apart from the present mental and nervous condition of the American public, as revealed in the anti-Red hysteria, the fears concerning Russia, and the popular terror stimulated by unceasing announcements and conjectures concerning the A. and H. bombs."[4]

Chambers's need to confess and expose had helped Nixon fulfill his need to exorcise. Hiss was essential to the deeply flawed, self-wounded, young Californian because he gave Nixon a political compass bearing and a set of prejudices and assumptions that the freshman congressman would never abandon on his long, tortuous road to the White House. Already contemptuous of liberals because of his experience battling Jerry Voorhis, Nixon found Hiss anathema. His account of the case reveals a sense of bitter resentment and envy toward a man who had everything, whereas he had struggled. Hiss was the worst (or best) example Nixon would ever find of what Republican zealots later sneeringly labeled "limousine liberals." Son of a prosperous Baltimore merchant, Hiss had gone to Johns Hopkins, not Whittier. He had earned an Ivy League law degree (Harvard), whereas Nixon had been forced to settle for Duke. He had clerked for the immortal justice, Oliver Wendell Holmes. Good-looking, urbane, and knowledgeable, Hiss had moved quickly up the career ladder, serving in several New Deal agencies, the State Department, and as secretary-general of the San Francisco conference that established the United Nations. In January 1947, the still young man had become president of the prestigious Carnegie Endowment, traditionally a stepping stone to the highest offices of government. And all the time he had been a communist traitor—or so Chambers said. Nixon had been determined to bring down this symbol of wealthy liberal arrogance, and he had.[5]

But after helping to expose Hiss, Nixon prudently stepped aside. Chambers's triumph suggested that a conservative resurgence could be best attained by right-wing populism. Nixon had no stomach for that. For all his deep resentments, he aspired to respectability; he did not want to be a mere rabble-rouser. Once he had made his point about communists in government, he moved on to more lofty issues. When necessary he would exploit anticommunism, such as helping to responsor the Mundt-Nixon internal security bill the next summer and successfully campaigning for the Senate in the autumn of 1950 against the "pink lady," Helen Gahagan Douglas. But he yearned to be a statesman, not a politician. He left the door wide open for others to reap what he had sown. Within days of Hiss's conviction and the unmasking of Fuchs, Joe McCarthy took up the challenge.

❖ ❖ ❖

A small-town Wisconsin lawyer and trial judge, McCarthy had once been reprimanded by the state supreme court for arbitrary and arrogant action in suppressing evidence and falsifying court records. Twice he had been exposed for income-tax evasion. He had won his Senate seat in 1946 with the help of Col. Robert McCormick and the *Chicago Tribune.* His campaign tactics had included identifying the Fair Deal with communism, giving himself a bogus war record, and then persuading the public—and himself—to believe it. In 1949, he had publicly defended Nazi SS men who had mercilessly executed more than one hundred American servicemen during the Battle of the Bulge. Many of his Wisconsin constituents were of German descent, and it was said that a good number had read *Mein Kampf.*

A short, dumpy, balding Irish-American pressed tightly into double-breasted suits and smitten with a fatal passion for alcohol, McCarthy was the consummate political adventurer. Like Nixon, he had a mirthless chuckle whenever he sensed a political kill or believed that he had suckered another journalist or politician into believing what he said. McCarthy possessed the charm and temperament of a storm trooper, and his thought processes were similar. His bonhomie had a Hermann Göring-like quality to it—menace thinly veiled in gusto. Whatever he could get, whatever he could take, was good because Joe McCarthy wanted it. His effrontery was both breathtaking and invincible.

The motives behind McCarthy's Wheeling, West Virginia, speech of February 9, 1950, remain obscure. Some have claimed that the senator knew he was in deep trouble back home and was frantically searching for an issue that would ensure his reelection in 1952. When he asked several close friends and advisers what he should do, they urged him to exploit the issue of communist subversion. McCarthy's staff was totally ignorant on the subject but were quickly steered to the conservative press establishment for help in writing a speech. Two of Cissy Patterson's reporters on the Washington *Times-Herald*, Ed Nellor and George Waters, together with Willard Edwards of the *Chicago Tribune* wrote what McCarthy would read that night in Wheeling. At least one contemporary observer, however, Ernest K. Lindley believed that McCarthy was completely unprepared for the incredible reaction to his remarks. The junior senator had simply "made some charges [for] which he did not expect to receive national publicity and for no purpose, apparently, beyond doing his bit to raise the morale of his party and help it collect campaign funds."[6] Lindley may have been right, for McCarthy reacted with conspicuous surprise to the stunning effect of his charges.

The plates of creamed chicken patties had been barely cleared from the tables of the Colonnade Room in Wheeling's McClure Hotel when McCarthy rose to denounce Acheson as "a pompous diplomat in striped pants with a phony British accent" who dared to quote the Bible in defense of a convicted traitor. He then articulated in a few sentences all the accumulated grievances, resentments, frustrations, and suspicions of conservative Americans long out of power and seething with a sense of unfair displacement.

> The reason why we find ourselves in a position of impotency is not because our only potential enemy has sent men to invade our shores, but rather because of the traitorous actions of those who have been treated so well by this nation. It is not the less fortunate, or members of minority groups who have been selling this nation out, but rather those who have had all the benefits the wealthiest nation on earth has had to offer—the *finest homes,* the *finest college educations,* and the *finest jobs* in government that we can give. This is glaringly true in the State Department. There the *bright young men who are born with silver spoons in their mouths are the ones who have been worse.*

"I have in my hand," he continued, "57 cases of individuals who would appear to be either card-carrying members or certainly loyal to the Communist Party. But they are nevertheless still helping to shape our foreign policy."[7]

Whether the administration or the State Department should have responded to claims that seemed preposterous on the surface is a moot point. John Peurifoy, the department's top security official, upset by the revelations about Fuchs, the Hiss case, and a swelling popular denunciation of Acheson's biblical defense of his former colleague, really had no choice. As soon as he learned about McCarthy's charges, Peurifoy called a press conference to deny them. The State Department had "fine-combed" its employees with thorough security checks. There were no disloyal diplomats in the U.S. foreign-policy establishment.[8]

McCarthy had achieved the reaction he wanted. Traveling on west, the senator expanded and clouded his charges. There were either fifty-seven or eighty-one but certainly "a lot" of communists in the American diplomatic corps. At first the national press printed what he said rather perfunctorily;

after all, most of the senator's assertions simply echoed Nixon's recent speech on the House floor. For a moment, the Wisconsin senator surrendered to desperation. On February 11, he sent Truman an impudent cable from Reno, telling the president "that the State Department harbors a nest of Communists and Communist sympathizers who are helping to shape our foreign policy. I further stated that I have in my possession the names of 57 Communists who are in the State Department at present." Of course, McCarthy continued, the department denied all. He did not have files in hand, the senator added, but "I know absolutely" that of one group of approximately three hundred diplomats "certified to the secretary for discharge," only eighty or so had been removed.

> I understand that this was done after lengthy consultation with Alger Hiss. I would suggest therefore, Mr. President, that you simply pick up your phone and ask Mr. Acheson how many of those whom your [internal security] board had labeled as dangerous, he failed to discharge. . . . Failure on your part will label the Democratic party of being the bed-fellow of inter-national communism. Certainly this label is not deserved by the hundreds of thousands of loyal American Democrats throughout the nation, and by the sizable number of able loyal Democrats in both the Senate and the House.[9]

If McCarthy expected to steal a march on the president, he was immediately disabused. Truman had been bred in the always rough, occasionally vicious Kansas City school of politics, and he not only knew when he was being shaken down, but he knew how to respond. He instantly drafted a blistering reply, telling McCarthy that he had read the senator's cable "with a great deal of interest and this is the first time in my experience, and I was ten years in the Senate, that I ever heard of a Senator trying to discredit his own Government before the world." Honest public officials did not do such things. "Your telegram is not only not true and an insolent approach to a situation that should have been worked out between man and man but it shows conclusively that you are not even fit to have a hand in the operation of the Government of the United States."[10] Whether such a spirited riposte might have nipped "McCarthyism" in the bud we shall never know. Someone in the White House prevailed on the president not to send his reply, and McCarthy continued his reckless attacks.

The senator was discovering that when curious local reporters pressed for specifics, the best tactic was not to produce evidence but to promise more sensational revelations when he returned to Washington. He quickly found that he could keep the political drama going indefinitely by waving pieces of paper, making sensational charges, never responding to demands for precise proof, and above all never relenting in the attack on communists in government. It was not McCarthy's job to put out the fire but simply to jump up and down and yell that the fire was there, to present an indelible image of an internal enemy. It was certainly not the first image of internal subversion presented, but its sweep and lack of details (unlike the specific charges of Bentley or Chambers and the earlier long lists compiled by Eugene Lyons) were its strengths. Peurifoy fed the allegations and McCarthy's own growing notoriety by sending the senator a telegram asking him to document his assertions.

McCarthy repeated his tale over and over again in February, March, April, and May of 1950.[11] The State Department had been "taken over" by a "group of twisted-thinking intellectuals," led by the effete Acheson, who had made Truman their "prisoner." Acheson was not only a "Red" or at least very "pink"; he was also trying to pass himself off as a British aristocrat as he played England's game in Europe with Americans' hard-earned dollars. The "57" or "81" or "over 200" State Department "intellectuals" were "card-carrying Communists," either sympathetic to or part of an "espionage ring" that controlled the same loyalty board that was supposed to ferret them out. Thus, constant protests by Acheson and Peurifoy that such men as John Davies and John Service had been repeatedly "cleared" as security risks were discounted by McCarthy and his growing band of supporters and well-wishers. Communist agents and spy rings were "well entrenched" in the various intelligence agencies around Washington, and everyone knew it. They were thus able to block investigations and "gain access to all secrets." Because they dominated the State Department's personnel office, they could place their communist friends and other communists in the highest diplomatic policy-making positions.

The State Department also administered the Voice of America, Washington's worldwide radio propaganda network, so it, too, was heavily infiltrated with Commies. "The easiest way to get in" to the Voice of America, McCarthy charged, "is to be a well-known Communist. . . . Unless one has a Communistic background, one cannot qualify for a position with the Voice of America." Finally, to conceal all of these traitorous activities, State Department officials falsified records and threatened to fire any loyal official who dared to tell the truth. The State Department thus contained a huge, malevolent, and out-of-control spy ring of communist intellectuals at the core of the U.S. government.

A week after Peurifoy's press conference, with McCarthy back in Washington, Democratic Senate Majority Leader Scott Lucas of Illinois told a reporter that although he could not defend Acheson's emotionalism in the Hiss case, McCarthy was nothing but a glory-seeking headline hunter. McCarthy had to respond. Starting just before dinner on the evening of February 20, he kept his colleagues in the Senate chamber for over six hours as he provided rambling, often semicoherent details of eighty-one alleged cases of State Department disloyalty. McCarthy's charges seemed to be based on notes from the department's own security files, and he referred to them simply by number. When pressed, he refused to give names but said he would supply them to interested senators for their information. Word soon leaked out that one of the cases involved John Carter Vincent, minister to Switzerland and a former official in the State Department's Far Eastern section. Soon another name cropped up: Owen Lattimore, a prominent academic who had worked for the government during the war. Both men had been sympathetic to young foreign service officers in Chongqing, who in 1944 and 1945 had insisted that Mao and his communist followers should be considered the true voices of China.[12]

In the context of the Hiss and Fuchs affairs, Lucas, like Peurifoy, could no longer ignore McCarthy's claims, however wild and unsubstantiated they might have seemed. Two days after McCarthy's marathon performance on the Senate floor, Lucas received permission from the Democratic congressional conference to propose a resolution authorizing a subcommittee of the Senate Foreign Relations Committee to look into McCarthy's indictments. It passed unanimously. Shortly thereafter, Herbert Block, the renowned political cartoonist of the *Washington Post*, coined the word "McCarthyism." The term was meant to be condemnatory; McCarthy shrewdly exploited it as a movement.[13]

And a movement it swiftly became. For more than forty years, scholars and journalists have argued about whether McCarthyism was rooted deep in the American past or was simply a spasmodic response to postwar frustrations. Was it a broad movement of social protest or merely a reaction by angry Republicans to repeated defeats and embarrassments?[14] McCarthyism remains elusive because its critics have concentrated on the man and have extrapolated the movement from what he said and what he did. Political scientist Willmoore Kendall wrote in 1963 that "the issue was Joe McCarthy himself." Thirty-two years later, another political scientist, David H. Bennett, insisted that McCarthyism "could not endure" beyond McCarthy himself and the immediate postwar conditions that made him. Once Eisenhower fashioned a new, more moderate political culture in 1954, McCarthyism lost its rationale and drive.[15] But Kendall and Bennett are wrong. McCarthy was not a lone political vigilante as he is often depicted; he was not a shoot-out artist who single-handedly blazed away at the liberal establishment. He symbolized a broad, reactive impulse in the early postwar American political culture that would multiply and grow in the decades after midcentury until it finally came close to capturing—or recapturing—the American spirit.

McCarthy immediately energized every campus Red-hunter, every member of a state legislative investigating committee, every conservative journalist, writer, and columnist, every professional anticommunist, and every ex-Communist Party informer.[16] At last, by God, someone prominent was speaking out against the Red Menace and not just once or twice, like Nixon, Mundt, or Hickenlooper, but repeatedly. When the exhausted senator called J. Edgar Hoover soon after his February 20 speech on the Senate floor and asked for help in documenting the presence of communist subversives, Hoover ordered his aides to comb Bureau files. Freda Utley, Louis Budenz, and other professional anticommunist crusaders telephoned McCarthy, pledging their support and, most important, promising to pass him their lists of "known subversives." A group of prominent conservative newsmen—including Hearst reporter Howard Rushmore, columnists George Sokolsky and Westbrook Pegler, Trohan and William Edwards of the *Chicago Tribune*, and Woltman and Smith of the Scripps-Howard chain—rushed in to write McCarthy's subsequent speeches. They joined Ed Nellor who had turned down the senator's request to be his speechwriter for a more lucrative offer at *Look*, only to be told by his editors at the magazine that he would be kept on the payroll while working full time for the burgeoning McCarthy crusade. Everything had been arranged through the good offices of Republican National Committeeman Arthur Summerfield. All of the conservative journalists had forged close links with Hoover and the FBI and, through them, McCarthy was assured continuing access to a gold mine of rumor, innuendo, half-truths, and speculations that formed the basis of the Bureau's anticommunist files. One of the most affluent Red-hunters to join the swelling McCarthy crusade was an obscure New York importer of Chinese textiles, Alfred Kohlberg, who in 1943 had become embroiled in a bitter political feud with the Institute of Pacific Relations (IPR), an obscure left-wing but noncommunist think tank that had published the journal *Amerasia*. Despite a lack of any evidence, Kohlberg firmly believed the IPR was "led by the nose down the Kremlin path by Lattimore," the State Department's Philip Jessup, and others.

The systematic hunt for Red America was finally under way, moving inexorably from the fringes to the center of national debate. And a large, diverse constituency was out in the country waiting to respond. McCarthy himself may have been an amoral political freebooter, but those who attached themselves to his crusade had grander objectives. They assumed that exposing liberalism as an anti-American fraud would return basic conservative values to the forefront of national life.

McCarthy already belonged to a small but powerful Senate faction, "a hard nucleus," in reporter William S. White's words, of what political scientist Earl Latham would later label "fundamentalist conservatives."[17] Included in this group were Mundt, Hickenlooper, Wherry, Kem, Bricker, Jenner, Bridges, and on the periphery, moving in and out as expediency dictated, Robert Taft. Occasionally, Knowland could be persuaded to join the group. If Truman had his cadre of able, often supercilious "wise men," the long besieged and bedeviled Republicans from Plainville and Middletown had finally formed their own aggressive counterfaction.

The Great Depression and World War II had accelerated fundamentalist conservatism's growing estrangement from the political mainstream. In 1946, a perceptive English observer, Graham Hutton, noted that in terms of effective political power Republicanism "has become more of an agricultural and small-town faith, as it was in the beginning. So Maine and Vermont are linked with Kansas, Nebraska, the Dakotas, Colorado, Iowa, and Wyoming" and also with those states "that have many prosperous farms and a disproportionately large number of small towns—Ohio, Indiana, and Wisconsin." In prominent agricultural states where big or middle-sized cities were numerous, where industry and organized labor were strongest, as in Illinois and Michigan, liberalism and the Democratic party remained unbeatable.[18]

The Midwest and middle border states (the Dakotas, Nebraska, Kansas) were *Chicago Tribune* country, where people responded positively to Colonel McCormick's latest jeremiads on the decline of American life and values. In

1947 popular journalist John Gunther devoted ten pages of his discussion of the Middle West to the power and influence of the *Tribune*.[19] It was more than a newspaper, Gunther reported, "more even than the 'World's Greatest Newspaper,' as it fondly calls itself"; it was "a property in several dimensions, a domain, a kind of principality" whose owner and governor was bizarre. At midcentury, Robert Rutherford McCormick was a tall (six-foot-four), imposing seventy-year-old, a shy, aloof man, "handsome in a riding-to-hounds sort of way," who cultivated a phony British accent. After graduating from Yale in 1903, he had served in Chicago politics in various capacities until the Great War, when he had gone to France with the Illinois National Guard. Upon his return, he had inherited partial ownership of the *Tribune* and, in 1926, became its sole publisher.[20]

By 1940, McCormick had transformed a few simple, powerful passions and prejudices into "vast wealth, vast prestige, vast influence." He ran his newspaper like a medieval seigneur and saw and spoke only to those people he chose to. His perspectives were based on a "furious Americanism and patriotism," which he equated with rugged individualism and free enterprise. He was so proud of the armed services and his own wartime contribution that when his adored first wife died, he buried her with full military honors. Despite his pretentious accent, he detested the British empire, hated Franklin Roosevelt and the New Deal for ostensibly transforming America into a neo-Bolshevist state, and was convinced that communists ruled the nation's capital. His prejudices perfectly matched those of his readers, who shared his conviction that somehow the New Deal, with its handouts, pro-labor policies, silly (or sinister) concerns about the Negro, and determination to crush private enterprise, had destroyed the moral fiber of the country. Gunther was struck by "the zealous anti-Britishness of so many midwest Americans," which politicians like Hickenlooper, Wherry, and Nebraska's other senator, Hugh Butler, exploited in their incessant conflicts with Acheson. Hutton added that "the Midwest in all its relatively short history has been as insulated from the currents of world affairs as the heart of Russia." Like the center of Russia, the postwar Midwest could no longer resist or ignore the tides of world affairs that beat repeatedly and strongly at its shores, and it responded with instinctive mistrust and much suspicion.[21]

McCarthy never forgot McCormick's initial and crucial support and never let his benefactor down. The senator's incessant assaults not only on communists in government but on Acheson's "British" manner and bearing were never-ending acts of homage to the *Tribune* and its publisher.

As the fundamentalist conservatives in Congress began punishing the Democrats with the Hiss case and the issue of communist moles and sympathizers in the State Department and elsewhere, they attracted the fervent allegiance of a strange and disparate coalition. Heartland evangelical anti-communists like young Billy James Hargis joined corporate religious anti-communists embodied by the Roman Catholic church; China missionary anticommunists, led by media king Henry Luce; and reformed communists from New York and Chicago such as Eugene Lyons, Utley, and Budenz, who possessed their own religious fervor. The coalition also included hustling anticommunist entrepreneurs (the liberals sneeringly called them "patrio-teers") such as Ted Kirkpatrick and Ken Bierly, who discovered that publishing a blacklist of alleged communists in the entertainment industry was another way to succeed in business without really trying.

No one upheld fundamentalist conservatism more staunchly or served McCarthy more loyally than Senate minority floor leader Kenneth Wherry, a burly, assertive fifty-seven-year-old lawyer and mortician. Wherry denied that he was a conservative. He considered the term "altogether inadequate to describe his position," William White reported in early 1950.[22] Wherry preferred the term "fundamentalist" because it "denote[d] a political person who wishes to have done with many of the political ideas of recent years and return to a simple past."

Wherry was convinced that a "'socialistic welfare state'" was "fastening a tightening grip on the country." Examples of rampant socialism included public housing assistance programs, federal aid to education; "socialized medicine"; the Marshall Plan (which "subsidized" the British labor government and gave money to European bureaucrats and planners rather than to businessmen); and all foreign aid programs that went beyond direct feeding of the world's hungry. Wherry was even occasionally suspicious of Taft for harboring "dangerously radical" ideas, such as accepting the need for a limited public housing program to sustain the American family. The only federal economic and social program Wherry favored was price supports for farmers, but even there his hatred of the federal bureaucracy was boundless. Those "damned foreigners" from Washington went out to the Cornhusker State to "tell the farmers what to plant."

Wherry was known in his hometown of Pawnee City as "Lightning Ken." Off the Senate floor, he was a good storyteller, "a generous, friendly, and good-humored man. The kind that sparkles brightest at a convention or a Chamber of Commerce luncheon." He was voted "jolliest Senator" by the "girls" in the only Senate office building that Washington possessed in 1950. A Nebraska editor once wrote that Wherry could "infuse enthusiasm and abounding good cheer into an inquest." But that was not quite true. He did not find communism or the Fair Deal amusing. "Whenever Truman acts," journalist Paul Healy said, "Wherry reacts as spontaneously as a conditioned reflex."[23]

Wherry's gruffness was legendary. His booming voice was pure club car American, cutting through the cigarette smoke and the whiskey fumes to rattle the eardrums of anyone within a hundred feet. Arthur Vandenberg once said that Wherry could make even "good morning" sound belligerent. Wherry's mouth always moved faster than his mind. Even when he was not talking, the Nebraska senator's lips were in constant motion, "visibly at work, apparently going through a dry run for his next forensic blitz." Without verbal warm-ups, Wherry's phrases tended to tumble out askew. He once excitedly referred to the "Chief Joints of Staff" and on another occasion reminded a colleague that "the Senator made the motion from Texas." In the midst of an angry exchange he admonished: "The Senator from North Dakota will have opple amportunity to reply." In a debate on Southeast Asia he talked about "Indigo-China," and he once referred to the Senate Rules and Administration Committee as the "Rules and Illustrations Committee."[24]

A person of rigid conviction and total candor, the Nebraskan expressed his "'oppositionism' . . . with a kind of impersonal fury, struggling hour upon hour in the Senate in his effort fully to convey his anxieties and misgivings." Wherry was the classic midwestern small town businessman of the nineteenth century. "The most liberal thing in the world," he told White, "is to preserve the free enterprise system in the United States. What else has anyone got to offer?" He added that he did not like the term *democratic process* because it was "too close to socialism. That's too direct for me. . . . I believe in a *representative* government."[25]

White had not the "slightest doubt" that Wherry was "a man with a mission . . . to end, so far as may be possible, the Roosevelt-Truman New-Fair Deal, and to do so, if at all possible, in ways that would appeal particularly to the civic luncheon clubs of the country." That audience was, of course, precisely what McCarthy appealed to that February night in Wheeling, West Virginia. Until Wherry's death in 1951, he supported McCarthy with undiminished fervor.[26]

Despite his malapropisms, Wherry was no buffoon. In 1942, he had defeated progressive Senator George Norris in the Nebraska primary. Observers found it difficult to assess accurately Wherry's influence because he was one of seven or eight senators who held politically extreme positions. But White concluded that there was "no doubt that Mr. Wherry holds a midwestern following which, while not easily calculable, at all times commands political respect and sometimes political fear."[27]

The Roman Catholic church had been a public foe of international communism well before midcentury. The party and the church, the two great world institutions seeking dominion over the human spirit, were totally at odds with each other. But stirring below the surface of American evangelical Protestantism was an equally powerful hatred of the Red menace, which had originated in the rabid patriotism and biblical fundamentalism of the 1920s. At midcentury, a new generation of rousing young preachers began exhorting their parishioners from the pulpit and by radio to beware of godless communist moles who had burrowed into the nation's churches, schools, and government under the guise of political, social, and religious liberalism.

During the war years, Billy James Hargis had absorbed the foundations of evangelical anticommunism at Ozark Bible College in Texarkana, Texas. From the beginning, he was a free spirit. Restriction to a particular Christian fellowship, denomination, or brotherhood made him restless and unhappy. "I take my orders from the Lord," he later wrote.[28]

Shortly after the war, the restless and somewhat aimless young man met evangelist A. B. McReynolds, who had a small church in Oklahoma's Kiamichi Mountains. Hargis was immediately impressed by the man's political-religious outlook. One day McReynolds gave the young preacher a copy of *The Road Ahead,* in which John T. Flynn claimed that the liberal Federal Council of Churches "was the biggest ally the international Communists had in the United States." Little by little, McReynolds provided Hargis with an understanding of Christian conservatism. His arms loaded with books and pamphlets, the young man returned to the small church in the Tulsa suburb of Sapulpa, where he had been temporarily hired, and read "the truth about 'Internationalism,' 'Socialism,' and 'Liberalism.'" Epiphany came. Earlier Hargis had naively preached that world government was the "ONLY solution" to earthly affairs; as a good Christian, he believed that he had to be a pacifist and speak out against war and violence. Now he suddenly realized the folly of believing that "a conglomeration of political philosophies and nations, void of national pride and political identity, [was] the only way out."[29]

One day in 1948, McReynolds told Hargis his destiny: to leave his congregation, to go out into the world and warn the people, to "expose Communism in the churches and the country." Hargis would not be a politician; he would be a prophet of God. "God showed me once and for all that I was to crusade the rest of my life for righteousness and truth, no matter what the cost. . . . I was by then completely convinced that I was called of God to launch a mass movement of resistance to the trend in American life to world government, apostate religion, and appeasement with deadly, satanic-inspired Communism." From the beginning, Hargis added, "I have never treated Communism as a political issue but as a religious issue."[30]

At first the road was hard, the message diffuse and difficult to explain. "I had Gethsemanes that I never dreamed of. God tried me and whipped me in a dozen ways." Most of the Christian churches turned against him as he sought to "lead God's people out of the complacency and apathy which seemed to have settled upon Christ's Church in the world." The young evangelist was rejected not because of his message but because of his stubborn itinerancy.[31] He would not be pinned to one place. For two years, Hargis crisscrossed middle America, preaching in villages, towns, and cities, wherever he could drum up a small audience. He was only one of thousands of independent preachers who felt compelled to spread their version of God's truth. Ozark Bible College denied it had ever known him. At one point, he had to sell his car, but he persevered, scrounging funds where he could. He went further than his colleagues, publishing, when possible, a magazine called *Christian Echoes*. His first break came in early 1950, when he obtained a small amount of time on two radio stations, KRMG in Tulsa and KUOA in Siloam Springs. In a few months, his rising popularity enabled him to get enough funds for a little radio time on a northern Mexico station, XEG, whose signal reached all of the southwestern United States.

One evening, a widowed, childless farm woman in the Oklahoma panhandle, hearing Hargis's voice booming over the airways from Mexico, was moved to give him much of her small fortune. Then the Baptist Bible Fellowship of Springfield, Missouri, representing a nationwide denomination of Baptist churches, offered to support him in his "prophetic role of warning the churches about the religious implications of Communism and especially of the subversion of the National Council of Churches."[32] The preacher was on his way.

His travels as a Christian anticommunist had taken him across the Bible belt, from Sciotoville in southern Ohio through central Missouri to western Arkansas, Oklahoma, and rural Texas. Here was his constituency, and this was his message:

I was permitted by the Lord to see the danger of Communism when almost no one else took its threat seriously. I saw how its satanic ideology was creeping into the pulpit and influencing the theology of some of our Protestant denominations. I set out to expose apostasy in the churches; the decay of morality in society due to Communistic, socialistic influences; and the open attempt to subvert the succeeding generations through Liberal teachers who parrot 'the party line' in schools and colleges.

. . . The objectives of the Antichrist and Communism are parallel:

1. The establishment of a world government to bring every nation under totalitarian rule;

2. The establishment of a world church which will claim to be Christian, but will in actuality deny Jesus Christ and subvert the influence of the church to promote a godless world government. . . .

. . . America is not only the brightest hope of freedom in this world but it is the last stronghold of Christianity. . . .

If America falls into Communist hands—or even goes completely Socialist—by the nationalization of key industry—that will be the first step toward Communism. . . .

Satan knows this. America is a thorn in his plans to rule the world. This nation was raised up by God to fill a vital role in His plans for world evangelism. . . .

. . . Under the Marxist concept of Communism, which is the philosophy of Liberalism, there is no God—and man is superior. An elite few, who feel they are academically qualified to lead the ignorant masses, have assumed command in plotting our destinies and motivating men. God has been dethroned. No longer motivated by God and his Holy

Spirit, America is motivated by the social planners, the monolithic Liberal Establishment. Revolution is becoming the norm; anarchy the acceptable.[33]

Liberals cried "Fascist" whenever Martin Dies (first chairman of HUAC) or McCarthy "pointed out the imperfections of individuals within our democratic system. . . . The Liberal Establishment in America is far more charitable to the left-wing anarchist than it ever is to the patriots on the right whose desire is to eradicate internal Communism. The Liberals unite to stop—at any costs—the activities of a McCarthy, a Dies, a Velde, a Hargis."[34]

By 1953, Hargis would be financially strong enough to pull his first great publicity stunt, the "Bible Balloon Project," in which stacks of Bibles were launched by balloon from West Germany, over the Iron Curtain, to reach the Red devils in the East. The project "catapulted my message to national prominence."[35]

Other virulent anticommunist preachers were also abroad in the land at midcentury. Their chief patron was apparently the "Reverend" Carl McIntire, who in 1936 had been ousted from the Presbyterian Church U.S.A. because of charges that he had defamed the characters of fellow Christians and violated some of the Ten Commandments. McIntire quickly formed a rival, ultraconservative religious group, the American Council of Christian Churches. According to a 1964 study, McIntire's hatred of both Protestant "modernism" and Roman Catholicism was intense. By 1950, he concluded that the liberal National Council of Churches was his prime enemy because it had become communist-inspired and communist-infested. That year he traveled to Sydney, Australia, with fellow evangelist T. T. Shields of Toronto and discovered Fred Schwartz, a mesmerizing, energetic man "with a folksy way of speaking and an infectious, waggish grin on a ruddy face." Schwartz had the platform manner of a scholar at ease with his subject, but he could deliver the fire and brimstone when necessary. His message was simple: Christian men and women were imperiled by an insidious, pervasive communist menace whose dimensions were nearly inconceivable, and it was the duty of Schwartz and others like him to inform the free world. This was the message McIntire wanted to hear, and he invited Schwartz to the United States for a two-month lecture tour under the auspices of the American Council of Christian Churches. Two years later, Schwartz made a permanent move to the United States.[36]

Acheson and his fellow wise men would certainly have scoffed at the manipulative blatherings of Hargis and Schwartz if they had known of them, but a growing number of post-New Deal Americans identified with their message. Big government had proved an unmitigated disaster for evangelical Protestantism. Washington bureaucrats had replaced the local churches as arbiters of social agendas and values; distant, faceless officials had assumed the role of social mediators, determining who would be on welfare, who would qualify for this program or that, who were the needy, and what they would get. Now it was government, not the church, that suffered the poor to come unto it. The churches suddenly seemed to lack moral and social purpose. Christianity had lost its basic role of social and moral arbiter and provider of last resort. Government, not the preacher, did God's work on earth and snatched from the churches Christianity's reward system for good deeds.* With its social purpose apparently destroyed, Christianity was left with conflicting theologies based on a two-thousand-year-old myth. Forty years later, the wife of a southern California congressman, herself a self-proclaimed religious guru, finally stated succinctly what Hargis had imparted so incoherently but powerfully to his increasingly restless and impassioned midcentury listeners. "The greatest tragedy of the modern welfare state," Arianna Huffington said, "is that we have allowed it to deprive us of a fundamental opportunity to practice virtue, responsibility, generosity, and compassion."[37] To thousands of evangelical Protestants, government by 1950 was a source of pain, not healing; it had become the anti-Christ.

McCarthy's determination to root out communists in the liberal federal establishment thus complemented the objectives of crusading Protestant fundamentalists, who normally mistrusted both Roman Catholics and Irish-Americans. These fundamentalists were not confined to village America. George Sokolsky, a prominent conservative columnist, told his urban readers repeatedly that communism's basic objective was "to prove that God does not exist."[38] Liberalism and communism seemed to share a basically pragmatic and materialistic view of life, and when that partnership was emphasized to millions of fundamentalist Americans (and then apparently demonstrated by Hiss and Fuchs), liberalism became odious. For

---

*This was as true abroad as at home. The Peace Corps agenda and programs in Africa in the 1990s were almost identical to the missionary objectives of ninety years earlier. Compare U.S., Peace Corps, "Africa Region Integrated Planning & Budget System, FY95-97: Strategy Statement and Individual Goal Report" (typescript provided by Peace Corps, Washington, D.C., n.d.), with Robert H. Milligan, *The Jungle Folk of Africa* (New York: Fleming H. Revell Company, 1908).

many people, McCarthyism quickly metamorphosed from an exercise in political extremism to something approaching social and religious cleansing.

Liberal American foreign policy had clearly betrayed the Christian missionary impulse in China and, in the process, alienated the most powerful figure in the national media. By 1950, even sophisticated Henry Luce had become susceptible to Red-baiting, although he was never completely comfortable with McCarthy. At first he rejected the Wisconsin senator, and after 1953, with Eisenhower in the White House, he urged the country to ignore McCarthy and his wild charges. But in the critical spring and summer of 1950 Luce briefly came to McCarthy's aid.

It is difficult now to understand the destructive influence of Nationalist China on American opinion in the 1940s and 1950s. Somehow China and Chiang's Kuomintang government had become a tabula rasa for America's most egregious aspirations. In 1940, Wherry had brought a wildly cheering crowd to its feet by pledging that "with God's help, we will lift Shanghai up and up, ever up, until it is just like Kansas City."[39] China's slow, agonizing "fall" to the "Reds" between 1945 and 1949 had focused the venom of anticommunist crusaders on the wise men of Washington's foreign-policy establishment.

America's romance with China contained several ingredients. Unlike the British or French, imperialists in every meaning of the term, Americans never knew well any part of Asia except China and, of course, the Philippines. China became their only playground on the Asian mainland, and, by the end of the nineteenth century, large numbers were there, believing they were both influential and indispensable in the daily life of this exotic land. Their presence was grounded firmly in missionary proselytization. The reverends and their wives fought for the spirit and future of China. Many, if not most, were remarkable people who had left their towns and fields, families, friends, and college classrooms to toil for many frustrating years in often harsh Chinese vineyards.

Missionaries are often crudely depicted as poorly educated, narrow-minded, credulous, hypocritical souls who do God's work with literal adherence to scripture. But the center of American missionary work at the beginning of the twentieth century was Yale University. Out of this hotbed of zeal came Henry Winters Luce, who sailed for the Orient in 1897 to uplift heathen souls. But Luce was no bigot. He soon learned to admire the richness and sophistication of Far Eastern religions and Chinese life. He passed his appreciations on to his young son, Henry Robinson Luce, who began schooling at Chefoo and then studied in England and at the Hotchkiss School in Connecticut before entering Yale in 1916. After brief wartime service, Henry became a journalist, and, in 1923, with an equally young colleague, he founded *Time* magazine to keep busy capitalists and would-be capitalists abreast of national and foreign affairs.

Luce and other missionary offspring were as remarkable as their parents. Like the equally precocious children of foreign service officers, they were often rootless people, never completely comfortable in either their lands of nativity or their country of official citizenship. Americans by legal fiat but only tenuously by culture, they spent their childhoods and often their adolescences in Asia. Dispossessed from the start, not fully experiencing the life of Shanghai, Kansas City, or Manhattan, they were strangers in every land they visited or inhabited. Yet these bright, articulate people carved distinguished public and private careers for themselves as diplomats, professors, and publishers. In the process, they defined China for several generations of Americans and understandably urged its transcendent importance. Tragically, they also reflected the serious divisions within China itself.

Luce created a media empire that, by 1944, spanned the United States and the world. In that year, *Time* itself had a weekly circulation of 1,160,000 plus classroom, various overseas, and servicemen's editions. *Life's* circulation exceeded four million U.S. subscriptions weekly plus another 370,000 abroad. *Fortune's* subscription list stood at 170,000. The news serial *March of Time* appeared monthly in ten thousand movie houses throughout the United States and abroad. Like nearly all the others who were later identified closely with China—including Lattimore and Vincent—Luce was a complicated, controversial man. He possessed a strange, quirky mind, and like many of his China colleagues in the early postwar years, he tended at crucial moments to express his ideas and thoughts in rambling, only marginally pertinent anecdotes.[40]

As the Japanese began their march through China in the late thirties, Luce became an ardent champion of Chiang Kai-shek. In 1941, he and his wife, Clare Boothe Luce, made the perilous journey to wartime Chongqing and were captivated by the "Gissimo" and his brilliant, American-educated wife, the "Madame." The Luces knew they "had made the acquaintance of two people, a man and a woman, who, out of all the millions now living, will be remembered for centuries and centuries."[41] Luce never lost his admiration for Chiang despite China's ordeal during and after the war.

When the Kuomintang, racked by corruption, incompetence, and demoralization, finally fell to Mao's Chinese Communists in 1949, forcing Chiang and a comparative handful of survivors to flee to Formosa, Luce was as embittered as any professional anticommunist. He believed that Acheson's effort to explain the long drawn-out catastrophe by issuing a two-volume compendium of diplomatic documents was a contemptible cover-up. Short on truth and long on sensation, *Time*'s summary of the *China White Paper* and its deficiencies reflected Luce's anguish and anticipated every theme that McCarthyites and "Asia firsters" would soon use to demand and justify an inflexible policy of confronting communism throughout the Far East.[42]

The loss of China, *Time* said, was a "chilling calamity," for the Nationalists had been America's "most important ally in the world outside Western Europe. . . . Gone beyond recall beneath the Red tide . . . was the whole great heartland of Asia; the millions who had suffered first and longest the Axis onslaught, who had survived to resume their old fight against the armies of Communism." The white paper was "a savage indictment" of Chiang, who, according to the State Department, had wasted more than $2 billion in U.S. aid before finally conceding to communist demands.

Such a charge was outrageous, *Time* maintained, as was "the State Department's brazen assertion of its own utter guiltlessness." How could the United States lose a nation for which it had spent $2 billion trying to save unless there was incompetence—or worse? The white paper was, in Republican Minority Leader Joe Martin's phrase, "an 'Oriental Munich.'" Arthur Vandenberg condemned as a "'tragic mistake'" the department's "'impractical insistence'" that Chiang join a coalition with the communists. But *Time* maintained that the record was more sinister than such congressional condemnations suggested. Roosevelt's Yalta Accords, "negotiated behind China's back," had opened up Manchuria to Soviet armies, and the State Department's insistence that Stalin could have seized the region with or without an agreement was merely "shallow cynicism" and overlooked FDR's "covert legal and moral sanction" of communist expansion.

Ignoring wartime praise of the Chinese Communist leadership by such prominent apologists as Wendell Willkie, *Time* dismissed as "fantastically gullible when set against today's knowledge of Communist General Mao's fealty to Moscow" the reports and recommendations from embassy officials at Chongqing, who claimed in 1944 and 1945 that the communists were "moderate democrats." Again and again, *Time* writers returned to the basic question: If Nationalist China had been such a hopeless cause, "U.S. policy apparently made a bad marriage with despair and defeat many years ago and wasted billions on the dowry." But the white paper indicated that Chiang had actually been extremely strong in 1945 and that, in the autumn of 1947, Lt. Gen. Alfred E. Wedemeyer had recommended continuing extensive military aid to the Nationalists. The facts were obvious: By assuming from the start that the Chinese Communists somehow possessed a moral or political legitimacy, American policymakers and the fools at the embassy in Chongqing had opened the door for Soviet domination of all of Asia.

China, *Time* proclaimed in a spirited summary, should teach American officials some powerful truths "as bitter as they were plain." American diplomats, from embassy personnel to the secretary of state, had been confronted with "fiercely stubborn problems, equally stubborn men." Yes, the Chiang regime occasionally possessed "many of the worst vices known to governments: corruption and disunity, incompetence and indecision." But that was no reason to abandon either the regime or the effort to save it. The Greek government in 1947 had been as morally corrupt as that of Nationalist China. Yet the Truman administration had protected the Athens regime and saved it from communist infiltration and triumph. "In a world racked by the evil and destruction of first fascist, then Communist aggression," *Time* lectured, "the American job was to work with the world it found and know what world it wanted." Washington had never demonstrated in China the same stamina and courage that it had displayed in checking communism in Europe. "For its Asia policy, it had filed a petition in bankruptcy" and "seemed desperately to be seeking solvency in platitudes and recriminations."

Here was a masterful, compelling indictment of partisan decision making that no Washington politician, bureaucrat, or statesman could ignore. The Truman administration had simply deserted a cherished Asian ally in its hopeless pursuit of a moderate response to a monstrous international communist conspiracy and thus had gravely compromised national security. Luce provided enemies of the New and Fair Deals with an entire arsenal of arguments. In foreign as in domestic policy, he suggested, pro-communist liberals had betrayed American traditions and ideals. They had sold out China at Yalta, promoted communist interests during subsequent negotiations in Chongqing and ignored traditional American desires to uplift Asia while busy saving European warmongers (i.e., the Germans) from their own folly. They had repeatedly appeased or been outmaneuvered by Stalin and his slick international communist apparatus and conspirators. Liberals did not seem to know what kind of world they wanted beyond a kind of fuzzy, do-good social order dedicated to the advancement of every individual, regardless of his political creed or economic interests. Apparently every con artist on earth was exploiting this liberal goal to subvert American ideals and strength.

Truman quickly provided his critics with more ammunition. As soon as Chiang was exiled to Formosa, Britain prepared to recognize the new communist regime in Peking (Beijing). Conservatives, already upset by this new example of British perfidy, became enraged when the president in January 1950 reconfirmed his decision to discontinue aid the Nationalists.

Luce intuitively understood the mores and values of middle America. If the United States was to be forced out of isolationism—out of the era of free security that it had known and enjoyed before 1941—it had a right and a duty to play the role of world leader according to its own traditions and perspectives.

Americans were the first to perceive the planet as a great village, and they later did more than anyone else to make it one. According to Main Street, inhabitants of this village functioned not as cold practitioners of balance of power politics but as neighbors—interested, involved, deeply concerned, yet always aware of their overriding self-interests. The village had its bullies and adversaries, cranks and drunks, extortionists and embezzlers. But that, as Acheson had said, was life. Main Street, however, disagreed with the secretary about the best response to such realities. People and nations should form shrewd friendships based on shared interests, if not shared values. They should not try to befriend those who disliked or opposed them, and they should not casually abandon or discard the friendships they had made. A man (or a nation) might gossip about friends and complain of their profligacy, their failure to return the tools or machinery they had borrowed, and their insufficient gratitude for favors. But nations and men watched over their friends and helped them out in times of crisis and need. Chiang had been such a friend. If he ultimately proved to be one of the profligate town drunks, he was nonetheless America's drunk, and Americans had let him down. As a result, the United States had lost much of the global village to the town bullies, whose agents had penetrated the most intimate and important corners of the American household to compromise both decency and the will to resist. Americans could never again allow themselves to be placed in such a shameful position. Their first job was to roust out the foreign agents in their midst.

❖   ❖   ❖

A small but strident band of professional Red-baiters and communist-hunters was ready to fulfill the mission that Luce and others had defined. They were city dwellers, not country folk; often broken-hearted liberal humanists, not Christian fundamentalists. Because of their bitterness, they possessed the same evangelical emotionalism that defined Hargis; they had become missionaries for the same capitalistic system that Wherry and Luce espoused with such ardor. That system had badly abused them in their youth, but they had concluded that the communist system they had briefly embraced in reaction was much worse. They had waited a long time for a consistent champion. McCarthy would be their man.

Many professional Red-hunters had impressive credentials. Eugene Lyons grew up in the fetid slums of lower east side of Manhattan during the first decade of the century. "In America we still romanticize the glories of a hard, poverty-ridden youth," he wrote bitterly in 1937. "Our rags-to-riches legends and literature overlook the fact that Tony the Bootblack ends up as a hod-carrier or a gangster more often than a millionaire." The New York of Lyons's youth "teemed" with crowded, chaotic conditions resembling "the underside of a moss-grown stone." Tenements were "odoriferous garbage heaps" filled with the same "over-abundant life" as the streets below. "We knew coarseness, vermin, want, so intimately that they became routine commonplaces." Poverty was only half the ordeal. The other half was an acute awareness of being aliens and intruders in a nation of Anglo-Saxon Americans. Textbooks, movies, and newspapers described a world of farms and warm, embracing towns, of snug one-family homes, baseball games, and national heroes cutting down cherry trees or freeing black slaves that was completely beyond the imagination or experience of immigrant children squeezed into city tenements.[43]

Lyons emphasized that the tenements and streets of New York broke most children. They became petty crooks, small-time hustlers, or elevator repairmen. A few, like Lyons, escaped, and often the means of their liberation were the socialist schools of their neighborhoods, where Karl Marx reinforced in flaming prose what they already knew about the inherent unfairness of life. Bull sessions and reading lists at City College confirmed their radical dedication to sweeping social change, and many drifted into communism without much thought.

Lyons was one of them, and, as a young man, he had moved swiftly up the hierarchy of CPUSA until he finally received the cherished invitation to work for the cause in Moscow. Like a handful of others, he found the experience devastating. He encountered incredible incompetence, hypocrisy, deceit, injustices, and, above all, terror and repression in a state that permitted no serious criticism. Words and facts suddenly lost their meaning and took on a new and "objective" reality to fit overriding bureaucratic needs. Sanctions against free thought and free thinkers were draconian. In the communist paradise, where party dictatorship defined all reality, there was no real hope for change. Deeply flawed as capitalistic America was, Lyons concluded, its open institutions might allow reform, perhaps even generous social change. After several years, the party had recalled Lyons from Moscow, and he soon left its ranks, determined to reveal everything: not only the intrinsic abuses and dangers of communism but also the threat to the nation posed by "those narrow circles in America where purblind Soviet fanaticism feeds upon self-deception."[44]

In early 1941, near the end of the Nazi-Soviet Pact, which had caused many overidealistic Americans to renounce any affiliation with communism, Lyons published *The Red Decade: The Stalinist Penetration of America*. Over the next twenty years, the book ruined careers and lives. Lyons professed not to care. The face of communism he had seen in Russia was so odious, so terrible, that any efforts to destroy it were legitimate.

All Red-hunters shared one overriding assumption: Anticommunist America did not know the true, insidious nature of communism. Most people "do not yet understand," Budenz wrote as late as 1954,

> how the Communist actually functions, nor the world of carefully studied directives in which he lives, and its effect on his non-Communist environment. . . . Instructions from Moscow for the benefit of Soviet aggression are passed through the American Communist Party out into local non-Communist organizations. They are proposed and often adopted as policies in these organizations, frequently without being recognized or challenged by patriotic Americans.[45]

Red-hunting seemed an especially legitimate occupation for Russian immigrants. Jacob Spolansky was one of several who became prominent in the early fifties as McCarthy's star steadily ascended. Arriving in the

United States as a typically penniless young immigrant, Spolansky soon settled in Chicago, where he founded a Russian-language newspaper. In 1918, the War Department asked him to join the army as a confidential intelligence agent. In love with his adopted land and eager to demonstrate his patriotism, the young man immediately accepted the offer. Soon after the war, he transferred to the FBI. From the first Spolansky's duties "were concentrated almost exclusively around Communists and their organized webs."[46] By 1950, he had served thirty years for the cause of anticommunist counterintelligence.

Spolansky described the communist penetration of America as widespread and covert. "To those who are worried about the Communist threat to go underground," he wrote in 1951, "I can say only that the principal activities of the Communists in America, from the very beginning, have never been anything *but* underground." Communists would use any method, legal or illegal, to accomplish their objectives. Spolansky reemphasized what HUAC, Lyons, and Carlson had asserted about communist and Nazi attempts to subvert the United States: It was precisely the strongest weapon—the Constitution—that could be most effectively used against America. The people had to abandon their folly and gullibility and realize that they were threatened most by free speech. In a world of monstrous conspiracies such an indulgence had become an unaffordable luxury.[47]

Democracy could not be trusted to rescue itself from disciplined tyranny. "The Red target is always the same," Spolansky wrote. "These engineers of the underground machine seek to destroy family ties, the church, the democratic way of life: in short, everything that blocks the Communist juggernaut's path."[48] Communist agents corrupted youth, penetrated trade unions and government agencies, and worked ceaselessly through the churches, schools, and other agencies to advance the world conspiracy of their masters in the Kremlin.

In 1946, Ted Kirkpatrick, Jack Keenan, and Ken Bierly decided to exploit the swelling public fascination with internal subversion. They persuaded Alfred Kohlberg to finance the creation of American Business Consultants, a professional blacklisting agency that published a regular newsletter called *Counterattack*. Bierly quarreled with his colleagues in the early fifties and began publishing his own list, *Red Channels*.[49]

For years, these two blacklists determined who would be employed and who would not in the U.S. entertainment industry. Screen stars, radio personalities, Broadway theater people, and entertainment executives lived in daily fear, knowing that at any moment an anonymous informer could finger them as Red dupes, former members of a communist front organization, or just parlor pinks. Careers could be instantly ruined by an unknown enemy or competitor, who would use any means to smear an individual's reputation. There were so many lists of unapproved or simply suspected organizations with attractive names and apparently pure motives that one might have belonged to or that one's agent might have innocently lent one's name to three years ago, during the war, or at the height of the depression. When McCarthy enshrined anticommunist witch-hunting in 1950, fear escalated to outright terror, and the blacklisters hounded several talented and decent people, most notably actor John Garfield, literally to death.

McCarthy's most essential support did not come from excitable or morbidly suspicious persons or from cold-blooded exploiters of hysteria but from respectable conservatives and their spokesmen. The Republican party used Joe, and Joe used it in a marriage of mutual convenience. The vows were repeated when Taft, "Mr. Republican," charged the New and Fair Deals with championing communism and harboring pro-communists. And when Bob Taft spoke, Main Street America listened.

Taft's hatred of liberalism was intense. In a national article in fall 1949, he asked how much government American capitalism could stand. Free enterprise had built the nation. It's definition was simple: "Fundamentally, it is the right of any man to engage in any occupation or business and to run it as he sees fit so long as it doesn't interfere with the right of others to do the same." It was a system that provided "universal and continuous incentive" to invest, to work hard, to innovate, and, if a person was a true genius, to create, "because of adequate rewards." Government had undoubted roles in such a system: to ensure standards of fair competition formulated by the business community; to prevent restrictive monopolies and other artificial business practices; and to regulate a few potentially chaotic enterprises such as civil aviation and electronic communications. In a rich nation like America, the people could even ask government to ensure a basic standard of general welfare.[50]

But government had no right to regulate prices, set minimum wages, allocate resources, or dictate specific standards of business conduct. It had no right to favor one interest group in the economy (labor unions) over another (management). Above all, government had absolutely no right to use its questionable power of taxation to fulfill agendas in social engineering or to confiscate and punish free enterprise. But this was precisely what Roosevelt and Truman had done. It was time to call a halt.

A man of Taft's temperament and perspective was easily persuaded that a government that punished free enterprise was receptive to communism. Although Taft believed that Truman (and perhaps Roosevelt) were loyal Americans, they had been duped and outmaneuvered by Red cabals deep inside the federal establishment. He was as outraged as Luce when Truman decided to cut off aid to the Nationalist Chinese government. The supposed goal of American foreign policy, Taft said on the Senate floor in January 1950, was to contain existing communism on the premise that one communist advance would stimulate others. But in China "for some reason, the State Department has pursued a different policy from that followed throughout the rest of the world." It "has been guided by a Left-wing group who obviously have wanted to get rid of Chiang and were willing at least to turn China over to the Communists for that purpose." Not only were these men traitors to the containment objectives of American diplomacy, they had, "in effect, defied the general policy in China laid down by Congress."[51]

McCarthy thus had a broad and restless constituency waiting when he began his stormy, dramatic crusade, and, within six weeks of his Wheeling speech, he clearly had the nation transfixed and the administration on the defensive. In mid-March, Acheson was in San Francisco, where he spoke to an admiring audience at the Press Club. In response, the reporters regaled the secretary with a parody in the spirit of the famous Gridiron banquets back in Washington. To the tune of "On the Road to Mandalay" they sang:

> On the Road to Maryland
> With his brief case in his hand
> Thats [sic] the place that makes him happy
> Like Antaeus he loves the land

Our honoured guest loves "peace and quiet"
So we all can understand
(There ain't no) Senator Joe McCarthy's [*sic*] in the
    heart of Maryland[52]

After making his initial charges, McCarthy had to start producing proof. He admitted that this might be impossible unless the Senate Foreign Affairs Committee could obtain the State Department loyalty files. Truman promptly responded that he would not authorize release of these confidential documents.[53] But McCarthy had friends and resources of his own. Utley and Budenz brought him their files. According to McCarthy biographer David Oshinsky, Nixon turned over materials from his own investigations. McCarthy also undoubtedly had access to HUAC files.

With the White House and State Department entrenched against him, the senator had to begin naming names. The first was Haldore Hanson, a State Department specialist in foreign trade since 1942. Another name mentioned was Esther Caukin Brunauer, a minor official at the United Nations Economic and Social Council (UNESCO) whose husband allegedly had admitted he was a communist. Revelation of the third name—John Service—sent the State Department into an immediate panic. Service was one of the young diplomats in Chongqing in 1944–45 who had begged for a more even-handed policy toward the Chinese Communists. Peurifoy promptly cabled Service, who was in Yokohama, Japan, on his way to a new post in India, to return home immediately to face another grilling by the Department's loyalty board. Then Peurifoy issued a public statement, claiming that the department had reviewed Service's file on three previous occasions at the insistence of Red-hunting legislators and investigators. He had been cleared every time. "Here, in the person of Jack Service, we have an able, conscientious, and . . . demonstrably loyal Foreign Service Officer, a veteran of seventeen years with the department, and one of our outstanding experts on Far Eastern affairs," Peurifoy added.[54]

McCarthy retorted that Peurifoy and State were simply covering up. By making this statement, Peurifoy was seeking to influence the department's loyalty board. "This is the sort of thing we know goes on behind closed doors," McCarthy stated in a press release. "But this is the first time the department has had the effrontery to publicly tell their own loyalty board how to prejudge the case before hearing the facts."[55]

But McCarthy was not escaping unscathed. When he released the name of Dorothy Kenyon, a former New York municipal court judge who had served briefly as U.S. delegate to the UN Commission on the Status of Women, she fought back spiritedly. Appearing before the Senate Foreign Relations Committee, the "matronly, plump woman of 62, dressed in unmodish black silk and wearing a black hat with three feathers," stated that she was not a communist, not a fellow traveler, and that she had not knowingly affiliated with any organization that could possibly be considered a communist front. At the end of her angry, defiant testimony the audience burst into applause.[56]

McCarthy refused to quit. If Hanson, Service, and Brunauer were insufficient pegs on which to hang charges of wholesale communist infiltration of the State Department and if people like Kenyon could not be bullied, then it was time to go after Acheson. Throughout the last half of March, McCarthy and the Republican congressional leadership, working separately and together, prepared a plan of attack.[57] Taft and others claimed they supported McCarthy completely. Later Taft, perhaps deliberately imitating FDR's famous 1933 inaugural address plea—to try something and if it did not work try something else, but above all in a time of unparalleled national emergency, try *something*—urged McCarthy to keep after the State Department; if one case or charge did not work, try another. The administration was tough, tricky, and determined, but there was a chance that Joe might really uncover something that could be used as a devastating campaign issue in the fall congressional elections and perhaps even the 1952 presidential race. Nonetheless, the Republican leadership knew it had an issue that could backfire if no communists were exposed. Thus Taft, chairman of the GOP policy committee, announced that although he was personally urging his young colleague to make his sensational charges, they were "not a matter of party policy." If McCarthy failed, there would be time and justification to repudiate him.

McCarthy was far out on a political limb of his own making. Taft did ask his close friend, Styles Bridges, to form a "brain trust," which would "whisper hurried advice" to McCarthy between sessions of the Senate Foreign Relations subcommittee. Once hearings in the Democratic-controlled subcommittee began, however, McCarthy was strictly on his own, and chairman Millard E. Tydings of Maryland was determined not to let his Republican opponent control the proceedings for the benefit of the GOP.

Unfortunately the administration's Asian policies were so muddled in the months after the fall of China that critics easily found a number of issues with which to assault Acheson and the State Department. In late February, someone on Gen. Douglas MacArthur's staff at Far East Headquarters in Tokyo leaked the contents of a confidential "guidance" memorandum from the State Department, which told officials "to prepare for the loss of Formosa to the Chinese Communists." Congress erupted. Who prepared the message? Two men, the Department responded sheepishly. Well, who were they? Get their names. Taft and the others insisted on holding a hearing to expose the devils. Acheson went to the Hill and appeared before the Senate Foreign Relations Committee in executive session. Chairman Tom Connally, the shrewd Texas Democrat, believed it would be prudent to invite five Republicans as "guest observers." Acheson boldly told the senators that Formosa was not needed for American defense of the western Pacific, and he took full responsibility for the guidance cable without mentioning who had actually drafted it.[58] The Republicans were not amused.

Acheson had numerous defenders in Congress, although many were lukewarm at best. They complained weakly that the secretary was being branded an appeaser in hindsight for following wartime policies of cooperation with the Soviets that nearly everyone had supported. In 1945, U.S. officials and citizens had justifiably expected cooperative Soviet behavior to continue; it was the American way to trust a friend until he proved otherwise. And there was no evidence that a tougher policy toward Stalin would have worked. The Red Army could not have been kept out of Eastern and Central Europe in 1945 unless the British and Americans had mounted an extensive attack beyond the Elbe, which surely would have transformed World War II into World War III in a few days. Acheson was no appeaser now, "even though plans for the H-bomb had made a 'new approach' popular." The Hiss case was an individual tragedy; there were no more communist agents in the State Department, and clumsy attempts to find them would destroy the careers of innocent public servants and blacken America's reputation with friends abroad.[59]

McCarthy disagreed vehemently. He charged that at least one unnamed flagrant homosexual had remained in the department at Acheson's request and that the "Red Dean," as McCarthyites soon branded Acheson, had thrown out Joseph Anthony Panuch in 1947 for trying to uncover Reds and perverts. Panuch quickly denied the charge, and Republicans and Democrats on the subcommittee promptly engaged in a bitter argument. Tydings demanded to know the name of the accused homosexual official, and Brien McMahon backed him. McCarthy retorted that Tydings's request was irrelevant; a snarling Hickenlooper agreed. Tydings then threatened to subpoena McCarthy's files if the senator refused to provide the name. McCarthy replied that Democratic subcommittee members were "tools" of the State Department. They wanted his files, and they wanted him to supply names so that Acheson and his colleagues could fire loyal State Department officials who were helping to root out Reds. "You are not fooling me," he shouted, prompting a white-faced McMahon to reply that he was shocked by McCarthy's "irresponsible" accusations of fellow senators. "When you start making charges of that sort against me," McMahon said, "you better reflect on it, and more than once."[60]

Early spring days dragged by with bitter arguments, charges, and countercharges. At one point, McCarthy stated that Ambassador-at-Large Jessup had "an unusual affinity with Communist causes." Jessup promptly appeared before the subcommittee armed with letters from Eisenhower and George C. Marshall, the revered former army chief of staff and secretary of state. Jessup lectured the subcommittee. "McCarthy's innuendoes" were making the United States a laughingstock abroad, eroding the confidence of America's anticommunist friends in the steadiness and wisdom of Washington's leadership. When McCarthy tried to cross-examine Jessup, Tydings immediately shut him up. Jessup had not been present to cross-examine McCarthy when he made his charges, and as a matter of policy, Tydings stated, he would not allow McCarthy to question anyone who came before the subcommittee unless the full membership was present. Since this rarely occurred, the young senator was squelched.[61]

In desperation, McCarthy made a final bid for respectability. He knew, he said, that a man "connected with the State Department" was in fact "'the top Russian espionage agent'" in the United States. McCarthy asked to go off the record and give the committee the individual's name. He stated that he would stake his entire reputation on this claim. "If I'm wrong about him, then I am discredited as a witness." But to make his charge stick, McCarthy said, he needed access to the man's FBI files. Soon the word leaked out, undoubtedly from McCarthy himself or from his small but intensely loyal staff, that the individual named was Owen Lattimore, who was then traveling in Afghanistan on a UN mission. "Anybody who knows anybody in Washington knows who McCarthy's target is," twittered syndicated columnist Doris Fleeson. "Those whose curiosity is killing them" could probably find out during "a 30-cent taxi ride from Union Station to the Capitol."[62]

McCarthy's revelation caused a slight but unmistakable turn in public opinion. *Newsweek,* which had closely followed the McCarthy story with considerable skepticism, now observed that although Lattimore had only been on the State Department payroll once, "it was equally true . . . that as a leading authority on China he frequently had been consulted by the Administration on foreign policy and was considered the principal architect of the specific policy which had ended with the victory of the Communists in China."[63]

But other, more powerful voices condemned McCarthy for destructive witch-hunting. Truman's attorney general, J. Howard McGrath, and FBI Director J. Edgar Hoover told the Tydings subcommittee that they could not make security files public without compromising national security. Because McGrath and especially Hoover were known to be dedicated to both Red-hunting and the preservation of national security even at the risk of curtailing essential civil liberties, their words had enormous influence. By mid-April, it seemed that the McCarthy crusade "had fizzled rather pathetically." Except for the Hearst and McCormick-Patterson papers, the "vast majority" of the nation's newspapers—Republican as well as Democratic—remained "highly critical" of McCarthy.[64]

In Washington state Tullius J. Brown, editor of the weekly *Grandview Herald,* tried calmly and rationally to put the entire anticommunist campaign in perspective. "Let's not condemn everyone as a communist who thinks he sees in the Russian government indications that it is not as bad as it might be," Brown stated in the first midcentury issue. "Americans merely want assurance that the Russians will not try to remold this country to fit the soviet [sic] pattern." Everyone "despise[s] Stalin and his police state," Brown later wrote, but "there is more phony patriotism wrapped up in anti-communist outbursts than can be imagined." As the first McCarthy investigations continued, Brown became more impatient. "If someone should demand that we take a loyalty oath we would feel just a little put out by the challenge." It would be like asking a horse thief whether he was honest. The horse thief wouldn't mind, but the really honest person would rightly believe that the demand was an insult.[65]

"Senator McCarthy and Secretary Acheson call each other bad names," Brown added at the end of March. The people just wanted this bickering in high places to end, for the result of such endless recrimination "is loss of confidence in everybody occupying high government posts. The Kremlin could ask for nothing better." The next week, Brown turned completely against McCarthy. The year before, the senator had toured the state, speaking in Yakima County, where he made a good impression and many friends. A brilliant future was predicted for him. "But that admiration has curdled and many of the same people are sick and tired of the Wisconsin man's continuous but unsupported attacks on Secretary Acheson and the state department. No such charges such as the senator made should be aired in public unless known to be unquestionably supported by facts, and even then, they should be otherwise handled if at all possible."[66]

Perhaps most devastating to McCarthy's crusade was the reaction of Luce. In early April, *Life*'s editorial writers urged Americans to reject McCarthy and preoccupation with former policy errors. The nation was experiencing a totally unexpected postwar economic boom that went on and on despite the gloomy predictions of a few. Americans were living better than ever before, better than they had ever imagined. But the Kremlin remained a fearful adversary. Under the circumstances "the past cannot be undone. We Americans desperately need to pull ourselves together to wage really effective political warfare against Soviet Communism—*now*." If people really wanted to do their part in stopping communism, they could begin by "not . . . join[ing] in the McCarthy lynching bee" but demanding "more vigorous and more foresighted" national policies in both Europe and Asia.[67]

McCarthy fought back desperately. "For ten years," he cried, "the State Department had pampered, rewarded, and mapped strategy with someone whose FBI dossier read 'Joe Stalin's top agent.'"[68] But he seemed cornered. Then, on March 30, Truman inadvertently bailed him out, entering the anticommunist debate again with disastrous results. He would never understand that "McCarthyism" in its broadest context was much more than a partisan assault on bipartisan foreign policy. It was the first and most piercing middle American protest against all the real and apparent soullessness and incompetence of a large, distant, often unresponsive and, above all, liberal government.

Perhaps a frustrating vacation explained the president's foul mood. He had gone to the Florida sunshine for a week or so of complete relaxation after a bleak winter of decisions and tension in Washington. But the trip to Key West had been miserable. Truman had decided to travel on the presidential yacht, but the Atlantic in early spring had been predictably rough, especially off Cape Hatteras. The *Williamsburg* had rolled and pitched heavily, and although it was never in danger of foundering, seasick reporters interviewing the presidential party by radio from a nearby press boat were told that the White House contingent was in some distress. By the time Truman reached the Keys, his anger about those who were "doing all they can to ruin Dean and the foreign policy," was intense. "The paper says this morning that the 'great' Styles Bridges has joined the pack," he wrote his wife on the twenty-sixth. "Well, we'll take 'em to town as we did before." The same day he wrote his cousin Ralph that "I am in the midst of the most terrible struggle any President ever had. A pathological liar from Wisconsin and a block-headed undertaker from Nebraska are trying to ruin the bipartisan foreign policy. Stalin never had two better allies in the country. I must make an effort to stop that procedure."[69]

Four days later, the obviously irate president summoned reporters to a feast of hot dogs, hamburgers, lemonade, and beer followed by an impromptu press conference on the lawn of the "winter White House."[70] He began by telling them that they could ask any questions they wished, and when the conversation turned to McCarthy and foreign policy, as it quickly did, Truman vented his spleen. After 1948, the Republicans had tried everything to discredit the Fair Deal at home and abroad. "Statism" had not worked, nor had "welfare state" or "socialism." Even "that old malodorous dead horse called 'isolationism'" had failed to arouse public anxiety. So now they were trying to sabotage bipartisan foreign policy with a hysterical witch-hunt in the State Department.

The administration had established an employee loyalty program in 1947 that was both effective and fair to all parties, Truman added. Of the 2,200,000 government employees screened, approximately 205 had left federal service. "Now, if anybody really felt that there were disloyal people in the employ of the Government, the proper and the honorable way to handle the situation would be to come to the President of the United States and say, 'This man is a disloyal person. He is in such and such a department.' We will investigate him immediately, and if he were a disloyal person he would be immediately fired." But this was not what the Republicans wanted. They wanted sensationalism. Truman believed there were plenty of legitimate issues to argue about and stated that he would be glad to meet with his GOP opponents and debate any one of them. But the Republicans really wanted to "torpedo the bipartisan foreign policy." When asked which Republicans besides McCarthy, Truman replied: Wherry and Bridges; "that's about as far as I care to go." Acheson would be remembered as a great secretary of state; Jessup was an able, distinguished citizen. Lattimore was a

Johns Hopkins professor and "a very well informed person on foreign affairs." Truman concluded by stating that he had ordered McGrath and Hoover not to turn over government security files to McCarthy and his allies on the Tydings subcommittee.

Truman's outburst was damaging in two ways: First, because of his widely suspected record against communism and communist subversion in recent months, many people believed he was not the person to lash out at McCarthy and Bridges; second, the president's remarks forced Taft and the Republican leadership to either embrace or repudiate McCarthy. If Truman had only berated McCarthy, Taft might not have needed to respond. But linking McCarthy with other Republicans revealed the widening network of Republican support for McCarthyism in the Senate. Not only Bridges and Wherry but Hickenlooper, Kem, Bricker, and Taft himself had repeatedly warned of a communist ring and bad security risks in the State Department.

Moreover, even the strongest Republican defenders of bipartisan foreign policy were beginning to doubt the wisdom of entrusting it to a president who seemed incapable of either understanding or confronting the growing communist menace at home or abroad. From his Michigan sickbed, Arthur Vandenberg painfully typed out a plea for a new nonpartisan national commission to restudy all aspects of American diplomacy, including foreign aid, and to "formulate a new peace policy." Even patrician, mild-mannered Senator Leverett Saltonstall of Massachusetts publicly wondered whether McCarthy might actually have a case against Lattimore. After hearing McCarthy outline his charges, Saltonstall replied: "This is terrible, Joe. I'm really disturbed." Taft thus had no choice: He had to embrace McCarthy after Truman's attack or lose his position as "Mr. Republican." In endorsing McCarthy, Taft legitimatized the man, his charges, and his methods. "The greatest Kremlin asset in our history," Taft said in response to Truman's news conference, "has been the pro-Communist group in the State Department who surrendered to every demand of Russia at Yalta and Potsdam and promoted at every opportunity the Communist cause in China until today Communism threatens to take over all of Asia." How could Stalin and his colleagues possibly profit from efforts to unmask these traitors and remove them from the responsibility of U.S. foreign-policy making? Administration spokesmen promptly retorted that Taft was no one to talk about surrendering to communism; he had voted against every collective security measure proposed since 1947, including the Truman Doctrine, the Marshall Plan, NATO, and the subsequent military assistance program.[71]

But it was too late. Respected businessman and self-styled statesman Bernard Baruch pontificated that the nation was lurching from crisis to crisis and proposed creating a "general staff for peace" to win the cold war. William Bullitt, a long-time critic of New Deal–Fair Deal foreign policy, dolefully warned of continuing communist gains around the world. So did banker Marriner Eccles, a prominent early New Dealer. All three men stressed the same point: America was now losing the cold war.[72]

With no further formal assistance from either the FBI or the Justice Department, McCarthy turned to the only others who could help him attack Lattimore and prove his case: informers Utley and Budenz, whose testimony had helped convict eleven communist leaders in New York the previous October.[73] McCarthy, Utley, and Budenz, along with the senator's staff, isolated themselves in a Washington hotel room for days, living off plates of chicken and Wisconsin cheese sandwiches as they poured over the Utley-Budenz files. Then, on Thursday afternoon, April 7, McCarthy entered the Senate chamber, his briefcase bulging with mysterious papers. Within minutes, the Senate press gallery superintendent yelled at milling reporters, "McCarthy's up!"[74] The newsmen, who knew what was coming, rushed to their seats, while a similar mad scramble took place in the public galleries, where late spectators were allowed to line up shoulder to shoulder against the walls. On the floor below, the small chamber was packed with senators and staff people.

McCarthy began speaking at 2:06 and concluded at 6:18 that evening, pausing only to gulp an occasional glass of cough syrup or milk. He covered the entire range of U.S. postwar policy failures in the Far East and charged that Lattimore not only had greatly influenced America's Asian policy since 1945 but was still influencing it. He quoted selected passages from Lattimore's writings to prove that he was an out-and-out Marxist essential to the Kremlin's cause. He swore that he could produce witnesses who would state under oath that Lattimore was "high up in Communist circles" and had been in Moscow in 1936 doing Stalin's bidding. The press realized almost immediately that the unnamed witnesses were Budenz and Utley. McCarthy then charged that a defecting Soviet general had learned from a colleague that Lattimore was "helping" the Kremlin and that during the war Lattimore had written a friend in the Office of War Information, asking the man to employ only Chinese with communist sympathies. Immediately contacted by reporters, Lattimore called McCarthy a madman and reminded the newsmen that his writings had been condemned by Soviet, Chinese Communist, and Mongolian critics.[75]

But Tydings panicked. In a long, somewhat rambling, but often shrewdly argued memorandum for the president, dated April 12, the Maryland Democrat stated that before McCarthy the country had generally been satisfied with the direction of both domestic and foreign policies. "Now, the present Communist inquiry has to a large extent robbed the Truman administration of some of the united support which our people had given to the foreign program. People who united to fight Communism abroad likewise unite to fight it at home. They feel that many of the advantages which come from spending their money to fight Communism abroad are lost unless equal effort is made to fight Communism at home." The Republicans were using McCarthy "first, to divide and weaken support for the Truman program at home, and, second, incidentally weaken the solidarity of our people for the Truman program abroad." To head off the increasingly successful Republican assault, the president should, in effect, throw Lattimore to the wolves. Truman should tell the people that he was in this one instance "breaking a long precedent because of the unusual nature of the times" and giving Lattimore's file to the subcommittee once that file was fully purged of the names of all informants. "Follow that up by saying you are making available to the Committee in secret" several other files that McCarthy was eager to get his hands on. "Stick to your position that you will *not* make the FBI files public, using the statement of Mr. J. Edgar Hoover that he is opposed to this procedure."[76] The White House sensibly ignored the memo, perhaps realizing that if it followed the Tydings scenario precisely, Hoover would have practically obtained official approval to make FBI files consistently available to McCarthy on a sub rosa basis, thereby joining and shaping this latest and most spectacularly effective anticommunist witch hunt.

Lattimore appeared before the Tydings subcommittee that week. Before he arrived, Tydings hinted coyly to reporters that a big story was coming. But it was not until Lattimore finished testifying and the Republicans started questioning him that the chairman dropped his bombshell. The administration had decided on a limited change of policy regarding State Department files. In strict confidence, McGrath and Hoover had shown Tydings a twelve-page analysis of the government's security file on Lattimore, which completely cleared the man of any communist sympathy or affiliation. McCarthy had left the room, but when queried by reporters he simply said: "If Tydings said that, then he is not telling the truth. Period." Tydings replied that he would let his reputation for probity and accuracy speak for itself. The next day Hickenlooper asked to see the file and said he was still dissatisfied. "I completely disagree with Senator Tydings's statement," he told reporters.[77]

Slowly, inexorably, the flood of charges never proved but never retracted began to change public opinion. "Was Lattimore a Communist?" the Luce journals asked. Budenz was, after all, a respectable informer. He had been editor of the *Daily Worker* before "bolting" the party in 1945. He certainly must have had access to names, files, and gossip. He was currently a professor of economics at Fordham, one of the most prestigious Catholic universities in the country. On April 20, after Lattimore's testimony before the Tydings subcommittee, Budenz took the stand and substantiated all that McCarthy had said. He claimed he had seen documents initialed "L" and "XL" in CPUSA "Politburo" meetings and that these letters referred to Lattimore. Budenz added that former CPUSA boss Earl Browder had appointed Lattimore director of all communist writers in 1937. The *Daily Worker* and other domestic and foreign communist publications had condemned Lattimore's writings to preserve his cover. Actually such critical reviews, if read correctly, could be seen as "praises with faint damns."[78]

What was the truth and who was telling it? No one could say. But after Hiss and Fuchs, it was clearly unwise to ignore the issue. Neither smear nor whitewash would work, the *New York Times* stated, only an earnest, ongoing search for the truth.[79] Tydings called Browder and other known or suspected communists to testify about Lattimore, but they were frustrating witnesses. All denied that Lattimore was a communist, but one, Frederick V. Field, disdainfully insisted that he had not been a communist, although Budenz had said he was. Browder refused to name anyone who had been to communist meetings during his tenure as head of the party. Although Field and Browder were cited for contempt, the question of Lattimore's loyalty or affiliations remained unanswered.

On May 15, Luce capitulated carefully but unmistakably to McCarthyism. He was clearly offended by both McCarthy and his methods, but he saw a link between McCarthyism and what he identified as "The Conservative Revival." Conservatives had finally found a value and an issue around which to rally. Clinton Rossiter's recent despair over the lack of a conservative identity could now be dispelled.[80]

What was the meaning of recent tumultuous events? Luce's editorial writers asked. Their answer was simple: "This country is going conservative—with a little *c*, take notice—and without particular regard to political labels." Roosevelt's New Deal had been simply "a phase of ferment" in American history: "creative ferment, yes, but also destructive of much that Americans are now trying to regain." Luce's men speculated that "in order to save and find itself" America had needed to live through the New Deal experiment just as it had earlier needed to experience the self-destructive boom of the 1920s. Both epochs had been characterized by a sky-is-the-limit mentality. Now Americans were finally coming back to earth.

Conservatism with a little *c*, Luce's men wrote, denoted "a conscious desire to 'do right'" and a decent respect for money as the product of work, for honest bookkeeping and a desire to carefully preserve all the best of America including the strength of the nation, the family, and the individual. The "biggest news story of the day" was the "fundamental" bond between "reviving conservatism" and anticommunism. Communism was "*wrong*" and thus was "hostile to all that is good, solid and enduring in the American spirit. Therefore it must be kept out and, to the extent that it has penetrated life and government, it must be hunted out. So, we believe, runs the mainstream of American thought and purpose." In a backhanded slap at McCarthy, Luce's writers admitted that some manifestations of anticommunism were "stupid, and worse." But the "rightness of [the] anti-Communist purpose ought not to be in question."

The polls seemed to confirm Luce's assessment. According to a Gallup survey conducted on May 21, 84 percent of those questioned had heard the charge that McCarthy was doing the country more harm than good. Only 29 percent of those polled agreed with the statement; 39 percent thought McCarthy was helping the nation by making public the issue of communists in government; only 16 percent had no opinion. *Newsweek* interpreted the Gallup figures differently, stating that 46.4 percent of those asked thought McCarthy was doing "a good thing for the country"; only 34.5 percent thought he was not, and 19.1 percent had no opinion.[81] Taft now stated publicly his belief that "the pro-Communist policies of the State Department fully justified Joe McCarthy in his demand for an investigation."[82]

The problem for McCarthy's opponents was that the man simply would not shut up and would not quit. Truman made one more effort to stop him. In a whistle-stop tour of the West in mid-May the president told audiences in Wyoming and Montana "that the way to avoid the danger of domestic communism was to keep from power 'little men with acorn minds'" who "saw only little acorns and not the giant oaks that grew therefrom. White House aides interpreted the trip—and, implicitly, the message—as a resounding success."[83]

Throughout May and early June, McCarthy and Hickenlooper kept the Tydings subcommittee in an uproar by using five interrelated tactics. First, when an individual accused of communist affiliations refused to answer or vehemently denied the charge, McCarthy simply put Budenz or Utley (or both) on the stand to rebut. The second strategy was to deny evidence or interpret it to suit McCarthy's needs. Soon after returning from the West, Truman finally pinned down the senator on the eighty-one names of alleged communists in the State Department. He then made the department's security files available to the Tydings subcommittee but with definite restrictions. Tydings, Henry Cabot Lodge, McMahon, McCarthy, Hickenlooper, and the others would be allowed to examine the files in the White House cabinet room one day. They could take notes if they wished but would have to leave the notes behind. McCarthy first claimed that the administration's offer was worthless because the State Department had "stripped" and "raped" the files before releasing them to the White House, a charge that Peurifoy promptly and vehemently denied.[84] Then, after the committee had examined the files, Hickenlooper brazenly insisted that Tydings's public assertion that they contained absolutely no evidence of disloyalty was simply wrong. Hickenlooper did not provide details, but he did not have to because the White House had already blundered by not allowing unrestricted access to and discussion about the files.

The third tactic was to condemn critics as communists. McCarthy was particularly adept at controlling the press by this means. Whenever a Wisconsin paper or a reporter criticized his behavior, the senator sent a staff member to the offender's hometown to dig up dirt and to label the critic a Commie, a dupe, a degenerate, or worse.[85]

The fourth strategy was to shift the emphasis of an existing issue. By mid-May, it was clear that the Lattimore-Budenz fight had been fought to a draw, which, of course, was exactly what McCarthy, Hickenlooper, and their friends desired. Lattimore had been smeared, not cleared. His testimony revealed that, during the late thirties and the war years, he had been associated with the Institute of Pacific Relations and its journal *Amerasia*. In 1945, an official of the Office of Strategic Services (OSS), the wartime predecessor of the CIA, claimed that an article in *Amerasia* contained exact quotations from a memorandum he had recently written. The OSS began watching the office of *Amerasia* and its editor, Philip Jaffe. Finally breaking into the office late at night, an OSS team found literally hundreds of classified government documents (the final, authoritative number was 1,700). Where had Jaffe gotten them and how?

Jaffe was arrested, and soon his network of informants was uncovered. One of them was John Service. When told about the evidence, Truman demanded a full inquiry, but somehow it never took place. Service did not come to trial, Jaffe and a few others received minor fines, and the incident subsided, although it was never forgotten by professional Red-hunters.

Clearly something more could be learned from the *Amerasia* case; McCarthy and his friends had finally found a potentially substantive issue. In mid-June, the New York City grand jury that had previously indicted several communist couriers began calling witnesses. Once again McCarthy and his friends were riding high, and once again the blundering Democrats helped them by seeming less than candid or intelligent. Assistant Attorney General James M. McInerney labeled the stolen government documents found in Jaffe's possession "silly stuff" and "teacup gossip," and Tydings persistently stalled in implementing his promised "full and complete" inquiry into the *Amerasia* incident. Hickenlooper then took charge, revealing that the "teacup gossip" documents in *Amerasia*'s possession in 1945 included a top secret message from Roosevelt to Chiang, the navy's wartime organization plan for establishing counterintelligence operations in the United States, a document giving the exact location of twenty-five U.S. submarines blockading a named strait in the last months of the Pacific war, and a detailed analysis of the composition of Allied troop formations in Malaya. When the Justice Department claimed that Hickenlooper had manufactured these particular documents, the Iowa senator produced one, prompting a curt "no comment" from the administration.[86]

The final method McCarthyites employed was to raise an entirely new issue. "The homosexual angle had been a completely unexpected by-product of the McCarthy hullabaloo," *Newsweek* reported in late May. In February, Peurifoy, testifying before the Senate Appropriations Committee, had blurted out that the State Department had recently "separated" ninety-one homosexuals from its staff. Wherry immediately capitalized on Peurifoy's admission. If the department had purged ninety-one homosexuals (Acheson alleged that such men were, by both definition and their own admission, security risks), how many more were on the federal payroll in sensitive positions? Unable to obtain what he considered a satisfactory answer, Wherry suddenly appeared at District of Columbia police head-quarters in early April and talked with "tough old" Lt. Roy E. Blick, head of the Washington vice squad for eighteen years. Wherry asked Blick for any information he had on sexual deviants in the government. Blick soon appeared on the Hill before a District of Columbia appropriations subcom-mittee, where he closed his testimony "with a real shocker." There were at least five thousand homosexuals in Washington, he stated, and 3,750 worked for the federal government. Between three and four hundred of them were in the State Department. The subcommittee immediately ordered that Blick's testimony be locked up and that his files be impounded so they could not be stolen. Then Wherry and Democratic Senator Lister Hill of Alabama were named as a sub-subcommittee to investigate the charges fur-ther. Hill promptly immersed himself in a reelection campaign, giving Wherry, who had four years left in his current term, the sole responsibility.[87]

Wherry "plunged into the job" but quickly discovered a "wall of executive [branch] resistance." Nonetheless, after constant prying and prodding, he learned that thirteen of the original ninety-one homosexuals fired by the State Department had found jobs elsewhere in the federal government. Peurifoy blocked, then denied outright, Wherry's request to check State Department personnel records against Blick's files. On May 27, Wherry and Hill submit-ted separate reports to the District of Columbia appropriations subcommit-tee, which immediately accepted Wherry's demand for a sweeping inquiry "into another sort of infiltration" of federal agencies. The subcommittee would conduct a "full-scale investigation of sexual perverts in government."[88]

The fundamentalist conservative faction in the U.S. Senate thus promised to keep the federal government in an uproar at least through the summer and probably much longer. McCarthy was usually the leader and certainly the symbolic head of this group. As Bricker told him: "Joe, you're a dirty son of a bitch, but there are times when you've got to have a son of a bitch around, and this is one of them."[89] McCarthy reacted with delight. But the senator also knew, as Bricker's remark suggested, that he was no longer (if he had ever been) a lone pariah.

A myth has grown that McCarthy's opponents were cowed from the beginning.[90] This is not true. As the senator became more vociferous, more outrageous in his charges and claims, Tydings and his fellow Democrats became infuriated and determined to do something about it. They held several supposedly secret strategy meetings at Tydings's home (which quickly became known to both the press and McCarthy and his friends) to develop plans for discrediting McCarthy and Budenz in both houses of Congress.

Late on the afternoon of May 8, Representative Frank M. Karsten, Democrat of Missouri, began the assault against McCarthy. Through deceit and fraud, Karsten maintained, McCarthy was trying to hoodwink the American people. State Department security files had been thoroughly combed, and no one had found any evidence linking diplomats to communism. Representative John J. Rooney, Democrat of New York, vigorously supported Karsten but inadvertently weakened the case by casually observing that the FBI was now investigating four of the eighty-one alleged security risks already cleared. Two days later, Senate Democrats resumed the attack after the press commented favorably on the Karsten and Rooney charges. Scott Lucas began arguing that McCarthy had never revealed precisely how many communists he had supposedly "found" in the State Department and that the man was. . . Before he could finish the sentence, Wherry leaped to his feet and demanded that the president pro tem seat Lucas for violating a Senate rule that prohibited calling another senator a liar. Vice President Alben Barkley directed the Illinois senator to sit down, but after a vote Lucas was allowed to continue and make his point indirectly.

Two other Democratic senators, Harley Kilgore and Matthew Neely of West Virginia, called McCarthy a Cain who was leading his country to destruction. Then Dennis Chavez of New Mexico said that as a Roman Catholic he was appalled by Budenz, who had rushed out of the Communist Party to embrace the church and was using his current religious affiliation as "a shield and a cloak" to protect his "un-American, un-Christian dubious testimony." Budenz's behavior, Chavez charged, showed that he was an enemy of the government he professed to defend. Budenz's current employer, the Very Reverend Laurence J. McGinley, president of Fordham, sniffed that such personal vilification was even lower than that indulged by the *Daily Worker*.[91]

The White House firmly supported McCarthy's critics. An unsigned memo to presidential aide Seth Dawson on the day Karsten and Rooney began the congressional assault indicated that the senator's congressional critics had raised serious issues about McCarthy's truthfulness and honesty. The White House should help sustain this attack "to the fullest extent in order that the Senate and the people of the United States be made to understand not only that McCarthy has lied but also that he perpetrated a collosal hoax." Senatorial critics should emphasize McCarthy's consistently disruptive tactics, his use of fraudulent data, his revelation of executive session testimony "openly on the Senate floor," and his blatantly false depiction of testimony before it had been given.[92]

Two weeks later, Acheson was asked about a recent McCarthy speech in which the senator had "said that in the process of concealing communism in the Department you [Acheson] are engaged in a vicious and desperate fraud." The department "has been making a practice of analyzing the inaccuracies of each of Senator McCarthy's statements and speeches," Acheson replied calmly, "and we expect to follow that same process and give you an analysis of the inaccuracies that were included in his speech last night." The department's anticommunist record and policies spoke for themselves, Acheson said, adding that it would be "extremely difficult to hide a conspiracy, to conceal communism in the State Department from a group of correspondents such as you when 28 of you have seen every important official" to discuss their work and when there had been no less than "280 individual, half-hour background press conferences" in the four months since McCarthy had first leveled his charges.[93]

But by this time, McCarthy and his allies knew they could not be stopped except by their own folly. With *Amerasia*, they had potential evidence that might yet discredit Lattimore and the entire State Department. As *Newsweek* said, somebody somewhere was hiding something about communist subversion.[94]

As the anticommunist excitement mounted, Americans began spooking themselves. In the early evening of May 19, a dozen train car loads of ammunition and dynamite being loaded on barges in South Amboy, New Jersey, suddenly exploded. Approximately thirty people were killed. The town's residents promptly concluded that they were under Soviet nuclear attack. One man, after picking himself out of the rubble of his home, heard his wife screaming that the Russians were in town.[95]

A week or so before, a widely reported social experiment had taken place in the little town of Mosinee, Wisconsin.[96] The approximately two thousand inhabitants of that hamlet held "a firm belief in Americanism." So Mosinee, hoping to warn the country of the dangers of the Red menace and to get some national publicity, "put itself behind an iron curtain for a day."

A group of American Legionnaires, carrying empty rifles and pistols, took over the town early one morning, seizing the library, mills, and schools on behalf of "the United Soviet States of America." The Legionnaires acted openly because a "Red invasion would more likely appear in native trappings." To help establish communist-style order, the town called in two experts: Benjamin Gitlow, formerly a high official in the CPUSA, and Joseph Z. Kornfeder, once a party organizer.

The local weekly newspaper, the *Times,* was published that day as *Red Star* and was printed on pink paper. The local movie house, renamed the People's Theatre, showed Soviet propaganda films, which were periodically interrupted with portraits of Stalin flashed on the screen while the audience was ordered to cheer. Security police herded the town's civic and religious leaders into a makeshift concentration camp, where they were soon joined by managers and some of the staff of the local mill. The police chief was "tortured," and a small child on his father's shoulder was photographed making a gesture of the "Red salute" during a "Red" parade. *Life* reported that citizens of Mosinee submitted good-naturedly to being pushed around all day by "Red" police. Those who complained that it was all a dumb stunt were not bothered. "Zack" Kornfeder, head of the Council of Peoples Commissars, was photographed with a sinister sneer on his face, the lower half of which was highlighted. Late that evening the barbed wires were torn down, the Red banners were torn up, Zack and the other "communists" reverted to being good Americans, and the town gladly abandoned its one-day experiment.

If Americans did not consider McCarthy quite respectable, if he was, truth to be told, somewhat frightening, they still supported his crusade. By the summer of 1950, McCarthy, with vigorous help from his friends, had become a political institution. Anyone who has any recollection of Main Street America during this time remembers the many men and women who said with some embarrassment that, of course, McCarthy was going too far, but still. . .

Then in June, after reactions to revelations over the Gold-Greenglass-Rosenberg spy ring had died down, excitement and hysteria abruptly subsided. McCarthy went off by himself for a while to write some new speeches. Washington withstood Stalin's latest threat to seize West Berlin, proving, as *Newsweek* observed, "that Russian aggression, which fattens on appeasement, crumples before a show of strength." Acheson returned home from a meeting of the NATO foreign ministers and reported that economically as well as militarily Western Europe was finally beginning to emerge from the rubble of war. French economist Jean Monnet had just proposed integrating the French and German coal and steel industries, which could hasten the economic and moral resurrection of the Continent. Some of the nation's "top" military "strategists" were beginning to say that with a little time and luck it might indeed be possible to defend Western Europe against a Soviet dash to the Channel. Twenty divisions—ten armored, ten infantry—and twenty good tactical fighter-bomber air groups might be enough to "hold back the Russians."[97]

In its last issue of the month, *Newsweek* reported that the sun was shining on "Harry" once more. The grand jury up in New York, instead of "lambasting" the administration over *Amerasia* and encouraging more McCarthyite attacks, had tentatively supported the government's earlier handling of the affair. Legislation to extend government rent controls further had unexpectedly passed in Congress after some effective last-minute prodding from the White House. Prospects seemed bright for passage of a new social security bill that would substantially increase benefits. The president had just signed a law, passed despite vociferous objections by Pat McCarran and other congressional xenophobes, that would greatly expand the admission of Jewish and Catholic refugees from communist Europe. Finally, Truman had declared in a press conference that the international scene was less threatening than at any time since 1945.[98]

It seemed that the political scene was calming down, that the administration might overcome the McCarthy challenge, the Fuchs affair, and the related Rosenberg spy ring scandal as it had so many other foreign and domestic crises and distractions during the brief postwar era. On June 11, Truman wrote his wife that he had just been plowing through the Sunday New York, Baltimore, and Washington newspapers. "For a wonder, there's not a mean remark in them—even the Sops [Joseph and Stewart Alsop], [Drew] Pearson, and old Mark Sullivan are friendly." Both St. Louis papers, the *Post-Dispatch* and *Globe-Democrat*, "had friendly editorials. I am sure I'm slipping."[99]

The last weekend of the month brought the first steamy burst of summer to the nation's capital, and official Washington scurried out of town to find peace, quiet, and cooler weather. Truman went to Baltimore on Saturday morning to dedicate the new Friendship International Airport (now Baltimore-Washington International Airport) and then flew home to Independence for several days with his wife and daughter. He hoped to go down to the family farm at Grandview on Sunday to talk to his brother, Vivian, about personal and business matters. Acheson drove to his Maryland farm to do some gardening and reading. Much of the country went to the ballparks or listened to major league games. Many wondered what the lowly Philadelphia Phillies were doing so close to first place.

Then the roof fell in.

6

The Guns of Summer

❖ ❖ ❖ ❖ ❖ ❖ ❖ ❖ ❖ ❖ ❖ ❖ ❖ ❖ ❖

It was raining in Korea as gray dawn broke over the thirty-eighth parallel on Sunday, June 25, 1950. Twenty-five miles south, Seoul lay wrapped in sleep. Many junior and senior officers of the Republic of Korea Army (ROKA) were in the city along with most of America's small Korean Military Advisory Group (KMAG). Everyone knew that North Korean armed forces had been slowly massing at the parallel over the past several months: "Yaks [propeller-driven, Russian-made fighter planes], and a few Ilyushins [Russian-made bomber aircraft], a few tanks. Also the return of two elements of North Koreans that had been with the Chinese Communists." But no one expected anything more than the usual border incidents and probes that had been occurring "from the end of '47 until the spring of 1950."[1] Shortly before daylight, however, North Korean artillery and mortars suddenly shattered the stillness; shells came crashing down on thinly held South Korean defense lines. The cannonade moved progressively eastward from the Ongjin Peninsula on the Yellow Sea 150 miles to the Sea of Japan; obviously something more than another border incident was happening.

Suddenly about ninety thousand men of the North Korean People's Army (NKPA) attacked across the entire parallel. For several hours, undermanned ROKA units stoutly resisted. Near midmorning, Gen. Chai Ung Jun unleashed his armor—150 T-34 heavy tanks supplied by the Soviet Union—against the ROKA lines and his Yak fighter planes against Kimpo Airport just outside Seoul. The NKPA tank battalions began overrunning ROKA positions despite often suicidal resistance. Soon the T-34s, followed by hundreds of truckloads of NKPA infantry, began pushing down the narrow

Uijongbu corridor, the historic invasion route that led to Seoul. Confused, overwhelmed, and now demoralized, the ROKA forces fell back in headlong retreat.

Ambassador John Muccio immediately cabled the State Department about the alarming events at (and soon south of) the parallel. It was still Saturday evening, June 24, in the United States. Acheson, who had just finished a good day in the garden and a splendid dinner, was in bed reading himself to sleep when the secure phone from the department began ringing. As soon as he was done speaking with the duty officer, Acheson called Truman in Independence. It was just after nine o'clock in western Missouri when the president picked up the secure phone in his library, where he, his wife, and daughter had settled down for some small talk. He heard the secretary of state say: "Mr. President, I have very serious news. The North Koreans have invaded South Korea." Truman responded that he would return to Washington at once, but Acheson urged him to wait until the next morning when the dimensions of the crisis had become clearer. Truman agreed.[2]

In the next several hours, official Washington began to awake to the crisis. John Hickerson, the assistant secretary of state for United Nations affairs, and his wife were at home, "a nice little house with a lovely garden in [the] Cleveland Park" section of the city when the phone rang about ten o'clock. "In those days, night calls weren't unusual," Hickerson remembered many years later. "Some problems one could deal with over the telephone, others you couldn't. I had by that time fallen into a habit that was somewhat descriptive of the hectic life we led. If the telephone rang after 9 o'clock, as I started to the telephone, I involuntarily picked up my car keys, just in case."

The call was from the watch officer in the department's Bureau of Far Eastern Affairs. There had been a "development," and Hickerson should come in right away. Driving through night-blackened Rock Creek Park, the diplomat concluded that the Chinese Communists had invaded Formosa. At the department, he quickly learned otherwise. A "massive" and "unexpected" invasion of South Korea was under way, and the ROKA, "pretty demoralized," was falling back in confusion. Assistant Secretary of State for Far Eastern Affairs Dean Rusk soon appeared, and the two men gathered their small staffs to begin work on the problem. Across the Potomac, Army Secretary Frank Pace, Jr., reached his office in the Pentagon and began his own assessment of the situation.[3]

By Sunday morning, it was obvious that a full-scale communist assault on South Korea was under way. Acheson, tie askew and jacket off, rushed

back to the State Department in his automobile. U. Alexis Johnson, director
of the Office of Northeast Asian Affairs, which oversaw Korean affairs at
State, was tracked down supervising a boy scout outing in the Blue Ridge
Mountains. A ranger took him to a forest camp phone, where he was told
by his wife that he had to return immediately. The connection was so bad
that Johnson did not really learn why his weekend (and that of his two boys
and their fellow scouts) had been so abruptly curtailed until he reached
home. As astounded by the news as everyone, Johnson immediately raced
to the department, where he remained for the next four days. Truman was
whisked to his airplane at Kansas City Municipal Airport and was soon airborne. Looking down as the farmlands of Illinois, Indiana, and Ohio rolled
by ten thousand feet beneath him, the president brooded. Here was the
Japanese invasion of Manchuria and Hitler's march into the Rhineland all
over again. Stalin was presenting the West with the ultimate challenge.[4] In
fact, the Korean conflict was the result of tragic miscalculation and grossly
misunderstood objectives on both sides of the Iron Curtain.

The origins of the Korean War can be traced to a series of decisions, statements, and meetings that took place in Washington and Moscow during the
last days of 1949 and the first weeks of 1950. At the end of December, Truman approved National Security Council (NSC) document 48/2, which was
designed to reorient Asian policy in light of the communization of China.[5]
The NSC paper committed the United States to promoting stable, friendly,
and self-sustaining noncommunist governments in the Far East while
diminishing or eliminating the "preponderant power and influence of the
USSR in Asia to such a degree that the Soviet Union will not be capable of
threatening from that area the security of the United States or its friends."
In other words, America would not exploit Asia; it would only defend the
area so that the Soviets would not use it as a springboard to attack the
United States or its non-Asian friends. To achieve these objectives, Washington would "support non-Communist forces in taking the initiative in
Asia; . . . exert an influence to advance its own national interests," and "initiate action in such a manner as will appeal to the Asiatic nations as being
compatible with their national interests and worthy of their support."

Such phrases were only glittering generalities devoid of any meaning
beyond a vague determination to prevent further encroachments by either

Stalin or Mao. Moreover, Washington would not extend its support to just any noncommunist nation. "Any association formed must be the result of a genuine desire on the part of the participating nations to cooperate for mutual benefit." The United States could or would offer little more than "vigorous prosecution of the [1949] Point IV" technical aid program (which had so far had limited application and benefit), maintenance of a liberal U.S. trade policy, "stimulation of imports from Asia," and "encouragement of private United States investment in non-Communist countries." The NSC document offered no proposals or suggestions of ways Washington might encourage American private enterprise to increase its investments and presence in a part of the world that was still primitive by U.S. standards. The government's chief objective would be to "exploit, through appropriate political, psychological and economic means, any rifts between the Chinese Communists and the USSR." But again the paper did not provide any specifics. Finally, "the United States should continue the policies of avoiding military and political support of any non-Communist elements in China [i.e., Chiang Kai-shek and his Nationalist Chinese rump government on Formosa] . . . unless such support would . . . contribute to the over-all national interests of the United States."

Thus, NSC 48/2 unmistakably indicated that, as of midcentury, Washington's cold war priorities remained firmly fixed on the Atlantic, not the Pacific rim, and that was where U.S. dollars, defense, and interests were concentrated. In his four years in office, Acheson traveled to the Continent eleven times and to Latin America twice. He never once set foot in Asia—undoubtedly because MacArthur, the U.S. overlord in Japan, discouraged him from doing so. Others in the administration were also focused on Europe. Two weeks after Truman signed NSC 48/2, George Kennan, author of the postwar "containment" policy, which allegedly committed the United States to confronting communism at every point around the globe, opened a routine meeting of the State Department's Policy Planning Staff by observing that "the military problem in Europe . . . is at the core of many problems, including not only the arms program but our whole approach to the cold war." A CIA paper of September 1949, cleared by the intelligence offices of the State Department and the army, concluded that "it would, therefore, remain the primary and most immediate concern of the United States to ensure the continued security of the European-Mediterranean area." The Joint Outline Emergency War Plan, ratified by the Pentagon while Truman was approving NSC 48/2, assumed that Western Europe would be the principal theater of action in a future world war with Russia. The Red Army would erupt westward across the north German plain, and the United States and its handful of militarily weak allies would attempt to hold a bridgehead somewhere on the Continent or, failing that, would try to return as soon as possible. "In the Far East, the United States would defend the Philippines, Japan, and Okinawa, and would attempt to deny the enemy the use of Taiwan." South Korea was ignored; it was considered either impossible to defend or not worth the effort in the broader context of World War III.[6]

Whether the United States could even wage war had become a pressing question by the end of 1949. Captain Harry Truman had returned from World War I harboring a profound contempt for generals and admirals, which he never lost. Professional military men of all services were "wrong a good deal of the time. . . . They're most of them just like horses with blinders on. They can't see beyond the ends of their noses." To the man from Missouri, MacArthur embodied all that was wrong with the nation's military leadership. The great war hero, supreme commander of the allied occupation powers in Japan and commander in chief of all U.S. military and naval forces in the Far East, seemed nothing but an egotistical poseur, "Mr. Prima Donna," a "play actor," and a "bunco man" who had stubbornly refused to come home to receive the thanks of a grateful nation and instructions from his civilian commander in chief. During his retirement, Truman's recollections of MacArthur became vitriolic. He claimed that some of the general's closest associates thought the man was no better than "a common coward." He told interviewer Merle Miller that George Marshall, whom Truman revered as army chief of staff, then as secretary of state and later of defense, had derided MacArthur as a "four-flusher" who "never was any damn good." Truman showed no more respect for high-ranking air force officers, whom he dismissed as "glamour boys" who liked to make wild claims.[7]

After 1945, Truman gladly presided over the virtual demobilization of one of the most powerful military and naval forces of the twentieth century. On V-J Day, America had 12 million men and women in uniform. By December 1948, at the end of Truman's first term as commander in chief, the standing forces had shrunk to a mere 1.5 million men and women. The military establishment "had slight combat effectiveness and was everywhere in desperate need" of new equipment and weapons, effective leadership, and adequate logistics. The 3,000-ship, two-ocean navy of World War II had been reduced to 289 combat vessels including just 11 heavy and light fleet aircraft carriers. The six-million-man, one-hundred-division army that had helped crush Hitler's Wehrmacht now contained only ten divisions, a total of 530,000 indifferently trained and equipped soldiers. By mid-1950, the army supposedly had 100,000 more men, but its actual strength remained below 600,000. Truman had reluctantly reinstated a modest selective service program in 1948, and half of the army was composed of draftees, marginal boys who had no compelling reasons or significant skills that would exempt them from military service. These young men found the lush occupation life in Europe and Japan delightful, and they were difficult to train as serious soldiers. Omar Bradley complained that this force was "in a shockingly deplorable state," possessing "almost no combat effectiveness." It "could not fight its way out of a paper bag."[8] The U.S. Air Force was just a shadow of the robust service that had appeared over Europe and Japan a few years before; its 218 groups had been reduced to 38.

At the beginning of his second term in January 1949, Truman appointed as secretary of the new Department of Defense fifty-eight-year-old Louis Johnson, a large, coarse individual whose soaring ambitions were exceeded only by a striking lack of tact and common sense. Johnson had become a political embarrassment to FDR but had made major financial contributions to Truman's 1948 campaign, and the president felt obliged to reward him appropriately. The new secretary soon made it clear that he wanted Truman's job, and the best way to get it was to fight and bicker with every other cabinet officer while pandering to congressional budget cutters and conservatives, who were demanding both further reductions in the armed forces and a resumption of military assistance to Chiang. "By June 25, 1950," historian Clay Blair has concluded bitterly, "Harry Truman and Louis Johnson had all but wrecked the conventional military forces of the United States." Johnson was cordially hated by all of his colleagues in the administration, but especially by Acheson, who realized that the defense secretary was providing not so secret encouragement to Taft, Wherry, and the others in their incessant assaults on the administration's China policy.[9]

Truman and his colleagues in the diplomatic and defense establishments had allowed the American armed forces to descend to such a deplorable state because they honestly believed there would be no world war in the foreseeable future and they had no experience with or conception of what would soon be known as "brushfire wars." The services had just concluded a vicious and debilitating squabble among themselves over missions and responsibilities in the cold war era, and no one at State, the Pentagon, or the

White House seemed able to conceive of combat on any level less than full-scale war with the Soviets.[10]

America's military weakness at midcentury and its drastically limited ability to mount global economic programs and offensives beyond Western Europe have been obscured for years by the obsession of much of the academic community with NSC 68 as an ostensible master plan for U.S. global domination. Word of the existence of this top secret National Security Council report, which was commissioned by President Truman at the end of January 1950 and completed in mid-April, began leaking out of Washington in the late sixties. For nearly a decade thereafter, tantalizing bits and pieces of the still highly classified document appeared along with more or less accurate summaries of its contents and often extravagant claims about its importance. In 1976, the full report was finally published.[11] It proved to be much less dramatic than the academic sensationalists had asserted.

Truman specifically asked for the study "in the light of the probable fission bomb capability and possible thermonuclear bomb capability of the Soviet Union."[12] If the president was expecting fresh ideas on the cold war as a result of sudden Soviet nuclear and thermonuclear capabilities, he would be disappointed. Bureaucratic inertia, combined with persistently underfunded military and foreign aid programs, ensured that NSC 68 would essentially be little more than a restatement of NSC 20/4, which the president had approved at the end of November 1948.

NSC 20/4, whose conclusions formed the basis of NSC 68, stated that the Soviet Union constituted the greatest immediate threat to the security of the United States because of the "hostile designs and formidable power of the U.S.S.R." The Kremlin was determined to weaken America's new and legitimate place in the world and might employ open warfare to gain its objective. The United States therefore should remain militarily strong (which in terms of conventional forces it was not) while avoiding the economic instability that had crippled the nation during the recent depression decade.[13]

Although NSC 68 was suitably hortatory in tone, it quickly became clear to the drafters, if they had not known it before, that the American military cupboard was virtually bare of all but nuclear weapons and that the economic cupboard contained only enough goods and services to undertake the formidable task of reconstructing Western Europe. Except for the Point IV technical assistance program, which had an uneven impact on various host countries, the United States and its allies were powerless south and east of the Elbe. NSC 68 therefore decreed that key U.S. objectives beyond Western Europe somehow could be achieved through moral strength. "It is only by practical affirmation, abroad as well as at home, of our essential values, that we can preserve our own integrity, in which lies the real frustration of the Kremlin design." American example, as much or more than dollars or soldiers, would "be such as to foster a fundamental change in the nature of the Soviet system."[14]

The report openly questioned the ability of the United States and its Western allies to match Soviet military power and production. The U.S. military budget in early 1950 was 6 to 7 percent of the gross national product; the NATO allies were devoting less than 5 percent of their national product to military purposes. The Soviet figure was 13.8 percent. The United States and its allies were both much wealthier and had larger production bases than the Kremlin, but "the Soviet Union is using 14 percent of its ingot steel, 47 percent of its primary aluminum, and 18.5 percent of its crude oil for military purposes, while the corresponding percentages for the United States are 1.7, 8.6, and 5.6." Stalin was "actually using, for military purposes, nearly twice as much steel as the United States and 8 to 26 percent more aluminum."[15]

The only way the Americans could successfully challenge the Soviet Union was through a major rearmament program that would jeopardize cherished benefits, "which they have come to associate with their freedoms." Moreover, "at any point in the process of demonstrating our will to make good our fundamental purpose, the Kremlin may decide to precipitate a general war, or in testing us, may go too far." Such risks, however, were less than "those we seek to avoid."[16]

The report closed with the usual series of conclusions and recommendations. Probable Soviet possession of nuclear weapons and possible possession of thermonuclear bombs "have greatly intensified the Soviet threat to the security of the United States."

This threat is of the same character as that described in NSC 20/4 (approved by the President on November 24, 1948) but is more immediate than had previously been estimated. In particular, the United States now faces the contingency that within the next four or five years the Soviet Union will possess the military capability of delivering a surprise atomic attack of such weight that the United States must have substantially increased general air, ground, and sea strength, atomic capabililties, and air and civilian defenses to deter war.[17]

In other words, any increases in U.S. military spending had to be devoted to bolstering national security, including civil defense and research and development. Soviet possession of atomic and hydrogen bombs thus stimulated a defensive, not an offensive reaction in American government circles.

Washington's pursuit of an effective containment policy was weakened not only by severely restricted economic and especially military power but also by public debates and divisions inherent in the western democratic tradition. Within weeks after Mao formally proclaimed the People's Republic of China, Britain and most of America's European allies had either recognized the regime or were publicly committed to doing so. The Europeans argued that however distasteful the Chinese Communists might be, it would be foolish to ignore their existence or their legitimately won status. In early June 1950, an English observer, K. Zilliacus, concluded that "the policy of the western powers towards the Communist-governed two-fifths of the world appears to be getting at cross purposes with itself." He stated that an unnamed "American cold warrior" was complaining that "if the west went on arming full tilt [which it was not doing] we should produce bankruptcy, starvation and revolution at home, whereas if we stopped rearming we should be at the mercy of the Soviet Union." Only Winston Churchill, Zilliacus argued, had the right idea: Conduct immediate negotiations with Stalin before the four- or five-year "breathing space," caused by each side's dread of nuclear war with the other, disappeared, giving Russia the advantage. "The view that the west is falling behind in the arms race appears to be spreading." Western European, British, and American citizens were being told they might have to impoverish themselves to maintain a collective deterrence against the aggressive Kremlin. But in France, and perhaps elsewhere, a counterargument was appearing: Europe should think about "'neutrality'" or "'independence'" from the cold war.[18]

Acheson tried to clarify American cold war policy in a speech to the National Press Club in Washington on January 12, 1950. Nearly fifty years later, the speech remains one of the most controversial expressions of American foreign policy ever made. Drawing on the provisions of NSC 48/2, Acheson stated flatly that Washington had no desire to intervene in the Chinese civil war. He publicly warned Mao (who was in Moscow for lengthy negotiations) that the Kremlin was not a trusted ally and that Washington was ready to explore the possibility of diplomatic relations with Peking. In his remarks, the secretary stated that the United States would, of course, defend its own legitimate interests in the Far East, which included Japan and the Philippines. Relations with the other nations of Asia would be conducted on the basis of "mutual respect and mutual helpfulness," but, as with Formosa, Washington could not "guarantee [them] against military attack."[19] Acheson clearly implied that South Korea was one of the other nations.

But what did the secretary really mean and what was he really saying? John Muccio, the U.S. ambassador to South Korea, later argued vociferously that Acheson's ideas were "not correctly presented to the American people" (presumably by the press). "This was not a *new* position." What Acheson did say, Muccio insisted, "was that the United States unilaterally would *have* to fight any aggression committed against the periphery of Asia [i.e., Japan, the Philippines, Formosa]. And then he goes on to bring out that in case of aggression beyond that it was a problem for the United Nations, not for the United States unilaterally. And that's exactly what happened in Korea."[20]

Perhaps. But NSC 48/2 clearly excluded South Korea from Washington's own defense calculations. If Acheson meant to send a different message, his precise position and intent are not clear from his speech. If Muccio was right, the secretary committed the classic blunder of the insider who assumes that outsiders know as much about his policies as he does, and it would eventually cost the nation dearly.

Acheson's real intent seems to have been to cut the United States irrevocably loose from Chiang. When Acheson had formally transmitted the State Department's two-volume *China White Paper* to the president in August 1949, his covering letter reeked with barely concealed contempt for the Chinese Nationalist leader. Two months later, the CIA concluded that extending substantial political, economic, and logistic support to the remnants of Chiang's forces on Formosa and elsewhere would not significantly alter "their present hopeless situation."[21] Truman's subsequent renunciation of the generalissimo had prompted Taft's response that Washington had either abandoned its China policy or had twisted it to serve the interests of a pinko conspiracy in the State Department.

Halfway around the world, Stalin and Mao watched the bitter and very public Washington policy struggles with keen interest. The two men finally met in mid-December, when Mao, fresh from his triumph in China, came to pay respects to his communist master in Moscow. Stalin was avuncular, even gracious, to his new and much younger partner. Mao was eager to accommodate, to win critical material support and diplomatic advantage, but he refused to defer completely to Stalin. At what was apparently their first conference on December 16, Mao flatly told the Soviet leader that China's "most important" need was a period of three to five years "to bring the [Chinese] economy back to prewar levels and to stabilize the country in general." Stalin concurred, observing that currently the new regime in Peking faced no threats. "Japan has yet to stand up on its feet and is thus not ready for war; America, though it screams war, is actually afraid of war more than anything." Mao added that although Britain and several other countries were eager to recognize China, "we must first bring about order to the country, strengthen our position, and then we can talk to the foreign imperialists." Stalin again agreed and took the opportunity to warn his Chinese colleague against creating "conflicts" with either the British or the Americans. "The main point is not to rush." Stalin did not mention Formosa, but it clearly weighed on the minds of both men.[22]

In another meeting five weeks later, the two briefly alluded to the overall situation in the Far East before turning to hard bargaining over respective spheres of influence and mutual support. Mao openly worried that while the two great communist powers were melding into a single mighty force, they could not "rule out the possibility that the imperialist countries [would] attempt to hinder us." Stalin acknowledged the danger, adding that a powerful undercurrent of militarism remained in Japan, which "will certainly lift itself up again, especially if Americans continue their current policy."[23]

But the two communist leaders were aware of the momentous events of the past five weeks. "History" seemed to be flowing as communist ideology dictated. In the first place, much to the dismay and disgust of the American public, if not their government, Britain and India had rushed to recognize the new Peking regime. Acheson had followed with his National Press Club speech, which Stalin interpreted as a "new American doctrine for the Far East, a crucial change in the international situation which seemed to signify a U.S. retreat from the Asian mainland and implicit acceptance of the Sino-Soviet alliance as a new geopolitical *fait accompli.*"[24]

This had not been Acheson's intention at all, of course, but Stalin clearly signaled to Mao his belief that China and Russia could do as they pleased on the Asian continent. Japan would have to be closely watched for a dangerous resurgence under American auspices; China had to avoid conflict with U.S. interests in the western Pacific, which meant staying its hand in Formosa for the present. Otherwise, the communist powers were free to act as they wished in the Far East. The Kremlin leader applauded Mao's intention to assault Tibet: "It's good that you are preparing to attack. The Tibetans need to be subdued."[25]

At the end of January 1950, Mao and Stalin signed a treaty of friendship, the Kremlin formally recognized Peking, and Acheson's overture to the Chinese Communists became irrelevant. Mao promptly initiated a series of provocations against American property and citizens in China. Consular buildings were seized, diplomats were beaten, and one consular official, Angus Ward, was arrested, tried as a spy, and placed under house arrest for many months while Washington unsuccessfully negotiated for his release.

In April 1949, a CIA intelligence paper, cleared by the State Department and the army, had warned that "it is the intention of the Soviet Union to advance toward its goal of eventual world domination by adding to the Soviet orbit the enormous territory and population of China, and by employing China to facilitate Soviet expansion into other Far Eastern areas." The Soviets might encounter resistance from dissident groups in the Chinese Communist Party (CCP), but "until evidence is available that an effective opposition is developing, it is concluded that the CCP will remain loyal to Moscow."[26]

Events of the first three months of 1950 had confirmed every point in the CIA paper, and, on March 15, Acheson publicly denounced the Sino-Soviet treaty as "an evil omen of imperialistic domination" in Asia and accused Mao and Chinese Foreign Minister Zhou Enlai of selling out China to Stalin. Five weeks before the outbreak of the Korean War, John Foster Dulles, one of Acheson's chief advisers, stated that the Chinese Communists seemed willing to "work in Asia as junior partners of Soviet Communism."[27]

Characteristically, Dulles was only half right. Mao was no slavish follower of Stalin. Nor was North Korea's fanatically ambitious young ruler, Kim Il Sung. Both men had agendas of their own, which forced the Kremlin's "revered leader" to react to events and pressures as much as or more than he shaped them. From the beginning, Stalin's ostensible Asian puppets acted more like impatient leashed tigers. The division of Korea between Soviet and U.S. forces in August 1945 made Kim totally dependent on Moscow for economic and technical assistance. Far from restraining Kim, however, this reliance stimulated his appetite. Seizure of South Korea was unthinkable while American forces remained on the peninsula, but once the last troopship carrying Yankee occupation forces sailed from Pusan in the summer of 1949, Kim began plucking Stalin's sleeve, and the old man gradually warmed to the idea of supporting a forcible reunification.

As early as September 1949, just after the Soviet Union tested its first atomic bomb, Stalin briefly considered, then rejected, supporting a limited North Korean military thrust to neutralize Syngman Rhee's noncommunist regime in Seoul. Even before Mao left Moscow in early February 1950, Kim was begging the Kremlin for a visit. On January 31, the Soviet ambassador to Pyongyang, Gen. Terentii Fomich Shtykov, cabled Stalin that he had met Kim the previous day "in accordance with your order," and "your agreement to receive him and your readiness to assist him in this matter made an especially strong impression." In view of the events of the next few months, Shtykov's reference to Stalin's "assistance" in "this matter" could only refer to Kim's determination to seize the south by force. After all, Stalin had just encouraged Mao to take Tibet. Why should Kim be denied a chance to expand dramatically the boundaries of Asian communism? Because the Americans "screamed" for war but feared it, Mao and Kim's flagrant destabilization of all of East Asia could become a favorable overture to the "final third-round showdown with the West."[28] Kim promptly escalated his campaign, dispatching the first of forty-eight telegrams to both Moscow and Peking and following them up with visits to the Soviet capital in March and April and to Peking in mid-May.[29]

Meanwhile Mao was busily disregarding both Stalin's prudent advice about not straying beyond the Asian mainland and his own concerns about not confronting the "imperialists" before China had been reorganized and restored. Even before he left Moscow, Mao cabled Peking, ordering the army to organize parachute units for an assault on Formosa. During the next month, the Chinese leader orchestrated both a diplomatic offensive and military preparations "for the armed attack that [he] regarded as inevitable." Mao's fractiousness placed Stalin in a bind. On the one hand, no one could tell how far the younger man's ambitions might extend. Was he dreaming of one day supplanting Stalin and the Soviet Union as leader of the world communist movement? On the other hand, he was far too valuable an ally to repudiate. "We definitely will render all possible assistance to the new China," Stalin had told a colleague in May of 1948. "If socialism is victorious in China and other countries follow the same road, we can consider the victory of socialism throughout the world to be guaranteed. No unexpected events can threaten us. Because of that, we must not spare any effort or resources in assisting the Chinese Communists."[30]

When Kim in early April 1950 pressed Mao for an invitation to Peking, a Soviet representative in Pyongyang was told that the Chinese leader had agreed. Mao "connected the proposed meeting with the question of the unification of Korea, indicating in this regard that if there is a concrete plan, . . . then the meeting should be organized secretly"; otherwise Kim would simply be invited for a routine state visit. Mao kept urging his North Korean colleague to mount an early assault against South Korea. According to Soviet sources, Mao told the North Korean ambassador to China, Li Zhou-yuan, on the eve of Kim's visit in mid-May "that the unification of Korea by peaceful means is not possible, solely military means are required to unify Korea." There was no need to fear the Americans. They would not "enter a third world war for such a small territory."[31]

Kim was already gearing up his war machine. He informed Shtykov on May 12 "that with regard to the question of the preparation of the operation he had given all necessary orders to the chief of the general staff, who already has begun to implement them, that his wish is to begin the operation in June, but he is still not convinced that they will manage it in this period."[32]

Mao's motive in egging on his communist ally in Pyongyang was obvious. A North Korean invasion of the south would either bring the Americans into a major war on the Asian mainland, tying down their resources for months if not years, or would cause Washington to back away from confrontation, which would make it extremely difficult if not impossible for the Truman administration to respond to communist probes anywhere else in the Far East. With either scenario, the way would be paved for Peking's seizure of Formosa and the final reunification of China under communism.

Soviet archives indicate that Kim envisioned a three-stage process of preparation. First he would concentrate his NKPA near the thirty-eighth parallel. Then his foreign ministry would issue an appeal to Rhee for peaceful reunification of the peninsula. Finally, Kim would initiate military activity after receiving Rhee's expected rejection of his offer. In his cables and visits to Stalin and Mao, Kim argued that the ROKA was not strong enough to contest the NKPA and that when the North Korean army drove south of Seoul, several hundred thousand loyal communists in Taejon, Taegu, Suwon, Osan, and the countless villages that dotted the rice paddies and hills of the south would arise spontaneously to liberate their homeland from the hated Western yoke. The drive to Pusan would be a cakewalk. Having so recently acquiesced in the fall of China, Washington would never try to rescue a much weaker and strategically questionable Asian country. But if American intervention did come, it would be too little and too late to affect the outcome. There was thus no risk of prematurely igniting World War III (which Stalin believed would come after 1954, when the Soviet nuclear stockpile was sufficient). The Americans would be disgraced throughout Asia whether they stood aside or tried to fight. Korea was a no-lose situation.

Stalin was apparently more difficult to convince than Mao, but the Kremlin leader finally capitulated to Kim's persistence with two stipulations, which revealed a lingering apprehension over the risks involved. First, the war had to be won quickly. Only a fool would completely discount possible intervention by Washington and perhaps the entire Western community under UN auspices. Kim was thus forced to plan the kind of sudden, massive, armored assault that Western military circles had long feared would happen in Europe. This imparted to the North Korean invasion a powerful and unlooked for symbolic aspect that invited an equally massive Western response. Stalin's second stipulation was that Soviet forces would not have to rescue the NKPA in case of an unexpected catastrophe.

Once convinced by Kim, and with his reservations clearly articulated, Stalin plunged in all the way. He ordered that every North Korean request for arms and equipment to form additional NKPA units be met at once. Peking provided Pyongyang with a division formed from Koreans who had been serving in the Chinese army and also promised to send large shipments of foodstuffs once war began. An entire Chinese Communist army was moved closer to the North Korean border "in case the Japanese enter on the side of the South Koreans."[33]

Once Mao became certain that Kim was about to plunge the Korean peninsula into war, he accelerated his own battle plans. "In late April, around the time Kim was in Moscow, Zhou sent a cable to the Soviet defense minister, Nikolai Bulganin, requesting a speed-up in the delivery of such naval requisitions as ships, airplanes, and coastal artillery." Zhou asked for a Soviet commitment of such supplies by the summer if possible and no later than the spring of 1951.[34]

In retrospect, Mao's planned coup de main seems the height of madness. A decade before, Hitler, with a small but powerful and efficient navy and a large, frightening air force, had been unable to hurl his splendid Wehrmacht across twenty miles of English Channel. Now Peking was planning to send a peasant army across nearly one hundred miles of water separating the mainland from Chiang's island stronghold with an almost nonexistent and decrepit navy and a small, inexperienced air force. Mao apparently believed that a sudden parachute assault against Formosa by several elite divisions of his People's Liberation Army (PLA) would panic the demoralized remnants of Chiang's Nationalist regime into surrender.

Perhaps he was right. Certainly MacArthur believed that Formosa was highly vulnerable. In mid-October 1949, as the last of Chiang's forces reached the island, Arthur Hays Sulzberger, publisher of the *New York Times*, sent a discreet query to Tokyo. Did MacArthur believe that "it is consistent with our military policy to defend the island against the Chinese Communists"? The supreme allied commander in Japan replied immediately. "The fall of Formosa to the Communists . . . would seriously breach" the current offshore island defense line that ran from the Aleutians to the Marianas, placing

a potentially hostile force on our flanks, establishing a dangerous wedge between Okinawa and the Philippines. . . . A Communist attack upon Formosa would undoubtedly take the form of an amphibious assault launched in motor-powered junks under cover of darkness from the China coast. Such an attack without air cover could easily be turned by either air or sea power but neither has heretofore been effectively employed by the Chinese Nationalists and there exists no unity of command essential to insure the proper coordination of such an operation. General Sun exercises no control whatsoever over the air and naval commanders. Worse than this, there appears to be constant bickering among senior officials with little unity of purpose. Furthermore, general morale among the Chinese forces is so low, and smouldering hostility on the part of the indigenous population so evident, that the possibility of internal defection may not be ignored. In these circumstances Formosa's defenders cannot be counted upon long to resist a determined enemy amphibious assault.[35]

Whether or not Mao could have actually invaded Formosa, the prime condition for success was the neutralization of America's admittedly very limited air and sea power in the Far East, either through intimidation or the distraction of another crisis. The Chinese leader must have awaited North Korea's lunge across the thirty-eighth parallel with keen anticipation.

❖   ❖   ❖

To the average American congressman, bureaucrat, and citizen in early 1950, South Korea was "one of those names seen out of the corner of the eye. Everyone was vaguely aware that the U.S. was committed to Korea, but only vaguely committed."[36] Rhee was unpalatable to many in Washington who had known him during his long decades in exile. For nearly thirty years, the man had waited impatiently in the United States for the yoke of Japanese occupation to be lifted, and, in 1946, he had finally come to power behind American bayonets. His patriotism was undeniable; so was his brutality and repressiveness. Once in power, he had proven to be a classic oriental despot. Popular opposition to him and to his regime had been widespread from the beginning. The CIA concluded in 1949 that, although subversive communist activities in South Korea were at a low level "and probably will be further reduced if the Republic continues its present trend toward increased stability," nonetheless "the number of South Koreans who have consistently braved various degrees of police action to assist the Communist program may exceed 600,000, while the total number of Koreans enrolled in Communist front organizations may exceed 10 percent of the 20 million population."[37]

Understandably obsessed with internal security, Rhee employed his small, poorly trained army as a domestic police force. John Hodge, commander of U.S. occupation forces in Korea, had been uncomfortable with U.S. support of Rhee, but, after 1948, Washington and most of the United Nations viewed South Korea as a besieged republic, not a struggling dictatorship. An October 1948 CIA paper concluded optimistically that Rhee had organized "the new government . . . with widespread popular support" and that despite inexperience with parliamentary institutions and Rhee's autocratic tendencies, "the present administration is apparently making good initial progress in the development of responsible government."[38] The Americans attempted to leave Korea after the United Nations recognized the republic. The occupation was straining the limited resources of the postwar U.S. Army, but continued domestic turmoil in the south and the growing threat from the NKPA forced a delay. When the Yanks finally departed in the summer of 1949, they left behind the KMAG to help organize and train the ROKA. But Washington, fearing Rhee's aggressive appetites, refused to provide him with either the air or armored forces that could be used in a thrust northward.

Acheson's exclusion of the peninsula from America's Asian defense perimeter caused immediate concern in Seoul. Rhee's intelligence reports indicated that Kim was preparing an assault. Throughout the spring of 1950, Korean officials in Washington probed for clues to the administration's thinking. Dean Rusk, then assistant secretary of state for Far Eastern affairs, told them that the defense line that Acheson had alluded to was merely an enumeration of those sectors in the western Pacific where the United States had firm military commitments—that is, in Japan, where it was the occupying power, and in the Philippines, where it had a long-term special interest in a former territory. When Ambassador John Chang pressed Rusk on Korea's status, the assistant secretary was evasive. He could not comment, but surely the Koreans could guess their relationship with Washington. After all, the United States was providing significant military aid and political support to the republic.[39]

Rhee remained understandably worried. After Acheson's January speech, the U.S. House of Representatives, in a burst of isolationism, had rejected the administration's $60-million Korean aid bill by two votes. Three weeks later, the congressmen had reluctantly reversed themselves, but it had been a close vote. Unknown to either Washington or Seoul, Kim exploited the Korean aid bill issue by arguing to Stalin and Mao that it was one more example of American disinterest in Korea. By April, Washington had become alarmed at the galloping inflation that was decimating the South Korean economy and undermining the modest U.S. aid program. In early May, Senate Foreign Relations Chairman Tom Connally (Democrat of Texas) had airily dismissed South Korea as an area that had little or no importance for the United States. Rhee promptly called in Chargé Everett F. Drumright and "in a deeply bitter and sarcastic manner" condemned Connally's remarks as "an open invitation to the Communists to come on down and take over South Korea." Two days later, on May 11, Drumright reported that the South Korean Defense Ministry had stated publicly that two divisions of Chinese Communist troops had arrived in North Korea during the past nine months, raising "the fully armed, effective fighting force there to 183,100" men.[40] (These were actually the North Korean soldiers who had been fighting with Mao's army for the past few years and whom Mao had made available to Kim as part of North Korea's invasion force.)

But those who have assumed then and now that the United States either deliberately or thoughtlessly invited the North Korean assault through a policy of neglect fail to take into account a critically important exchange between Acheson and the Washington press corps in early May 1950. Senator Connally had just stated his belief that the United States should pull out of "southern Korea," and the secretary of state was asked for his reaction at the beginning of his May 3 press and radio news conference. "Well, I think that the view of the Department in regard to southern Korea has been made very clear in numerous hearings" on Capitol Hill, Acheson replied.

> We have stressed, as you very well know, the importance which we attach to southern Korea. We have recounted our efforts to establish Korea as an independent nation. We have told how the Soviet Union made it impossible to unify the whole country and how under the United Nations Commission we went forward with the other nations in establishing southern Korea; that we have been and are now giving them very substantial economic help, military assistance, and advice. Now I have not seen the interview with Senator Connally, but I should doubt very much whether he takes a different view from what I have just stated.[41]

Presumably the Soviet embassy monitored all public statements by high administration officials in 1950 as closely as it did in subsequent years. Acheson's voice was on radio; even if the newspapers failed to pick up or adequately interpret his forthright statement, Soviet intelligence agents could and presumably did. Nearly two months before the North Korean invasion of the South, Moscow, Peking, and Pyongyang should have realized not only that the United States considered South Korea an important component of its foreign policy but that Washington would surely invoke UN assistance and support if South Korea were assaulted. Stalin, Mao, and Kim had no one but themselves to blame for their impending and catastrophic misjudgment of American and Western intentions in the Far East.

There had been rumors of a coming North Korean attack across the parallel since at least 1948. Washington knew that Kim had been slipping guerrilla forces across the border for more than a year, although, by the spring of 1950, most of these bands had been rounded up by the ROKA and the South Korean constabulary. Ambassador Muccio, while on home leave in April, warned Congress that, although the threat of guerrilla activity had diminished considerably, "the undeniable matériel superiority of the north Korean forces would provide north Korea with a margin of victory in the event of a full-scale invasion."[42]

Far East Headquarters in Tokyo shared Muccio's view but not his concern, and intelligence sources in the KMAG seemed blissfully confident that Kim would not send his forces south. MacArthur's intelligence people were a strange group. They were nominally directed by Maj. Gen. Charles Willoughby, a long-time MacArthur crony, whom uncharitable critics of the general characterized as a bootlicker. Willoughby spent much of the first half of 1950 gathering materials and writing the initial draft of a laudatory biography of his commander. His subordinate, Col. Lawrence G. Smith, commanding officer of the 441st Counter Intelligence Corps Detachment (proudly referred to as "the eyes and ears of the Occupation"), seemed to enjoy indulging in the dramatic, labeling Asian Communist armies "Red Hordes." As the 441st's motto suggested, Smith and his subordinates concentrated most of their attention and energies on real or alleged communist subversive activities in Japan; Korea was definitely a peripheral interest. But Smith did acknowledge five months into the Korean War that "sources" had told him that "the North Korean Army, having been trained and equipped by the Soviet[s], would invade South Korea, possibly in July 1950." According to Counter Intelligence Corps information dated May 27, the entire peninsula would supposedly be under Pyongyang's control by autumn.[43]

Presumably MacArthur was privy to this remarkable assessment. Washington and Seoul may or may not have been. On June 19, the CIA circulated a paper based on information available up to May 15. Titled "Current Capabilities of the Northern Korean Regime," the document was cleared by the State Department, army, navy, and air force intelligence services. The agency cautiously stated that "northern Korea's armed forces, even as presently constituted [i.e., without substantial logistical support from the Soviet Union] . . . , have a capability for attaining limited objectives in short-term military operations against southern Korea, including the capture of Seoul." But "it is not certain that the northern regime, lacking the active participation of Soviet and Chinese Communist military units, would be able to gain effective control over all of southern Korea."[44]

On June 15, Secretary of Defense Johnson and Joint Chiefs Chairman Bradley left Washington for a hasty tour of the Far East. They returned only hours before the North Korean attack. While in Japan, Johnson and Bradley met with Gen. Lynn V. Roberts, chief of the U.S. military mission to Korea. Roberts had been telling visiting congressmen and officials for months that the KMAG was doing a brilliant job of training the ROKA, which might be the best military force in the Far East. Now he told Bradley and Johnson that he "had no special problems." The ROKA was making "genuine progress . . . [and] unless Russia furnished actual troops . . . the South Korean forces could handle any possible invasion by North Korean forces." Johnson and Bradley were so pleased with this news that they directed Roberts to submit a plan "shortly" for "the gradual reduction of the Korean Mission."[45]

Little more than a week before Roberts spoke with Bradley and Johnson, Kim began implementing his invasion scenario, reversing stages one and two. The official newspaper of the North Korean Communist Party in Pyongyang published a manifesto in which the "Central Committee of the United Democratic Patriot Front" called for all-Korean elections for a "national" parliament, which would convene in Seoul by August 15. This clear signal that something was up was immediately followed by massive North Korean troop concentrations near the thirty-eighth parallel. Between June 12 and 23 the North Korean command moved all of its regular army units—seven infantry divisions, one armored brigade, one separate infantry regiment, one motorcycle regiment, and one border constabulary brigade— into planned lines of departure all across the parallel. According to a report from Shtykov in Pyongyang, "the redeployment of troops took place in an orderly fashion, without incident." Shtykov added that American intelligence had "probably detected the troop redeployment, but we managed to keep the plan and the time of the beginning of troop operations secret." And he concluded: "The planning of the operation at the divisional level and the reconnaissance of the area was carried out with the participation of Soviet advisers." The ninety thousand North Korean soldiers advanced to their start lines at midnight local time June 24-25, 1950; four hours and forty minutes later, North Korean artillery opened up and the war began.[46]

Historian Bruce Cumings, reflecting a generation of leftist scholarship, has argued that Willoughby, Rusk, various South Koreans, and others may have manipulated intelligence data in order to condemn Pyongyang for an aggression actually begun by Rhee.[47] He is wrong. In the absence of South Korean armor and air power, Washington and Tokyo obviously prayed that the most recent North Korean buildup signified only another round of routine war games and that if the NKPA did attack, it would either be repulsed by the ROKA or would not advance south of the Han River, giving MacArthur and Truman time to develop a proper response.

But the NKPA, better trained, well supplied, and more imaginative than MacArthur, Roberts, or anyone else had believed, not only rushed across the parallel and captured Seoul, but after a week's delay marched on toward

Pusan. Communism had thrown down the gauntlet to the free world, and the next move was up to Truman.

As the president's plane landed in Washington, maps of Korea were going up on nearly every Pentagon wall, and there was much excited coming and going in the big building near the Potomac. Reporters recalled the somber days just before and after Pearl Harbor nearly a decade before, when the old Munitions Building on Constitution Avenue was filled with officers and soldiers bustling about purposefully. Truman, alone in his Blair House office (the executive mansion was being renovated), dashed off a few lines to his wife back in Independence. He hadn't been so badly upset, he wrote, "since Greece and Turkey fell into our laps." He wanted to avoid full national mobilization, but news from the Korean war front was worsening by the hour. "Let's hope for the best."[48] For the next five evenings, the president convened his chief advisers around the Blair House table. Each day the situation in Korea deteriorated.

Liberals and moderate conservatives were equally apprehensive. Liberals believed fervently that the United Nations was the best hope for prolonged world peace. If the UN membership was not going to challenge the North Korean assault, all prospects for a secure future would be dashed. Moderate conservatives believed that the United States was the only sure guarantor of peace. If it did not act (either alone or with others), communism would be further encouraged to continue its aggressive march across the planet. Monday night, June 26, was especially tense as Washington and the nation waited impatiently to learn whether Truman would respond at all. "Anybody who was Anybody" in town "knew what Truman was going to do." Weak, vacillating Harry Truman "was going to appease." He would pass the buck to the United Nations, offering them, as some wit sardonically put it, "'all aid short of help.'"[49]

Truman stunned them all. At 12:07 the following day, the White House released an executive order. Washington would offer unlimited military aid to South Korea and send U.S. air and naval forces currently in the Far East against the steadily advancing NKPA (jets from MacArthur's Far East Air Force promptly shot down three Yak fighters over the port of Inchon). At the same time, the president ordered elements of the Seventh Fleet to the Formosa Strait to prevent the Korean conflict from widening. American sailors and fliers would ensure that Formosa was safe from communist attack while preventing further assaults by Chiang's aviators against coastal areas on the Chinese mainland. Each step coincided with press and congressional opinion. As one liberal journalist observed, the Truman pronouncement was a diplomatic masterpiece, for it "sterilized" both Formosa and the Republican Right. "The political opposition was left to the *Daily Worker* and the Chicago *Tribune,* and it is not the first time that this strange couple has shared a bed."[50]

Moderate conservatives were equally incredulous and equally impressed. Tom Dewey cabled Truman, pledging his whole-hearted support for the Korean and Formosan decisions, which "should be supported by a united America." Recalling the announcement five months later, Henry Luce wrote that on this one occasion Truman had "taken a bold line in Asia." The communist "attack in Korea contradicted every assumption and every calculation which then underlay American policy in Asia. So did Mr. Truman's decision to meet the attack head-on."[51] Fundamentalist conservatives in Congress were predictably critical. Wherry, Knowland, and others blamed the North Koreans' assault on the administration's failed China policy.

Administration supporters and editorial writers first expressed hopes that the ROKA could stem the invasion on its own with U.S. air and naval assistance. Liberals were delighted to discover a broad national consensus that the problem should be brought to the United Nations, for the North Korean assault was the clearest violation of the charter since the founding of that organization. As the dimensions of the crisis became clearer, public reactions sharpened. The North Koreans would never have streamed over the parallel without orders from their masters in the Kremlin. "Soviet imperialism moves through its puppets like an amoeba," the *Washington Post* declared, "always into soft spots, halting only in the face of obstruction." If the United States did not counter Stalin's aggression, the Soviets would nibble away at Western power all around the world. America had to respond to the sudden crisis in the Far East with military aid and, if necessary, with troops. "This country is committed to repel the aggressor," the *Post* editorialized on June 26, "by every reason of prestige in Asia and of moral obligation to the Koreans." Three days later, national columnists Joseph and Stewart Alsop wrote: "It is surely obvious that short of a general war, Southern Korea must be held at whatever cost and by whatever means, including the commitment of American troops and strategic bombing."[52]

Seoul fell to the North Koreans on the twenty-ninth. Two days earlier, MacArthur had flown to the peninsula and watched as the first elements of the ROKA retreated across the Han River bridges beyond the city and fled south. He returned to Tokyo convinced that only U.S. troops could prevent South Korea from becoming, like Czechoslovakia, another communist trophy captured by violence. He promptly conveyed his views to Washington.

Acheson, the supposed Commie appeaser, had been orchestrating two UN resolutions authorizing intervention. Their passage was almost guaranteed because Stalin had called home Soviet UN Ambassador Jacob Malik in a pique, apparently over the failure of the United Nations to kick out Nationalist China and seat the Peking regime in its place. The first resolution, which the Security Council had passed on June 25, just hours after news of the North Korean assault reached New York, demanded that the NKPA return to its positions above the thirty-eighth parallel. When that order was ignored, the Security Council passed another on June 27, branding North Korea an aggressor and calling on UN member nations to "render such assistance to the Republic of Korea as may be necessary to repel the armed attack and to restore international peace and security to the area."[53]

The precise "area" that the Security Council meant was never made clear and would eventually cause endless problems. But at the moment the international community concentrated on bolstering the South Korean regime. Britain promptly pledged ships and men, and, by the end of the month, Truman had ordered to the peninsula elements of MacArthur's 100,000-man Eighth Army, which was on occupation duty in Japan. He also permitted the Far East Air Force to strafe and bomb targets throughout North Korea and ordered the navy to begin a blockade of the North Korean coast. On June 29, the first U.S. troops started disembarking at the port of Pohang on the eastern coast of South Korea after the short trip across the Sea of Japan. The United States and the United Nations were in the Korean War, and Washington was committed to an enterprise that many military men had vigorously argued against in earlier years: an American war against Asians on the Asian mainland.

Nearly everyone in the noncommunist world applauded the decision, and nearly everyone believed that the Soviet Union had been behind the North Korean thrust. In his first cable from Moscow after news of the invasion raced around the world, Ambassador Alan G. Kirk charged that the "aggressive NK military move" represented a "clear-cut Soviet challenge" that had to be met if the United States wished to continue its "leadership of [the] free world against Soviet Communist imperialism." Within hours of the North Korean assault, State's Office of Intelligence Research had drafted a paper concluding that North Korea was "completely under Kremlin control and there is no possibility that the North Koreans acted without prior instruction from Moscow. The move against South Korea must therefore be considered a Soviet move." During the long, hot summer evening meetings at the end of June that led to American intervention, the question of Soviet intentions was never far from anyone's mind. If the Russians were behind this fundamental destabilization of Asian affairs, would Stalin rush his troops in to save the situation if the North Korean invasion were repulsed? According to one participant, Army Secretary Frank Pace, the issue "was thoroughly discussed, and it was the conclusion of most people involved that the Soviets would *not* come in, . . . but there were different shadings of concern about it." If assessments were wrong and the Red Army entered the Korean War, "this really was something that had to be faced and dealt with, because otherwise the impression would be left with the Soviets that they could undertake any kind of initiative anywhere in the world and we'd be afraid to counter it." The consensus around the Blair House conference table was that the Soviets had blundered; they did not think Washington and the "free world" "would react to this action." Moscow "had come to the conclusion that this was an isolated part of the world, that our basic interests were not there, and that they [the Soviets] were in a position, using North Koreans, to go ahead and take over that whole area." Possible Chinese intervention "was not discussed."[54]

The mood at Blair House echoed that in the country. "Russia had timed its move shrewdly," Luce's editorial writers said. The United States had to respond with both boldness and caution to save South Korea but still avoid World War III. Americans had been shocked awake, *Newsweek* asserted. They had not expected the Soviets to start hostilities until at least 1952, when their nuclear arsenal would roughly match that of the United States. Now the "Kremlin-controlled armies of North Korea" were on the march. What did it mean? As the United States committed its first troops, the answer began to emerge. Washington had put up a "stop" sign for the communists in the Pacific. The Reds would have to move east and south of China at their own peril. "U.S. is committed to guard all oceans, half the earth. Formosa won't fall to Communists by default. Indo-China isn't to be let go, either."

With U.S. troops on the ground in Korea, *Newsweek* published a headline that unwittingly summarized U.S. foreign policy for the next half-century: "Uncle Sam Takes Role as World Cop."[55]

"Korea brought Europe to its feet," John J. McCloy recalled. The Soviets had added a new dimension to the cold war. Whether from desperation or calculation, the Kremlin seemed ready to use armed force to extend its power on the Eurasian landmass. When Charles Bohlen and Averell Harriman, then in Paris, heard that Truman had decided to commit U.S. troops, they promptly brought the news to French Foreign Minister Robert Schumann. "Thank God," Schumann responded with teary eyes, remembering the appeasement follies of the 1930s, "this will not be a repetition of the past." The *Economist* stated that the "American response to the Communist challenge in Korea has been swift and resolute. . . . It has been a heartening spectacle." The House of Commons, which "had been deep in a party debate only a few hours earlier closed its ranks behind Mr Attlee when he announced, without qualification, British support for the American decision. In Europe, opinion—save among the Communists—has proved remarkably steady, obviously relieved that a great moral and political decision should have been taken so quickly." As the North Korean tide continued to engulf the South in the first week of July, the *Economist* urged its readers to have faith in an eventual UN victory.[56]

There had been some talk at Blair House about getting a congressional resolution in support of committing U.S. troops, but Acheson squelched it. Truman supported him. Public and congressional opinion was clearly behind the administration; it would be unwise to give a handful of obstructionists the opportunity to talk the issue to death, thereby suggesting to the Kremlin that American and international resolve was not total. Wherry reacted bitterly; once again Acheson had outmaneuvered Congress, and Wherry would neither forgive nor forget.

Acheson stubbornly refused to characterize either the Korean invasion or the U.S.–UN response, but pundits had no doubt that the world was entering a new era. The "cold war (which was neither cold nor war)" had ended. "What was this new thing the U.S. was in," *Time* asked. "World War III? Could Armageddon begin with so feeble a fanfare as the muffled Battle of Korea?" Could the "push-button war" that modern science had introduced into civilization "start among the grass roofs of a land where men had hardly caught up with Galileo?"[57]

The American public never wavered in its support of Truman during the early weeks of the war, although well-informed individuals sensed that the

Korean ordeal might be prolonged.[58] "Every American hopes with all his heart that this will be a short war and a quick UN victory, but there is no guarantee that this will be true."[59] Nonetheless, George Gallup found that 80 percent of the people he polled on July 1 approved of the decision to intervene in Korea. One man commented that the action was the "best thing Truman's done in five years." A majority of those polled (57 percent) believed that American intervention would increase the chances for world peace, presumably by showing the Soviets that the United States and the "free world" would no longer countenance communist expansion.[60]

Luce sent reporters out to Sycamore, a northern Illinois town of six thousand in the middle of what had been the heart of the isolationist belt only a decade before. Of the fourteen people interviewed for the July 10 issue of *Life*, only one, druggist David Hamilton, expressed concern about Truman's decision. A carpenter, an advertising man, a teacher, a lawyer, a housewife, a mailman, a laborer, a veterans' counselor, a janitor, and a salesman, among others, all had the same general opinion: The Kremlin had unquestionably ordered the North Korean attack, and it was time to stand up to the Soviets. "I don't know if we're doing right or not," seventy-four-year-old Fred Buck said, "but the sooner you stop the Russians, the sooner we're getting somewhere." Twenty-eight-year-old teacher Eric Henigan added that "Russia is like [Nazi] Germany, taking countries one by one. If war comes, I'll go back to the Marines." All the veterans in the group echoed Henigan's sentiments. They had served once to stop tyranny; if necessary, they would serve again. George Roden, a fifty-eight-year-old tailor, summed up the consensus:

> Sure I got boys, and [a] son-in-law, too. I still agree with Truman. We have let Russia get too many countries, and too many footholds. We ought to protect those countries and get those Commies out of there. We ought to let those people in Europe and Asia run their own countries, but we ought to see [that] they get good rulers. And when they have an election we ought to see that they have a fair and honest election. That's what this country's for.[61]

From the start, the Korean War went wrong for everybody, but especially for the invaders. Most of the ROKA, after a few gallant stands, dissolved into what seemed a routed rabble. But time and again the North Korean Army failed to exploit its early victories. Seoul was only twenty-four miles south of the thirty-eighth parallel. Ambassador Muccio expected advance NKPA units to be in the city by invasion night at the latest "because they had such preponderance of armor and mobility, and they had control in the air." Yet it took the NKPA three and a half days to reach a city it should have seized "in that many hours." Muccio attributed North Korean dilatoriness to three factors: the brave stand of many South Korean units before being destroyed or dissolved; the torrential rain on the morning of the invasion, which impeded initial North Korean air and armored assaults; and, most important, a flawed North Korean strategy. "I think that what the Communists had in mind," Muccio told an interviewer in 1971, "was to rush into Seoul, capture the government, and then they'd be able to present to the world that Rhee and his government had no support from the people of Korea, and the whole issue would be settled right then and there before the U.N. or the Free World could do anything."[62]

But Rhee and his government did not wait supinely for capture; they promptly moved south to Taejon and eventually to Pusan. Within a few weeks, the ROKA began to bounce back spectacularly from the sucker punch it had received along the parallel. Above all, the North Koreans failed to exploit the military advantage they so briefly enjoyed. At Taejon, Muccio saw the railway yards "jammed with gasoline, ammunition, and all kinds of equipment," which had been hastily brought over from Japan and "dumped" at Pusan and brought up to Taejon as part of the initial U.S.–UN buildup for a counteroffensive. With the U.S. intervention, control of the air had become contested but had not yet passed completely to the Americans. Enemy forces in front of the slowly advancing NKPA were scattered and initially ineffectual. Swift, bold moves by the North Korean military could have led either to the seizure or destruction of enemy supplies as critical to the North Koreans as to their opponents. Yet the NKPA made no rapid thrust on Taejon, and the North Korean air force made no effort to destroy the city's marshaling yards. Muccio speculated that the seizure of two North Korean spy rings by the Seoul police the previous February and April had not been reported back to Pyongyang and that therefore Kim and his colleagues expected a network of saboteurs, who in fact no longer existed, to emerge behind the retreating South Koreans.[63] Whatever the reason, the criminal slowness of the NKPA in advancing into South Korea would cost it the war.

Indeed, as the North Korean army crawled across the Han, it saw no sign among the South Korean peasants and urban workers of the promised popular uprising that would guarantee a triumphant three-day march to Pusan. Instead, scattered U.S. forces began to appear in hastily prepared blocking positions ahead of the advancing NKPA armored and infantry columns, while long lines of refugees fled south, complicating NKPA troop movements. Pusan began to seem far away.

Kim, Mao, and Stalin were stunned, alarmed, and embittered by the swift response of the United States and the United Nations. On July 1, the Soviet leader anxiously asked Shtykov in Pyongyang about Kim's intentions. Were the North Korean comrades going to suspend their advance or push on? "In our opinion the attack absolutely must continue and the sooner South Korea is liberated the less chance there is for intervention." Within hours, Shtykov dispatched a dispirited reply. American propaganda and bombing campaigns across the entire peninsula had begun to erode the political mood of the North Korean people. Elements in the North Korean politburo were "speaking about the difficulties of conducting a war against the Americans" and were cautiously asking Kim about the prospects of a Soviet intervention. Three days later, Shtykov cabled Stalin, reporting a continuing "seriousness of the situation at the front and in the liberated territories." The North Korean high command was especially sensitive to "the danger of landings by American troops in the rear or at the North Korean ports or airborne landings of troops." Such fears soon prompted Kim to ask Stalin for further arms shipments in order to form two more divisions, twelve battalions of marines, and additional internal security forces. Stalin, clearly alarmed, cabled Zhou Enlai the next day that "we consider it correct to concentrate immediately 9 Chinese divisions on the Chinese-Korean border for volunteer actions in North Korea in case the enemy crosses the 38th parallel. We will try to provide air cover for these units." Mao began to mass troops along the North Korean border, and Stalin hurried him along with an urgent suggestion that Peking establish a military liaison with the NKPA as soon as possible.[64]

Mao vented his spleen at a meeting of the Central People's Government Council on June 28, the day after Truman ordered the Seventh Fleet into the Strait. "The U.S. invasion of Asia" could only "touch off the broad and resolute opposition of Asian people." The president had publicly stated on January 5 that he would "not intervene in Taiwan." He had lied, and in the process "shredded all international agreements related to the American commitment not to intervene in China's internal affairs."[65] The handful of modern U.S. warships that appeared in the Formosa Strait revealed the crippling weakness of Mao's naval and air forces and the unrealistic nature of his dream to seize the island.[66] Truman and his lackeys were nothing but imperialist dogs who needed to be taught a lesson.

For the next two and a half months, the NKPA did just that. Instead of taking time to establish a firm and defensible front to check the North Korean offensive, Eighth Army commander Gen. Walton H. ("Johnnie") Walker and his subordinate, Gen. William Dean, ordered the first units of the Eighth Army reaching Korea to rush north and west in a more or less blind search for the NKPA. The results were predictable. An axiom of combat is that inexperienced soldiers cannot stand up to an aggressive enemy on first contact, and the units of the Eighth Army were no exception. On July 3, elements of the Twenty-Fourth Infantry Division, moving west and north from Pohang, got as far as Pyongtaek just south of Osan on the Suwon Road, where they met the first NKPA forces moving carefully out of their Han River bridgehead. The Americans hastily prepared defensive positions but could not hold them against the skilled enemy, who infiltrated, outflanked, or in some cases simply overran the defenders. The Twenty-fourth held on as long as it could at Pyongtaek, then fell back to Chonan and stood again before retreating to Taejon, where it rallied once more, only to be terribly mauled and forced to retreat toward Pusan in company with two other infantry divisions and supporting artillery and armor that had come up to join it.

The fighting was bitter and heartbreaking. Young men who a week before had enjoyed inexpensive drinking binges, light housekeeping with native girlfriends, and dabbling on the black market in Japan suddenly found themselves in a strange, hot, rainy, smelly land, surrounded by sullen, uncommunicative people. By train, truck, or foot, they were rushed to this village or that town, to a rice paddy or a ridge line, where they were told to establish a blocking position with insufficient arms and ammunition. For how long, they asked. Never mind that, their commanders told them, just hold it! All they had to do was show themselves to the craven Commies, many officers maintained, and the NKPA would simply melt away. The soldiers believed it.

Soon the enemy materialized, either silent infantry or clanking tanks. For a while, the Americans resisted with whatever machine guns, mortars, and light antitank weapons they possessed. But these could not stop the T-34s, and the enemy infantry did not scatter as it was supposed to but advanced steadily in disciplined formations. The North Koreans knew the stinking paddies and the high, exhausting hills much better than did the Yanks. To one anguished young soldier, the men of the NKPA looked like the whole city of New York coming toward him. Frightened troopers from Arkansas, South Dakota, and Massachusetts tried to hold on as the first withering blasts of enemy fire swept toward and over them. The heat, dust, and rain added enervation to the shock of combat and the sudden screams of shot or blasted comrades. As enemy fire kept coming and the NKPA appeared all around their positions, troopers broke and ran, leaving behind their dead and wounded. As they bolted, they discarded arms and equipment, food and clothing. A new word came into the Eighth Army's vocabulary: *bug-out*. Platoons and companies were cut off from each other; battalions were decimated. Men lost touch with their comrades and wandered across the strange countryside for hours or days until most were captured. Only a few caught up with their steadily retreating lines.

Initial press reports from the fighting fronts were shocking. In its first battles since the triumphs of 1945, the U.S. Army had been badly beaten by a rag-tag bunch of Asian peasants. At a makeshift base somewhere in Korea, wounded men with "dull, bloodshot eyes and the haggard faces of complete exhaustion" told journalists the same thing over and over again: "Those bastards were everywhere all around us. They had everything."[67] Young soldiers cursed their government for sending them into such a hellish situation so totally unprepared. Junior officers became embittered and cynical as their men cut and ran; senior officers were frantic. Was this the same force that had decimated Hitler's Wehrmacht just a few years before?

The hysteria reached all the way to Tokyo and Washington. On July 10, MacArthur demanded that the Pentagon raid the army's general reserve and immediately send all of its units, along with the entire Fleet Marine Force, to Korea before the Eighth Army units on the peninsula were pushed into the sea. Influential national columnists condemned "the debacle in Korea" and demanded that the administration recognize that the "'initial reverses'" were more than temporary. "We have a major war on our hands, by the poor standards of existing American strength," the Alsops concluded.[68]

Truman did not panic, but he was understandably worried that Korea might be just the beginning of a limited but multipronged Soviet military thrust around the periphery of the Eurasian landmass. His service secretaries, however, exhibited considerable hysteria. As late as August 1, the three sent a memorandum to Defense Secretary Johnson calling for "an urgent and frank re-appraisal of the global position of the United States military potential. . . . There is no margin left." Until such an evaluation was complete, "no additional commitments of United States support should be undertaken." Then "we must make clear through diplomatic and other channels the extent to which United States support may be expected. Having made such declarations, there should be no deviation therefrom until such time as world conditions moderate or the military potential of the United States is substantially increased."[69]

Immediately after deciding to intervene, Truman had asked the State and Defense Departments for estimates of the areas most vulnerable to a Soviet assault. Characteristically the two agencies could not agree, but at a cabinet meeting on July 14, Acheson observed that the international situation was sufficiently dangerous and unpredictable to demand a substantial increase in American fighting strength. Truman concurred and during the next several days abruptly reversed five years of military spending policy, undermining Louis Johnson in the process. In a report to Congress five days after the cabinet meeting, the president emphasized the need to strengthen the national military establishment and to prepare not only to deal with the war in Korea "but also to increase our common defense, with other free nations, against further aggression." Congress readily agreed, and emergency appropriations and grants of presidential powers tumbled over one another, "sometimes in such haste that supplemental appropriations virtually accompanied the regular fiscal-year bill they were supplementing."[70] America was rearming for an age of peril whose end no one could predict.

Truman requested that the nation's military bill, which had been around $13 billion annually (Johnson had wanted to slash it to $10 billion), be extended to roughly $17 to $18 billion. The president increased draft calls and sent to the Hill hurriedly written legislation that expanded the armed forces to two million men. The Pentagon quickly summoned 25,000 volunteer reservists to duty; 135,000 more would be called up in the next year. Ninety-two National Guard and Army Organized Reserve Units were mobilized. The navy began taking warships out of "mothballs" as fast as possible and transferred vessels from the Atlantic to the Pacific Fleet as a stopgap measure to cover the new commitment in the Far East. At San Diego the Pacific Fleet Marine Force received orders to ship out immediately for

Korea. The air force began estimating immediate airlift capabilities from the West Coast to Japan and southern Korea.[71] From California piers and airfields and at urban and small town railroad stations and bus depots all across the country, American women once again began waving goodbye to their war-bound men. Soon those same piers, airfields, and railroad stations would ring to the sound of funeral dirges as the first caskets arrived from Asia. Not quite five years had passed since the end of the most devastating and widespread war in history.

On the same day (July 19) that he sent his first message to Congress on rearmament, the president delivered a "fireside chat" over national radio. He insisted that the communist offensive in Korea must be perceived in global terms. Nothing less than American national security and world peace were at stake on the peninsula. Reports from the front were cautiously optimistic, but the road to victory might be long and hard. He closed by expressing confidence that the American people shared his own detestation of "Communist slavery" and were therefore united behind the war effort.[72]

Six weeks later, Truman again escalated the nation's military strength. Warning "the leaders of international communism" that "the United States would employ its great power without limit to uphold the rule of law in the world," the president announced that he would ask Congress for funds to support a three-million-man national defense establishment. As before, public and congressional opinion strongly supported the move.[73]

In Korea the Eighth Army and the ROKA steadily retreated before the NKPA, but as the Americans and their South Korean allies gained experience in combat, they began fighting back with courage and tenacity. Air force and navy tactical air support began to play an important role in breaking up enemy formations and disrupting enemy supply lines. Every bridge over the Han River was bombed to pieces, and American B-29s and fighters roamed over North Korea from the parallel to the Yalu, torching cities and blowing up bridges, factories, electrical plants, railroad marshaling yards, and strategic highways. Under this pounding and a stiffening American defense, the NKPA advance crawled to a halt.

By the beginning of August, the Eighth Army and the ROKA had been pushed into the Naktong River valley north and west of Pusan. With its open spaces and river barrier, the region constituted the natural defense perimeter that Walker and Dean should have established in the first place. By this time, the conflict had officially become a UN police action. On July 7, the Security Council (with Malik still in Moscow) had authorized the creation of a UN command in Korea and deferred to American suggestions that MacArthur lead it. Two weeks later, the first units of the British army, two brigades from Hong Kong, including the famous "Glo'sters," disembarked at Pusan and moved immediately into the front lines. Soon thereafter the army's Second Infantry Division and Fifth Regimental Combat Team, along with a marine regimental combat team, arrived in Korea. These units brought armor and vehicles with which to wage either a fluid defense or an aggressive war of movement if developments suddenly made a breakout possible. "UN Forces," as they were now designated, held a semicircular 120-mile-long front along the Naktong River barely 50 miles from Pusan and only 15 miles in front of the key communication and transportation center at Taegu. On July 19, MacArthur revealed the first of many mood changes that would plague him and his superiors in coming months. The defeatist tone of early cables was suddenly jettisoned for a new jauntiness. "With the deployment in Korea of major elements of the 8th Army now accomplished," he informed Truman in a personal message, "the first phase of the campaign has ended and with it the chance for victory by the North Korean Forces."[74] MacArthur was right, but the fighting became more, not less bitter for the next six weeks, as General Chai desperately flung his dwindling NKPA columns at the UN lines. American, South Korean, and British casualties were high; North Korean losses in men and matériel were frightful.

At the end of August, Stalin tried to stiffen the resolve of an obviously badly shaken Kim. He told the North Korean that the Central Committee of the Soviet Communist party formally "saluted" its North Korean comrade and his gallant troops in "the great liberational struggle of the Korean people." On a personal level, Stalin urged Kim not to be "embarrassed" by the lack of "solid successes in the war against the interventionists." Periodic setbacks were a part of war. Kim replied several days later with a gushy note of thanks to "you, our dear teacher" and promised "final victory" against the evil Americans.[75]

Almost as soon as the United Nations had voted on June 27 to oppose aggression in Korea, British Prime Minister Clement Attlee nominated himself as peacemaker. He instructed his ambassador in Moscow, David Kelly, to contact Deputy Foreign Minister Andrey Gromyko to determine the Soviet attitude. Gromyko responded with his own question: Did London have any proposal to make? Status quo ante, Kelly promptly replied. Nothing more was heard in the West about the Attlee proposal. Stalin cabled Peking on July 13 that he considered Kelly's suggestion "impertinent and unacceptable."[76] When Kelly's American counterpart, Alan Kirk, heard of the démarche, he promptly cabled Acheson in Washington that status quo ante had to be clarified. It should mean, Kirk added, that North Korea had to comply absolutely with the United Nations' June 27 call for a cease-fire and withdrawal of all NKPA units to north of the parallel.[77]

This was also the position of some in Washington. When Acheson on the day of the UN resolution asked George Kennan to brief the NATO ambassadors "on what it [the United States] was trying to do in Korea," Kennan "innocently assured them that we had no intention of doing more than to restore the *status quo ante*."[78] But China's international status complicated the situation.

In early July, British Foreign Minister Ernest Bevin told U.S. Ambassador Lewis Douglas that an "'influential'" group in the British Foreign Office was eager to use the Korean War as a means of getting the Chinese Communists into the United Nations. Bevin then wrote Acheson that, according to British sources in Moscow, the Kremlin really did wish to restore the status quo ante in Korea but that Truman had made this impossible by reversing the U.S. position on Formosa. Bevin urged that Truman not endanger "Western solidarity" by advocating continued Formosan independence from Peking but to use the June 27 resolution solely to work for peace in Korea. Acheson went to Truman, and the two men drafted a reply, dated July 10, in which they bluntly told the British that American policy was "aimed at as early and complete a liquidation of the Korean aggression as was militarily possible, without concessions that would whet Communist appetites and bring on other aggressions elsewhere." Moreover, the Formosa issue would be "disposed" of either through a peace treaty with Japan or by the United Nations. If the United Nations dealt with the questions of either Formosa or Chinese representation, Truman and Acheson added, the United States "regarded it essential" that the issues "be considered on their merits and not under the duress and blackmail then being employed."[79]

Having suffered stinging rebuffs in both Moscow and Washington, Attlee and Bevin backed off after warning the Americans that the West should not drive Communist China into Stalin's arms and insisting that Britain wanted both the Soviet Union and Red China on the UN Security Council. The government of India then took up the issue, but several weeks of muddled communications among New Delhi, Peking, Moscow, Washington, London, and New York only stiffened American resolve to cut no deals with communism to end the war.

But the British and especially the Indian initiatives had raised a question that had to be answered. Assuming that UN forces could hang on in Korea, what was the future of the peninsula to be, and who would define it? Kennan found to his horror that as the stressful days and weeks of July and August passed, his colleagues were becoming convinced that Washington, working through the United Nations, should determine the future of all Korea.

Discussions began during the preparation of responses to London and New Delhi regarding Chinese Communist admission to the United Nations. Peking could not be allowed to threaten or shoot its way into Lake Success; that would be rewarding the aggressor because Washington and the country were becoming convinced by the end of the summer that the Chinese Communists not only had been behind Pyongyang's invasion of South Korea but might soon intervene themselves to ensure communist dominance of the peninsula.

Washington and MacArthur's headquarters in Tokyo had been vaguely aware of the "reciprocal accommodations" between Kim and Mao. They knew that during the Chinese civil war North Korean units had "shuttled" into Manchuria and back "to gain battle seasoning fighting the Nationalists," and some Red Chinese units, "under heavy pressure" from Chiang's forces, had "used North Korea as a sanctuary, crossing into one corner of it when pursued, pausing a while for rest and rehabilitation, and then slipping into Manchuria again across Korea's northwest border." In the vicious fighting around Taegu in early July a unit of the hard-pressed Twenty-Fourth Division claimed they had captured a Chinese soldier; some days later, an NKPA prisoner of war reported that several units of the PLA were operating on their own north of the battle line. Both reports and several others during the next month or so were checked out; none proved to be true.[80]

But Washington and the country were unnerved. As early as July 5, Acheson was asked at his weekly press and radio conference whether he had "any information about what the Chinese Communists are trying to do in Korea." No, Acheson replied. "There are various rumors and reports that reach us but there are no authenticated data on the subject at all." The issue was again raised at the end of August. In the context of an Indian proposal to let six nonpermanent members of the Security Council work out a Korean settlement, Acheson was asked what Washington was doing "to discourage the Chinese communists in getting into the war in Korea." The secretary's response was two-edged and in terms of the unfolding realities of the Korean War was ambiguous and even misleading. Both in word and deed, Acheson maintained, through the Voice of America and other channels, the United States was seeking to reassure Peking that it had no aggressive intent either in Korea, the Formosa Strait, "or in regard to any other question" involving China. But American forbearance had decided limits: "Now, for any one to join with the North Koreans, in the hostilities in Korea, is to join in what the United Nations has branded as an aggression. . . . That is being made very clear to everybody, not only through ourselves but through all the members of the United Nations who are supporting the action."[81]

While Washington pondered the possibility of Chinese intervention, the Chinese were asking why the United States was meddling in a local revolutionary struggle. Washington's response to the NKPA invasion had been so swift, its protection of Formosa so immediate, that Mao feared the United States had designs on the fledgling Chinese Communist regime and would use the Korean conflict as an instrument and excuse for starting a war against Peking.[82] As soon as the North Koreans moved across the parallel, Mao ordered antiaircraft units of his PLA to cross the Yalu to the Korean city of Sinuiju in order to protect the bridges crossing the river. Less than two weeks later, he ordered seasoned PLA units into Manchuria.

Washington soon learned of these activities, and its alarmed reaction quickly spread to the public sector. A week after PLA forces arrived in Manchuria, *Newsweek* reported that elements of the Chinese Communist army were "moving up to the [North] Korean border." These actions suggested to the editors of the magazine that Stalin was trying to get Washington embroiled in an outright war with Peking, which would further tie down America's strategic forces in a remote corner of the world, permitting Soviet military adventurism elsewhere. Throughout the remainder of July and August, the prospect of a sudden Chinese Communist intervention in Korea to help the NKPA knock out the Naktong bridgehead haunted both policymakers and pundits.[83]

The summer of 1950 was clearly not a good time to make concessions to Peking—or so many Washington officials believed. Just two weeks after Truman had ordered the Eighth Army to Korea, Presidential Assistant George

Elsey queried the National Security Council about future strategy. To the best of his knowledge, Elsey wrote, no decision had been reached about what would happen once the NKPA was driven back to the thirty-eighth parallel. Was the question even being discussed anywhere in the government? The Pentagon seemed to be making assumptions about men and equipment required in Korea "without knowing whether our forces are to stop at the 38th parallel or continue north to the Manchurian Border. It seems to me," Elsey concluded, "that this matter should be considered at a very early date by the United States Government, and that we should press for the United Nations' answer to this question." Elsey asked NSC Executive Secretary James Lay for an early appointment to pursue the issue.[84]

But it was State, not the White House, that first began discussing the issue in some detail. As early as July 1, John M. Allison, director of the department's Office of Northeast Asian Affairs wrote to Rusk that any suggestion in the president's forthcoming speech on Korea that UN forces would stop at the parallel was foolish. "Peace and stability in Korea" could only be assured by terminating the "artificial division at the 38th parallel."[85] Kennan, however, thought that intelligently conceived concessions to the communist world might be the only way out of a deepening quagmire. His arguments merely hardened positions against any policy that would not give Washington—or at least the United Nations—control over the future of all Korea.

Kennan was becoming deeply disturbed that Dulles, Rusk, and others were beginning to convince Acheson and Truman to pursue an aggressive rather than a defensive policy in Korea. Dulles was a captive of public opinion, Kennan believed. "With Rusk and some of the others, I think there was a real sense of moral indignation about the Chinese Communists." Kennan first became alarmed just before Acheson's daily morning meeting on July 21, when two of his staffers came in to express concern "that we were not making clear our determination to stop at the 38th parallel in Korea." Kennan stated his own anxieties a few moments later to Acheson and his colleagues. Although the U.S. intervention had been undertaken "for good political reason," it was essentially "an unsound thing, and . . . the further we were to advance up the peninsula the more unsound it would become from the military standpoint." If UN forces went much beyond the neck of the peninsula, "we would be getting into an area where mass could be used against us." It is not clear whether Kennan's reference to the "neck" meant the thirty-eighth parallel or the region about sixty miles above it that ran from the east coast port of Wonsan to Pyongyang. It was essential, Kennan concluded perceptively, that the United States and United Nations be "able to terminate our action at the proper point."[86]

Kennan enjoyed initial support for his position from the Pentagon. On July 21, the Joint Chiefs submitted a paper to the National Security Council in which they warned against any "excessive commitment of United States military forces and resources in those areas of operations which would not be decisive." Should America's slender military resources become tied down on a remote Asian peninsula, the Kremlin would be free to move into Western Europe and the Middle East and the Chinese Communists into other parts of Asia that were of much greater importance to American security objectives than Korea. Ten days later, however, the Chiefs reversed themselves, informing Truman directly that occupation of North Korea was desirable if the Soviet Union did not intervene and "the United States would mobilize sufficient resources to attain the objective and strengthen its military position in all other areas of strategic importance."[87] In other words, war in Korea was worthwhile if it would stimulate a major rearmament program—which it did.

The same day that the Joint Chiefs began advocating a military advance into North Korea, Kennan received a draft paper in which the State Department's Bureau of United Nations Affairs urged that if and when the Security Council began debating the future of Korea, U.S. Ambassador Warren Austin should propose not only that the NKPA withdraw to the thirty-eighth parallel but that the UN commander (MacArthur) disarm the North Korean army and that Pyongyang then transfer government authority to him "in order that he might create order throughout all of Korea." Elections under UN auspices would then be held in every part of the peninsula. Dulles was already exploring the option of a UN advance beyond the parallel, which appealed to conservatives on Capitol Hill. It also appealed to MacArthur. As early as Independence Day, he had tasked his subordinates to begin considering the feasibility of an amphibious landing behind enemy lines, which, with proper reinforcements, could begin as early as July 22. On July 7, the day he was appointed UN commander, MacArthur informed the Joint Chiefs that he first planned to halt the North Korean advance and then mount the amphibious operation that would "'compose and unite'" Korea. On August 17, in response to an Indian request for a U.S. statement of peace terms, Austin informed the General Assembly that the Security Council had set as its first objective ending North Korea's breach of the peace. "'This objective must be pursued in such a manner that no opportunity is provided for another attempt at invasion.'" Two days later, Austin told the Security Council that Korea could not be left "'half slave and half free.'"[88]

Kennan had begun to present an alternative during Acheson's morning meeting on July 11, even as the first stories about a possible Chinese Communist intervention in Korea were alarming the country. There seemed to be "a serious difference of policy between the Soviet and Chinese Communist governments," Kennan told his colleagues, and the dispatch of the Eighth Army to the peninsula was, after all, only a "negative response" by the United States and United Nations to an obvious communist provocation. Washington should not ignore other possibilities for solving the crisis. Above all, the seating of Red China in the United Nations and termination of the Korean conflict should be separated to allow a maximum opportunity to split the Chinese Communists from the Russians "on issues of real importance." Moscow, Kennan continued, could be seriously embarrassed by a sudden U.S. willingness to admit Peking to the United Nations and the Security Council. The United States could simply make clear to the rest of the world that it neither supported nor approved of the Peking regime, but since that regime had come to power in an internationally recognized fashion, Washington would neither block its admission to the United Nations nor feel obliged to open diplomatic relations with it.[89]

The whole controversy was silly, Kennan concluded. Peking's admission to the United Nations would not harm the United States. Then Kennan went too far: "I hate to see what seems to me a minor issue, on which we should never have allowed ourselves to get hooked in the first place, become something which the Russians can use to our disadvantage in the Korean affair."[90] The Soviet archives clearly indicate that Kennan badly misread the relationship that existed between Moscow and Peking in 1950. But he was correct in assuming that that relationship was not and never could be static. To ignore Peking's existence in the context of the Korean War and to demand that the international community do so was simply foolish.

Yet that was exactly what Dulles, Rusk, and others did. "I was shouted down," Kennan wrote in his daily diary. Dulles emphasized that if Washington allowed Peking's admission to the United Nations "in the belief that we were thereby buying some Russian concessions about Korea; . . . it would therefore look to our public as though we had been tricked into giving up something for nothing." This was not what Kennan had said, but he did not respond to Dulles's outburst.[91]

Eleven days later, the issue was again debated at the secretary's meeting. Either then or sometime that same day, Paul Nitze, Kennan's deputy on the Policy Planning Staff, raised further objections to the forcible reunification of Korea. Any such effort would be militarily risky. The United Nations would never sanction it, and the Soviets would correctly perceive it as a clear threat to their national security. Driving the NKPA out of the South with heavy casualties would be sufficient. Kennan repeated his conviction that Washington should accept Peking's UN admission in order to provide the United States with foreign-policy options not available if the Chinese Communists were continually ignored. "I can see, myself, no fundamental objection from the standpoint of US interest to the seating of the Chinese Communists, provided we still wish to cling to the principle that the UN is a universal organization and can eventually be of some use in the adjusting of relationships between East and West." Kennan reminded his associates that when the United Nations had been founded five years earlier, Americans were highly skeptical of Russia's commitment to democratic values and procedures. Moreover, to gain Stalin's support, FDR had agreed to the separate admission of the Ukraine and Belorussia to the United Nations although they were obviously integral parts of the Soviet Union. But everyone had known then and should know in 1950 "that we would be dealing with an organization in which a certain number of the other members had political purposes antagonistic to ours." The United Nations had not been established as a reward for peace-loving countries but as an international peacekeeping agency with members included because of "existing fact."[92]

Dulles again led the opposition. If the Red Chinese were seated at Lake Success, "it would confuse American public opinion and weaken support for the President's program looking toward the strengthening of our defenses." Acheson agreed. Kennan, although he understood Dulles's argument, "shuddered over the implications of it; for it implied that we could not adopt an adequate defense position without working our people up into an emotional state, and this emotional state, rather than a cool and unemotional appraisal of national interest, would then have to be the determinant of our action."[93] It was too late. The nation was already captive to the emotionalism that Kennan so rightly feared.

7

The Politics of Hysteria

❖ ❖ ❖ ❖ ❖ ❖ ❖ ❖ ❖ ❖ ❖ ❖ ❖ ❖ ❖ ❖

Modern conflict involves three realities—taxes, casualties, and controls—
repugnant to democratic peoples everywhere. To overcome that repug-
nance, to place their sons and their dollars under the absolute direction of
a distant federal government, Americans have worked themselves up—and
allowed themselves to be worked up—into frenzies of commitment that
flowed easily into persecution of various "alien" elements within their
midst. During the Civil War, northern intellectuals strove to define an
acceptable ideology of "Americanism," insisting that the "'sacred cause of
government itself'" justified sweeping suppressions of unpopular speech
and organizations. In this century, long-simmering prejudices against specific immigrant or ethnic groups—German-Americans in 1917–18, Japanese-
Americans, blacks, and Hispanics during World War II—quickly exploded
into outright persecution. Woodrow Wilson understood his countrymen's
temperament perfectly. "Once lead this people into war," he told New York
journalist Frank Cobb in the spring of 1917, "and they'll forget there ever
was such a thing as tolerance. To fight you must be brutal and ruthless, and
the spirit of ruthless brutality will enter into the very fibre of our national
life, infecting Congress, the courts, the policeman on the beat, the man in
the street."[1] In 1950, another war focused public rage more obsessively than
ever before on another long-perceived enemy of the established Anglo-
American way of life: the Communist.

❖ ❖ ❖

Joe McCarthy was largely silent that summer, but his influence grew steadily. On July 20, the special Senate Foreign Relations subcommittee had finally completed its report on the validity of McCarthy's charges against the State Department. They were, Millard Tydings and his colleagues formally stated, groundless. There were no communist spy rings in Acheson's shop, no pro-communist foreign policies, nothing. Tydings and the others were respected men, and many of them had seniority in the upper chamber. McCarthy was a reckless political freebooter. The issue should have been dropped. It was not.

For in a few short months McCarthy had become twentieth-century America's first and most effective political gossip- and scandalmonger. He brought to Washington the techniques of sensationalism, revelation, and celebrity bashing recently perfected elsewhere by people like Walter Winchell and Louella Parsons. Roget's *Thesaurus* classifies gossip as news and vice versa. McCarthy did as much as anyone to blur any distinction between the two. The upheavals of the 1920s and 1930s—the abrupt cycles of boom and bust, the sudden dominance of urban life and values, the emergence of a consumer economy, and, perhaps most important, the creation of an information industry grounded in mass circulation newspapers, radio, and the movies—had created an excitable, freewheeling, and impersonal popular style in the nation. A handful of intuitive, opportunistic entrepreneurs like Winchell, "Cholly Knickerbocker," and later Leonard Lyons in New York and Parsons and Hedda Hopper in Hollywood exploited the situation. They used gossip and scandal to tear down the walls that wealth, privilege, power, and fame had erected. They revealed that the glitterati—the few on Wall Street, Broadway, and Hollywood who shaped the public economy and public taste—were just like the rest of the country and often a good bit worse.[2] Gossip both created and reflected the cult of celebrity. Its task was to inform and titillate but also, under masters like Winchell, to hold the high and mighty to account and to humiliate them whenever possible. The ultimate goal of any really good gossip was scandal and its handmaiden disgrace.

Gossip as news and politics came late to Washington, D.C., because the capital had been a national backwater until World War II. Even the New Deal had not changed its folkways. Before 1941 the power center of the country was in New York City—on Wall Street and Broadway and in the great publishing houses that lined Fifth Avenue and were scattered around other parts of Manhattan. Throughout the twenties, presidents had been dull and Congress even duller. During the depression decade, a dynamic

FDR dominated the city and indeed the country, but he was not a rich source of rumor despite strenuous efforts by hostile press lords to demean his wife Eleanor and his occasionally rakehell sons.

But as Washington became a national and then a world power center after Pearl Harbor and as its bureaucratic population burgeoned, a culture of gossip and scandal began to emerge. There was Cissy Patterson, owner of the *Washington Times-Herald*, an inveterate Roosevelt hater who manufactured wild, irresponsible tales about the president. There was Drew Pearson, the ultimate gossip. "When an embittered government employee, a jilted woman friend or an angry former wife had dirty and embarrassing information and wanted to settle a score, Pearson was the man to call. He promised and delivered anonymity. He took telephone calls in drugstores and sidewalk phone booths" because he was convinced that his phones were tapped. "It made him famous, made him rich, and since he thought being attacked by politicians and publishers made him more credible to the reading public, he was delighted when Roosevelt at a press conference called him 'a chronic liar.'" He was equally pleased when he heard Patterson say that she wished she was still in Chicago "'so I could have that son of a bitch rubbed out.'"[3] But Patterson and even Pearson engaged in little more than petty bickering inside the Washington community. Before McCarthy, no one had held that community up to the ruthless, unrelenting scrutiny of the country at large.

To be effective, gossiping and scandalmongering need an important subject. By 1950, Korea, communism, and big government gave McCarthy all the subjects he needed. The U.S. government was now deeply involved in the most intimate aspects of nearly everyone's life. It set the rules that allowed the citizen to get welfare, and it told that citizen how long and under what conditions he or she could have it. Washington told the farmer what to plant and how much he would get for his crops. It told the businessman what guidelines he would have to follow when conducting his business and dealing with his workers. The government shaped the future of America's young depending on its military manpower needs. And after June 25, Washington told many of America's youths that they, like their older brothers, fathers, and grandfathers before them, might have to die for their country.

The Nebraska farmer, the Chicago businessman, the unemployed San Francisco or New York husband, and the Georgia or Idaho schoolboy did not care whether a deputy assistant secretary of state or commerce, the head of the Bureau of Labor Statistics, or any other faceless bureaucrat was cheating on his wife or whether Senator Jones or Congressman Smith was jumping from bed to bed. But they definitely cared when McCarthy suddenly gave one of those faceless bureaucrats or congressmen an identity and revealed to all that he had caused the kind of mischief that was sending American boys to die in Korea. When a U.S. senator—given authority merely by his position—began gossiping about communists in government and produced for the cameras and reporters a sweating diplomat or professor-consultant who really did shape national policy, the public became just as intrigued as it was with the peccadilloes of a Hollywood star or a drunken Wall Street tycoon.

There were so many questions about these formerly faceless people who had wielded such control over American lives from behind the scenes: Who had helped Acheson "lose" China? Who might have whispered in Truman's ear that the effort to root out Commies in the postwar federal establishment was a red herring? McCarthy provided the answers.

Korea made McCarthy a star. Without the war, the senator probably could not have sustained his crusade of gossip, scandal, and innuendo. The war suddenly made the Red menace an immediate instead of an abstract reality. Soured Republican conservatives could proclaim in 1938 that there were communists in the New Deal and in the industrial labor unions that Roosevelt had encouraged. Later they could condemn Yalta or Potsdam. But, for the average American, these were abstractions. Even Soviet possession of the bomb was somewhat of an abstraction because the Russians had not yet seemed inclined to use outright military aggression to achieve their imperialist ends. Korea changed all that. Suddenly communists were killing hundreds and then thousands of American boys. Main Street and rural America could read the mounting casualty figures every week in a small box prominently displayed on the first news page of *Time*. Communism had become a clear and present danger, and Joe McCarthy was asking why this had happened, using the attractive context of gossip and scandal, which relied on the unsubstantiated allegation for maximum effect.

McCarthy did not go away simply because Tydings and the Senate Foreign Relations subcommittee implied that he should. He had raised too many questions and stung too many sensibilities within Washington's liberal establishment. Instead of ignoring him, liberal and even moderate columnists obsessed about McCarthy throughout the midcentury summer, enhancing and legitimatizing what had earlier seemed an unsavory or at least a questionable reputation. Eleanor Lattimore wrote a two-part essay in *Harper's Magazine* describing what it was like for her husband to be maligned by such a miscreant. Alfred Friendly, a veteran *Washington Post* journalist, combed the record of McCarthy's springtime assault on the State Department and showed how shabby the senator's allegations and conduct had been. Liberal Supreme Court Justice Robert H. Jackson, who had earned a reputation as an outstanding international jurist during the Nuremberg trials of 1945–46, declared that if the delicate balance between liberty and authority were to be maintained, Congress had no right to pass laws "that call for a disclosure of belief unconnected with any overt act."[4]

At the end of July, Joseph and Stewart Alsop published an essay in the *Saturday Evening Post* titled "Why Has Washington Gone Crazy?" They described a city experiencing a "miasma of fear and suspicion," where "no man entirely trusts another," and emphasized and reemphasized how new this feeling was. Of course, personal hatreds, jealousies, and conflicts had always existed within the capital's political community. There had been confusions and ineptitudes that were inevitable in a democratic form of government. But such tensions and failings had occurred in a context of "friendly openness," which set the city "off from any other world capital" and had derived "essentially from a simple, unshakable confidence in the American future." Now that confidence was "seeping away."[5]

Until 1945, it had been easy to forge and maintain political friendships in Washington. Politicians and newsmen had considered themselves allies rather than adversaries. Reporters had been the liaison men between responsible government and the public, explaining Washington's policies and the rationale behind them. Now the U.S. government, "like a man on the edge of a nervous breakdown, has . . . suddenly and sickeningly lost its confidence in itself."[6]

The symbols of this loss of confidence were the wiretap, the endless and repeated security checks, and a growing cult of secrecy. The Alsops spoke with an "energetic, intelligent" civil servant who calmly talked about who might be wiretapped and who would not. Acheson's security people, he said, routinely came into the secretary's office one night a week at different hours to search for bugs. "An able foreign-service officer" with an expertise in those communist heresies especially intolerable to Stalin remarked casually but with a tinge of bitterness that he was undergoing his fifth loyalty check. By this time, it had become axiomatic that anyone who was interested in communism might be a communist. The man expected he would be cleared again, but he could never be sure. Bureaucrats whose doors were formerly open to journalists now refused to see them. Many officials had recently concluded that the policies of the U.S. government were "none of the American public's damned business," an understandable view when frank explanations of policy could get an individual labeled as a communist traitor or at least a "dupe." To protect themselves from slanderous and baseless charges, government people "tenderly stamp[ed] TOP SECRET in lavender ink on almost any piece of information, however meaningless or however publicly available."[7]

Who was responsible for this neurotic atmosphere at the center of government? The Alsops rightly placed substantial blame on Truman. He was, after all, the president, and he had permitted a schizophrenic atmosphere to develop throughout his administration. On the one hand, Acheson preached about the need to stand up to the real and powerful Red menace, to make the necessary sacrifices in taxes, controls, and service to country to confront effectively and wear down eventually Stalin's "new Soviet empire." On the other hand, Defense Secretary Louis Johnson had allied with the Republican conservatives in Congress, who constantly preached economy in government and applauded Johnson every time he said (as he often did) that "we can lick hell out of Joe Stalin." Truman, the Alsops observed acidly, believed both of his subordinates.[8]

There were two Harry Trumans, the Alsops maintained. One had told George Marshall in 1947 that he would back him unconditionally, that he, the president, would do whatever was required for the national security and defense. The other went behind Marshall's back the next year and proposed sending Supreme Court Justice Carl Vinson on a diplomatic mission to Moscow to cut a deal with Stalin. There was the presidential Truman, the fighter against communist encroachment who supported the Marshall Plan, aid to Greece and Turkey, and the Point IV technical assistance program. There was also the graduate of the Pendergast school of Kansas City machine politics, "who likes to put his poker-playing cronies, the Harry Vaughans and the Mon C. Wallgrens, in positions of trust and power." The first requisite of leadership was to tell the people the truth, however unpalatable or painful. But Truman fed his fellow citizens "a bewildering mixture . . . of some truths, many half-truths, and quite a few untruths."[9]

Yet the president was not exclusively or even primarily to blame. America had endured weak leadership before. The real villains were the fundamentalist conservative Republicans in Congress. Still deeply tinged with prewar isolationism, unwilling to grant the federal government the needed funds and power for an international movement to contain communism, the Tafts, Wherrys, and McCarthys had successfully covered up their own "pinch-penny response" to the dangers of Soviet world domination by assiduously proclaiming that the paramount threat to American security and liberty came not from without but from within. By choosing this political path, the fundamentalist conservatives had aligned themselves with some of the most unsavory persons in national life.[10]

Diplomats had good reason to fear that McCarthy's agents were spying on them. A visit to the senator's Capitol Hill "lair," the Alsops reported, was like touring the set of a cheap Hollywood gangster movie. "The anteroom is generally full of furtive-looking characters who look as though they might be suborned State Department men." McCarthy, "despite a creeping baldness and a continual tremor which makes his head shake in a disconcerting fashion" (the onset of severe alcoholism, although the reporters were too polite or too intimidated to mention it), played the role of the square-jawed, tough Hollywood private eye. Telephone in hand, shouting cryptic messages ("'Yeah, yeah, I can listen, but I can't talk. Get me? Yeah? You really got the goods on the guy?'"), the senator constantly glanced up at visitors from above hunched shoulders to see the effect of his dramatics. ("'Yeah? Well, I tell you. Just mention this sort of casual to Number One, and get his reaction, okay?'")[11]

It was not only tawdry; it was childish. But because McCarthy's tactics worked, they imposed childishness on the entire government and country. The Alsops observed with distaste Wherry's attempt "to elevate the subject of homosexuality to the level of a serious political issue" involving national security. Such prurience degraded everyone. An inquiring reporter for the *Washington Post* had innocently asked a man standing in a movie line where he worked. "Rather sheepishly" the gentleman replied the State Department. "The whole line broke into snickering laughter." Another journalist asked a cab driver to take him to the department's new building in Foggy Bottom. "The taxi man turned round in his seat and grinned. 'Fruits,' he said, 'the whole place is fulla fruits and treachers [i.e., traitors].'"[12]

The results of this spreading rot of paranoia were threefold. First and foremost, the worst factions in the U.S. political system were persuading the country "that the cheap pleasures of the smear and the spy chase are an adequate substitute for the long, hard effort which this country must make if the free world is to survive." Second, many good men were leaving government service permanently. The Alsops mentioned two. One was a highly respected, thoughtful State Department official with years of experience observing the Soviet system (probably Kennan). His insights were irreplaceable. Instead of continuing to try to promote and protect the national interest, he was going to a university, where he would spend the remainder of his working life pondering and perhaps doing a little teaching. The second individual, a big, red-faced, cheerful air force general, was the antithesis of the State Department man, whom McCarthy would undoubtedly label another "twisted intellectual." The general had played professional football in the twenties, gotten interested in flying, and had achieved a superb combat record during World War II. He was leaving the Pentagon because "I just decided one day the whole thing stank, and the hell with it." A "smog of mediocrity" had settled over the capital, and he would not work in such a climate. "If there's another war, I can get back in," he told the Alsops; then he corrected himself: "When there's another war."[13]

The last observation deeply disturbed the two journalists, for the general and the diplomat, so different in temperament and background, shared one conviction, the third result of declining political courage and morality. Because Truman's America was blundering about in a fog of fear and an obsession with internal security, because it had responded so ineffectively to a Korean War that should never have happened, there would inevitably be a World War III. The general, the diplomat, and many others like them had lost faith in their country's ability to avoid calamity by returning to common sense and courage.

Moral erosion first expressed itself in predictable but respectable calls to *do something.* Senator William Benton (Democrat of Connecticut), sporting a bright blue suit and a pink carnation, told colleagues on the Senate Foreign Relations Committee that Korea might never have happened if the United States had possessed a strong propaganda machine. America needed to take the ideological offensive against the Reds. David Sarnoff, chairman of RCA, promptly submitted a fifteen-page statement proposing to "ring" the iron curtain countries with a powerful radio network. It would cost only $200 million, Sarnoff added. The climax came long-distance. Movie mogul Sam Goldwyn called the committee from New York and insisted that the United States needed a Hollywood press agent with a billion-dollar budget to overcome Moscow's ideological offensive. *Newsweek* printed a page-long story detailing "snafus" in the Point Four technical assistance program that could have inadvertently weakened the ability of Chiang's forces on Formosa to resist an impending communist invasion.[14]

In July and August, as the stalemate continued along the Naktong perimeter with no resolution in sight, the mood in Congress and the country turned ugly. The pent-up frustrations of nearly a year of setbacks, real and imagined, were behind Wherry's impassioned cry that "the blood of our boys in Korea" was on Acheson's shoulders. Moderate Republicans privately admitted that the secretary's policies in Europe had been about as successful as was possible. But he had failed in the Far East, and since 1950 was an election year, that failure had to be exploited. "The Amerasia case, the Alger Hiss case, and the charges of Sen. Joe McCarthy had left a deep imprint on the public mind," *Newsweek* concluded. "The Far Eastern fiasco, to the Republicans, was Dean Acheson's baby and they were set on leaving it at his doorstep." The four Republican members of the Senate Foreign Relations Committee, including hospitalized Arthur Vandenberg, added more fuel to the foreign-policy debate by charging that Roosevelt's "'blunders'" at Yalta and Truman's follies at Potsdam had given Stalin a "'green light' in the Far East." Republican presidential hopeful Harold Stassen came close to what angry fundamentalist conservatives were really thinking when he stated that the Truman administration "has sown so many pink seeds that now the American people must reap a red whirlwind."[15]

MacArthur compounded the administration's woes. At the end of July, he made a quick trip to Formosa, which was authorized by the Pentagon but not the White House. The general immediately embraced Chiang (whom he had never met before) as a valiant fellow fighter against the Red menace. The White House could say nothing; this was no time to engage in public debate with the supreme UN commander. But liberals were appalled, declaring that MacArthur had injected the United States into the Chinese civil war and in the process had "shouldered aside the civilian authority and policies of the US Government." Was the general drawing the United States and the United Nations into a war with Communist China?[16]

On August 24, Mao publicly condemned the United States for meddling in Chinese internal affairs, and a week later Malik, who had returned to

New York at the beginning of the month to resume his Security Council seat and assume the Council's rotating chairmanship, placed Mao's accusations on the Council agenda. MacArthur apparently felt compelled to respond to this modest communist diplomatic offensive with a counterattack. He replied to a routine request by the Veterans of Foreign Wars for a message to their annual convention by stating flatly that Formosa had become essential to free-world security. Then he challenged the authority of his commander in chief: "Nothing . . . could be more fallacious than the threadbare argument" of those who advocated appeasement and defeatism in the Pacific that "if we defend Formosa we alienate continental Asia." Those who employed such reasoning did not "understand the Orient."[17]

Truman and his wise men were outraged. The president ordered Louis Johnson to wire MacArthur, demanding an immediate retraction. Johnson promised he would but then went to the Joint Chiefs, who cravenly complained that it would not do to embarrass the great man in Tokyo. Eventually Truman had to telephone Johnson and dictate the recantation order to MacArthur. Within days, the president used the incident to force his weeping secretary of defense to resign. Meanwhile Luce had published key portions of MacArthur's message in *Time*.[18]

Truman's "gag" of MacArthur generated a fresh burst of fury from both fundamentalist conservatives and Republican moderates. Senator William Knowland claimed that the president's action was just "another in the long series of efforts to keep the truth from the American people." Wherry promised that Truman's action "will be resented by every American," and Joe Martin, the Republican House leader, declared that the public would view Truman's action as "another flagrant example of the incurable bungling which delivered Manchuria and most of China to the Communists and which culminated in the Korean war."[19]

Truman immediately became embroiled in another quarrel with his conservative tormentors when he nominated Marshall to replace Johnson. The nomination was popular with almost everyone except the fundamentalist conservatives, who had never forgiven Marshall for ostensibly contributing to the fall of China by failing to bring the communists under Nationalist control during his 1946–47 mission and for blaming Chiang as vigorously as Mao for the breakdown in negotiations. Another "Comsymp" was about to return to government. Knowing Marshall's towering reputation as one of the architects of victory in World War II, Taft and Knowland shrewdly argued that the former general was forbidden by the provisions of the 1947

National Security Act from becoming defense secretary because he had been out of uniform less than ten years. Clearly the law would have to be modified. This was not good enough for William Jenner, who denounced the nomination as "a staggering swindle, a horrifying hoax." Marshall "is not only willing, he is eager to play the role of a front man for traitors. . . . Marshall is a living lie."[20] Even Luce was infuriated by Jenner's extremism. Liberal and moderate senators gripped the arms of their chairs while Jenner spewed his hate, but he was neither censured nor reprimanded.

In fact, Americans were tired of the Reds thumbing their noses at the United States and getting away with it. Someone had to pay, and if the Reds abroad could not be stopped, those at home could be. "The people of this country want to see Communists tried for treason," Florida Democrat Charles E. Bennett cried out on the floor of the House. Republican John Jennings, Jr., of Tennessee echoed the cry: "Let us go after them . . . let us leave no stone unturned and no law unwritten."[21]

The impetus for such comments was a bill that passed the House by a count of 354 to 20 on August 30. It was an expanded version of the Mundt-Nixon internal security legislation, which had failed in 1948. Once again Nixon sponsored the bill on behalf of HUAC.[22] His version treated communism "as an outright international conspiracy to overthrow democracy throughout the world." Thus, according to the bill's preamble, "'a clear and present danger faces United States security.'" Employing this premise, the legislation required the Communist Party to register and list all of its members and agents and their activities. This part of the bill could be considered tough but not unreasonable given the feverish climate of the time. The Communist Party *was* dedicated to the violent overthrow of the government of the United States, and an aggressive communist nation was shedding American blood on a distant battlefield.

But the bill's specific provisions would move the United States in the direction of a police state. Most disturbing was the "concentration camp" clause for the internment without trial of all communists during a war or national emergency. Almost equally disquieting was the vague definition of "communist." "Front" organizations, "many of them concededly having as members, many dupes," as the *New York Times* reported smugly, would have to register with the Justice Department. The "dupes" would have the choice of remaining with the front and facing the consequences or getting out and hoping that zealous Red-hunters would abide by the bill's provision that they could do so "without the matter going to the public record." Fines as high as $10,000 and prison sentences of up to ten years would be levied on government officials and employees who knowingly let communist spies get hold of military or other classified materials, and the statute of limitations for this crime would be extended from three to ten years. Federal employment would be denied to communists and their allies, whoever they might be. Normal income tax exemptions would be denied to individuals and groups that helped communist or front organizations financially. Communists and "fellow travelers" would be denied passports and could use the mails for propaganda only when they plainly labeled it as such. The definitions of a communist, a dupe, an ally, a front organization, and a fellow traveler would be left to the discretion of a three-person "subversive-activity control board" created by the legislation.

The comparative handful of critics complained in vain that the proposed bill was unconstitutional and "unconstructive," that it violated basic rights of freedom of speech and of assembly, that it created in the subversive activity control board an unaccountable star chamber that would decide who and what was politically correct and who and what was not. It might be a criminal conspiracy, for example, for two men to agree informally that one of them would run for Congress on the ticket of a party that a particular grand jury had considered subversive. Decisions of the control board regarding alleged communist front organizations could be appealed to a U.S. District Court, but the legislation provided that such decisions would remain conclusive "'if supported by the preponderance of the evidence,'" whatever that meant.

The legislation's many defenders in the House replied, as had so many before them, that the Constitution did not give hostile outsiders the right to destroy the American political system. Nor were the champions of the Nixon bill willing to consider the counterargument of eminent Harvard law professor, Zechariah Chafee, who stated that real subversives would do exactly what Irish rebels in the early part of the century had done when faced with almost identical British legislation. "Every time a particular society [like the Communist Party] was declared unlawful," Chafee fearlessly reminded HUAC, "its former members started a new society to do exactly the same thing." If the new version of the Mundt-Nixon bill became law, "we can expect the formation of a large number of Shakespearian societies,

Dante institutes, chess clubs, indoor-baseball associations, etc. Meanwhile, you will no longer know whether there are 70,000 who are Communists at heart—or 700,000." Chafee's argument was devastating but irrelevant. Nixon, Mundt, and others were not fighting domestic communism. They were persecuting the Fair Deal, and the unwitting public was right behind them.

"From coast to coast," *Time* reported at the end of August, "indignant citizens took after Communists, their party-line friends, and some they just suspected of being party-liners." The *Seattle Times* urged its readers not to be misled by liberal critics who charged that the pending anticommunist legislation was a modern version of the Alien and Sedition Acts of 1798, which Thomas Jefferson, James Madison, and others had denounced so eloquently. The HUAC-inspired bill should be judged on its own merits.[23]

NBC Radio postponed the fall start of its highly popular program *The Aldrich Family* because actress Jean Muir, who had contracted to play the mother, had been identified "as a leftie" by the right-wing blacklisting sheet *Counterattack*. Several national publications subsequently claimed that the Muir case was possibly an example of mistaken or overzealous anticommunism. But no one thought to rehabilitate a talented woman's reputation.[24]

In New Hampshire, Wentworth-by-the-Sea Hotel canceled a scheduled talk by Owen Lattimore after half the guests said they did not want to hear him. In Hollywood, Harry L. Warner, president of Warner Brothers Studios, called a half-hour midday break in the first week of September to lecture two thousand executives, stars, and technicians on the evils of communism. Warner said his studio wanted no communists on its payrolls. "'If they'll come to us,' he added, 'we'll pay their expenses to Russia.'" Over at Metro-Goldwyn-Mayer, Louis B. Mayer approached writer-director John Huston about a project. "Joe McCarthy," Mayer said, "was one of the greatest men of our time." Then he looked at Huston speculatively and said, "John, . . . you've done documentaries. . . . How about doing one that is a tribute to McCarthy?" An appalled Huston replied, "L.B., you're out of your God-damned mind!" and walked away.[25]

The board of the Screen Directors Guild held a referendum in which "a large majority" of those polled voted to make noncommunist oaths mandatory for all members. The board promptly took steps to implement this sentiment by deciding that such an oath should be written into the bylaws of the organization and that anyone refusing to take the oath "should be considered as no longer in good standing." Hollywood's bedroom communities also took action. Los Angeles County and the city of Burbank put new ordinances into effect that week, "requiring all Reds to register as such," and a similar ordinance went before the Los Angeles City Council.[26]

The House internal security bill reached the Senate in early September, as Johnnie Walker was shuffling his reserves around the Naktong perimeter and trying to mount effective counteroffensives while beating off incessant NKPA thrusts and probes. The United States had already suffered fourteen thousand casualties in Korea (killed, wounded, and missing in action), and the numbers kept growing. The White House condemned the House bill and submitted draft legislation of its own that included no provisions for muzzling free speech or registering front groups but did contain a concentration-camp clause to placate the extremists. Truman publicly vowed to veto any legislation of the sort passed by the House.

For nearly three weeks, the senators heatedly debated whether to accept or amend the House bill. Homer Ferguson (Republican of Michigan) sponsored the House legislation in the upper chamber, and Democrats Harley Kilgore of West Virginia and Paul Douglas of Illinois championed the administration's counterproposal. Then Pat McCarran, Nevada's reactionary Democrat and self-styled "lone wolf" of the upper chamber, nominated himself as power broker and submitted a new bill that contained every provision of the House legislation except the concentration-camp clause.

McCarran was an institution in the Senate. Possessing an oversized torso and head capped by a wavy mane of silvery hair, the Nevadan viewed the world with shrewd and wary blue eyes. Few people called him "Pat"; even his wife's best friends called him "Senator." To all, he was a power to be reckoned with, and he fought viciously for those issues that attracted his fancy.[27]

The Senate quickly focused on the McCarran bill, and toward the end, debate became bizarre. Certifiable liberals like Douglas, Hubert Humphrey of Minnesota ("the most vocal of the Fair Deal Senatorial contingent"), and Senate Majority Leader Scott Lucas pleaded for the "moderate" White House proposal, which would establish wartime concentration camps for known communists (whether active or not), but ultraconservatives like McCarran condemned such camps as "a working blueprint for dictatorship" while urging more broadly repressive legislation. No one apparently questioned whether the Korean conflict was a war rather than a "police action." If it was, then presumably all known Reds should be immediately incarcerated under the administration's proposal. It was all complex and confusing, and battered liberals were in a quandary. "I had pictured myself as defending civil liberties," Douglas sighed at one point. "And yet," he added plaintively, "there is a Communist danger in this country."[28]

Douglas and his colleagues argued that the McCarran bill was both impossible to administer and a violation of traditional American freedoms. "The Congress of the United States," Humphrey intoned in the midst of an impassioned four-hour speech, "will regret the day it ever passes S. 4037. . . . It will prove to be one of the darkest pages in American history." McCarran and Ferguson promptly tacked on the administration's concentration-camp clause, then sanctimoniously proposed language that included constitutional guarantees of trial by jury and confrontation of accusers and added it to the McCarran omnibus package. Lucas, clearly outmaneuvered, sighed, "We'll have signs on our concentration camps. They'll read, 'It's not comfortable, but it's constitutional.'"[29]

The McCarran bill passed by a large margin, giving the anticommunist extremists everything they had wanted since Mundt-Nixon.[30] Liberal Democrats were appalled, but they proved to be Democrats first and liberals second. The public mood was aroused, and few dared confront it forty-five days before an off-year election. Several weeks earlier, George Gallup had written that "Washington moves" for more drastic curbs on espionage and sabotage had been widely accepted throughout the country. "But in handling U.S. Communists the public would in some respects go further than President Truman proposes to go." Even before Korea "the overwhelming majority of American voters" favored requiring all members of the U.S. Communist Party to register with the government. "Furthermore, the public would like to see steps taken now to remove all members of the Communist Party from jobs in industries that would be important in war-time. . . . Sentiment for rooting 'bad security risks' out of private employment in war industries is overwhelming—15 to 1." On August 10, American Legion National Commander George N. Craig had demanded a federal law making communism in the United States a crime. In 1947, Gallup wrote, a survey found that Americans favored outlawing the party by a margin of two to one. By December 1949, the ratio had risen to four to one. Finally Gallup reported that in his most recent polls he had asked what the United States should do with communists during a war with the Soviet Union. Imprisonment was the most popular solution, but 13 percent of the public approved of shooting or hanging every one.[31]

Gallup also observed that the public should not be blamed for current "U.S. weakness." The people had long known what wimpy Fair Deal liberals had apparently not learned. In June 1946, 58 percent of Americans polled had said they believed that Soviet Russia was preparing to rule the world. Four years later, just before Korea, the number had risen to 70 percent. In November 1945, 75 percent of those asked had said they favored universal military training. When asked about Truman's statement in early June 1950 that the world was closer to peace than anytime since the end of the war, 57 percent had disagreed. The inference was obvious: The people had recognized the Red menace from the beginning and had been willing to resist it. Liberal Washington was clearly responsible for the country's distress abroad and at home.[32]

Under the circumstances, only a foolhardy politician would identify himself as a Fair Deal liberal when it came to the communist issue. Douglas, Humphrey, Lucas, and nearly every other Democrat voted for the McCarran bill. "They moved," *Newsweek* observed trenchantly, "to protect the Democratic Party from manslaughter at the polls." They did so reluctantly and with much soul-searching. But in the end, they voted not only politically but also emotionally. A war and six months of steady, virulent anticommunism finally wore down the common sense of even the most generous and rational politician.[33] If the war in Korea became a debacle, public outrage might become illimitable.

8

Hubris

On the eighty-third day of combat, as the world peered anxiously at the smoke of battle billowing up from the Pusan perimeter, Douglas MacArthur transformed the Korean War.

The September 15 Allied landing at Inchon that soon had the NKPA reeling back across the thirty-eighth parallel has achieved the status of legend, of heroic myth, for a generation of American conservatives and professional military people. Indeed, Inchon was the last unambiguous U.S. military triumph for forty years. In its wake came a dangerous temptation to alter the East-West balance of power in ways that Stalin and Mao could never accept.

❖   ❖   ❖

Inchon seemed to be MacArthur's finest hour. Whether he was its real architect or whether a contingency plan for such an operation had existed for some time in Pentagon files is unimportant. The assault was inherently dangerous, perhaps foolhardy; "Mac" alone was willing to risk it. In August, Truman had sent a delegation to Tokyo to warn his Far East commander not to get the United States involved in a war with China. MacArthur turned the visit into a warning: Time was running out for the West in Asia. Because of the perceived weakness of American and South Korean forces, Stalin and Mao might throw their armies into Korea at any moment. Only an early victory over the NKPA could forestall a possible prelude to World War III. Moreover, a winter campaign in Korea was a dreaded prospect. Korean winters were as severe as those "in my native state of Wisconsin," and frostbite would be as great a threat to UN forces as enemy bullets.[1] The tide of battle had to be turned immediately, and Inchon was the place to do it.

MacArthur believed that on the one day of September when the tides at Inchon were sufficiently high, the navy could bring X Corps (the First Marine Division and the army's Seventh Infantry Division) across the mud flats guarding the port and that the marines could swiftly scale a daunting seawall and seize the town. Thereafter, the navy would continue to reinforce and resupply X Corps through the single narrow, treacherous channel of water that cut through the flats, permitting U.S. forces to march the twenty miles to Seoul, cut the NKPA supply lines from the north, and trap Chai Ung Jun's forces between the hammer of X Corps and the anvil of the Eighth Army breaking out from the Naktong perimeter.

MacArthur's critics were appalled at his audacity. Seizure of Inchon first demanded a lightning strike to neutralize the island of Wolmi, which sat astride the mud flats and commanded the approaches to the port. Even if the navy got the marines ashore, they would surely be pinned down at the seawall by NKPA forces holding houses on the high ground just above. There would be chaos as the U.S. forces landing behind the marines would also be pinned down on the narrow beach. Surely the communists were aware of Inchon's importance and would garrison the town accordingly.

In fact, intelligence specialists in Moscow and Peking had concluded by mid-August that UN forces, spearheaded by U.S. troops, would soon launch a counteroffensive. Because MacArthur's headquarters made no effort to hide the amphibious buildup occurring in Japan, it was clear that the Americans were preparing to invade one of Korea's six major ports. It was easy to guess Inchon because of its proximity to Seoul. Mao immediately passed the intelligence assessment to the North Korean ambassador in Peking, who quickly sent it to Pyongyang. At the same time, Soviet field advisers "strongly cautioned" their NKPA colleagues "that the Americans would be fools not to attack behind enemy lines to cut the North's communications." Incredibly, Kim Il Sung refused to heed these warnings, and Inchon remained largely undefended.[2]

In a series of August meetings with apprehensive delegations from Washington, MacArthur beat down every criticism, every fear of the Inchon operation.[3] The old warrior was into his eighth decade now, and he projected the ideal image of the American soldier. With his crisp but informally worn khakis, his firm, square jaw, his mouth often clamped tightly around a corn-cob pipe, his resonant voice, and the big sunglasses worn beneath an osten-

tatiously crushed general's cap, MacArthur was every central casting director's dream to play the purposeful general, the father figure to his adoring
men. MacArthur's self-conceit was boundless; he honestly believed that any
part of the world that did not revolve around him or did not immediately
interest him was of little or no account. As Army Chief of Staff in 1932, he
had exceeded his orders from President Hoover and had chased the raggedy
and pathetic army of bonus marchers across the Anacostia Bridge and had
burned their camp because he believed the veterans were the vanguard of
a communist takeover of America. Ever after, MacArthur believed himself
to be one of Moscow's chief targets. "It was the beginning of a definite and
ceaseless campaign that set me apart as a man to be destroyed," he wrote
years later, "no matter how long the Communists and their friends and
advisors had to wait, and no matter what means they might have to use.
But it was to be nineteen years before the bells of Moscow pealed out their
glee at my eclipse."[4] After thirteen years in the Orient, including command
of the allied forces that had won World War II in the Pacific, MacArthur
believed that the Far East belonged to him, and he was eager to destroy the
one man who challenged him: archcommunist Mao Zedong.

Army Chief of Staff J. Lawton Collins later wrote that the landing at Inchon
was the "masterpiece of one man, General Douglas MacArthur."[5] The navy
and marines cooperated brilliantly, the North Koreans were completely surprised, and X Corps raced into Seoul, where the North Korean garrison,
modestly reinforced from above the parallel, put up a ruthless defense before
yielding the ruined city and retreating toward the border. The loss of Seoul
doomed the entire NKPA, for it had been the hub of the North Korean supply, transportation, and communication routes to the Naktong perimeter.

After breaking the NKPA defense of Seoul, X Corps moved south and
east, destroying escape routes. Chai had to withdraw his depleted forces
from the Naktong front, and Johnnie Walker's Eighth Army slowly gathered itself and set out in pursuit. The NKPA withdrawal soon became the
rout that MacArthur had predicted as each man and unit scrambled desperately to escape being trapped between X Corps in front of them and the
Eighth Army behind.

❖   ❖   ❖

The first inevitable moral ambiguities of the war appeared. Critics charged
that indiscriminate use of American firepower had destroyed Seoul.

Defenders of X Corps blamed the NKPA garrison, which had ruined the city through looting and murder just before the Americans arrived and then had deliberately invited further destruction by conducting a useless house-to-house opposition. "The defense of the Korean capital in such a way as to compel its liberators to shatter it was a horrible act of psychological warfare from which it could readily be concluded that the cause was the wanton extravagance of U.N. firepower rather than the wantonness of defenders who called forth such firepower."[6]

Outraged American troops fighting their way through the city saw open graves, into which the enemy had hastily shoveled the bodies of thousands of executed South Korean civilians. Eighth Army troopers moving out of the Naktong perimeter a few days later came across a little knoll on which fifteen or sixteen trenches had been dug. A captain, seeing his men pause and hearing their harsh voices, went over to look. "Buried waist-deep, hands wired behind their backs, agony imprinted on their stark faces, were 500 ROK soldiers and 86 GI's. Some had been bayoneted to death; some had been clubbed; some mercifully, shot. Doc Phelps, looking ill, determined the men had been killed the evening before."[7] Several weeks later, back in power, Syngman Rhee began committing his own atrocities, ordering his dreaded security police to round up thousands of suspected "communists" among Seoul's pitiful survivors. They were promptly marched off to concentration camps, where many were killed.

Famed newsman Edward R. Murrow had come to Korea some weeks before the breakout from the Naktong and had witnessed bitter fighting, retreats, and advances as Walker struggled to hold his lines. The violence of the conflict appalled Murrow, and back in Tokyo, after informing the American public that no one could tell when the war might be over, he reminded his audience that Korea was a "fleabitten" land where the simple peasants had lived on the "knife edge of despair and disaster for centuries." American firepower had created "dead valleys" and "villages to which we have put the torch by retreating." Murrow wondered whether Korea's simple folk could ever understand America's motives or forgive American actions. His message was never broadcast. CBS News decided to suppress it because it was too controversial, but other American editors were more responsible. A month before Inchon, the liberal New Republic had reported that MacArthur "has employed B-29's in area bombing [of north Korea], destroying cities and factories as well as warehouses and railways yards" in "600-ton devastation raids." The peoples of Asia remembered the B-29 from the

terrible last days of World War II. They considered it "a weapon of indiscriminate destruction," not a harbinger of liberation. Did the United Nations
really believe that area bombing of Korea would not entail inestimable political costs?[8]

Such concerns were of little importance to Americans in the month after
Inchon. There was a sudden, giddy transformation in public opinion. To a
nation in which winning was not everything but the only thing, victory itself
obscured its moral as well as human costs. "Clear the track," *Time* exulted,
adding: "Within a matter of hours last week, the nation's whole military
posture changed. . . . After 83 days of defeat, retreat and dogged defense on
the [Naktong] perimeter" MacArthur had launched a strike "which might
well shorten the Korean war by months." *Newsweek*'s headline proclaimed:
"Now It's Put Up or Shut Up for Reds." The United Nations would either
win a "quick victory," or the Kremlin would dictate "a much bigger war,"
and the latter seemed quite unlikely. A week later, *Newsweek* concluded that
reports from Korea were "almost too good to be true. The North Koreans
were going down to swift and bloody defeat with Seoul besieged and their
armies split asunder by American drives." At the end of September, Truman
sent an adulatory message to his field commander, telling MacArthur that
"few operations in military history" could match his "brilliant" delaying
actions in July and August and the audacious Inchon invasion.[9]

Suddenly it seemed that the Korean War had not been so great an ordeal
after all. It was the triumph of World War II replayed in dramatically tele-
scoped time and at greatly reduced cost. On September 24, the *New York
Times* observed that it had been "just three months ago today" that the
NKPA had begun its "war of aggression against the Republic of South
Korea." Seoul had fallen in four days; at that time, the nearest American
troops had been three hundred miles away in Japan, and adequate
weapons for them had been seven thousand miles away in California. Six
weeks later, a comparative handful of American soldiers and their ROKA
allies had been pressed into the narrow Naktong perimeter "with their
backs to the sea." But now "the forces of the United Nations were everywhere on the attack. They were closing in on the bulk of the enemy's
forces." The climactic battle for Korea was about to take place, and the
Times left little doubt as to the outcome. Pictures were worth a thousand

words. The front page of the Sunday *New York Times Magazine* for October 1 showed a South Korean soldier confronting a North Korean soldier with his hands up; the one-word caption read: "Surrender." Two weeks later, the magazine's cover pictured a large truck convoy of U.S. infantrymen on a dirt road with the caption: "Northward in Korea." The *New Republic's* Korea story on October 30 began with the phrase: "with liberation of Korea in sight."[10]

Perhaps this time the enemies of decency had learned their lesson. The editor of the *Portland Oregonian* undoubtedly spoke for many Americans when he observed on September 22 that "if the Korean unpleasantness under the new circumstances ends reasonably soon—and the Russians do not break out somewhere else in the meantime—there will be an answer to certain manpower problems that have been having a grave effect on the temper of the American people." To Washington, "manpower" was simply "a vast array of statistics." But "on Main Street, in the east end, in suburbia, and on the farm" it meant something else. To "the young husband and father who has a start on his home," it meant "'what is the postman going to leave today?'" To the veteran, it meant "'am I going to go back into uniform again? It was cold in the Bulge and I sure hated that captain!' It means to the father, the mother, the aunt, the uncle, the wife: 'Is Joe to be called?'" If the "Korean situation" were indeed going to be "mopped up" soon, stability might return to American life. "Our younger people may at least guess as to where they are likely to be in the next few minutes."[11]

But the imperatives of world power and world politics were remorseless. Washington policymakers and UN ambassadors continued to ponder the wisdom and necessity of taking the war north of the parallel to the doorstep of Communist China. Two weeks before Inchon, the National Security Council, finally responding to growing pressure from within and beyond the White House, noted that three previous UN resolutions had established as political objectives the achievement of a completely independent, united Korea. "If the present United Nations action in Korea can accomplish this political objective without substantial risk of general war with the Soviet Union or Communist China, it would be in our interest to advocate the pressing of the United Nations action to this conclusion." Four days before Inchon Truman approved the NSC recommendation as national policy.[12]

MacArthur won a brilliant victory at Inchon, but the stubborn North Korean defense of Seoul and Walker's hesitancy in moving out of the Naktong perimeter had subsequently compromised it. Instead of battering the

NKPA in conjunction with Inchon, Walker had waited passively until Chai began pulling his troops back, then pursued sluggishly. The expected entrapment of the NKPA between the Eighth Army and X Corps was only partially realized during the last two weeks of September, and although the NKPA was severely damaged, it was not completely destroyed. Washington and its UN allies could no longer evade the question of what to do about Korea.

❖   ❖   ❖

After Inchon, the Truman administration pursued an impossibly ambitious set of policies. On the one hand, it sincerely wished to limit the Korean War and to avoid provoking Peking or Moscow into an intervention that might quickly escalate to World War III and a nuclear exchange. On the other hand, Washington could not resist the opportunity to forcibly reunify Korea under UN auspices. These conflicting policies all swirled together in an off-the-record briefing that Acheson gave on September 2—just thirteen days before Inchon—to four carefully selected reporters from the Washington and New York papers. Acheson knew of the operation; his interlocutors presumably did not. The secretary began with a dramatic introduction to the Korean issue: "Between now and the first of October more important decisions have to be made than perhaps at any time in the history of the Department of State." The United Nations was on record as favoring a politically, socially, and economically united peninsula. How the war would be conducted over the next month within that context "and how we come out of it will have to be discussed and decided." The "business of the 38th parallel" and what the UN forces might do there depended absolutely "on how we get there." Should there be "no sizable armies to fight," should North Korean troops be so thoroughly routed that they "break and run helter-skelter back to North Korea, lose their uniforms, and say they have been working in the fields all the time," then South Korean military and political forces "would probably take care of the situation." But "should Red Korea be defeated and should Russia decide to re-occupy North Korea, that would be another situation."[13] Exactly how the United States and United Nations would react to this "other situation" or whether such a situation would also be created by the intervention of Chinese rather than Soviet troops, Acheson did not say.

In the days just before and after Inchon, policymakers somehow convinced themselves either that they could destroy a communist buffer state, bring unfriendly troops to the borders of a communist superpower, and condemn communist war-mongering without provoking a substantial response or suffering a significant consequence, or that should a communist response materialize it could somehow be handled and contained without the threat of a major war. The only explanation—and excuse—for such a frame of mind is that it was the product of a bitterly divisive and confused domestic politics of anticommunism. Truman, Acheson, and the State Department had been harried, hounded, and humiliated for months over communism in general and China in particular. Now MacArthur had given the administration a spectacular victory that begged to be exploited, and the lawyers at the National Security Council had given the president and administration the legal justification for doing it.

On the day after Inchon, Acheson attempted to open a dialogue with Peking. His medium was the government of India; his tone was a mixture of bravado and apprehension. In a cable to Ambassador Loy Henderson in New Delhi, Acheson asserted that the "situation in Korea has reached [a] critical stage for aggressors." Henderson should inform Indian Foreign Minister Girja S. Bajpai that UN forces might be able to restore peace throughout the peninsula within weeks. The international organization would "view with grave concern Chi Commie intervention." Bajpai was asked to pass these sentiments to his ambassador in Peking, Kavalam Panikkar, who should assure Chinese authorities that the "character of UN action" and "continued UN interest in Korea" would constitute a "solid guarantee" that no threat would "come to China" from a politically united peninsula if peace were restored "along UN lines."[14]

Mao was understandably unimpressed. He remained convinced that "the American war of invasion in Korea has been a serious menace to the security of China from its very start." Peking believed that "the United States deliberately concocted the assault of the Syngman Rhee gang against the Korean Democratic People's Republic in order to expand its aggression in the East and then, on the pretext of the situation in Korea, dispatched its naval and air forces to invade the Taiwan Province of China; [and] announced that the so-called problem of Taiwan's status should be solved by the American-controlled United Nations."[15]

During the first week in August, Mao had concluded that Kim's effort to reunite the peninsula by force had failed. The NKPA needed help against American aggression. When and how that help would be provided depended on the fortunes of war, but Mao was certain that the main struggle for Korea lay ahead and that China's military involvement was inevitable. By September 1, he had mobilized 100,000 troops in northeastern Manchuria near the Yalu River border with North Korea. Hundreds of supporting field hospitals and first-aid stations were established.[16]

For many weeks, "leading Party members" questioned whether the regime should battle "'the world's foremost imperial power.'" There was so much to do at home: The country needed to be reconstructed politically and administratively; huge swatches of the countryside had not been cleared of local guerrilla and warlord forces; the army was still recovering from its struggle against Chiang, the national economy was in shambles; and relations with the Kremlin remained equivocal. Mao was isolated; but with his usual personal courage and stubborn determination, he clung to his position and worked slowly and carefully to persuade his apprehensive colleagues to accept the necessity of intervention.[17]

Inchon threw the entire communist world into a state of paralysis and despair that took nearly a month to dissipate. Of the three major communist players in the Korean War, only the old man in the Kremlin immediately recognized that the old man in Tokyo had fashioned a master stroke. Nine years before, when Hitler had treacherously assaulted the Soviet Union, Stalin's shock had lasted for weeks. Now he reacted decisively. Recently opened Soviet files indicate that whatever Soviet field advisers might have been telling their NKPA clients, Ambassador T. F. Shtykov and General Vasiliev (the chief Soviet military adviser to the NKPA) agreed that Inchon was merely a minor diversion, a mere pinprick meant to distract the North Koreans from mopping up the Naktong front. In their first cable to Stalin after X Corps had forced its way ashore, Shtykov and Vasiliev openly questioned the need for Chai to pull any of his troops away from the Naktong. One final, decisive thrust would throw the UN forces off the cliffs of extreme southeastern Korea, whereupon Chai could dispatch a division or two to wipe out the few Americans around Inchon and Seoul.[18]

Stalin knew better. Mao was ambivalent. Within twenty-four hours after the first elements of MacArthur's troops stormed ashore, Moscow "warned our Korean friends that the landing of the U.S. troops at Chemulp'o [Inchon] had great significance and was aimed at cutting off the First and Second Army Groups of the North Koreans from their rear in the North." That day or the next Stalin cabled Mao, "bluntly stating that China had to save Kim Il Sung." Mao then wrote one of his generals: "Apparently it won't do for us not to intervene in the war. You must accelerate preparations."[19] On the eighteenth, Stalin cabled Vasiliev and Shtykov, ordering them to insist that Kim remove at least four divisions from the Naktong front and send them north to parry the American thrust that had reached Seoul. At the same time, he ordered his defense minister to draft plans for the entry of the Soviet air force into the war, "including the transfer of several . . . fighter squadrons with maintenance crews, radar posts, and air defense battalions from their bases in the Maritime Provinces of the Soviet Far East (including the strategic port city of Vladivostok) to the airfields around Pyongyang."[20]

Stalin's initiative raised more problems for Mao than it solved. How sincere was the Kremlin leader? Would he rush the Red Army into Korea if Chinese troops also failed to stem the UN advance? Would intervention lead to open war with the United States? If so, Formosa might be lost forever. Such a conflict would also involve the United Nations and thus be viewed as defiance of the world community. Could China's Communists risk such an incredible gamble only a year after seizing power?

A strange lassitude befell both Pyongyang and Peking. By September 27, Stalin was livid, and he dispatched a blistering cable to Shtykov and Gen. M. V. Zakharov, whom he had just sent to North Korea to reinforce the Soviet military advisory group in Pyongyang. The old tyrant, who had played a significant role in Soviet defeats and victories less than a decade before, now lectured his subordinates as if they were blundering platoon leaders. "The serious predicament in the area of Seoul and in the South-East in which the Korean People's Army has found itself lately," Stalin began, "has to a great extent been caused by a series of grave mistakes made by the Frontline Command, the Commands of the Army Groups and army groupings in matters related to command and control over troops, as well as to the tactics of their combat use in particular." But the NKPA was not solely at fault for the developing disaster; "it is our military advisers who are even more to blame for these mistakes." They had failed to "implement" Stalin's request that Kim extricate his forces on the Naktong from the rapidly developing trap, "despite the fact that at the moment of adopting this decision such a possibility existed."[21]

Such follies reflected "the strategic illiteracy of our advisers and their incompetence in intelligence matters." Vasiliev, Shtykov, and the others had utterly "failed to grasp the strategic importance of the enemy's assault landing in Inch'on, denied the gravity of its implications, while Shtykov even suggested that we should bring to trial the author of an article in the 'Pravda' about the U.S. assault landing." Because Stalin may well have planted that article himself, Shtykov was clearly in serious trouble. But his master was not through. The NKPA's armored forces had consistently been deployed poorly; "such paramount matters" as communications, command, and control of troops, the organization and dissemination of intelligence, and basic combat decisions were "exceptionally weak." As a result, NKPA troops, "in essence, are beyond control; they are engaged in combat blindly and cannot arrange the coordination between the various armed services in battle."[22]

Stalin's cable reached Pyongyang just as Kim finally realized that his dream of driving the UN forces out of the Pusan perimeter had failed. In a cable that crossed Stalin's bitter tirade, Zakharov reported that the NKPA, "suffering heavy losses, mainly from the enemy's airforce," was at last withdrawing from the Naktong front. Even then, however, Kim had no understanding of the dimensions of the disaster that had overtaken his troops. The North Korean leader hoped to end the NKPA retreat at Taejon "for further levelling off the front line" that would stabilize on a new Seoul-Taejon axis. Two days later, on September 29, Shtykov reported that Kim had asked his advice, admitting that continued, severe pressures by UN forces had made the flight of Chai's troops from the Naktong "particularly troublesome." Kim added that "the situation in Seoul is also murky." Shtykov reported that he had no advice for Kim.[23]

Within hours the North Korean leader dispatched his own cable to the "DEEPLY RESPECTED Iosif Vissarionovich STALIN." Kim admitted that his once magnificent army in the south had been completely cut off from its northern homeland and was being "torn into pieces." He begged for "special assistance, . . . direct military assistance," as soon as the enemy crossed the thirty-eighth parallel, which it definitely would. Stalin immediately turned to Peking and after briefly reviewing the situation told his Chinese allies that "the way toward the 38th parallel" was "wide open." Given the current situation, Mao should "move at least five–six divisions toward the 38th parallel at once so as to give our Korean comrades an opportunity to organize combat reserves north of the 38th parallel under the cover of your troops." Of course, China would not officially enter the war; the troops she sent would all be "volunteers." Stalin concluded: "I have not informed and am not going to inform our Korean friends about this idea, but I have no doubt in my mind that they will be glad when they learn about it."[24]

Almost immediately Mao sent an astonishing response to Moscow. "We originally planned to move several volunteer divisions to North Korea," the Chinese leader stated, but "having thought this over thoroughly, we now consider such actions may entail extremely serious consequences." The Chinese People's Liberation Army was "extremely poorly equipped," and Mao had "no confidence in the success of military operations against American troops." Moreover, even an attack by "volunteers" against American forces "will provoke an open conflict between the USA and China, as a consequence of which the Soviet Union can also be dragged into war, and the question would thus become extremely large." The basic problem, Mao admitted, was China's continued administrative and political as well as military weakness. A Sino-American war would simply destroy the communist regime. Mao closed by emphasizing that the decision not to enter the Korean War was a preliminary one and would be reconsidered in coming days and weeks by the Chinese politburo and leadership.[25]

Stalin refused to be deterred. He sent a long reply to Mao sometime between the third and seventh of October. Although this letter has not been found among the Soviet documents, Stalin quoted at length from it in a letter to Kim dated October 8. The Soviet leader told Mao that the United States was simply not ready "at present" for a big war, and Japan, still weakened by wartime damage, was not in a position to offer any significant military assistance in Korea. Therefore, if the Americans and their handful of UN allies were confronted by determined Chinese power, "behind which stands its ally, the USSR," Washington "will have to agree to such terms of the settlement of the Korean question that would be favorable to Korea. . . . For the same reasons, the USA will not only have to abandon Taiwan, but also to reject the idea of a separate peace with the Japanese reactionaries." In short, if Mao simply stood up to the U.S. paper tiger, everything that he ever desired would be his.[26]

But what about the "big war" that Mao feared? Stalin revealed how far anger and frustration had carried him since Inchon. The communist world should not fear World War III "because together we will be stronger than the USA and England, while the other European capitalist states (with the exception of Germany which is unable to provide any assistance to the United States now) do not present serious military forces." Then the bitter old man abandoned all restraint: "If a war is inevitable, then let it be waged now and not in a few years" when a revived and militaristic Japan would join the United States in tipping the balance of Asian power decisively away from communism.[27]

Stalin informed Kim on October 8 that his exhortations had convinced Mao. He was wrong. Mao had long been convinced of the need for intervention. During the first week in October, he bent all of his formidable energies and talents into convincing his still reluctant colleagues on the politburo that national security demanded no other course. Finally, on October 5, following several days of intensive meetings, he at last won them over. On October 7, Mao wrote Stalin expressing "solidarity with the fundamental positions discussed in [Stalin's September 30] letter" and promised to send "nine, not six, divisions" to Korea. Mao added, however, that he would "send them not now, but after some time." However fearsome the crisis, Mao simply could not bring himself to become Stalin's toady, and if he could obtain solid Soviet support in the form of air power over the battlefield so much the better.[28]

Policymakers in Washington and at UN headquarters in New York had their own problems. Rhee was insisting that the United Nations forcibly reunify Korea. More important, UN General Assembly resolutions of 1947, 1948, and 1949 had declared that the people of Korea had the "right to be free, independent and united." These resolutions, along with UN activities in Korea between 1947 and 1949, carried great weight with American liberals. The UN Commission in Korea had reported in the latter year that "the people of Korea are remarkably homogeneous. Ethnically and culturally they are one. They have a passionate longing for unity and independence and profound desire for the peaceful unification of their country." Secretary General Trygve Lie stated flatly that "the authority of the UN is identified with the unification of Korea." John Allison of the State Department's Office of Northeast Asian Affairs continued to exert his not inconsiderable influence over Washington policy makers. As early as July 24, he had raised perhaps the most disturbing question of all. If the United States and United Nations only fought to preserve the status quo in Korea, what would prevent the NKPA from regaining strength and trying again? Status quo ante would merely bring matters back to where they had been in 1947. "The aggressor would be informed that all he had to fear from aggression was being compelled to start over again."[29]

Would China intervene? In New Delhi, Prime Minister Jawaharlal Nehru urged caution, but Consul General James R. Wilkinson at the Hong Kong listening post claimed that reports he was receiving indicated that the "Chinese Communists would not get involved" in the Korean War or fight "in any area outside China unless attacked." O. Edmund Clubb, director of the State Department's Office of Chinese Affairs, took the same approach to a Chinese intervention as did politburo critics in Peking: "Domestic tasks facing the

Communists are keeping them very busy at home," he wrote on September 27. But reports of Chinese troop movements into Manchurian areas immediately adjacent to North Korea were disturbing.[30]

During the last two weeks of September, the Truman administration labored to define the basic elements of a Korean solution. On the twenty-seventh, Acting Secretary of State James Webb, with the approval of the Pentagon, "urgently recommended" to the president that he authorize MacArthur to broadcast, at his discretion, a message to Chai demanding unconditional surrender of the NKPA to United Nations forces wherever elements of that army might be situated. Truman immediately approved the draft message, which Webb had included in his memorandum.[31] Although the president carefully avoided admitting publicly that any decision either to cross the parallel or to reunify Korea had been made, the U.S. delegation to the United Nations on September 28 completed a plan calling for unification of the peninsula under the terms and conditions of the 1947, 1948, and 1949 UN resolutions. With strong elements of the NKPA unsubdued and UN forces still engaged in mopping up exercises south of the thirty-eighth parallel, a military solution seemed the only feasible course. Acheson thus included in the U.S. plan a provision that "aggressors must lay down their arms and submit to UN settlement."[32] If the NKPA chose to do this immediately, there would presumably be no need to send UN forces north of the parallel, and a UN Commission could organize and oversee popular election of an all-Korean parliament throughout the peninsula. But if fighting remnants of the NKPA managed to stumble back across the border, MacArthur's generals and troops would have to go after them. The British delegation immediately volunteered to submit the formal proposal to the General Assembly.

On September 27, while Truman was approving the surrender demand to North Korea and Stalin was railing at his military advisers and ordering units of the Soviet air force to Pyongyang, the Joint Chiefs of Staff transmitted another directive to MacArthur, signed by George Marshall and formally approved by the president and Acheson. "Your military objective is the destruction of the North Korean armed forces," the Joint Chiefs stated.

> In attaining this objective you are authorized to conduct military operations, including amphibious and airborne landings or ground operations north of the 38 parallel in Korea, provided that at the time of such operation there has been no entry into North Korea by major Soviet or Chinese Communist forces, no announcement of intended entry, nor a

threat to counter our operations militarily in North Korea. Under no circumstances, however, will your forces cross the Manchurian or USSR borders of Korea and, as a matter of policy, no non-Korean ground forces will be used in the northeast provinces bordering the Soviet Union or in the area along the Manchurian border.[33]

Washington thus chose to widen the Korean War. Marshall explicitly emphasized this change two days later in a clarifying message to MacArthur. Word that the Eighth Army might pause at the thirty-eighth parallel to regroup would cause "embarrassment" at the United Nations, which wanted to avoid having to vote on whether to order UN forces to proceed into North Korea. "We want you to feel unhampered tactically and strategically to proceed north of [the] 38th parallel," Marshall asserted. In his initial directive he had also ordered MacArthur to "immediately make an intensive effort, using all information media available to you, to turn the inevitable bitterness and resentment of the war-victimized Korean people away from the United Nations and to direct it toward the Korean Communists, the Soviet Union, and depending on the role they play, the Chinese Communists." But Marshall reemphasized that no "non-Korean" troops were to go anywhere near the Yalu. Washington was determined not to give Moscow or Peking any pretext for intervention.[34]

MacArthur responded quickly. The Eighth Army would move across the parallel to capture Pyongyang; X Corps would be shipped out through Inchon and around to the east coast, where it would engage in an amphibious assault against the North Korean port of Wonsan. Then it would move west 110 miles across the "waist" of Korea toward Pyongyang, sweeping all remaining units of the NKPA before it to crush them against the Eighth Army. Unopposed ROKA forces would then march north to the Yalu, and UN political units would arrive to prepare for all-Korea elections.

Washington's decision to widen the war produced divided opinions in the Western community. British, Commonwealth, French, and U.S. intelligence assessments completed in the fortnight after Inchon generally agreed that if the United Nations stayed out of North Korea, "Russia would intervene to resuscitate Kim Il-sung by one means or another," thus inviting a second Korean War. But if the United Nations tried to forcibly reunite North with South Korea by moving toward the Yalu, "there would be no danger of Russian physical intervention." Truman and Acheson believed this; so did British Foreign Secretary Ernest Bevin.[35]

Others, however, argued that MacArthur had done enough and that an invasion of the north would only be counterproductive. John Slessor, marshal of the Royal Air Force, told the British Chiefs of Staff on October 2 that he was baffled by Bevin's insistence that leaving North Korea as an independent political entity would give Stalin a victory. "I should have thought that the complete defeat of this obviously Soviet-inspired Communist aggression, the destruction of the whole North Korean industry [by UN bombing] and the elimination of the" NKPA "represents a triumph for the UN on any count." Slessor warned his colleagues that successful UN operations above the parallel would transform opinion in those Asian nations that had strongly supported UN actions to expel North Korea from the south. "I still think," he concluded, "that, while unification of all Korea under UN is no doubt desirable, the one *essential* is that the UN position in Korea must be no worse than if the [North Korean] invasion had never happened."[36]

But the Truman administration was not interested in either strategic considerations or prudence. It was determined to smite the Commies hip and thigh. The administration would win the Korean War politically as well as militarily; it would not only discomfit Stalin and Mao but silence Taft, McCarthy, Wherry, and the rest of the fundamentalist conservatives in Congress. At a Security Council meeting on September 18, the U.S. delegate to the United Nations, Warren Austin, submitted the fourth report of a commission appointed to examine the conduct of the war. The commission charged that the Soviets had supplied equipment and the Chinese had provided manpower to expand the NKPA from a defensive force to an offensive army. As he read this part of the report, Austin reached behind his chair and with a flourish drew out a Soviet machine gun recently captured in Korea and labeled "1950." He later posed dramatically with the weapon. The report condemned Mao for "releasing [to the NKPA] a 'vast pool' of ethnic Koreans" who had served with the Chinese Communist forces in their victory over the Nationalists.[37]

On September 30, Peking replied in ominous tones. Zhou Enlai "declared to the world [that] 'the [Chinese] people absolutely will not tolerate foreign aggression, nor will they supinely tolerate seeing their neighbors being savagely invaded by the imperialists.'"[38] London learned of the statement almost immediately and forwarded it to Washington; the Pentagon quickly passed it on to Tokyo. Initial reaction at the highest levels in the State Department was subdued: Zhou was probably bluffing, although China experts warned that his remarks should be taken seriously. Certainly Bevin heard what Zhou was trying to say. For weeks the British Foreign Secretary had been saying publicly what many in Washington agreed with privately: that the People's Republic of China existed legitimately because of its military victory over Chiang. To ignore this regime and the more than half-billion people it represented was idiotic. The British government was sympathetic to Peking's growing insistence that no solution in Korea could be reached without China's participation. But Truman and Acheson brushed aside London's misgivings.

On October 3, three evenings before the Americans crossed the parallel, Zhou summoned Panikkar to an interview and for the first time explicitly clarified China's position. Of course he said nothing of the continued opposition to intervention within the politburo that would require another seventy-two hours of steady pressure by Mao to resolve. Instead, Zhou informed Panikkar that Mao was ready to tell Stalin that "we have decided to send some of our troops to Korea under the name of [Chinese People's] Volunteers [CPV] to fight the United States and its lackey Syngman Rhee and to aid our Korean comrades." China's first objective would be to fight and to "annihilate the American troops . . . , principally the Eighth Army (an old army with combat effectiveness)." Mao was plainly worried, perhaps even frightened, by the prospect of battle-hardened U.S. soldiers soon appearing on the other side of the Yalu within sight of some of Communist China's most important industrial facilities.[39]

Zhou stated twice that U.S. troops were going to cross the thirty-eighth parallel in an attempt to expand the war and that "we will intervene." Zhou's bitterness toward Washington was as deep as Mao's. He had learned (undoubtedly through Panikkar) that on September 1 the foreign ministers of the United States, Britain, and France had agreed that the parallel would not be crossed without prior UN approval. But MacArthur's troops were already doing just that on the east coast, and the United Nations had not acted. "The U.S. Government is unreliable." China sincerely wanted both peace "and the localization of the Korean incident," Zhou continued. "Our idea for localizing the Korean incident is just to make efforts to keep the aggression of U.S. troops from expanding into an incident of worldwide dimensions."[40]

Panikkar fueled Zhou's anger. The portly, middle-aged professional diplomat with the carefully trimmed moustache and lightly graying goatee replied that "some signs suggest that the U.S. Government will probably violate the agreement reached at the meeting of the three foreign ministers." Reports from Korea indicated that South Korean troops had already moved nine miles above the border, and "U.S. troops will probably cross the 38th parallel within 12 hours." It was all MacArthur's fault, Panikkar added. He was exerting "great pressure" on Washington to obtain a decisive victory. It was probably too late to stop him. "That is the Americans' business," Zhou replied brusquely as he terminated the interview. "The purpose of this evening's talk is to let you know our attitude."[41]

When the outlines of the Zhou-Panikkar interview became known the next day, the noncommunist world was shocked. The Indian press of October 5 and 6 reported that a "neutral authority" had stated that a "major conflict in Korea now 'looks almost inevitable.'" Nehru begged Zhou to "'hold his hand for the present.'" The Chinese premier repeated that Peking had no intention of taking any action if U.S. forces did not cross the parallel "but was determined to do so if American troops moved into North Korea."[42]

On October 7, as Mao informed Stalin of China's decision to intervene, the first units of the Eighth Army did just that. The same day the UN General Assembly passed Resolution 376 (V), introduced by Great Britain and seven other delegations after being revised and cleared by Acheson. The resolution recommended that "all appropriate steps be taken to ensure conditions of stability throughout Korea" and that "all sections and representative bodies of the population of Korea, South and North, be invited to co-operate with the organs of the United Nations in the restoration of peace, in the holding of elections and in the establishment of a unified Government." The resolution also included a promise suggested by the British military chiefs of staff that no UN forces would remain in Korea after these steps were accomplished.[43]

Under the uncertain canons of international law, Korea no longer belonged to communism. The admittedly small sacrifices of the Red Army in 1945 had been obliterated with the stroke of a pen, as had all of Moscow and Peking's substantial political, military, economic, and ideological interests in the peninsula. Anyone who assumed that the communist world would not react to such a setback was ignoring reality.

Yet that was precisely what the U.S. government and people did. On October 9, the Joint Chiefs sent another directive to MacArthur, amplifying Marshall's orders of September 27 and 29: "Hereafter in the event of open or covert employment anywhere in Korea of major Chinese Communist units, without prior announcement, you should continue the action as long as, in your judgment, action by forces now under your control offers a reasonable chance of success. In any case you will obtain authorization from

Washington prior to taking any military action against objectives in Chinese territory."[44] Within hours MacArthur issued a "final" surrender order to the NKPA. If it was not heeded, MacArthur stated, "I shall at once proceed to take such military actions as may be necessary to enforce the decrees of the United Nations."[45]

George Gallup had been repeatedly polling public opinion about the war. He found that the country supported the administration and was soberly optimistic about an early victory. Even before Inchon, when UN fortunes were at their lowest, 65 percent of those asked thought that Truman had been right to send American boys to defend Korea. A week after Inchon, 51 percent of those questioned thought the war would be over in at least six months—by March of 1951. Only 14 percent thought hostilities would last more than a year. On October 13, Gallup's pollsters asked the public whether the fighting should stop once the North Koreans had been "push[ed] . . . back over the line from where they started" or whether "we should continue to fight in their own territory until they have surrendered." A majority (64 percent) replied that the fight should be taken into North Korea; only 27 percent said that restoring the prewar boundaries of the Republic of South Korea was sufficient. That same day Gallup asked: "If the United States got into a war with Communist China, how much chance do you think we would have of winning it?" Of those polled, 57 percent replied that the United States would have an "excellent or good" chance; 21 percent said a "fair" chance.[46]

Americans would soon be able to test their hypothesis, for Mao was now ready to enter the Korean War. The day after the UN resolution calling for the reunification of the peninsula and the entry of the first Eighth Army units into North Korea, the Chinese leader issued an official order "to resist the attacks of U.S. imperialism and its running dogs." He then cabled an ecstatic Kim, confirming Stalin's cable of the same day, that "in view of the current situation, we have decided to send volunteers to Korea to help you fight against the aggressors," and he asked the North Korean leader to send several members of his politburo to Manchuria to coordinate activities. Significantly, Mao did not tell Kim exactly when or under what circumstances the Chinese intervention would begin.[47]

Within hours London picked up a broadcast in which Kim exhorted his people to resist the approaching UN columns. The North Korean leader cried out defiantly that "the Korean People are not standing alone in our struggle and are receiving the absolute support of the Soviet Union, the

Chinese people, etc." Bevin became deeply alarmed. He could not know about Mao's message of commitment, but he immediately understood that the North Koreans were flinging MacArthur's surrender order back in his face. It was clear to the British foreign secretary that Washington was responding to MacArthur, not vice versa, and that MacArthur was running the Korean War as he pleased. He had to be restrained. Bevin cabled his ambassador in Washington, Oliver Franks, to go to the State Department and impress on Dean Rusk and the others the British government's conviction that the situation on the peninsula was becoming a crisis. The most "serious consequences . . . would flow from Chinese intervention in Korea." It was impossible to assess the actual potential for such an intervention. Perhaps Peking was bluffing, but no one could be sure. Bevin urged that Truman issue "categorical instructions" to MacArthur that even if the Chinese intervened, he should not "take action outside Korea without the express orders of the President."[48]

Suddenly there was a flurry of consultations on both sides. Truman decided to meet with MacArthur to reassess risks and opportunities, while the ever suspicious Mao sent Zhou to Moscow to determine once and for all the nature and dimensions of Soviet support for China's impending war against the United States and the world community.

The decision to schedule a Truman-MacArthur meeting was reached abruptly during the weekend of October 7–8 while the president was sailing down the Potomac with a handful of White House aides and staff on the *Williamsburg*. According to George M. Elsey, MacArthur was not consulted nor were secretaries Acheson and Marshall. Charlie Ross, another presidential aide and close, longtime friend of the president, formally drafted a memorandum on Monday, October 9, setting forth the justifications for the meeting and suggesting the makeup of the traveling party, which would include neither Acheson nor Marshall but instead Army Secretary Frank Pace, Rusk and Harriman from State, and several others. Truman wanted to see his Far East commander in person, take his measure, and give him the same opportunity to see and know his commander in chief. Recent incidents had convinced the president that MacArthur had completely lost touch with events in his own country. The general no longer understood "the world-wide picture," although Truman had repeatedly tried to present it to him through envoys such as John Foster Dulles, Averell Harriman, and members of the Joint Chiefs of Staff. And if news from London and New Delhi were true, it was time to sit down and talk about how to handle a possible Chinese intervention. Finally, off-year national elections were less than a month away, and MacArthur had become a godlike hero to many Americans after his brilliant victory at Inchon. The president dared not risk being upstaged by a man who had been formally nominated as a presidential candidate in the last two Republican conventions.[49]

To many Americans, MacArthur was a savior in a time of bitter partisanship and apparent government bungling. After a hurried trip to Japan and Korea in early August, Harriman had told the army's Deputy Chief of Staff Matthew B. Ridgway that "political and personal considerations should be put to one side and our government [should] deal with General MacArthur on the lofty level of the great national asset which he is." Newspapers were filled with letters and columns praising the general, likening him to Wellington and Washington. On the eve of the MacArthur-Truman meeting, Harold Stassen, widely regarded as a seasoned and influential young politician-statesman, urged on national radio that the president effectively turn over all Asian policy, civil and military, to his Far East commander. Truman should accept MacArthur's advice on Asian and western Pacific affairs; he should allow MacArthur to shape U.S. policy in and out of the United Nations regarding Communist China, Formosa, and Indochina. He should place MacArthur in supreme command of American military policy and interests in all of the Asiatic-Pacific area and "follow [MacArthur's] advice."[50]

Under the circumstances, Truman was willing to go to the general. At first the president suggested a meeting in Hawaii. But MacArthur demurred. He was busy running a war, Hawaii was too far away, and he "didn't like to fly at night, only wanted to go fly as far as Wake because he could make a daytime journey." This suited Truman, who had already scheduled a prior speaking engagement in San Francisco that he could fulfill on his way back from the Pacific. After briefly considering and rejecting the option of joining MacArthur in Korea so that he could see things firsthand and be with the troops, Truman agreed to meet the general at Wake Island, a famous World War II battle site some twenty-five hundred miles southeast of Tokyo and seven thousand miles west of Washington. Elsey hurriedly drew up a "suggested organization of talks" from early Saturday morning, October 15, through lunch, afternoon, and dinner before final staff talks on Saturday evening between the presidential and Tokyo parties to tie up "any loose ends."[51]

On Tuesday, October 10, the White House released a statement in which Truman stated that one of the purposes of the meeting would be to express to MacArthur the "appreciation and gratitude of the people and Government of the United States" for the "imagination, courage, and effectiveness" with which the general had carried out his Korean assignment and, indeed, all of the missions entrusted to him throughout a long career "as one of our greatest military leaders." The president and general would then "discuss . . . the final phase of United Nations action in Korea," including "the establishment of a unified, independent, and democratic" country organized under "United Nations relief and reconstruction program[s]."[52]

Both the president and the general approached the meeting with a private grimness that belied the confident public assertions. One of Truman's most sophisticated biographers, Alonzo Hamby, has emphasized the president's deep insecurities, which led him not only to personalize grievances but to bottle them up and then unleash them after the event, often with destructive results. One of the president's naval aides, Robert Dennison, remembered several occasions when Truman apparently had a normal conversation, then remarked after the caller left that he had really set the man straight or "'let him have it.'" Dennison failed to realize that Truman was exhibiting "a common behavioral pattern: the friendly conversation that smoothed over or failed to touch on some difficulty with another person, then the surging feelings of aggression when that individual was out of range."[53] Truman clearly envied and despised MacArthur yet could not bring himself to confront the man and his all-encompassing arrogance. Instead, the president would fawn over the general in their only meeting, refusing to ask hard questions or sustain a mood of tough-minded inquiry that might have shaken MacArthur's self-confidence and forced him to consider interests and perspectives other than his own. The country would pay dearly for the character flaws that both men exhibited at Wake Island.

Truman was nonetheless sufficiently concerned by recent events to ask for an immediate intelligence assessment of Soviet and Chinese capabilities and intentions in Korea. The hurriedly compiled study, titled "Critical Situations in the Far East," reached the White House just before the president left for the Pacific and was included in his briefing book for the Wake Island meeting. Truman undoubtedly read the document during his long flight west.[54] Scanning it for substance, he was probably comforted by the last part of the third sentence: "There are no convincing indications of an actual Chinese Communist intention to resort to full-scale intervention in Korea" despite recent statements by Zhou, Chinese troop movements to Manchuria, and propaganda charges from Peking of atrocities and border violations by UN forces (U.S. aircraft had inadvertently bombed installations on the Manchurian side of the Yalu several weeks before). The crucial term, of course, was "full-scale," for the CIA admitted that, despite the absence of air and naval power, the Chinese were "capable of intervening effectively, but not necessarily decisively, in the Korean conflict."

Truman was certainly familiar by this time with all the formidable obstacles to Chinese intervention: chaotic domestic problems, the certain loss of any opportunity to oust Formosa as the representative of China in the United Nations, the inevitably high cost of battling UN forces without substantial Soviet air and naval support, and the danger of becoming identified by Asians as just another lackey of the Kremlin and by international observers as an outlaw state. The president could have been either gratified or frustrated by the CIA's summation: "While full-scale Chinese Communist intervention in Korea must be regarded as a continuing possibility, a consideration of all known factors leads to the conclusion that barring a Soviet decision for global war, such action is not probable in 1950. During this period, intervention will probably be confined to continued covert assistance to the North Koreans." But 1950 was nearly over. The agency had carefully and effectively covered itself to avoid future charges that it had completely rejected the likelihood of a Chinese intervention. And did Chinese involvement automatically mean that the Kremlin would start World War III if Washington responded vigorously? The document raised more questions than it answered, and if Truman read it carefully, he must have been especially eager to meet MacArthur and get his views firsthand.[55]

The president left Washington on Wednesday October 11. Reporters observed that he barely nodded to photographers as he climbed down from the presidential plane *Independence* for a brief rest stop in California. The next morning in Hawaii, the pretty wife of Pacific Fleet Commander Arthur Radford attempted to put a lei around the president's neck and kiss him on the cheek. He looked uncomfortable and took off the floral offering "as if it were poison ivy." When he lunched at the Pearl Harbor Officer's Club after seeing the rusting hulks of the battleships *Arizona* and *Utah*, he spoke seriously about his hopes for world peace. His jocularity returned only when he visited wounded soldiers at the army's Tripler General Hospital. He joked lightly and gently with the men before heading back to the airfield and the last leg of his flight.[56]

The *Independence* touched down at Wake, a small coral atoll in the middle of the Pacific Ocean, early on Sunday morning, October 15. Contrary to later stories, MacArthur had arrived the previous evening. He had also been in a peevish mood during his flight from Tokyo. John Muccio, who accompanied the general, said he was "surly, uneasy, and mad," "irked," and "disgusted" at having to leave his duties even for a day. MacArthur knew, as did Truman, that the meeting would be more of a confrontation between sovereign rulers of separate states than a conference between superior and subordinate.[57]

But MacArthur was pleasant when he greeted his president. It was just after dawn when Truman and his party arrived in two aircraft. The sun had begun to silhouette a large, black thundercloud east of the island. In the dim light, the Washington contingent could see dozens of rusting Japanese tanks along barren beaches. As the *Independence* circled overhead to land, Harriman stepped out of the first plane, walked toward MacArthur's quarters, and met the general halfway to the airstrip. What was this meeting all about, MacArthur wanted to know. "I told him," Harriman remembered, "that the President wanted to discuss with him how political victory in Korea could be obtained now that MacArthur had won the brilliant military victory. Also Japanese peace treaty and all matters in Far East." Harriman recalled that MacArthur seemed relieved, saying "'Good. The President wants my views.'"

Given the tension inherent in the meeting, Harriman may have then committed an indiscretion by reminding MacArthur of the "strong support the President had given him for the [Inchon] operation." MacArthur replied that, although the action was successful, he too had "taken a grave responsibility." Harriman "pointed out that perhaps the President's was at least equally grave in backing him." With that unpromising exchange, the two men walked onto the airstrip, where the *Independence* had just landed.[58]

The president and general shook hands warmly. "I am glad you are here. I have been a long time in meeting you, general." "I hope it won't be so long next time, Mr. President."[59] The two men cheerfully posed together for the photographers. Truman was in a suit and tie; MacArthur wore his khaki shirt open at the neck and his general's cap fashionably crushed. He had shaved. In the pictures he seemed to have a more commanding presence than did Truman.[60]

The two men then went off by themselves for a private chat. The meeting had been so hastily arranged that there was only one automobile on the island: a dusty, two-door 1948 Chevrolet. Truman and MacArthur piled in for a short drive to the latter's quarters in a World War II Quonset hut. Reporters saw the two men sit down in wicker chairs just before the door was firmly shut, and what transpired for the next forty minutes only Truman and MacArthur would know. MacArthur always refused to discuss the conversation. In his memoirs, Truman stated that MacArthur told him "that the victory was won in Korea" and that Japan was ready for a formal peace treaty. MacArthur then apologized for any inappropriate remarks about Formosa that might have caused embarrassment, and Truman brushed it off. The president told his Far East commander about developments in Europe, and MacArthur assured the president that one division could be transferred from Korea to Germany in January. The only person who heard what the two men said to each other before joining the main meeting was the secret service agent, who sat in the front seat as MacArthur and Truman were driven to the conference room. He later stated that the president had asked about the possibility of Chinese intervention and that MacArthur had dismissed it, adding that if the Chinese did enter the war "his UNC [United Nations Command] forces could handle them."[61]

The main conference was held in Wake Island's small, coral-colored administration building. Pace, Omar Bradley, Harriman, Rusk, and State Department special envoy Philip Jessup had come out with Truman (though on the first plane); Muccio and Gen. Courtney Whitney had accompanied MacArthur. The formal meeting began as soon as Truman and the general arrived. MacArthur began by stating categorically that formal resistance would end throughout North and South Korea by Thanksgiving once the remnants of the NKPA were mopped up.[62] When the discussion turned to postwar events, MacArthur stated that with a little intelligence Rhee could dominate the peninsula because all local officials in North Korea would have fled to Manchuria, and Rhee, as leader of the only legitimate government left in Korea, could make all new appointments.

Truman then asked point-blank: "What are the chances for Chinese or Soviet interference?" "Very little," MacArthur replied. Moscow and Peking had missed their opportunity. If the Soviet or Chinese armies had attacked the Naktong perimeter in July or August, they would have thrown UN forces into the sea. Now "we are no longer fearful of their intervention. We no longer stand hat in hand." The Chinese had 300,000 men in Manchuria, about a third of whom were stationed on or quite near the Yalu. But only about 50,000 to 60,000 of them could be transported across the river before the Far East Air Force and the navy's carrier planes destroyed the bridges and prevented amphibious crossings. Air power had become decisive in Korea, and the Chinese "have no Air Force." Because the United States now possessed air bases in Korea, any attempt by Chinese forces to "get down to Pyongyang" would result in "the greatest slaughter."

The potential for Soviet intervention was somewhat different. The Russians had a large, "fairly good" air force in Siberia, roughly two to three thousand planes including at least a few jet fighters. But because the planes and pilots "are probably no match for our Air Force," Stalin "would have difficulty in putting troops into the field. It would take six weeks to get a division across [the Yalu] and six weeks brings the winter." No one apparently remembered that seven years earlier the Red Army had proved that it was the finest winter fighting force in the world.

MacArthur then addressed the question of Soviet air cover for a Chinese intervention. It would not work, he declared, because "ground support is a very difficult thing" for air forces to accomplish. It required weeks if not months of coordinated training with troops in the field to be effective. "Between untrained Air and Ground Forces an air umbrella is impossible without a lot of joint training. I believe it just wouldn't work with Chinese Communist ground and Russian air. We are the best."

The hour-long conference soon closed with a gushy tribute from the president. Throwing aside Elsey's carefully crafted all-day schedule, Truman enthused, "No one who was not here would believe we have covered so much ground as we have been actually able to cover." His relief that he had not had to confront MacArthur was as obvious as MacArthur's conclusion that he had assessed his president and had mastered him.

Truman suggested lunch while a communiqué was prepared; "then I want to award a couple of medals to a couple of people and we can all leave after luncheon." MacArthur's reply was barely civil. He had work to do running a war and a command that embraced the entire noncommunist Far East. "If it's all right," he would like to leave immediately. Truman deferred. "The communiqué should be submitted as soon as it is ready and General MacArthur can return immediately. This has been a most satisfactory conference."

MacArthur apparently reached the same conclusion. Protocol demanded that Truman take off first in the *Independence.* This left MacArthur alone briefly with the rest of the Washington contingent, and he told Harriman that he had been "much impressed by the President. Newspaper accounts and articles did not do him justice." The hint of condescension was amplified by MacArthur's next comment. He would come home to a grateful nation, he announced to Harriman in lordly fashion, "after [the] Japanese peace treaty was concluded," which would consume perhaps a year or a little more.[63]

Arriving back in Tokyo that evening, MacArthur told reporters that the Wake Island meeting would "'arouse great enthusiasm throughout the Far East,'" symbolizing as it did "'a firm determination that peace shall be secured in the Pacific and that Asia shall be free, not slave.'" "Sources close to MacArthur indicated" that he was "well pleased with his talks with the President."[64] He had good reason to be. Truman's fawning attitude seemed to ensure for MacArthur continued freedom from interference and direction both in the conduct of the war and the running of Japan.

Two evenings later at the San Francisco Opera House, Truman addressed the nation on the results of the conference. His elation had not diminished. The long-range ability of the free world to maintain peace was being proved in Korea. "It is fortunate for the world that we had the right man for this purpose—a man who is a very great soldier—General Douglas MacArthur." The president was careful not to specify when hostilities would end, as MacArthur had done, but he made it clear that some of the boys might be home for Christmas or at least by the New Year: "The power of the Korean communists to resist effectively will soon come to an end." In a perhaps gratuitous gesture, MacArthur sent a personal message to his commander in chief, again lauding Truman's leadership. The San Francisco speech would have an "electric" effect throughout the Far East. "It will be almost universally interpreted as providing a dynamic leadership," and as "your field commander in this theater it has immeasurably strengthened my arm to meet the potentialities of military responsibility."[65]

On the other side of the world, the communist partners were finding that coordination of their Korean policies was a much more arduous task. Zhou finally tracked down the Soviet premier at his Black Sea dacha on October 10 and endured five days of anguish there and back in Moscow before he got what he wanted. Stalin began the first meeting by agreeing that the NKPA was obviously in extremis. Zhou replied that China lacked the means to conduct an effective war against a modern, mechanized army such as the

UN contingent in Korea. Moreover, the war had to be won. Intervention could not result in a stalemate, and it would not be child's play. "How can we get out of the war if we are caught in a whirlpool and cannot escape for several years?" Zhou then added a little blackmail. If the CPV did not drive the "imperialists" out of Korea with one quick blow, the resulting protracted war "probably will involve other fraternal countries." Zhou's implication was clear: If Stalin wanted China to rescue Kim's regime without sending the Red Army into Korea, he would have to provide Peking with funds, weapons, and transport.[66]

As Zhou spoke, Chinese supplies were pouring across the Yalu, although MacArthur's people ignored this development on the eve of the Wake Island conference. Listening to Zhou, Stalin became fretful. The Soviet Union was not yet prepared for a major confrontation with the United States, he told the Chinese envoy, "because as you know the Second World War ended not long ago, and we are not ready for the Third World War." But neither was the United States ready for a two-front war in Asia. It could not fight in Korea and China at the same time. Therefore, Peking could intervene in Korea with impunity. On the other hand, Stalin continued, if it did not, think of the consequences for China if an American army was permanently stationed on the southern bank of the Yalu. "The economic recovery of the Northeast probably will be out of the question," and the Americans could harass China forever "from the air, land, and sea." Mao should ensure that every possible industrial installation in North Korea and every North Korean soldier was removed to Manchuria until a great communist counteroffensive from China could drive the Americans out of Korea forever, for after all "it is far simpler" for such forces "to enter Korea from Northeast China than from the Soviet Union."[67]

Zhou was appalled. Stalin had concluded "without a blush" that the two communist superpowers would "have to bear the burden" in Korea, but, in fact, he was leaving Peking to carry the load alone. The Soviet leader was experiencing a sudden spasm of either cowardice or prudence. The disconsolate Chinese premier was further devastated when Stalin informed him a day later that the Soviet Union could not even provide air cover and support for the CPV. Zhou cabled the terrible news to Mao, who told him to keep negotiating. Eventually Stalin grudgingly agreed to supply the CPV with essential weapons, especially armor and artillery. Then, after Zhou left the Black Sea for Moscow, the Soviet leader abruptly changed his mind again and sent Vyacheslav Molotov to the Chinese embassy to tell Zhou that the deal was off. "We do not agree with the decision to send in your troops," the Soviet foreign minister told his amazed Chinese colleague, "and we also will not offer you military equipment." Zhou was enraged, but he could not change Stalin's mind. Recent sources indicate that Stalin may have thought Mao was trying to draw the Soviet Union into Korea and he was determined to resist. Nikita Khrushchev remembered Stalin saying at the time of the Zhou mission: "So what? Let the United States of America be our neighbors in the Far East. They will come there, but we shall not fight them now. We are not ready to fight."[68]

Stalin had placed Mao in an impossible situation. United Nations forces were now steadily advancing north of the parallel; within weeks if not days U.S. troops might be at the Yalu, and North Korea would disappear as a political and military buffer. Surely Stalin understood the strategic implications of an unconditional UN victory in Korea. The way to *make* him understand was to do nothing for the moment. So, on October 12, as Truman was flying to Wake Island, Mao ordered his military commanders to delay carrying out the October 9 "go" order until the completion of the Zhou mission. But Mao was not going to abandon intervention, as he made clear the next day at a politburo meeting, "for he had concluded that the Americans would not stop short of the Yalu or even at the Yalu."[69] "We saw through their tricks," Mao told his colleagues. "Nehru told me that [the UN forces] would stop 40 miles short of the Yalu River after crossing the 38th parallel. . . . Obviously this was the second time [for them] to fool us. If we did nothing, the aggressive enemy would surely continue its advance up to the Yalu River and would devise a second scheme" to invade Manchuria itself. China had to intervene.[70]

Meanwhile in Moscow, Zhou impatiently negotiated long distance with Stalin, who was still at his Black Sea dacha. Molotov remained the go-between. On the thirteenth, Mao sent Zhou the gist of his remarks to the politburo for transmission to Stalin, and by the next day, Zhou learned that the Soviet leader had again changed his mind. Molotov told Zhou that it would now be possible to supply Peking with a guaranteed amount of advanced weapons and equipment, and the two men promptly began devising ways to ensure the assembly and delivery of the material and to protect it from U.S. air strikes. Zhou was told that when Stalin read Mao's cable committing China to intervention regardless of the cost, the old dictator allegedly muttered: "The Chinese Comrades are so good. The Chinese Comrades are so good." It was said that he had tears in his eyes. Stalin then ordered the release of sixteen "air regiments" of fighter planes to China for use in Korea. Mao and his generals would have their air cover after all, and it would be invaluable.[71]

The die was finally cast. But it was unclear in mid-October when Chinese forces would be able to strike and where advancing UN columns would be when they did strike. The task would be more perilous the farther south Chinese forces had to advance. If MacArthur's troops held a strong line across the waist of Korea—from Wonsan through the interlocking mountain valleys beyond Yongdok to the coastal plains around Pyongyang—they would be almost impossible to dislodge. This was presumably what the Joint Chiefs had concluded on September 27, when they directed MacArthur to permit only South Korean troops to clear out far northeastern and northwestern parts of the peninsula. Easily resupplied from either Inchon or Wonsan and able to maneuver their armor in comparatively open terrain, the UN forces could chew up any Chinese offensive. But if American and other highly mechanized UN forces could somehow be lured into the mountainous far north, which guarded the approaches to the Yalu, they would be marching into disaster, for the only roadways above the waist open to the units of the Eighth Army and X Corps were either along narrow coastal corridors or through mountain passes overlooking deep, dark gorges. Supply lines would be difficult to maintain, and the threat of ambush from the mountain heights would always be present. At the moment, however, those concerns were obscured for the Americans by the joy of victory.

Korea had been a bitter, bloody war for American GIs. Suddenly summoned from Japan or California, wrestling their mechanized equipment and armor off ships in the miserably inadequate and overcrowded port of Pusan, thrust into defensive fighting in which patrols were decimated and limited offensives to straighten out a line often required assaults up steep hills against a determined enemy who held the high ground, the soldiers had not fought with distinction. MacArthur consistently overestimated the fighting qualities of his troops. Matt Ridgway, one of the twentieth century's great warriors, did not make this mistake. "The quality of soldier now engaged in Korea is not up to World War II standards," he reported after a trip to Japan in August. American troops were "easily stampeded," and instead of responding to attacks with the "fundamental infantry reaction to fire and movement," they called in artillery and air support. If it did not materialize immediately or was insufficient to blunt an enemy assault, they withdrew. "Our troops do not counter-attack an enemy penetration," Ridgway continued remorselessly. "Our forces do not maintain outpost protection nor flank protection. Weapons are not properly emplaced to obtain a good field of fire." Soldiers took up positions on tops of hills to ensure sight of the enemy, which was fine. High ground should always be seized, but they did not hold it when the enemy approached. "Our troops do not dig in and make no pretense at camouflaging their positions. They do not seek cover and concealment while moving by day." They were thus easily visible. Their frontline signaling was inadequate.[72]

Above all, Ridgway was disturbed by the lack of leadership and professional competence at the regimental and divisional levels. Soldiers were only as good as those who led them, and Ridgway was distressed to find in the field too many overage colonels and brigadiers, some of whom had failed at command during World War II. Only a few had been sacked, and Inchon and the ensuing breakout obscured the lingering incapacities of those allowed to remain at their posts.

The U.S. Army in Korea was, in short, soft, spoiled, and often poorly led. Units entering combat on the perimeter for the first time invariably performed in an "undistinguished and at times abysmal" manner. Some regiments that had been hard hit in earlier engagements "bugged out in droves."[73] The army's chief vice was being "road-bound"; it depended too much on tanks, other self-propelled armor, and artillery as well as poorly coordinated tactical air power. It would rather ride in trucks than march to its objectives.[74]

The marines were another story. Somehow during the years of peace, when Truman disdainfully referred to the corps as little more than a police force, the drill instructors at San Diego and Parris Island, the sergeants and captains at LeJeune and Pendleton, trained their young charges to be highly professional. The marines came to Korea to get at the enemy, kill him, and protect each other in the best way possible. Morale and competence were invariably excellent, and tactical air support was outstanding. Whenever a marine unit was pinned down, the big Corsairs came winging out of the east or west within minutes from hastily constructed airfields near the front lines or from the flight decks of small "jeep" carriers close offshore.

The fighting men who had the most bizarre experiences in Korea were undoubtedly the pilots of MacArthur's Far East Air Force. During the brief years of peace, these men had brought their wives and children to Japan as one of the privileges of occupation. Young couples spent their weekends in the bars or on the horse paths of fancy resort hotels in the Japanese "Alps," where food, liquor, and lodging were cheap. Families went to the beach, where the children played in the sand and mom and dad soaked up the weak northern Pacific sun.

Once the war came, families were not sent home because no one in Tokyo believed, at least initially, that Korea would be a prelude to World War III or even a regional war in Asia. So the conflict became a "commuters' war." The men got up early in the morning for breakfast fixed by their wives. The whole family—dad, mom, and the kids—then piled into the car for the drive to the airfield. While dad went in for his daily briefing, wife and children waited outside the fenced perimeter; then they waved gallantly as they watched him take off for work before going home or to school to sweat the day out. Dad was back for dinner (and sometimes lunch) or was dead or captured by the enemy.

Initially the war was a bit of a lark; dad or husband was doing what he had been trained to do, and the family was proud of him. But the first deaths shocked everyone. After that, wives began looking up from their clotheslines in the dependent housing area to count the planes coming back across the Sea of Japan. The throats of girls barely out of their teens tightened and hearts did flip-flops when only two or three of the wing's four jets or P-51 Mustangs came back from a mission. Soon the wing commander would arrive and quietly tell one of them that her husband was dead. The young woman was expected to take the news dry-eyed if possible. Air force people were proud of their community and believed that they understood one another. The new widow was immediately surrounded by friends, who talked her through her grief as best they could. A surprising number of the bereaved young women remained at the air base; there was always a job for them someplace, and who could console a recent widow better than a slightly older one.[75]

By the time they crossed the parallel, the American GIs were exhausted from ceaseless combat. By mid-October, more than thirty-six hundred U.S. soldiers had been killed in action. Another forty-two hundred were missing, and many of those would later be found dead, bound and shot or bayoneted by their captors. More than sixteen thousand Yanks had been wounded. When MacArthur reviewed F Company of the Fifth Cavalry Reg-

iment on October 20, he asked all those who had served since the unit first
entered Korea ninety-six days before to come forward. Of two hundred
men, only five stepped forth, and three of them had been wounded.[76]

It was time to win the war and get the boys back to Japan, Europe, or
home. But a few days after MacArthur returned from Wake Island, his
grand strategy for victory began to unravel.

At first things went smoothly. Crossing the parallel in the west, the Eighth
Army entered Pyongyang (inevitably called "Ping Pong" by the GIs) on October 19, and the next day MacArthur flew over from Tokyo to take formal command of the city. He was in a fine mood. It was the sixth anniversary of his
celebrated return to the Philippines during World War II. Now Pyongyang
was the first Red capital ever to fall. With luck it would not be the last. Stepping off his plane, the *SCAP,* MacArthur remarked jocularly, "Any celebrities
here to greet me? Where's Kim Buck Too?" Earlier he had watched an extensive parachute drop north of the capital, which was designed to catch the last
of the NKPA. The mission failed, but MacArthur did not know that. He told
reporters joyfully that the war was definitely coming to an end. "It looks like
we closed the trap," he said, and "closing that trap should be the end of all
organized resistance." He drove through Pyongyang, where portraits of Stalin
and Kim were still displayed on street posters. He received the Distinguished
Flying Cross from his commander of Far East Air Forces, Lt. Gen. George
Stratemeyer, and then returned to Tokyo, while the 800,000 remaining inhabitants of Pyongyang watched silently as UN troops tore down the communist
posters and Walker settled into Kim's old office.[77]

From one perspective, MacArthur had now won the Korean War. He had
captured the enemy capital; ROKA troops had established a firm defense
line across the waist of the peninsula. Soon X Corps would begin to fill in
that line after coming ashore at Wonsan, and ROKA forces could then be
sent north to complete the conquest of the peninsula. "Complete victory
seemed now in view," Ridgway would recall—"a golden apple that would
handsomely symbolize the crowning effort of [MacArthur's] brilliant military career." Far East Headquarters in Tokyo observed on the day of the
Truman-MacArthur meeting that "no definite [enemy] front line locations
can be determined." The Eighth Army, hustling north to Pyongyang, had

found only a few "points of contact" with the retreating, demoralized, frightened enemy.[78]

On October 21, MacArthur informed the Joint Chiefs that he envisaged that the Eighth Army's transfer to Japan would start before Thanksgiving and be completed by Christmas. The next day, he ordered Stratemeyer to release two B-29 bomber groups for return to the states. On October 25, Chief of Naval Operations Forrest P. Sherman formally notified the other Joint Chiefs that, because "the requirements for Naval air support of operations on shore in Korea is coming to an end, and the disadvantages of continuously operating the fast carrier force in the Yellow Sea and the Sea of Japan are steadily increasing," it was time for the Seventh Fleet to return to its normal operating areas in the western Pacific and the Formosa Strait. Soldiers in the First Cavalry Division boasted that on Thanksgiving Day they would parade on the *ginza* in Tokyo wearing their yellow cavalry scarves. As the unit began to move unopposed along the coastal road north of Pyongyang toward the Yalu, its supply officers ordered the men to begin turning in some of their equipment in preparation for their return to Japan.[79]

No one had counted on the irrepressible ROKA. This army was completely different from the disorganized rabble that had repeatedly fled before the enemy in late June and early July. During battle the officers and men had gained not only experience but confidence. They could defeat the NKPA whenever and wherever they found it. Unleashed across the parallel days before the Eighth Army, the determined divisions and regiments of the ROKA's I and II Corps had raced north, east, and west to spread across as much of North Korea as they could reach as quickly as they could. In the process, they disrupted every UN timetable and strategy. The experience of X Corps at Wonsan was only one example.

For Gen. "Ned" Almond's men the whole operation was a fiasco. The troops of X Corps did not finish embarking at Inchon until October 16, just three days before the Eighth Army entered Pyongyang. After arriving off Wonsan on the nineteenth, they had to wait a week to go ashore. While the transports and attack cargo ships traced lazy racecourse patterns in the gray seas off the North Korean port in what bored, seasick soldiers called "Operation Yo-yo," navy minesweepers cleared a passage through an unanticipated mine field that had been inadvertently discovered just in time. At last, on October 26, the First Marine Division (the frustrated, impatient men of the Seventh were temporarily held in reserve on board their ships) raced onto the sandy beaches near the Wonsan airport with armor and trucks and thundered into the city eager for a fight. All was quiet until the column came to an intersection where a big banner flew overhead: "Welcome to Wonsan courtesy of the KMAG of the I Corps of the ROK Capital and Third Divisions." The men of the First Marines had not known how far the ROKA had advanced north of the parallel. Now they knew. The marines were further embarrassed to be greeted not only by their South Korean allies but also by a marine air wing, Almond himself, and Bob Hope. Major General Oliver Smith, the marine corps commander, sheepishly admitted that "history got ahead of us."[80]

The South Koreans were getting ahead of everyone. When the last of X Corps finally came ashore at Wonsan, most of the ROKA I Corps was ensconced in Unsan and Huichon, nearly a hundred miles northeast of Pyongyang and more than 120 miles across the mountains from Wonsan. Unsan was at the southern base of the high escarpments that constituted the mountainous roof of far northern Korea; Huichon was in the center of those mountains, called the Taebaeks. As soon as I Corps took the two towns, its commander ordered the Sixth Division to head north to the Yalu. He boldly sent two thin, pencillike reconnaissance probes ahead of the division, and, at dusk on the twenty-sixth, a handful of ROKA troopers from the Seventh Regiment of the Sixth Division pushed their way through the town of Chosin and stood on the banks of the Yalu looking across at Communist China. "Just four months plus one day after the beginning of the Korean war, they became the first United Nations unit to cover the 350 miles from the old [Naktong] perimeter to the Manchurian goal line." Fanning out along the Yalu, "they found no Reds." The troopers headed back to the advancing ROKA lines. The other probe had reached an old guerrilla fortress in Kanggye, a town high in the Taebaeks about forty miles south of the river. A cursory glance convinced the soldiers that there were no communists there either, and they also turned back. Admiring Americans began calling their South Korean allies "the Ramblin' Roks."[81]

But all was not well. Kim and his government had managed to escape from Pyongyang. On October 25, they reached Sinuiju on the south bank of the Yalu in the extreme northwestern corner of Korea. Sinuiju was linked to the Manchurian city of Antung by a three-thousand-foot railway drawbridge and a parallel highway bridge. MacArthur's people estimated that the remnants of the NKPA fleeing behind Kim toward Sinuiju numbered no more than twenty thousand. Somehow this last outpost of communist defiance would have to be destroyed.

❖ ❖ ❖

In fact, MacArthur should have pulled back his forces, concentrated his command, including the ROKA, at the Korean waist, and let the Chinese come to him. But the old general wanted it all. American boys—and British too—would stand where South Korean boys had stood, at the Yalu. International communism would be taught to respect U.S. and UN resolve. The South Koreans could not be allowed to win the Korean War alone. At Pyongyang on the nineteenth, MacArthur ordered Walker and Almond to use "maximum effort" and immediately push north from the Korean waist to a new line running from Sonchon to Songjin. They were to prepare to send their troops on "continued rapid advance to the border of North Korea." Five days later, MacArthur abolished the restraining line for non-ROKA units in North Korea and exhorted Almond, Walker, and their men to "drive forward with all speed and full utilization" of their resources "to secure all of North Korea," although UN forces would be withdrawn from the provinces bordering Manchuria "as quickly as feasible" and replaced with South Korean units.[82]

As military leaders and analysts around the world watched with disbelief, MacArthur committed the most fundamental military blunder: dividing his forces in the face of a potential enemy. The general explained his rationale in the Far East Command Report for November, in which he emphasized that "certain inflexible limitations were imposed" on UN forces in North Korea "by terrain, communications and logistical realities. The mountainous spine" of the Taebaeks "splitting North Korea from north to south divided the area into two distinct parts for military purposes, dictating a similar division in the command and organizational structure of ground forces during the period—Eighth Army in the western part and X Corps in the eastern area."[83] MacArthur and his field commanders were convinced that the NKPA was finished as a fighting force and that neither the Chinese nor Soviet armies would intervene.

Forced to use both the main highway along the western coastal corridor and wretched secondary roads through the adjacent hills, the Eighth Army continued north from Pyongyang toward the Chongchon River and Sinuiju. The ROKA I Corps remained on its right flank at Unsan and Huichon, while elements of the ROKA II Corps marched with Walker's columns. Units on the poor hill roads had to move slowly through the uneven terrain. Some columns became so compressed that they could not provide an effective, interlocking defense. Others were so spread out that they could not help each other if faced with a sudden enemy assault. Radio sets left over from World War II were almost useless in maintaining communications.

In the east, X Corps, relieved of any duty to move west and hook up with the Eighth Army along the waist, also prepared to drive north. Almond replicated MacArthur's blunder by splitting his own command in two. The Seventh Infantry would move north along the coast toward Hungnam and beyond, trying to catch up with rapidly advancing ROKA forces. The First Marine Division would drive inland, ascending the mountain roads toward Hagaru to support ROKA forces that were rushing toward the huge Chosin Reservoir and its power plants, which lay in the middle of the Taebaeks.

United Nations forces had lost all cohesion. Supply officers concluded that there was little need to worry about logistics. MacArthur exacerbated problems by making the Eighth Army responsible for supplying X Corps. The tactical and logistical muddle could only be sorted out when UN forces reached the Yalu River valley and could be reintegrated into a single military force. Meanwhile, no one thoroughly reconnoitered the high, forest-carpeted mountains of the Taebaek Range in between the Eighth Army and the ROKA Corps in the west and X Corps and its South Korean units in the east to see if an unmechanized army might be gathering there, waiting to pounce with grenades, mortars, and machine guns on an unsuspecting enemy below. The ROKA I Corps commander had sent one probe into the mountains and found nothing. He did not send others.

By ordering a reckless, ill-coordinated advance, MacArthur had once more challenged higher authority. His October 24 order directly violated the JCS directive of September 27. He should have been fired or at least reprimanded. Instead, the Joint Chiefs again caved in to him. They expressed "concern" over MacArthur's action but added that they "realize[d] that you undoubtedly had sound reasons for issuing these instructions." They asked to be kept informed. Truman said nothing.[84]

Bradley, however, was playing a duplicitous game. At Wake Island, he had heard MacArthur say that the Chinese would not intervene and if they did, the UN command could handle the situation. But after his return to Washington Bradley told the British Chiefs of Staff, who had crossed the Atlantic for a meeting, that "we all agree that if the Chinese Communists come into Korea, we get out."[85] So MacArthur would walk into Mao's trap with badly splintered forces and with his military superior quietly vowing not to support him if he faced serious difficulties.

Signs of potential trouble appeared during the third week of October, but no one paid attention. On the eighteenth, American warplanes, on a sweep against Sinuiju, saw nearly one hundred Soviet-built fighters at the air base at Antung just across the Yalu. The CIA suggested that the Red Chinese might fight to defend the hydroelectric facilities near Sinuiju.[86] Both reports were discounted.

Indeed, the American press almost dared the Chinese to intervene at this time, carefully enumerating the enormous industrial complexes that lined the Yalu River and emphasizing their importance not only to North Korea but also to Communist China and the Soviet Union. As Walker's Eighth Army pushed north from Pyongyang toward Sinuiju, *Newsweek* observed that the Reds had "grudgingly" surrendered the key rail center of Chonju less than seventy-five miles from Sinuiju and the Yalu. Sinuiju itself was a "Japanese-built industrial city of 61,143 people" containing Korea's largest lumber plant, a match factory, and a soybean oil facility. Over in Antung were large explosives, power, and chemical plants. The Sinuiju airfield was "the closest in Korea to the twin Russian-occupied harbors of Dairen and Port Arthur." Up the Yalu, between Sinuiju and the village of Chosin, which the ROKA reconnaissance unit had reached on October 26, was Sakchu, "an even more sensitive spot" because it contained Korea's biggest hydroelectric plant. The Soviets had stripped this complex in 1945; then, realizing its capital importance, they had rebuilt it. "Together with smaller power installations," the Sakchu hydroelectric facility "feeds electricity not only to Korea but to the Manchurian industries at Mukden and Harbin and even to Soviet Dairen." Finally, along the Yalu between Sakchu and Chosin lay the 116-square-mile Supung Reservoir, which supplied water to the Yalu hydroelectric facilities. The Japanese-built dam was "Asia's largest," a modern, reinforced concrete structure rivaling Hoover Dam in size and capable of providing water to power 640,000 kilowatts.[87]

MacArthur's assumption that neither Mao nor Stalin would defend one of the world's major industrial power centers strains credulity. American publications observed that Washington had insisted that MacArthur's air force refrain from bombing the communist installations, even those on the Korean side, and that this message had been conveyed to the Chinese and Soviets to demonstrate American restraint. With UN columns approaching the Yalu, Mao and Stalin had legitimate grounds for believing that the

Americans were not bombing the Korean reservoirs and power plants because they wanted to use them.

By the fourth week in October, Mao's commitment to Korea had been matched by MacArthur's folly and Washington's blind deference to its field commander. All the elements for an American disaster had locked into place.

9

Disaster

❖ ❖ ❖ ❖ ❖ ❖ ❖ ❖ ❖ ❖ ❖ ❖ ❖ ❖ ❖ ❖

The nearly six weeks after Inchon were the calmest days of 1950, perhaps the quietest time the nation would know for many years. The news from Korea was so consistently good that Acheson spent much of his time in Europe and nearly all of his energy on European affairs. The politicians and the press focused on the upcoming state and congressional elections, while much of the nation concentrated on the fate of the Philadelphia Phillies, who had thrown off decades of determined incompetence to humble the mighty Dodgers and the arrogant Cardinals and win the National League pennant. The "Whiz Kids"—Granny Hamner, Mike Goliat, Jim Konstanty, Eddie Waitkus, and others—would enjoy one brief season in the sun before being swept by the Yankees in the World Series. By 1952, most of them would return to obscurity, but for a few exciting weeks in the early autumn they kept Americans glued to their radios and small television screens. Television dealers, still a novelty in those days, placed sets in their store windows so passing pedestrians could steal a minute or an hour to watch a crucial baseball game in progress hundreds of miles away.

Korea was another diversion, of course, but one that America's youth had no desire to experience firsthand. The war had not begun with a treacherous bombing of American property or a sudden loss of several thousand American lives. There was no symbol around which to whip up public opinion. There were no emotional mass enlistments, and draft calls were comparatively few. (In November 1943, New York City was told to produce 46,000 men for military service; seven years later, the government asked for only 4,180.) Pretty girls did not stare with contempt at young men not in uniform. To the adolescents of midcentury, World War II was long ago and Korea was far away. Selective service officials found that the youngsters who came before them were at best sullen and resigned. The chairman of Local Draft Board Number 14 in New York City realized that the attitudes of draftees differed "sharply" from the youngsters he had seen seven and eight years before. In 1942 the inductees had not griped as their younger brothers did in 1950. "The spirit—the sense of participating in something important, of doing a necessary job—that characterized World War II selectees is missing from the men being called up today," he told a journalist. "There isn't the same cooperation. All we can do is explain to them that they have an obligation to their country that they must perform." The young men were not convinced, and usually draft boards were unable to create "a little good will" among those they selected for military service.[1] But the selectees dutifully went into the armed forces as their grandfathers, fathers, and brothers had before them. It seemed that each generation had its own war to fight, its own moral imperative to vanquish the forces of tyranny.

Things were not much different in Wauseon, Ohio, population 3,500, thirty-five miles west of Toledo. The local draft board had called up perhaps a score of youngsters by October, but so far no one from the town had been killed or wounded or was missing in action. Wauseon's young men did not want to go to war, but, like their city cousins, they went when called.[2]

Those already on the Korean battle lines were just as reluctant. In the autumn of 1950, Bill Shirk, a nineteen-year-old gunner from Ohio serving in the Fifteenth Artillery Division, was in a hospital in Osaka, Japan, recovering from wounds received on the perimeter. He had been in Korea only a few weeks when an NKPA patrol had ambushed his truck convoy and nearly wiped it out, but like his buddies he had quickly grown to hate the smelly rice paddies, the pathetic peasant villages with their miserable huts and strange people, and the weird, frightening enemy who was collectively labeled "gook." "Like everybody else—I felt really happy to be getting out of this stinking place." To his disgust, he was sent back to the front as soon as his wounds healed.[3]

On October 25, Korea again dominated American headlines. Advancing Eighth Army and X Corps units, along with their ROKA allies, were suddenly and violently attacked by the enemy. A regiment of the ROKA Sixth

Division in the west was struck about forty miles north of the Chongchon River. Within forty-eight hours, it was annihilated. The rest of the Sixth Division, including the handful of troopers who had reached the Yalu hours before, was nearly wiped out as it moved north of Unsan. The other two ROKA divisions in the western advance, the First and Eighth, were also heavily attacked, producing a complete collapse of the ROKA II Corps and dangerously exposing the right flank of the Eighth Army, whose own units were widely scattered along the coastal corridor. The veteran Twenty-Fourth Infantry Division, which had been in action since July 3, had reached the village of Chonggo-Dong, only eighteen miles from Sinuiju and the Yalu. It and a British brigade, also well north of the Chongchon River, were now in danger of being trapped. Both units were ordered to retreat southward to the Chongchon as quickly as possible, while Johnnie Walker sent the First Cavalry and Second Infantry Divisions north to stop the enemy thrust. By November 1, the enemy had pushed far south of Huichon, was threatening Unsan, and was sending advance units south of the Chongchon toward Kunu-ri and Pyongyang.

Eastward, across the Taebaek mountain range, the ROKA Third Division, which was leading the drive toward the Chosin Reservoir, was suddenly confronted on October 25 by a heavy enemy armored attack at Sudong. The ROKA division held on for nearly a week before frantically signaling for help. Ned Almond sent the Seventh Marine Regiment to the South Koreans' aid. By November 2, the Seventh was engaged in furious battle, and for the next five days it badly mauled enemy units and columns while occasionally being outmaneuvered and shot up.

Who was this suddenly resuscitated foe? As prisoners began to be taken, it was clear that most were from the apparently revived "remnants" of the NKPA, but some were Chinese who called themselves "volunteers." The word raced from intelligence officers to headquarters, journalists, and the world. The Chinese were intervening in the Korean War, but no one knew how many and what their purpose was.

Washington's reaction was sluggish. Acheson would recall that "it took time for report of the events of October 25–November 1 to percolate from North Korea through Tokyo to Washington—if, indeed, it ever did percolate in recognizable form."[4] On October 28, he sent a directive to Tokyo, approved by the State Department, the Pentagon, and Truman, with guidelines for the occupation of North Korea. MacArthur would have another province to govern. A day earlier Consul General James Wilkinson at the Hong Kong listening post had told Acheson that, according to a "reliable source," Mao had sent two divisions of troops into Korea but would send no more. According to this source, the head of Peking's observation group in Korea had advised against intervention because Chinese forces could not cope with UN air power or artillery. Even if Stalin provided air support, MacArthur's bombers and fighters could disrupt China's internal transportation system, making it "very difficult" to get supplies to troops in Korea.[5]

By November 1, however, Washington had awakened to the peril. In a memorandum to Truman, the CIA concluded that Mao's "main motivation at present appears to be to establish a limited 'cordon sanitaire' south of the Yalu" to protect the "Suiho Hydroelectric Zone." Agency analysts also declared that "current reports" of "Soviet-type jet aircraft in the Antung-Sinuiju area" suggested that Stalin was ready to provide at least logistical air defense for the Manchurian–North Korean border region.[6]

The State Department's China desk expressed greater concern. Was the Chinese intervention the beginning of a worldwide Soviet military offensive? O. Edmund Clubb reminded Dean Rusk that Russia's UN ambassador, Andrey Vyshinsky, had recently repeated earlier claims that MacArthur was using or planning to use Japanese troops in Korea and might employ them as part of an invasion of mainland China. Vyshinsky could be laying the groundwork for a full-scale Soviet intervention in Korea. It was equally possible "that the Soviets plan action elsewhere to equal the Chinese Communist effort" in Korea. The presence of four Russian armies southwest of Berlin was ominous, for recent reports had indicated that Stalin might attempt to force unification of the city. Radio Peking had not mentioned protecting the Yalu hydroelectric installations but had repeatedly talked about assisting the North Koreans and resisting UN approaches to China's Manchurian border. By November 3, Wilkinson had become less optimistic and reported that articles and speeches fiercely hostile to the United States were appearing almost daily in major Chinese publications. The "line followed in all these statements" was that Washington was "bent on world conquest[,] that aggression against Korea" would be followed by an invasion of Manchuria, and that the "Chinese must aid Koreans in order [to] defend [their] own territory."[7]

Far East Command in Tokyo was equally slow to comprehend the peril, and when MacArthur finally acknowledged the Chinese intervention, his reaction was more petulant than alarmed. The Commies were not playing according to international rules of warfare. On November 4, the supreme commander issued UN Communiqué No. 11, reconfirming the defeat and destruction of the NKPA, which was not entirely true. Then, he continued, "the Communists committed one of the most offensive acts of international lawlessness of historic record by moving without any notice of belligerency elements of alien communist forces across the Yalu River into North Korea and massing a great concentration of possible reinforcing divisions with adequate supply behind the privileged sanctuary of the adjacent Manchurian border."[8]

The same day MacArthur sent Washington a draft special report for transmittal to the United Nations, describing in general terms the history of Chinese intervention. It had begun, MacArthur contended, as early as August 20, when Chinese antiaircraft guns on the Manchurian side of the Yalu had shot at American bomber and fighter planes flying near the river. Sporadic gunfire against U.S. aircraft had continued ever since. Some planes had been damaged, but none were lost. The first contact between Chinese and UN troops had taken place near the Chosin Reservoir on October 16 (the day after Mao began committing his forces), when approximately twenty-five hundred communist troops briefly engaged advance patrols of the ROKA army coming up from Hamhung. By October 20, five thousand Chinese troops had crossed the Yalu in the Antung-Sinuiju area, but they had not gone farther to make contact with the UN forces that had just captured Pyongyang. Thereafter MacArthur's report made little reference to the estimated size of the Chinese forces that had entered Korea.[9]

Truman, Acheson, and the Pentagon were understandably baffled by the latest developments. MacArthur's November 4 communiqué suggested that his assurances to the president at Wake Island three weeks earlier had been completely contradicted and that the supreme commander had been overly optimistic. Or was Washington misreading the situation? Truman ordered George Marshall to get an estimate from MacArthur. The general replied immediately that although a huge Chinese thrust into Korea was "a distinct possibility, and many foreign experts predict such action, there are many fundamental logical reasons against it." But he did not explain what these "logical reasons" were. He concluded that Mao was probably planning to provide the shredded NKPA with covert military assistance, possibly a few thousand volunteers, so the North Korean government at Sinuiju could "retain a nominal foothold in Korea." Or perhaps the Chinese had sent a few thousand troops in the mistaken belief "that no UN forces would be committed in the extreme northern reaches of Korea," leaving that area exclusively to the ROKA. MacArthur recommended "against hasty conclusions which might be premature." He believed "that a final appraisement should await a more complete accumulation of military facts."[10]

Washington was not satisfied with the general's vague assurances. Newspapers throughout the country were reporting new defeats on the Korean battlefront, and the world situation was suddenly ominous. On November 3: "Allies Line Thrown Back: Reds within 47 Miles of Their Lost Capital"; on November 4: "Trap 2 More Yank Forces: Chinese Slip Past Marines and Cut Road"; on November 5: "Reds Open New Tank Drive; Gain Two Miles near Allies' Western Line." A *Portland Oregonian* headline read: "Chinese in Korea Seen As World War III Hint."[11]

On November 1, the First Cavalry, rushing north to rescue the British and the Twenty-fourth Division, was suddenly struck by Chinese forces north of Yongsan, and one regiment was "routed." Soon the handful of exhausted survivors, dirty and unshaven, talked to reporters on one of the town's street corners. The "First Cav" had also been in Korea since the summer and had suffered some stinging defeats during vicious battles with the NKPA along the perimeter. But this "was a worse nightmare than Yongdong or the 'bowling alley' north of Taegu," Pvt. Ronald Swanson of Milwaukee said. "I never saw so many Gooks," he added. "We were hit from all directions at once. The Chinese were big fellows. Some were on horseback. They attacked with the blowing of bugles, just like the North Koreans sometimes do." Surrounded by Mao's forces, Swanson and a handful of buddies had to make several banzai charges to get away. "We jumped up and down and hollered and then charged them. . . . It worked. If we had not broken that road block we never would have got out." After shaking off the Chinese, the Americans walked to a village, where they discovered what they thought were South Korean troops. "But we found out different . . . when they started throwing hand grenades at us." For days survivors continued to trickle back to steadily retreating American lines. "We got mousetrapped, that's all," Cpl. Robert Stephen of Indiana told another newsman. Stephen was caught in enemy cross fire in the middle of a rice paddy but managed to escape when other GIs on a nearby hill provided covering fire.[12]

Acheson wanted to take the Korean problem to the UN Security Council immediately, although he knew that Jacob Malik would veto any resolution condemning Red China. But, as the secretary of state cabled Ernest Bevin on the sixth, MacArthur's appraisals did "not contain sufficiently detailed information to permit an immediate estimate" of Chinese intentions. "We are giving this problem most urgent attention both in Washington and Tokyo. . . . We should greatly appreciate any info or views which you might have on this most important point." Meanwhile State Department experts like John Paton Davies were warning that Soviet and Chinese objectives in Korea and elsewhere remained "veiled from us" and that "situations such as this tend to generate their own imperatives."[13]

On Monday, November 6, the day before the off-year elections, Truman was in Kansas City, waiting to cast his ballot in Independence. Suddenly Acheson was calling from a conference room in the State Department, where he was meeting with Under Secretary of Defense Robert Lovett. Word had just arrived from Tokyo that MacArthur had ordered a massive bombing raid by B-29s against the Yalu River bridge linking Sinuiju and Antung. Acheson was deeply disturbed that this action might send the wrong signal to Peking. Truman replied that he would authorize the raid only if UN troops were in immediate jeopardy from men and matériel crossing that bridge. Acheson and Lovett replied that there was no such danger, and MacArthur was ordered to cancel the air strike, which was scheduled to take off in less than two hours.

Truman's abrupt intervention in the Korean War quickly evoked an anguished response from MacArthur. He first wrote a request for immediate relief from duty, which his acting chief of staff, Maj. Gen. Doyle O. Hickey, persuaded him to rescind. Hickey argued that the UN soldiers would not understand why their supreme commander was bugging out at such an unpropitious moment. Perhaps remembering the bitter reactions to his recall from the Bataan front eight years before, MacArthur relented, but he vented his anger in a long cable to Washington. "Men and material in large force are pouring across all bridges over the Yalu from Manchuria. This movement not only jeopardizes but threatens the ultimate destruction of the forces under my command." He asked for an instant reconsideration of instructions and promised compliance with those already issued. The next day he amplified his concerns. "Hostile" aircraft were operating from bases just north of the Yalu "against our forces in North Korea. These planes are appearing in increasing numbers." Because distances from the Chinese airfields in Manchuria to the North Korean front were so short, it was almost impossible to intercept these planes. Morale and combat efficiency among UN ground and air units were plummeting, and "unless corrective measures are promptly taken this factor can assume decisive proportions."[14]

The last vestiges of optimism that had emerged from the Wake Island meeting had evaporated, and Washington could have been pardoned for thinking that MacArthur was losing his nerve. In forty-eight hours he had gone from nearly dismissing a Chinese threat to making it his major concern. But MacArthur could plausibly be defended for responsibly describing an entirely new and fluid military situation to his commander in chief in the most dramatic, attention-getting way possible.

Washington was torn. The Joint Chiefs responded to MacArthur's November 6 message by assuring him that "consideration [was] being urgently given [to the] Korean situation." But the Chiefs also warned the supreme commander that "one factor is present commitment not to take action affecting Manchuria without consultation with the British." Therefore, "until further orders, postpone all bombing of targets within five miles of Manchurian border."[15]

At the same time, the administration was quietly exploring use of the atomic bomb in Korea to counter any major Chinese military action. That possibility was first discussed on November 4 in a meeting between Brig. Gen. Herbert B. Loper, the Pentagon's top atomic energy specialist, and Paul Nitze, director of the State Department's Policy Planning Staff. Four days later, one of Rusk's subordinates submitted a long, thoughtful memorandum on the subject. He concluded that the bomb should only be used if UN forces on the peninsula were in extremis. He warned that any unilateral U.S. decision to use the bomb would have a devastating effect on the nation's moral position in the world and would undoubtedly destroy the UN unity needed to fight the war. Moreover, dropping the bomb on Chinese military columns or installations would confirm Soviet propaganda that the United States was "bent on initiating general war." Finally, the United States, like an alcoholic, could not stop with just one. "In order to obtain decisive results" against a full-scale Chinese intervention "we should undoubtedly have to engage in atomic warfare on a wide scale. This would involve us deep in Asia and make it difficult, if not impossible, to withdraw in order to fight in another theater of war."[16]

Washington and the Far East Command were uneasily aware that Sino-Soviet intentions could be most accurately determined from what was happening in the air above the Yalu. The sudden appearance on November 1 of "Red jets" over the battlefield was especially disturbing. It was not clear whether these aircraft were manned by Soviet pilots (it later transpired that some were), but their presence was a further indication of a major change in the war.

Omar Bradley had been so perturbed by the tone and content of MacArthur's November 4 and 6 messages that he read them to Truman over the phone, and the president, although aware of the "grave dangers" involved, reluctantly granted MacArthur permission to reschedule bombing of the Yalu bridges if they could be knocked down on the Korean side of the river. The communists responded within a few days. On November 16, Acheson passed a top secret message to Marshall. The State Department had just learned that the counselor to the Soviet Embassy in Peking had told Indian Ambassador Kavalam Panikkar "that if United Nations planes bomb Manchuria, they would be attacked by the Air Force of the Soviet Union." Acheson informed Marshall that he could pass the word on to MacArthur, but if so, "it is requested that special security precautions be used because of the extreme sensitivity of the source." MacArthur did not believe the Soviet threat was sufficiently imminent to force a cancellation of bombing along the Yalu.[17]

By November 7, Walker's intelligence officers estimated "that 3 Chinese Communist units of divisional size, totalling 27,000 personnel, are committed in the 8th Army Zone." That day Hickey, in a report titled "Order of Battle Information, Chinese Communist, Regular Ground Forces, Fourth Field Army," indicated that the Fourth, commanded by Mao's ablest general, Lin Piao, might enter Korea at any moment. Four days later, a CIA intelligence update on Soviet capabilities and intentions concluded that although "to date" there was no evidence that Stalin would bring Russian air, naval, and ground forces into the conflict, "the commitment of Chinese Communist forces, with Soviet material aid, indicates that the USSR considers the Korean situation of sufficient importance to warrant the risk of general war."[18]

The Joint Chiefs were now aware that the escalating crisis in Korea could get out of hand. On the eighth, they cabled MacArthur that the introduction of Chinese forces to the extent that he had reported created a "new situation" in which the earlier objective of destroying the NKPA might "have to be reexamined." MacArthur was incensed. He could not agree with that interpretation, he replied the next day. "In my opinion it would be fatal to weaken the fundamental and basic policy of the United Nations to destroy all resisting armed forces in Korea and bring that country into a united and free nation." If he continued to have the use of unrestricted air power over Korea, MacArthur added, he could prevent Chinese reinforcements from coming across the Yalu in sufficient strength to either threaten his command or thwart his "mission of driving to the border and securing all of North Korea" beginning "about November 15." MacArthur added that the United States should urge the United Nations to condemn Communist China for flouting the will of the international body, and if Mao did not withdraw his forces immediately, the United Nations should consider unspecified sanctions against Peking.[19]

In his monthly activities report for November 1950, MacArthur claimed that his people had "closely watched" the "buildup of CCF [Chinese Communist forces] strength in Manchuria." In July, Mao had only 116,000 regular troops on the border; by late September, the number had risen to 450,000 "and reached a total of 850,000 in Manchuria and Korea by 16 November." But no one could guess during the first ten days of November exactly what Mao and Stalin's intentions were. Walker, Almond, MacArthur, and their intelligence people "were not yet ready to accept the fact that Chinese forces of division and army size were already south of the Yalu." Walker told reporters that no one should assume that the Chinese were extensively committed just because a growing number of prisoners had been seized. "After all, a lot of Mexicans live in Texas."[20]

At home, the press nervously shared the same view and sought to reassure the public. The liberal *New Republic,* which from the beginning had concluded that the war was an essential test of UN strength and resolve, argued that there were good reasons to believe that a full-scale Chinese intervention was unlikely. Yes, Mao had probably 300,000 to 500,000 troops on the Manchurian border. But "the supply of munitions to such large forces fighting a destructive Western style war is beyond Chinese capability and would seriously strain Soviet communications to the Far East." Moreover, this was not the kind of war in which huge numbers of troops could be used effectively. MacArthur could easily defend the waist of Korea with no more than ten divisions, and there were already 300,000 Americans, Britons, and South Koreans under his command.[21]

General Carl A. Spaatz, former air force chief of staff and now a *Newsweek* columnist, agreed. Confirmed reports that Chinese troops were fighting in Korea were "disquieting." But "it is difficult to believe that the Chinese will commit their forces in major strength unless guaranteed at least the support of the Soviet Russian air force. And if it is true that Soviet Russia does not want to enter the conflict at this time, then the Korean war should be liquidated within a few months." Why, then, had the Chinese intervened? Probably just to put up "a token fight to save the face of their foreign minister [Zhou Enlai], who promised help to the North Koreans." Another, more plausible reason was to let the United Nations know that it must not threaten Manchuria's hydroelectric power installations along the Yalu basin.[22]

Air power was the key factor in the Korean War, Spaatz argued. Because the UN command retained its quantitative and qualitative superiority, the Soviet Union "has indicated up to now that it is not willing to risk its air force" in the conflict. Thus it was obvious that if the Chinese continued their force buildup and their fight, "it will be necessary for the United Nations to bomb supply lines and industrial targets deep in Chinese territory." This was the simple logic of war.[23] MacArthur shared Spaatz's view. He would never be convinced of the need for a limited war in the nuclear age. If your forces were attacked, you went after the enemy, if you could, in "hot pursuit." This was particularly true in aerial warfare, including aerial bombardment. There could be no sanctuaries during wartime.

Despite the reassurance of political neophytes like the editors of the *New Republic* and military professionals like Spaatz, the American people had been jolted by the news from Korea. Everyone knew that the United States was now engaged in a "fresh war with a fresh Red army." The first week in November had been the "blackest" time in the conflict since Inchon. Somehow, in ways that MacArthur and his people in Tokyo and Korea had never anticipated, Mao and his generals had pushed sizable numbers of troops across the Yalu and into North Korea. In fact, Mao had done more than the UN command had ever imagined. "Between October 13 and 25 the intelligence staffs of MacArthur's armies failed to discern the slightest evidence of the movement of 130,000 soldiers and porters" across the Yalu.[24]

How had Mao done it with the bridges under constant daytime surveillance? His success was partly due to Washington's initial refusal to let MacArthur's fliers bomb the bridges. But when such bombardments were authorized, darkness and the weather became Peking's allies. Most of the units that had moved into Korea had crossed during the night and had immediately hidden in the Taebaek Mountains, awaiting word on whether or not to strike. These Chinese People's Volunteers were tough and hardy. Veterans of the campaigns not only against Chiang's hapless forces but also the superb Japanese army of 1937–45, they carried at most ten pounds of supplies per day, not the sixty pounds that each UN soldier counted on to fight with. The units that Mao sent over the Yalu between mid-October and mid-November possessed little armored support, depending almost exclusively on deadly, well-handled mortars for their offensive power. The tanks that ROKA forces near the Chosin Reservoir claimed had attacked them were probably the remnants of NKPA units. Indeed, the NKPA, stronger and better equipped than MacArthur's staff realized, played a significant role in the late October–early November counteroffensive against UN forces.

The Chinese, in their quilted cotton uniforms and tennis shoes, could quick march or trot mile after mile up mountain tracks, "hauling all that they possessed in the world." Along with mortars for each unit, each man carried a personal weapon, eighty rounds of ammunition and a grenade or two, spare foot rags, sewing kit, chopsticks, and a week's rations or less— tea, rice, sugar, and small tins of meat or fish. "Thus, to sustain fifty divisions in combat, Peking needed to move only 2,500 tons of supplies a day south across the Yalu." Here was the source of MacArthur's tragic intelligence miscalculation. Peking could support a major army in Korea despite the most determined aerial warfare. That army would rely on sudden, overwhelming attacks for success. It would shock and demoralize its better armed and more maneuverable enemy, which had total air superiority.[25]

There was never any doubt that Washington would support MacArthur's determination to renew the Korean offensive, but since a formal decision was necessary, the National Security Council (NSC) met on November 9. The Joint Chiefs of Staff had already voiced their concerns. In a memorandum to Marshall they requested that "every effort . . . be expended" to settle the problem of Chinese intervention in Korea by "political means, preferably through the United Nations." But "pending further clarification" of Peking's military intentions, "the missions assigned to the Commander in Chief, United Nations Command should be kept under review, but should not be changed."[26]

Truman did not attend the NSC meeting, but all the other key players were present, and the president was immediately informed about the discussion and its outcome.[27] Before ratifying MacArthur's request to resume the offensive, Bradley, Marshall, Acheson, and others reviewed the situation carefully. Bradley believed that the Chinese had one of three objectives in mind. They might be merely trying to establish a shallow buffer zone in far northern Korea to protect the Yalu installations. If so, negotiations at the United Nations to demarcate areas of occupation might be "fruitful." Second, Mao might be considering an exhausting war of attrition that would tie down most of America's military resources for an indefinite period.

Third, he could be planning to drive UN forces "completely off the Korean peninsula." This would probably bring World War III. MacArthur should be authorized to at least hold his present positions in North Korea, but it was not clear "how much pressure we could stand" from a renewed Chinese offensive "without attacking Manchurian bases." Bradley believed MacArthur's claim that bombing the Yalu bridges would stifle further Chinese assaults was overly optimistic. Walter Bedell Smith, head of the CIA, warned that the Yalu would be completely frozen over in fifteen to thirty days, after which bombing the bridges would have no value whatsoever.

Marshall intervened. He thought MacArthur had spread his forces too widely and thinly. Well, Bradley replied, the supreme command had no choice if he was to carry out his UN mandate to occupy all of Korea and conduct national elections. Acheson then spoke up. He believed Stalin had two objectives in Korea: to keep the West tied down militarily and to protect the Yalu power installations. What about solving the problem by bringing a proposal to the Soviets in New York? (The United Nations had just moved into lavish headquarters overlooking the East River in midtown Manhattan.) Washington would agree to a twenty-mile demilitarized zone on either side of the Yalu enforced by a UN commission with a constabulary but no UN troops. But Acheson realized that the Soviets would only accept such a proposal if all UN troops left the peninsula, thus eventually allowing the communists to take over.

Acheson turned to Bradley and asked the central question. Would it not be best to order MacArthur to organize and hold a more defensible line? Bradley replied that the wisest course might be to pull back to the Korean waist, but doing so "might lose us the South Koreans' will to fight." Torn by doubt and uncertainty, the NSC then basically agreed to follow the previous recommendations of the Joint Chiefs. When Acheson later summarized the conclusion for Truman, he pointed out that "General MacArthur's directive should not now be changed and . . . he should be free to do what he could in a military way, but without bombing Manchuria." Truman was concerned about Chinese aggression all around eastern Asia. Growing evidence indicated that Mao was providing Ho Chi Minh and the Vietcong with the supplies needed to maintain their offensive against the increasingly demoralized French in Indochina, and the recent Chinese lunge into Tibet had troubling implications for the future integrity of India and Pakistan. But above all "I had no intention," Truman later wrote, "of allowing our attention to be diverted from the unchanging aims and designs of Soviet policy.

I knew that in our age, Europe, with its millions of skilled workmen, with its factories and transportation network, is still the key to world peace."

Winter came to Korea in mid-November, further aiding the Chinese buildup. American and British troops, who had slogged through the debilitating heat and driving rains of high summer on the perimeter and had then experienced the pleasant days of late September and October as they moved up the peninsula, now faced another change in climate. Temperatures dropped precipitously, snow began to fall, and, most important, ice formed on the Chongchon and the Yalu. As UN troops shivered in the cold (most were only half-prepared for winter weather), the frozen Yalu became a highway, not a barrier, for the Chinese. Troops, transport, and supplies streamed across the river at night, unmolested by allied air strikes. An entire Chinese army concentrated clandestinely in the Taebaeks, ready to burst out of the mountains at any point in a flood of troops and gunfire. But Mao had so far sent only a fraction of his mighty force against the advancing UN columns. It was a warning to MacArthur to retreat, to get out of Korea, before disaster struck.

United Nations delegates in New York were as uneasy and concerned as the administration in Washington. Clearly it was time to determine what China's intentions were in Korea. Trygve Lie invited Mao to send representatives to address the Security Council. They would come, the Chinese replied sullenly on November 11, but only to talk about American aggression against Formosa, not about Korea or any other subject.

The sudden turn of events in the Far East profoundly if not decisively affected the American national elections as, perhaps, Mao had intended. For all Republicans, moderates and conservatives, the news from Korea that first week in November could not have come at a better time. In an election year in a democracy the first rule is to win, and the disaster in Asia was a winning issue. Even moderate Republicans became enthusiastic Red-baiters during the final days and hours of the campaign.

The Republican National Committee issued a pamphlet titled "Background to Korea," charging that the Asian war was the culmination of half a decade of Democratic folly and worse. All the old chestnuts were called forth once more—Yalta; Potsdam; the partition of Germany, which ostensibly weakened the United Nations; and, above all, the rapid demobilization of the finest armed forces in the world—and laid at the feet of Harry Truman and the Democratic Eighty-first Congress. "The blindness of our leadership in ignoring the Communist attempt to capture the minds of men" had led to the loss of American initiative and "the influence for peace." Responsible Republican leadership had eventually forged an effective bipartisan foreign policy that had saved Western Europe, but in the Far East nefarious policymakers had convinced the country "that Chinese Communism was only a great agrarian reform movement." New Deal–Fair Deal Asia and China policies were characterized in terms of "subtle betrayals" and "sabotage," which had "turned over to Stalin the control" of Manchuria and Outer Mongolia. By its persistent "temporiz[ing]" the Truman administration had "given a green light" to communist domination of East Asia.[28]

The National Committee had provided Republican candidates a crude, powerful message, and hundreds of eager aspirants for public office exploited the opportunity. A candidate for local office in Illinois claimed on the eve of the election that a vote for the Democrats would be a ratification of "rationing controls, bungling foreign policies, and more military drafts." It would be "a vote for national socialism," World War III, and "the approval of Communist coddling and smear and sneer," which had forced those in large cities to endure atom bomb drills "because most of our sacred secrets have been turned over to Communist Russia by the New Deal spies and henchmen in official positions in high places in our government."[29]

Republicans charged that known communists were financing the Senate candidacy of liberal Helen Gahagan Douglas in California in order to ensure her victory over stalwart Commie-fighter Richard Nixon. California's William Knowland charged that Truman was trying to prevent the public from knowing that Chinese troops were in Korea, and Republicans in radio addresses expressed fury that the administration was now planning to draft men for two and a half instead of only two years. How could Scott Lucas claim that he was a Truman supporter when he had voted for the McCarran Act? The Democrats were in disarray as usual, and, as in 1946, it was time for a change.[30]

Everett McKinley Dirksen, a solemn, rubber-faced, deep-voiced man from rural and Middletown "downstate" Illinois, campaigned vigorously against Lucas. He sensed that the senator was in trouble and in a radio address condemned the Democrats for placing billboards throughout the Chicago area that read: "Vote Democratic for world peace." Where was peace when the draft and the national military establishment were being extended, Dirksen asked. Where was peace when the administration decided that the recent enemy, Germany, had to be rearmed, "thus undermining all the work done by dead G.I.'s"? The collapsing world situation was all the fault of the Truman administration. "You Democrats have botched and bungled all along the line," Dirksen concluded. "The world situation is a result of your stupidity."[31]

The *Chicago Tribune*'s Col. Robert McCormick wrote three days before the election that "another Acheson betrayal" had created the crisis in Korea. It was Acheson's fault that American and South Korean forces had suffered "serious reverses." The secretary of state was responsible for the humiliating defeat of the First Cavalry Division, whose men had abandoned wounded comrades. He was ultimately the culprit who had forced the Twenty-fourth Infantry Division to withdraw and retreat fifty miles. "Gen. MacArthur's campaign had smashed the North Korean army," but Acheson's diplomacy had destroyed everything the general had accomplished. Acheson had encouraged Chinese aggression by working cozily with the British Empire to get Peking into the United Nations. He had turned the entire Formosa question over to the world body instead of embracing Chiang. "Having got the United States committed to the Red cause before the U.N.," McCormick wrote, "Stalin has, as usual, pulled the rug out from under his dupe. More American boys are dying in Korea because our foreign relations are entrusted to Mr. Acheson whose chief qualification for the job is that he doesn't look like a fool or a Red sympathizer. Once again it can be observed that appearances are often deceiving."[32]

On election eve, Harold Stassen delivered the most stinging condemnation of administration policy over the Mutual Broadcasting System, reiterating virtually every charge that McCormick, Dirksen, and others had leveled at Truman and Acheson. Outside Wauseon, Ohio, Cliff Clevenger, the Republican candidate for Congress, put up numerous signs with a single message: "'SIMPLE ARITHMETIC — COMMUNISTS IN HIGH PLACES + BUNGLING LEADERSHIP = WAR IN KOREA.' Therefore, elect me."[33]

McCarthy was the master orchestrator of the conservative offensive. He pinned the charge of "'Communism, Confusion, and Corruption'" on the Democrats and made it stick. "GOP candidates in every important Senatorial and gubernatorial election hewed to this central line," and it paid off. The Wisconsin senator's chief target was Millard Tydings, the man who had humiliated him by rejecting his allegations of communists in the State Department. After appearing on behalf of Republican aspirants in eight other states, McCarthy stumped Maryland during the last week of the campaign.

His speeches were all the same and all effective. Acheson was "the procurer of the pinks and punks in the State Department." Truman and his administration formed the "Commiecrat Party." When the GOP won control of Congress, "you will see the greatest exodus from Washington of that motley crimson clique that this nation has or ever will see."[34]

On election day, the Republicans won impressive victories in Congress, the statehouses, and the governor's mansions as fundamentalist conservatives routed their liberal opponents. Dirksen defeated Lucas handily. Nixon had no trouble beating Douglas in California, and a nonentity in Maryland trounced Tydings. Fundamentalist conservatives were ecstatic. The *Chicago Tribune*'s political cartoon the morning after the election was typical. An evil-looking Stalin, pipe clenched in his mouth, stands on the shores of Europe. One hand holds a bloody bayonet; the other is clutching the top of a tombstone. He is looking across the Atlantic at the United States, where the feet and legs of a corpse (obviously the Democratic party) are covered with a huge pile of papers labeled "votes." Stalin is saying: "Buried alive—How barbarous!" "Congress has moved strongly from left to right," the *New Republic* moaned. "Senate Democrats were a battered army whose command post had been blown up," *Newsweek* added.[35]

A Republican matron asked a man attending his first postelection party at Taft campaign headquarters in Cincinnati to be patient if the celebrants seemed like overwrought children. "If you knew how many damned wakes we've attended here, you'd understand." The CIO and AFL combined had spent close to one million dollars, a huge sum in those days, to defeat Taft and other Republican candidates. The Ohio senator had begged his constituents to restore traditional America—a nation of docility, deference, and social and economic discipline—and they had responded. Taft piled up a smashing, totally unexpected victory that observers immediately compared to FDR's big 1936 win. In California, a victorious Nixon joyously reminded associates that he had intended all along to use the communist issue against Douglas. It also worked well in southern primaries against liberals Claude Pepper of Florida and Frank Graham of North Carolina. The 1950 elections, pollster Samuel Lubell subsequently concluded, had been "the most crushing setbacks Southern liberalism has suffered since the coming of Franklin Roosevelt."[36]

The Republicans did not win control of Congress, but they came very close, gaining five Senate seats to reach a near parity of forty-seven to forty-nine with their opponents and cutting the Democratic majority in the House from more than ninety seats to just forty. Three former GOP members of the

House Committee on Un-American Activities—Nixon, Karl Mundt, and Francis Case of South Dakota—moved up to the Senate. Not only were Lucas and Tydings gone, but so were the majority whip and the chairman of the Labor Committee. Their replacements were conservative southern Democrats Harry Byrd of Virginia and Walter George of Georgia, who were entirely comfortable with Taft, if not Wherry or McCarthy.

Newsweek correctly identified McCarthy as "one of the heroes" of the campaign. Soon after beating Lucas, Dirksen intoned that his goal was to be "a second McCarthy." Dispassionate observers concluded that now Truman would not be able to "defy" MacArthur on Far Eastern policy since the general was "a particular favorite of the Republicans." Formosa would be kept out of Chinese Communist hands "by whatever means necessary," and Acheson was clearly through. Not only were the Republicans out to get him, but Democratic party leaders realized that he had become a distinct liability.[37]

When Lubell later reexamined what had happened to Frank Graham, he discovered that racial hatreds and divisions had contributed much more to the Democratic aspirant's defeat than had any message that McCarthy might have delivered about Reds in government. But a close look at Lubell's evidence indicates that Nixon's assessment of the growing might of McCarthyism was not far off the mark. The white supremacists who passed out "shrieking" handbills accusing Graham of favoring a "'mingling of the races'" indulged in the same hysterical appeals to unreasoning fear and prejudice as did McCarthy. The association of black activism with the Red menace was easily made in the apprehensive environment of November 1950. In later years it would become habitual. Moreover, as has often been observed, history is not only what happened but what people think happened. For Republicans Red-baiting seemed the most effective way to regain control of the national political process. Roosevelt's secretary of the interior, Harold Ickes, writing a few days after the elections, charged the Republicans with mounting a "campaign of fear . . . ever since 1946" that had been "intensified during the last two years." In the most ruthlessly pragmatic terms, McCarthyism worked. If the situation in Korea did not improve, there was no telling how far McCarthy, Wherry, and the other fundamentalist conservatives might go.[38]

❖　❖　❖

As the American elections ended, Mao's soldiers suddenly disappeared from the Korean battlefields. MacArthur promptly concluded that the Chinese were no longer a major factor and that his men could rid the peninsula of communist forces by Christmas. In the east, he ordered X Corp's First Marines to clear any remaining enemy troops from the Chosin Reservoir and sent units of the Seventh Army north toward the Yalu at Hyesanjin. Part of the ROKA's II Corps was dispatched into the Taebaek Mountains on the marines' left flank to take over the wrecked town of Tokchon south of Huichon and establish a tenuous link with ROKA I Corps at Unsan. The I Corps would serve as the right flank of the Eighth Army, which had now moved back to the southern bank of the Chongchon, where it pushed a tentative bridgehead across the river. Thus, the UN command forged a tenuous but definite link between its two main thrusts along the east and west coasts in preparation for a final, victorious march to the Yalu.

The Eighth Army would drive to Sinuiju in the west, while the Seventh Division seized Hyesanjin in the east and the marines moved north from the reservoir. These three prongs would meet in the Yalu River gorges, then sweep up and down the south bank of the river in a kind of drawstring maneuver, closing the net on whatever NKPA and Chinese forces remained in northern Korea. This plan could have been based on only one assumption: that most of the Chinese forces along the Yalu had either withdrawn from or had never entered Korea. But battlefield reports, sifted and processed in Tokyo, were indicating another scenario—one so chilling that MacArthur apparently did not want to acknowledge it.

The command intelligence summary for November 12 indicated that during the previous week there had been a "continuous and obvious" buildup on the Eighth Army's front. The total estimated strength of enemy forces facing Walker's men had been 40,100 on November 4 at the height of the enemy offensive. A week later, on November 11, when the enemy had supposedly withdrawn or at least broken off contact, intelligence estimated that the 110,000-man Eighth Army was confronting 98,400 enemy troops. The most significant buildup "has been in the CCF units," roughly 18,900 men. But MacArthur's intelligence people suggested an interpretation of the data that left their commander free to resume his disastrous strategy. Remnants of the NKPA were also appearing on the battlefield as reorganized, reconstituted, and retrained units. Perhaps the Chinese had merely been relieving the North Koreans temporarily so they could catch their breath and reenter the fray. In that case, the Chinese intervention would not be serious or at least sustained.[39]

By November 21, MacArthur's intelligence officers knew of the existence and precise positions of at least three Chinese divisions totaling about 28,000 men. Two days later, on the eve of MacArthur's "last offensive," they had pinpointed several more Chinese divisions along with NKPA units.[40] Obviously the roughly 140,000 soldiers of the Eighth Army and X Corps were not going to have a cakewalk to the Yalu. Moreover, MacArthur, his intelligence staff, and his field commanders should have made two assumptions: first, the previous enemy offensive indicated that many more Chinese and North Korean forces might be in the Taebaeks than had previously been identified; and second, Mao could pour more thousands of troops across the Yalu at any time he chose.

Tokyo also willfully ignored a third ominous development. Since the beginning of the month, the Far East Air Force had been progressively harassed for the first time by enemy aircraft.

On October 14, Soviet Ambassador N. V. Roshchin in Peking had cabled Stalin, confirming Mao's intention to hurl his troops into Korea within hours. Mao's "past hesitations" over adverse international opinion, "questions about the Soviet assistance," and concerns about air cover, had now "been clarified," and the remorseless UN advance had to be stopped at once. The first nine divisions were preparing to cross the Yalu. Although this "echelon" was "poorly armed, it will be able to fight against the troops of Syngman Rhee. In the meantime, the Chinese comrades will have to prepare the second echelon." Under the circumstances, air power over the battlefield was essential. "The main thing we need, says Mao Zedong, is air power which shall provide us with air cover." The Chinese "hope to see its arrival as soon as possible, but not later than in two months."[41] Stalin easily exceeded that timetable.

On November 1, Soviet-built MIG-15 fighter jets downed two B-29s that were bombing suspected enemy supply lines and troop concentrations near the Yalu. An escorting P-51 Mustang was also shot out of the sky. No one could be certain who was piloting the enemy planes, but technological realities indicated that it could only be Chinese or, more likely, Russian aviators. In fact, that same day two F-82 twin Mustang jet fighters were shot down over the battle lines by a formation of MIG-15s commanded by "Comrade Belov," who had flown from the air base at Mukden, Manchuria. Two weeks later, on November 15, Mao cabled Stalin, agreeing to the Soviet leader's proposal "to reinforce Belov's aviation force by an additional delivery of MIG-15 planes to China in two lots, numbering 120 . . . pieces and to create a command apparatus for the [Soviet] air corps." Mao then expressed "gratitude to the Soviet pilots for the heroism and effort they have displayed in battle, and for the fact that over the last 12 days they downed 23 invading American planes."[42] But MacArthur did not turn a hair over the sudden appearance above the Korean battlefront of the most advanced aviation weapons in the communist arsenal, the shocking losses that these communist warplanes were inflicting on allied air power, or the probability that the Soviet Union had now entered the Korean War, albeit in a limited but highly dramatic fashion.

Instead MacArthur moved confidently, even recklessly forward. He was an old general; he had been a bold general. He failed to understand that in war there are few, if any, old, bold generals. His intelligence reports again provided the kind of speculations he wanted to read. Yes, there were Chinese in the hills of Korea, but they faced terrible problems of logistic support. Based on interrogation of POWs, MacArthur's staff knew that units of the CCF "embarked upon this Korean adventure with, in some instances, only three days rations and, at the most, with only ten days' supply. In addition, constant contact with the UN ground forces and harassment by UN air actions have had their effects on available supplies of ammunition." The more the UN forces pushed, prodded, and probed this inert Chinese mass, the more it would be drained of its already limited firepower. MacArthur's intelligence experts concluded on the evening before the big UN offensive that "although the full import of the effect of this poor logistic support cannot be readily determined at this time, it is reasonable to assume that [enemy] combat efficiency and morale have been considerably lowered."[43] MacArthur prided himself on his knowledge of the "oriental mind" and military capabilities. After years of experience fighting the Japanese army, he should have known that Asian boys fought effectively with far fewer comforts, amenities, firepower, and even essentials like food and clothing than did their Western counterparts. But he chose to ignore this fact.

His own troops were not faring well in the harsh winter that had now descended on the peninsula. Everywhere up and down the front it became bitterly cold, with temperatures hovering anywhere from twenty degrees below zero Fahrenheit to fifteen above. When the histories of the war were written, *Newsweek*'s Compton Pakenham cabled from Walker's headquarters near the Chongchon, they would not reflect a backdrop of friendly châteaux, charming farmhouses, warm barns, and convenient back-area cities as in the European theater of operations of scant years before. Korea was a repellent land where distant, snow-topped mountain peaks framed a squalid foreground of barren hills, tracks instead of highways, and the ever present rice paddies. The overall impression vaguely reminded one of the northwest frontier of India. The gray, thatched huts of the villages and towns were disgusting on the outside, "dark, dirty, and malodorous inside." An invariable "string of natives [seemed] eternally to be straggling along the roadsides toward some place that couldn't possibly be worth reaching." The expressionless women balanced fifty-pound bundles on their heads, while the tough, little men manhandled heavy "A" frames on their backs and the white-clad elders with fly-trap hats and two-foot pipes walked with "impenetrable, pathetic dignity" through dust clouds raised by jeeps and tanks.[44]

The dust was everywhere except when the rain turned the ground "to a yellow morass which grips like warm tar" or when it snowed as it began to do with increasing frequency. The constant wind kept everything flying, but the cold destroyed morale, sapping men's desire to fight and even to live. It reminded Pakenham of Robert Falcon Scott's last Antarctic diary. Under the tents and around the big fires at the nightly encampments, men could derive a sense of companionship. "But in the open one feels—though aware that hundreds of others are within a hundred yards—an intense sense of loneliness. The cold is inexorable. It drives men back into themselves. They can't mention it or complain because all suffer precisely the same discomfort and are equally armed" or disarmed "against it."[45]

Perhaps the coldest Americans of all on the eve of the offensive were the 360 men of the Seventh Division's Task Force Cooper, an infantry company reinforced with a few tanks and commanded by thirty-five-year-old Major Carroll Cooper. It was the second UN force and the first and only American unit to reach the Yalu. The men arrived at Hyesanjin on November 21, bundled up in overcoats, heavy pants, and thick scarves under their battle helmets. *Life* photographer Hank Walker, who accompanied them, took a shot of a stressed-out American battle commander. His eyes were keen but tired, breath streamed from his nostrils and mouth in heavy waves, and his entire body was weighed down with clothing and exhaustion. In the midst of battle and afterward, men were always trying to keep warm by building small fires. Sergeant Cox held up a pair of his long johns, frozen solid in the icy air.[46]

Digging in a few yards south of the river, which was iced over and covered with a light dusting of snow, Cooper's men were harassed by a two-hundred-man enemy force, which they chased for three days in and around the Yalu gorges and the small village of Posong-ni. When the communists abruptly crossed the ice to the Manchurian shore, Cooper told correspondent Roy Rowan: "To fight a war in these parts, you need a squad of lawyers." The ground was so hardened with frost that the men had to use pickaxes instead of shovels to dig foxholes. Cooper was understandably scared, nervous, and disgusted. His men were far out in front of the UN main lines, and he was not sure who they were fighting, who they *should* be fighting. "I want to get some of those bastards," Cooper said to Rowan. "I don't mean dead either. If they are Chinese, I want to know how many more are ahead of us."[47] Hank Walker went out on the snow-covered Yalu to photograph footprints heading toward the Korean shore, a sure sign that a Chinese patrol was not far away. But even in their exposed position, the men got Thanksgiving dinner with all the trimmings, air-dropped by the daring fliers of the Far East Air Force.

Who could or wished to fight for such a land? Who would die so that MacArthur could fulfill his dream of uniting Korea? Even before the last offensive, men were eagerly looking forward to getting out any way they could. Hugh Moffett, a correspondent for *Life,* reported from the Chongchon bridgehead that in the first hours of the offensive "a soldier advised us that the bug-out route was to the east if we found it necessary to shag during the night." It was also known as the "haul asbestos" route. One commanding officer instructed his motor pool sergeant to begin hoarding spare supplies of gasoline for possible use as "bug-out gas."[48] But MacArthur pressed on.

At home anxious conservatives could detect a defeatist attitude in the utterances of key administration officials. Perhaps they were right. The Defense Department's casualty figures of November 10 listed a total of 28,881 men dead, wounded, or missing in the 139 days of the war; 4,798 had been killed, and 4,343 were missing in action. The UN command was losing an average of one full company, or about 200 men, a day. Reacting to this sacrifice, Luce's reporters wrote scathingly of the cowardice pervading Washington. "The U.S. is living in fear of war. It is in a jam in Korea, and unable right now to defend Europe. In one breath it begs its enemies to hold their fire; in another breath it confesses its own weaknesses. It does not want to get in trouble with anybody; it just wants brotherhood and peace."[49]

To support this remarkable claim, *Time's* writers referred to Acheson's allegedly craven comments before a joint meeting of labor, industry, professional, and religious organizations in Washington. The secretary had said that the Chinese had not entered Korea as conquerors but merely as protectors of their legitimate property holdings along the Yalu, and he claimed that everything possible was being done to assure Peking "that their proper interests will be taken care of" by the United Nations and its forces. The next day, Truman, complaining of Chinese air attacks on U.S. planes over the Yalu, asserted that he and his administration had never "entertained any intention to carry hostilities into China. . . . We will take every honorable step to prevent any extension of hostilities into the Far East." Perhaps most disturbing were the recent remarks by Bradley to a convention of newspaper editors in Atlanta. "I do hope we can get together with China," the general declared, "and find out what they have in mind. I am sure we could work out something with them on a satisfactory basis. . . . War, if it comes, may mean the atomic bombing of our cities and homes. We have created the atomic bomb. Today, we would gladly trade it for a genuine course of righteousness in the world."[50] Bradley's earlier remarks to the British Chiefs of Staff—that if the Chinese mounted a full-scale intervention the Americans would leave (presumably taking the British and the rest of the UN command with them)—had clearly been no passing whim. Washington wanted no war with Peking.

Only days before the Eighth Army planned to jump off from the Chongchon River, Luce, who may have received intelligence estimates from other sources, had his writers inform the American public that Peking had moved sixty thousand troops into North Korea from Manchuria the previous week. "Aggressive China Becomes a Menace" was *Life*'s headline on November 20. Meanwhile, the *New Republic* observed that the United Nations had worked earnestly and delicately with the newly arrived delegation from Peking "to prevent the dangerous Korean situation from developing into the Third World War" and praised Acheson for his "statesmanlike" efforts and utterances.[51] The country was obviously upset, but MacArthur was oblivious. Far East Command did not try to disguise when or where UN forces would strike to end the conflict. Soviet and Chinese intelligence sources could read the American press and the handouts from MacArthur's headquarters and know exactly what was coming, where, and at what time.

The UN offensive began on schedule at dawn on November 24. Its objective, in the words of UN Supreme Headquarters and Far East Command, was to "complete the defeat of the North Korean army, disclose the intentions of the CCF and fulfill the UN mission of securing all of North Korea." Several hours after the assault began, the *SCAP* landed on the bumpy runway at Sinanju, and MacArthur jauntily stepped out into the icy sunshine and was welcomed by a cluster of his top brass. The supreme commander climbed into a jeep with his subordinates, pulled the hood of a pile-lined parka over his head, and drove off to the various Eighth Army command posts. When he asked how cold it was, one of his corps commanders replied, "About 15° [Fahrenheit]."[52]

MacArthur visited each of the various corps and division headquarters. He told Maj. Gen. John Church that he was recommending that the veteran Twenty-fourth Division receive a Presidential Unit Citation. "I have already promised wives and mothers that the boys . . . will be back by Christmas," he told Church. "Don't make me a liar. Get to the Yalu and I will relieve you." Then, skipping lunch, MacArthur reboarded his aircraft for a daring flight up to Sinuiju and then along the Yalu to Hyesanjin. No enemy MIG fighters rose to challenge the triple-tailed Constellation as it flew along the border. Above Hyesanjin the *SCAP* swooped low and waggled its wings in salute to Task Force Cooper. Then the plane headed southeast to Tokyo. It was a typical example of MacArthur's grandstanding, designed to demonstrate both his contempt for the Asian enemy and his confidence in his own troops and his own destiny. Back on the ground at Eighth Army headquarters, one general turned to another as MacArthur's plane flew over the hilly horizon. Everything should go all right, he said. After all, the supreme commander would not have come if the outcome was in doubt.[53] But within hours disaster struck across the entire UN front.

The first blow hit the ROKA II Corps, which held the weak twenty-two-mile center of the UN lines between the Taebaek mountain villages of Tokchon and Yangwon. During the darkest part of the night of November 24–25, tens of thousands of Chinese soldiers, blowing bugles, beating drums, and clanging cymbals, suddenly smashed into the South Korean lines in wave after wave. The ROKA units disintegrated, opening both the left flank of the marines at the Chosin Reservoir and the right flank of the Eighth Army on the west coast. Walker immediately dispatched the First Cavalry Division, which had been held in reserve, to Tokchon to stop the Chinese flood. It was like trying to plug a fire hose with a wad of bubble gum, one news account stated. The First Cavalry barely managed to avoid being surrounded and annihilated and retreated thirty miles in one day. After that, it just kept retreating.[54]

Once the center of the UN line was gone, the Chinese could roam the flanks and rear of the Eighth Army and X Corps at will. Suddenly Mao's troops were everywhere, hundreds of thousand of soldiers flooding out of the Taebaeks to envelop and engulf ROKA, U.S., and British forces all across the peninsula. Unit after unit of slowly advancing UN forces were cut off, surrounded, and overwhelmed by the sudden Red tide. The few companies that had established a bridgehead on the far side of the Chongchon were mowed down by cleverly concealed Chinese mortars and machine guns as they tried to retreat across the river. The marines at the Chosin Reservoir tried to push north, then west, in an effort to cut behind the Chinese offensive and pinch it off, but that was impossible on the snowy, narrow mountain roads. The marines were thrown back and besieged. They began a desperate but orderly withdrawal down the mountains toward the village of Hagaru, where they waited to rendezvous with retreating Seventh Division units including Task Force Cooper.

In the west the Eighth Army gradually became a rabble. South of Kunuri, a small village near the Chongchon River, a huge Chinese force enveloped the Second Infantry Division. This unhinged the entire Chongchon front, and companies, battalions, regiments, then entire divisions of the Eighth Army reeled back in confusion. A few units attempted to hold their positions or retreat carefully with their guns and vehicles intact. Some individuals and companies fought with incredible bravery. But as the Chinese pressed on hour after hour, day after day, without letup, panic broke out and quickly spread throughout the army. The supply system collapsed, adding the burden of hunger to men's distress. Discipline and pride disappeared. The bitter cold, the incessant ambushes along narrow hill trails, and the constant fear of being cut off and left behind turned each man into a loner.

The same stories were repeated over and over again. Platoons, companies, regiments, and divisions fought under ashen skies against an enemy that suddenly appeared everywhere: in front, on the flanks, to the rear. Commanders tried to hold a line—the south shore of the Chongchon, a blocking position at a key juncture of several trails, or a ridge line above an important mountain pass. But it was impossible. Trapped between high hills, besieged by constant mortar and machine-gun fire during the daylight hours and by human wave assaults at night, American, British, and South Korean soldiers could not hold their lines. Roads and trails became bloody gauntlets to be run in growing terror. MacArthur's Far East Air Force and fighter planes from the navy's carriers offshore tried to relieve the pressure, but pinpointing enemy positions above the UN columns during the day was much more difficult than MacArthur and his lieutenants had ever imagined, and no existing aircraft were designed for night bombing or strafing.

As the Eighth Army began its disorderly retreat, mortar fire from the surrounding hills disrupted columns, blowing apart men, trucks, guns, ambulances, and mobile field kitchens. Below the Chongchon, as the withdrawal gathered momentum and lost cohesion, the Chinese seemed everywhere all the time. There was no way to escape them. The retreat became a rout, a "big bug-out," as men abandoned any thoughts of fighting back. All they wanted was to get out of the hellish terrain, the terrible cold, the awful country. Far East Command rapidly revised the number of Chinese soldiers dramatically upward. Mao had sent at least 200,000 men to Korea, MacArthur's headquarters claimed after the first week of fighting; perhaps there were as many as 500,000 Chinese shooting, mortaring, and capturing UN soldiers. It was, the supreme commander complained publicly, "an entirely new war," and he demanded sweeping powers to bomb Chinese staging areas and air bases in Manchuria and to initiate a naval blockade of the entire Chinese coast.[55]

Mao's troops lacked two essential ingredients for total victory: mobility and supplies. In their attack by foot and horseback, they could not match the speed of the Eighth Army's withdrawal on wheels. More important, the Chinese were ill-clad and poorly provisioned. The troops suffered from hunger and frostbite as much as or more than their UN enemies, and they lacked the heavy firepower and ammunition to exploit their initial assaults. The Eighth Army soon escaped.

But the Chinese attack had been so sudden, concentrated, and shocking that it had completely unnerved most of Walker's men, who kept retreating long after there was any need to do so. The UN forces rushed south, heedless of any military realities, responding to the wildest rumors. During their flight, they began discarding gear. "Rocket launchers went first, then spare clothing, ammunition, even sleeping bags." The few roads and pathetic trails of northern Korea became littered with the equipment of modern war. In ten days, the Eighth Army retreated 120 miles, racing through Pyongyang, which it had entered in triumph only five weeks before. By December 13, it was back below the parallel and ready to evacuate Seoul.[56]

Experienced soldiers, both commanders and noncoms, were appalled as their army disintegrated. Lieutenant Karl Morton of the Fifth Regimental Combat Team thought the first reports of the retreat were incomprehensible. His men had hardly been engaged. Nonetheless, he ordered them to move south, only to discover that all transportation had disappeared. As they marched away from the Chongchon, they did not fight, but they heard rumors. "Faster, faster, they were constantly warned, lest you be cut off by the Chinese." One day at a roadblock they watched as the remnants of the Second Infantry Division staggered by "'in awful disarray.'" Another evening toward dusk, a solitary soldier came pedaling "maniacally" past them on a bicycle. They tried to stop him. What was going on "'up there'"? The cyclist kept going but called back "over his shoulder, 'Hell of a lot of Chinamen!'" A captain trying to push his jeep north toward a divisional headquarters through a constant stream of retreating vehicles and soldiers saw an old sergeant who had served with his father years before: "'This just isn't the goddam American Army—running away,'" the sergeant cried out in tears. "'We ought to be taking up positions.'" But nothing could be done. The two men watched helplessly as the listless troopers and drivers continued their numb trek toward the parallel and beyond.[57]

Hungry soldiers looted what they could from the supply depots that Walker had set up at Pyongyang to support the victory offensive. Men carried away anything they could—alcohol, tobacco, sugar—but acres of equipment and supplies were burned. "The great pillars of smoke from the fires were visible for miles to the retreating army." Perhaps that was because the fires were not controlled and soon raged over much of the city, which previously had not been damaged by war. The American press admitted that the Eighth Army had practiced a "scorched earth" policy in Pyongyang, something that only Nazis and bloodthirsty Asians were supposed to do. A British army officer who retreated from the city remembered mostly the intense cold, the dust, and the terrible disappointment. South of Pyongyang, a ROKA general met an old battlefield companion, Col. John Michaelis, commander of the Twenty-seventh Infantry Division. The Korean had been born in Pyongyang and had hoped fervently that it would become the provincial capital of a united Korea. What was going to happen now, he asked his American friend. "'I don't know,' said Michaelis. 'I'm just a regimental commander. But we may not be able to stay in the peninsula.'"[58]

On the east coast, Almond quickly decided that the only way to save his X Corps was to get the marines and the army's Seventh Infantry Division, plus ancillary ROKA and British forces, down to the ports of Hungnam and Hamhung, where the navy could evacuate them by sea to Pusan or Pohang. The Seventh Division ducked through the village of Hagaru and moved down the road to the coast before Chinese forces could cut them off.

The marines were not so lucky. From the reservoir down to Hagaru, they fought their way along narrow mountain trails of icy dirt with Chinese forces always above them, constantly lacing the roadway with mortar and machine-gun fire. Patrols scrambled up the snowy ridge lines in heavy winter gear to chase off the Chinese ambushers, who invariably reappeared somewhere else to pepper the long, retreating column. The temperatures reached twenty-five below and lower. Blood in syringes froze, and needles snapped as medics tried to insert them through the thick clothing of wounded men. But the marines stayed together and reached Hagaru on December 5. The next day, they began the final, terrible journey to the coast, bringing with them their vehicles, their personal equipment, their wounded, and their dead. "Retreat? Hell, we're just attacking in a different direction," cried Maj. Gen. Oliver P. Smith, a veteran of some of the most vicious campaigns of the Pacific war.[59]

As the marines left Hagaru, one regimental commander told his men that they were "all a part of a sad piece of history." Such a withdrawal was unprecedented for the marine corps, but the men had come this far with their pride and their fighting spirit intact, and he expected them to retain that pride and spirit until the end. His troops never let him down. They marched down one hill and up another on a corkscrew trail just wide enough for a two and a half-ton truck. Engineers had to blast their way past rocky ridges and forested bluffs swarming with dug-in Chinese.[60] But the marines kept their column intact and fought day and night despite dwindling ammunition, wounds, and frostbite.

Because the Chinese were determined to exterminate the marines, they exposed themselves recklessly, and tactical air power could finally be used effectively. MacArthur's air force jets came screaming in from Japan to drop napalm and antipersonnel bombs on hilltops and hillsides. Offshore the navy's carriers, the *Leyte* and the recently recommissioned *Princeton*, launched F4U Corsairs from rolling, spray-swept flight decks. The Corsairs rushed over the marine column to demolish Chinese positions, even killing Mao's soldiers in their foxholes with antipersonnel bombs armed with proximity fuses. But between dusk and dawn the battlefield belonged to the Chinese, and the marines suffered accordingly. The finest novel written about the road to Hungnam was aptly titled *Hold Back the Night*.[61]

Almond sent a relief column up the road toward Hagaru to link up with the marines, and, by December 9, they began pouring into Hungnam and Hamhung. The navy ringed the approaches to the two ports with heavy gunfire from the battleship *Missouri* and supporting cruisers and destroyers. No Chinese offensive could stand up to such punishment, and Mao's generals backed off. The day before Christmas, the last Americans had been evacuated and were on their way south.

But the magnificence of the marines' conduct could not disguise the magnitude of the defeat. By December 25, communist armed forces had swept the United Nations from North Korea forever.

The news from the battlefronts devastated the American people. No U.S. army had retreated so shamefully since First Bull Run ninety years before. American troops had swept all before them in 1865 and 1898; in 1918, they had hung on magnificently, then turned the tide against the Hun; in 1942, they had bought precious time at Bataan and Corregidor for the forces of freedom to gather their might and deal evil a shattering blow. Now suddenly American boys were running away without any thought of sacrifice or honor; they were just bugging out. Here was the final, awful betrayal of hope, the last disillusionment, of a traumatic year that had begun with Hiss and Fuchs and the decision to build the doomsday weapon and had continued with McCarthy's sensational charges and an ominous war in Asia. Now that war was being lost, and lost with it was the instinctive public sense that in the last analysis liberal Washington could be trusted to know and to do what was right.

"The disaster and its implications became the subject of endless shocked conversations," *Time* reported in early December. "Some of them were almost monosyllabic: men meeting on the street sometimes simply stared at each other and then voiced the week's most oft-repeated phrase—'It looks bad.'" The news was particularly traumatic for combat veterans of World War II, who knew or could easily guess what the men in Korea were enduring. A Purple Heart veteran in Des Moines told a reporter that he had quit turning on the radio—" 'I didn't want to hear the news.'"[62]

There was some outright hysteria. In Birmingham, Alabama, the women of the local Marine Corps League Auxiliary, who had given their men a rousing send-off in July, "held a tearful mass meeting, appealing to the President to 'use every weapon necessary' in Korea and to 'evacuate our troops immediately.'" In Tecumseh and Shawnee, Oklahoma, in Seattle, Los Angeles, and Denver, citizens organized themselves to demand that atomic weapons be used on the battlefield. In San Francisco, nervous residents of Chinatown braced for a wave of riots and looting that never came.[63]

MacArthur was severely criticized for the first time. His intelligence blunders were readily apparent even to the most casual observer; his strategic objectives had been questionable at best. Even if UN forces had reached the Yalu, they were too weak to hold the frontier against an all-out China-based attack. The river was too long a defense line in summer; in winter, it became a frozen highway for Mao's soldiers.[64]

The old soldier was unrepentant. In a long press conference on December 2, MacArthur defended his actions and policies with vigor and self-righteousness. He now claimed that since the first UN resolution of June 25, Chinese intervention "was always inherent and always present but impossible to avoid by any field maneuver or generalship." No nation or group of nations "can avoid the risks involved in the launching of aggressive warfare against it by another nation or group of nations." In response to the blunt query about whether the military command in Tokyo "over-exceeded its authority," MacArthur replied stoutly: "No. It has acted in complete harmony and coordination with higher authority." MacArthur asserted that his soldiers now faced "500,000 Chinese troops" and that although "our air and naval forces furnish invaluable assistance . . . under present conditions, their potential is limited by the fact that they cannot operate against any element of the Chinese forces not immediately situated in North Korea."[65]

The general's supporters tried to help the old man put the best possible interpretation on the catastrophe. Luce promptly cabled his reporters in Tokyo to seek an interview with MacArthur, who was quite willing to explain his position. He could not agree with critics "that we are in an 'impossible situation' in North Korea, or that we are even in a bad situation in North Korea." There could be no appeasing the enemy, no "deal" with communism. "He would do exactly what he is doing—that is, seek a military decision through destruction of the opposing forces, whether North Korean, Chinese or mixed." MacArthur emphasized that Munich provided a lesson to be avoided. One did not negotiate with aggressors; one crushed them. Implicit in his comments was criticism of Acheson and the Truman administration for allowing the United Nations to invite the Red Chinese to Manhattan.[66]

The general was even more scathing in private. Hugh Baillie, president of United Press, radioed a set of questions to MacArthur in late November, just as the Chinese offensive got rolling. On December 1, the UN Commander responded in a long letter, in which he emphasized the impossibility of fighting a war against an enemy who consistently enjoyed and exploited "the privileged sanctuary of neutral boundaries." MacArthur skirted perilously close to self-pity as he described the difficulty of directing a war in which enemy supply lines and offensive jump-off points became progressively shorter with each defeat while the UN armies were faced with growing supply and strategic problems with every foot of Korean soil gained. Anticipating later remarks to Congress on the overriding importance of Asia to Western security, MacArthur bombarded Baillie with a litany of complaints against "Europeans" who failed to realize the transcendent importance of the Korean battlefield. Nor was the Chinese intervention due in any way to MacArthurian strategy or triumphs. "The decision by the Chinese Communist leaders to wage war against the United Nations could only have been a basic one, long premeditated and carried into execution as a direct result of the defeat of their satellite North Korean armies."[67]

Four days after the general replied to Baillie, he received a fawning letter from Roy Howard, president of the nationwide Scripps-Howard newspaper chain. Writing under the paper's letterhead, he told MacArthur that, largely as a result of the Chinese offensive, those fools who had long insisted on Peking's admission to the United Nations were now on the run. Scripps-Howard's long fight to support Chiang and Formosa had been given a big boost. Nonetheless, it could not be denied that MacArthur himself was falling under increasing criticism for not having anticipated the Chinese offensive. Such charges were intolerable, and Howard begged the general to give him some sign of what Scripps-Howard's position should be on Far Eastern affairs, including "a controlled re-armament of Japan." Howard realized the "far-reaching potentialities of such a move" and told MacArthur that "you are the one best situated to determine both its desirability and its timing." Howard realized that it might be "inexpedient" for MacArthur to respond directly "even under my personal pledge of confidence, which you would of course have." But "would it not be possible for me to receive at my home address, 20 East 64th Street, New York, and marked 'Private' an unsigned memorandum that might come through General Willoughby, General Whitney, or from some source that need not be known to me, but which would chart a course which I could have reason to believe was in line with your ideas"?[68]

Two weeks later, Howard got his wish: MacArthur sent him a personal message, first stating self-righteously that since his reply to Baillie had been published, "confidential regulations issued from Washington required submission of future public statements prior to release. As a consequence, I have made no effort to clarify any further questions raised concerning the Korean campaign."[69] The general then proceeded in four single-spaced typed pages to further clarify his views on Korea. The campaign was no debacle, as "irresponsible talk" at home suggested, but rather a well-planned, well-executed strategic withdrawal. The last offensive had not been designed to drive the final remnants of the NKPA from Korea so much as to sniff out Chinese Communist intentions. It had succeeded brilliantly. True, ROKA units on the Eighth Army's right flank had been smashed, but the Chinese had not been able to turn the Eighth Army's flank. Responding to Howard's query about abandoning Korea, MacArthur believed it could be done in order to strengthen the overall strategic position of U.S. and UN forces in Asia so long as evacuation was accompanied or swiftly followed by some sort of "military retaliation against the Chinese Communists." MacArthur continued, "My views with respect to the strategic importance of Formosa have not been altered an iota." The "action of Mao in recklessly committing his armies to war against the United Nations and the United States in Korea should demonstrate to the most naive the use to which he would put the potentiality of such an offensive bastion as Formosa once in his control. With its threat to our littoral defense line, he could consolidate and advance his hold over Asia at will."

China, not Japan, was now the great danger in Asia; communist expansionism knew no bounds. Rearmament of Japan, MacArthur hinted, was surely desirable but unfortunately illegal given the foolish constraints imposed by the occupying powers. "Meanwhile within the framework of my own existing authority, when the Korean War broke out I ordered the creation of a 75,000-man police reserve which has been organized along the lines of a light constabulary."

In the end, MacArthur assured his friend, all had turned out for the best; he, MacArthur, had been on top of the situation all along and had mastered it. The general's peroration reflected a mind and temperament from which nearly all reality had departed.

This is written at some length, Roy, but I wanted to give you the full picture as it is here. Some criticism has been voiced over the optimism with which I launched our drive of November 24th. Such criticism by those who fail to understand the situation here is perhaps justified. But from this position, it was necessary for me to give final assurances to the Chinese Communists that once I had achieved my border goal, my intention was to withdraw the United States forces back to Japan leaving the ROK forces to police the country. Political reassurances to such end had failed and I was under constant pressure to give such military assurances. To avoid the impression of weakness, I felt I should give any such assurances incident to normal operations. Such assurances, indeed, were no less necessary to get the maximum fight out of our own army, tired from months of continuous fighting and faced by the bitter cold of that northern latitude. Had there been a degree of sincerity in the Communist position as so many British and Americans held that there was, my effort would have been successful. Failing this, we at least achieved a comprehensive understanding of the motives and intentions of Communist China and destroyed the myths which had been woven to obscure the truth. Based upon this information, I have now redeployed our forces and our country is at long last moving towards mobilization. That some should still cling to the illusion that international Communism can be dealt with as a legitimate political force is one of the wonders of this age. It defies explanation.

In the interim, the general cabled a brief and equally astonishing message to his superiors in the Pentagon. On December 8, MacArthur maintained that both Eighth Army and X Corps had "now successfully completed tactical withdrawals to more secure strategic positions from which to fight the enemy." This was not true. Eighth Army was still in the midst of its frantic escape across the parallel, while X Corps had not completed its withdrawal to the North Korean evacuation port of Hungnam. The "retrograde movements," MacArthur maintained, "have been conducted with tactical skill by field commanders and the display of much gallantry by all forces concerned" and with "complete order and unbroken cohesion among the various components." All units, MacArthur concluded, "are intact." Moreover, the enemy had suffered at least ten-to-one losses and "the suggestion widely broadcast that the command has suffered a rout or debacle is pure nonsense. It is an injustice to our troops and disservice both to our own nation and those allied with us in the battlefield." His command, MacArthur stoutly insisted, "is now in no serious immediate danger and in position, even with the existing limitations upon military, to deliver massive blows against" an enemy who could no longer exploit its initial advantages because of steadily growing supply problems.[70]

As the news from Korea steadily worsened and evacuation of the entire peninsula became a possibility, the mood in America became somber and angry. The only real armed forces the United States possessed seemed about to be demolished on a distant Asian battlefield. News photos coming out of the peninsula told an appalling story: dead-eyed American soldiers bundled up against the cold and staring vacantly out of trucks as they retreated south from Pyongyang; frantic North Korean refugees, who had earlier welcomed UN forces, now scrambling through the twisted girders of a bombed-out bridge over the Taedong River as they fled south; David Douglas Duncan's gruesome pictures of the marines stubbornly marching down from Hagaru, "heads bent against the furious cold," trudging along the lee of a hill "toward a sea that is always just beyond the horizon. . . . The living walk and the dead ride," stacked like cordwood, only their boots and trouser bottoms showing out of the sides of trucks and jeeps.[71]

Only hours after the Chinese offensive, press reports indicated another potential betrayal. The British Foreign Office was urging the Attlee government to distance itself from American foreign policy by announcing that henceforth Britain would rearm itself and renounce all reliance on U.S. military assistance. When Truman subsequently stated at a news conference that "we will take whatever steps are necessary to meet the military situation, just as we always have," and responded to a question about the atomic bomb by declaring that he would use "every weapon we have," Clement Attlee immediately flew to Washington to discuss the entire range of Anglo-American issues.[72]

Conservative press lords in the United States were both frightened and incensed. Baillie and Howard had MacArthur's own uncomprising views to draw upon. Luce placed a somewhat different spin on the MacArthur argument, but essentially reached conclusions with which the general could not disagree. The country had reached an "hour of mortal choice." Its soldiers had absorbed "a hell of a beating" in Korea, and the global prospect "is war." But "the heart of the news is that at last we know—we really know—our enemy."

> We know that our enemy is the Soviet Union. We know that the Chinese Communist armies assaulting our forces in Korea are as truly the armies of the Soviet Union as they would be if they wore the Soviet uniform. Maybe most of us thought that we knew this before. It has been said before. But never as it was said last week, by President Truman in

Washington and by his spokesmen [at the United Nations], with the knowledge and the certainty forced upon us all by the facts of Korea and by the enemy's cold voice of hate and purpose. . . . Overnight a little stranger named Wu, the leader of the Communist delegation from Peking, did for us what we could never quite do for ourselves. . . . With a single speech to the Security Council . . . he laid naked the total enmity of Chinese Communism, its total purpose to seize all Asia, its total identity with Soviet Communism and its total dedication to the Soviet program of world conquest.[73]

McCormick and William Randolph Hearst, on the other hand, urged a return to isolationism. "It is absurd to think that we can be any more effective militarily in Europe than we have been in Korea," McCormick stormed. "Therefore, instead of spending ourselves into Communism, we should pull in our expenditures, call out the National Guard to hold Northern Canada, and leave the treacherous so-called Allies in Europe to their own protection." Hearst added that "our sovereignty has been impaired by making us a virtual vassal of the United Nations which disrupts our councils and seeks to fly its mongrel flags over our public buildings. . . . We should get out of the United Nations . . . and end our unrequited efforts to support and supply an ingrate Europe."[74]

But most Americans understood that isolationism was no longer an option in an age of nuclear weapons. "Millions sadly accepted the probability that war of some kind, perhaps even World War III, had already begun and that their world might be sacrificed to it," *Time* reported in its December 11 issue. Detroit salesman Zacharias Cosmas urged Truman to "'hit the main Bolsheviks. The tail won't bite if you hit the head.'" A New Orleans policeman added that Washington should officially declare war on the Soviet Union "'and then drop all the A-Bombs we can on her.'" One of the most bitter expressions of dismay came from Capt. Eugene Guild of Glenwood Springs, Colorado, whose letter to the *Denver Post* appeared on the first page. Guild said he was writing as the father of "one of the 5,000 boys killed by the Reds in Korea. I let my boy down. . . . Our leaders in Washington and the mouse-men at Lake Success were too timorous and weasling to face up to the real aggressor." Because Truman had ordered MacArthur to refrain from bombing Manchuria or engaging in hot pursuit, all of northeastern China had become a sanctuary for the communist buildup in Korea, and "our sons were not given a fair fighting chance for their lives. . . . We are told we must not strike back in defending ourselves against the Reds. They make war on us but we must not make war on them because then they will make war on us; what supreme gibberish is that?" Guild could reach only one conclusion: The atomic bomb was a sound weapon of war.[75]

The voices of Congress, most of them anonymous, were just as disturbing.

A world war is possible at any hour. . . . "I never felt worse in my life. What in the name of God can we do?" . . . "I can't conceive of a worse crisis." . . .

This country is more poorly prepared than it was in 1941. We have delayed all-out mobilization. The Administration has fiddled with war preparations. The Munitions Board has fallen down in its job of stock-piling. . . .

The Defense Department is way behind on its military orders. . . . We picked a hell of a place to stand against aggression. . . .

Now we have got to stand and fight. No two ways about that. If we pull out of Korea without being pushed out, then whatever prestige we have is gone. The French will collapse in Indo-China. India and Burma will go under. The French and Germans will fold their hands in Western Europe.

Acheson is a weak sister. Truman is no international bargainer. . . .

If the Reds drive south of the 38th parallel, then we ought to hit Manchurian industries. . . .

If Russia makes a diversionary drive into Iran, Turkey, Germany, then we should recognize the existence of World War III and proceed to atomize Russia.

We should use the atom bomb at our own discretion—not the U.N.'s. Whenever the military says, "Drop it," the Senate and House will support them. It is time we recognize where we stand now and where we stand for the future.[76]

On December 5, Congressman Frank Boykin of Alabama wrote Adm. Sidney W. Souers of the NSC staff that "a crisis has come to our Country, the like of which has never before been experienced." There was irresponsible talk of a humiliating deal with the Chinese Communists in which the United Nations would be allowed to "keep" South Korea in exchange for Peking's admission to the United Nations in place of Chiang Kai-shek's government.

This "humiliation" would give the Chinese Communist aggressors a permanent seat on the Security Council. The only thing to do was pull out of Korea "in order to strengthen our outer" Asian "ramparts, Japan, Okinawa, Formosa and the Philippines," along with Western Europe. "From now on we shall arm and arm to the teeth, and when we are thoroughly ready, we can choose our own Theatre of Operations, just as our enemy has chosen it this time."[77]

Within the administration, anger and panic were just as prevalent. Once the dimensions of the disaster slowly became clear, Truman ordered the National Security Council into emergency session. It was an extraordinary meeting.[78] In his military briefing to the council, Omar Bradley estimated that the communist enemy could muster at least two hundred thousand troops and three hundred warplanes (two hundred of them bombers) for the battle of North Korea. Marshall stoutly insisted that "we must act on the assumption that United Nations forces can hold a line."[79] Above all, neither the United States individually nor the United Nations collectively should get into a major war with China; such a conflict was flatly unwinnable. Acheson emphatically agreed.

The nation's manpower supply, however, was disastrously low. Casualty replacements could be fed into the fighting beginning in January, but no new units could be sent to the front before March. MacArthur was the target of bitter comments. How could he have said that he would have the boys home before Christmas? Truman spoke up for the first time. The general had made the statement; he would have to be asked why he made it. Deputy Defense Secretary Robert Lovett and Army Secretary Frank Pace joined Bradley in weakly defending the general, but their remarks fell flat. Marshall concluded that the general's comments were "an embarrassment that we have to ride around in some manner."[80]

Vice-President Alben Barkley would not let the issue alone. MacArthur simply had not thought through the implications of his remarks. Truman intervened. No matter what anyone thought of MacArthur's statement, the administration would have to be very careful "not to pull the rug out from under him." Truman added that "we could not afford to damage MacArthur's prestige at this point." Barkley persisted. MacArthur's statement was "an incredible hoax" that had produced unhealthy speculation.[81]

Acheson spoke up. It was essential to view the Chinese assault in global terms. Undoubtedly the Soviet Union was behind Peking's intervention, but

Washington could not say so because of the risk of World War III if public opinion got out in front of government policy and "because we can't do anything about it now." The secretary admitted that he and the others around the table had misjudged the communist enemy. "Time is shorter than we thought, Mr. Acheson said. We used to think we could take our time up to 1952, but if we were right in that, the Russians wouldn't be taking such terrible risks as they are now." Clearly a third world war was very near.[82]

But would the country support the kind of restrained military and diplomatic policies that the crisis called for? Harriman referred to a recent *New York Times* article quoting a dispatch from Moscow titled, "Pravda Says U.S. Faces Deep Crisis." Well, the country was in crisis, Truman responded. Back in March at Key West, he had said "that the campaign of vilification and lies and distortion of the facts" indulged in by McCarthy, Wherry, and others "was the greatest asset that the Soviets had. He said he felt that Hearst and McCormick, and Roy Howard, had succeeded in doing exactly what the Kremlin wanted. They had divided our people and had shaken the confidence of the American people in their Government." Somehow, some way, this had to be overcome. Barkley took up the point. The recent Republican publicity campaign "'was the most diabolical thing I ever ran into.'" He had traveled around the country during the recent campaign and "found there was a real underground movement that he couldn't put his finger on. 'People you were trying to reach weren't there.' The minds of the American people were being poisoned by lies and rumors and untrue statements that caused them to worry and doubt their leadership. 'I don't know the remedy but it must be found.'" Truman concluded that the country faced a situation "like that in . . . 1840 (referring to the Know-Nothing movement) [*sic*]."[83]

Once the NSC meeting broke up, the president and most of his colleagues went into immediate session with the cabinet, where he summarized what Acheson, the Joint Chiefs, Marshall, and Barkley had said. "We are trying to find the proper means to meet this situation," Truman concluded. "It could turn into all-out involvement in a war. It is terribly serious."[84]

During the NSC meeting and in the next few days, Stuart Symington, head of the National Security Resources Board, urged a complete withdrawal of all UN ground forces from the peninsula followed by "an open and sustained [air and sea] attack upon lines of communication in China and Korea, and also upon aggression-supporting industries in Manchuria as considered militarily advisable." Acheson responded that such a policy would invite World War III; Marshall added that Symington's proposal was so radical that its implementation would require a complete rethinking of the entire range of national security policy. Nonetheless, Symington's proposals resonated in the highest circles. As late as January, Bradley and his colleagues on the JCS were giving serious thought to severely punishing China. During a discussion between Truman and Acheson in early December, Bradley burst out bitterly: "We used to say that an attack on a platoon of the United States troops meant war." Now the Chinese were sending hundreds of thousands of troops against the Eighth Army and X Corps and did not call it war. Yet "if we drop one bomb across the Yalu they say we are making war against them."[85]

The people were as apprehensive and unsure as were their leaders and opinion makers. The head of Atlanta's largest church remarked after a service in December that in his thirty-one years in the pastorate, which had included the worst of the Great Depression and World War II, "'today's congregation was by far the most sober and serious that I have ever seen.'" In Roosevelt County, Montana, two members of the draft board announced that they were unwilling to draft men "until the U.S. guaranteed to use the atomic bomb." The national commanders of the American Legion, the Veterans of Foreign Wars, the Disabled American Veterans, and Amvets wrote Truman a joint letter, urging him to give MacArthur discretion to bomb Chinese bases in Manchuria. Stassen urged the United Nations to demand that the Chinese pull out of Korea and to drop atomic bombs on targets in China if they refused. Reverend Billy Graham suggested that Truman and Attlee "hold a little prayer meeting, telling God, 'We don't know where to turn.'" Wisconsin Republican Senator Alexander Wiley asked the State Department to investigate whether Vyshinsky, who was delivering blistering anti-American speeches at the United Nations, could be arrested on some charge. The public was engulfed in gloom, doubt, confusion, and a sense of helplessness to reverse the debacle in Korea. But there was no panic. "The way ahead would be hard, and everybody knew it. It had to be traveled, and the nation knew that, too."[86]

Luce sent his reporters back to Sycamore to see how people in the heartland now viewed the war.[87] They found that folks were "grimmer, less ready with quick answers, more thoughtful. There was no doubt about it; the war was very close to Sycamore." Druggist David Hamilton, the only one who had expressed opposition to Washington's intervention the previous summer, now refused to speak to Luce's team. The situation was too serious for finger pointing. "'I don't feel I'm free to say anything. There are a lot of families in this town who have sons fighting in Korea.'"

Generally the people of Sycamore still believed that the war was "right," that American boys should be in Asia fighting communism, and that the U.S. position should not be compromised. "That quiet determination, sobered and tempered by anxious months, seemed as accurate a gauge of national feeling as their more confident words last June." But the way individuals expressed their feelings was as revealing as the total mood. George Roden, the fifty-eight-year-old tailor, said that Americans had to stick together and hold South Korea. " 'No deals, no bargains. If it's going to bring war, let it bring war. If peace, so much the better.' " The bomb should only be used "'to save our men.'" As for the home front, "'if a citizen sticks up for the Reds, we should ship him to a Red country.'" Phil Norman, the advertising man who in June believed that Washington had already appeased Stalin too much, now argued for a little appeasement to buy time to rearm. Mrs. John McNamara, who had stated earlier that "'we had to do what we did,'" had changed her mind. "'We should let them run their business and we run ours. It's been a slaughter.'" She was adamantly opposed to using the bomb. Fifty-two-year-old lineman Emmet Woods, who in June had said the United States should have been tougher in the past, still advocated firmness. "We 'should never pull out'" of Korea. "'If we back up, we're done for. Let's drop the A-bomb on them.'" Salesman Wayne Oeser believed in withdrawal, rearmament, and waiting for "'one big push.'" The majority opinion, although not a consensus, was that the country had to continue fighting both in Korea and against the communist menace in general.

A minority viewpoint in the country was strongly expressed by powerful men. Former president Herbert Hoover urged, as had McCormick, a retreat to fortress America. The nation could be economically and militarily self-sufficient, and it was time to return to isolationism. Financier Joseph P. Kennedy agreed. Speaking at the University of Virginia, where his son, Robert, was a law student, the former ambassador to Great Britain proposed the same brand of isolationism he had championed a decade before. "Today it is idle to talk of being able to hold the line of the Elbe or the line of the Rhine. . . . Why should we waste valuable resources in making such an attempt?" Postwar handouts to Western Europe had not brought the United States one "foul-weather friend," and the United Nations was a "hopeless" instrument of international peace. Korea was a "costly and staggering extravaganza." Americans "have never wanted a part of other people's scrapes," Kennedy concluded. "We can do well to mind our own business and interfere only where somebody threatens our business and our homes." Distinguished political critic Walter Lippmann responded that isolationism was not consistent with the intuitive common sense of most of the people.[88]

Taft Republicans predictably concluded that Acheson, not MacArthur, was responsible for the plight of the Eighth Army and X Corps. In early December, New York Senator Irving Ives and House Minority Leader Joe Martin drafted a Republican resolution, calling on the president to fire his secretary of state for losing the confidence of the legislative branch. Several hearings on the measure were held on Capitol Hill, giving Republicans the opportunity to vent their frustration. The besieged president immediately responded that he had no intention of getting rid of Acheson, and Republican Governor Thomas Dewey of New York labeled the Ives-Martin initiative a shameful act. Acheson's visits to the Capitol had always been ordeals. Now each time he appeared before the House or Senate Armed Services or Foreign Relations Committees, he was hectored unmercifully by the fundamentalist conservatives. He returned one evening to his State Department office gray with fatigue and joked to a subordinate: "Home is the hunted, home from the hill."[89]

The discussions with Attlee proved to be difficult, tiring, and time-consuming. Churchill had once described the little prime minister with the fussy moustache and prim, precise voice as a sheep in sheep's clothing. On another occasion, he had remarked that a long black automobile with no one in it had driven up, and Clement Attlee got out. During this moment of crisis the prime minister seemed the epitome of an appeaser, and he was so depicted by a number of political cartoonists. But he managed to say the right words at the right time to mollify all except the most rabid Anglophobes. Taking a break from his White House discussions, Attlee told a National Press Club audience: "You may be certain that in fair weather or foul, where the Stars and Stripes fly in Korea, the British flag will fly beside them. We stand by our duty. We stand by our friends." His dramatic declaration was slightly compromised when he then observed that, of course, "geographical conditions" imposed differing perspectives on various policy questions among even the most loyal friends. Nonetheless, president and prime minister somehow got through their meetings and smoothed out their differences. Truman convinced Attlee that the only basis for a solution in Korea was a free, united nation, and Attlee persuaded Truman to promise publicly to provide prior notification of any projected use of nuclear weapons.[90]

But in the last midcentury month these were peripheral concerns. The real question was Stalin's intentions. It was easy to conclude that his malice toward the West was unbounded and that he had brought the Chinese Communists into his orbit. But what would he do? Three days after the Chinese offensive, Truman decided that Stalin would never again have the advantage of exploiting weaknesses in the Western decision-making process. MacArthur could no longer be allowed to unilaterally make U.S. policy decisions that would send misleading signals to the Kremlin and Peking. Truman told Marshall that henceforth "all instructions to General MacArthur from the Chiefs of Staff be processed through the Secretary of Defense to the President personally." Marshall promptly passed the word to Bradley.[91]

Meanwhile, the CIA was ordered to prepare intelligence estimates of short-term Soviet intentions. The agency submitted reports to the White House on December 5 and 11, 1950, and January 10, 1951, after receiving concurrence from the intelligences offices at the State Department and in each of the armed services. The three documents were based on information available to U.S. sources between December 1 and December 15. Their depressing conclusions coincided with public opinion.

The December 5 report depicted the Soviet leadership as reckless and irresponsible. Stalin and his men "have resolved to pursue aggressively their world-wide attack on the power position of the United States and its allies regardless of the possibility that global war may result, although they may estimate that the Western Allies would seek to avoid such a development." China had intervened in Korea "in realization of the risk of general war" with the United States "and perhaps in expectation of such a development." They never would have done so "without explicit assurance of Soviet support," which soon might include direct involvement of Russian "volunteers."[92]

Six days later, the CIA projected an even gloomier scenario.[93] Soviet bloc responses to recent developments in Korea indicated that the Kremlin assessed its current military and political position "as one of great strength in comparison with that of the West" and that it would "exploit the apparent conviction of the West of its own present weakness."* Moscow, "seconded by" Peking, had made it clear "through a series of authoritative statements" that it was going to challenge the West in Asia as well as in Europe. Stalin intended to force U.S. troops to withdraw from Korea, establish Communist China as the predominant power in the Far East, and reduce Western control over Japan. "Moscow has given no real indication that it will compromise on any one of these points," the CIA declared. The Kremlin had also demonstrated repeatedly its determination to drive a wedge in the close working relations between the Western powers in order to isolate the United States and end all European efforts at rearmament. Finally, "the scope of Soviet bloc preparations and the nature and extent of Soviet Communist official statements and propaganda raise the question of Soviet or Satellite moves in other areas. The points that appear most critical are Berlin and Germany, Indochina, Yugoslavia, and Iran."

The third paper, devoted to the Soviet Union's capabilities in unconventional warfare, was the most chilling. The CIA concluded that there was a "high" probability that the Kremlin could successfully mount biological and chemical attacks against the United States in the event of hostilities between Russia and the West.[94]

Truman was determined to check the rapid erosion of government and public morale with vigorous action. On December 13, he met with top congressional leaders, including Taft and Wherry, to "inform them of my decision regarding the declaration of a national emergency." The president got an earful of congressional opinion, all of it alarmist. Senator Connally noted that Korea "had made everybody very jittery." Tydings added that "the United States was in deadly peril. The question now is whether we can survive."

---

*Soviet diplomats in Washington and New York had obviously been reading the American press carefully. Luce's reporters wrote scornfully about American unpreparedness (see "What Mobilization? Manpower Is Low, Training Is Long," *Life*, 11 December 1950, pp. 42–45), which was also a lively topic of conversation on Capitol Hill. The Federal Civil Defense Administration announced that it planned to spend two-thirds of its three-billion-dollar fiscal-year budget to provide bomb shelters for fifty million people in critical areas across the nation. State governors, who were expected to finance about one-third of the project, reacted sharply. No known bomb shelter could adequately protect against an atomic raid, they responded. The whole program was a boondoggle. See "Civil Defense: A Place To Hide," *Time*, 18 December 1950, p. 21.

Once again the people and government had "made a great mistake of under-estimating the power of the enemy and as a result we are far too weak." Korea had demonstrated communist military strength and effectiveness far beyond what had been assumed in the West. "'We still have some time left,' Senator Tydings said, 'but damn little. I am in favor of giving the President the power to get ready as fast as we can.'" Other Senate and House leaders more or less echoed Tydings's alarmism. The Chinese offensive had apparently demonstrated that communists were ten feet tall. It would take a mighty national effort to defeat them. Two nights later, Truman spoke to the country over national radio about his plans for dealing with the crisis in Korea and the threat from the communist world.[95]

It had been a bad week for the president. First Charlie Ross died suddenly. Then music critic Paul Hume of the *Washington Post* published a stinging review of daughter Margaret's Washington recital, which both Truman and Attlee had attended. Truman, struggling with a national crisis and personal grief, lost his temper and wrote a bitter letter to Hume that soon appeared in the press, further damaging the president's reputation among those who had long ago decided that the man was an incompetent fool.

There was nothing foolish in Truman's speech to the people. "Our homes, our Nation, all the things we believe in, are in great danger," he began. The Chinese intervention in Korea was the final proof that the communists "are now willing to push the world to the brink of a general war to get what they want." America had the strength to curb the international march of communism, and "here are the things we must do:" create a vast, permanent military machine; continue to support the United Nations and cooperate with free world allies; expand the national economy and "keep it on an even keel." The official presidential proclamation of national emergency followed within twenty-four hours.[96]

In some ways, the president's speech and proclamation were remarkably restrained. America would rearm, but there would be no wartime rationing, no brownouts or blackouts of coastal and key inland cities, and no resumption of crushing wartime controls on business. Detroit would not be shut down and reopened as a huge war plant, and Pittsburgh would not divert all steel production to wartime uses. There would be no bond drives and no calls for victory gardens, scrap iron, or nylon stockings to support the war effort. But Truman clearly put the country on notice that the United States had entered a new era of potentially unlimited confrontation with the nuclear armed forces of the communist world.

In Korea the situation continued to deteriorate. The Eighth Army completed its evacuation of the north, while the last elements of X Corps at last left Hungnam on Christmas Eve. Major General Frank Lowe sent a personal, priority message to the president, stating that he and his staff were on their way to Seoul via Tokyo and Pusan. "All secure safe and good health absolute minimum casualties in Tenth Corps and Third Div throughout entire operation." The troops had heard "reports of dire predictions at home of disaster here. Such erroneous reports must affect no less than 30,000 families. These reports should now be repudiated immediately as a Christmas act for the peace of mind of the men out here and their kin folk at home."[97]

By the end of the year, X Corps had landed at Pusan and rushed back toward the parallel, seeking a strong defense line. In the confusion of general retreat, Walker had been killed in a jeep accident; few in Korea or elsewhere dared to express the relief they felt. The general's reputation had understandably plummeted. Who would replace him? The Joint Chiefs had the perfect man in mind: Matthew Ridgway. If anyone could stop the retreat and halt the terrible erosion of morale, it was he. On Christmas Eve, Ridgway flew to Tokyo. His mission was to save the U.S. Army. Meanwhile the Department of Defense began to grease the skids for MacArthur's eventual departure.

On December 29, the Joint Chiefs sent a remarkable message to the supreme commander. It was marked personal and secret, and a typed draft bore the handwritten notation: "OK HST." The Chiefs began by stating that the message's existence was known to only a handful in Washington and that MacArthur should limit knowledge of its contents to himself and Ridgway plus their respective chiefs of staff. Then the Chiefs plunged in. "It appears from all estimates available that the Chinese Communists possess the capability of forcing United Nations forces out of Korea if they choose to exercise it." Peking could only be stopped by committing substantial additional UN forces, an action that would "seriously jeopardiz[e] other commitments including the safety of Japan." Because of "the increased threat of general war" the highest levels of the administration had decided that Korea was not the place to wage a major conflict or commit the bulk of U.S. ground forces.[98]

MacArthur's new orders were to hold onto the peninsula if he could, to grind down the Chinese Communist armies, and to compromise if not destroy Red China's military prestige. Acheson had already told subordinates in the State Department "that the President agreed that we should not pull out of Korea and leave our friends there to be murdered." But if UN troops were forced back beyond the Kum River and the Chinese massed huge forces against the UN lines, MacArthur should immediately withdraw all his forces. The Chiefs reminded MacArthur that his "primary mission" was the defense of Japan and that he possessed and would possess only the Eighth Army to carry out that mission. "Following the receipt of your views you will be given a definitive directive as to conditions under which you should initiate evacuation."[99]

This was a humiliating rebuke, and MacArthur interpreted it that way. He quickly responded, in effect urging Washington to widen the war into an explicit Sino-American conflict. The outraged Joint Chiefs immediately sent back a negative reply.[100] Korea was no longer to be the center of national and international attention and concern, as it had been in October. The West dared not make the Korean War a litmus test of either its competence or its prestige. The peninsula would have to become an expendable backwater, and MacArthur could no longer strut on the world stage as the heroic leader of an anticommunist crusade. The Chiefs finally declared unequivocally that they were ultimately in charge of the war. They would determine whether it was successful or unsuccessful and when and under what conditions it would be necessary to pull out. They had not only put MacArthur in his place; they had defined what that place was. For the next three and a half months, as Ridgway stabilized his army below the thirty-eighth parallel and then drove back to the old dividing line in a slow, crunching, and above all limited, offensive, the supreme commander twisted and turned, appealing to domestic opinion at home for restoration of his reputation and freedom of action, until at last his repeated insubordinations left his civilian commander in chief no alternative but to fire him.[101]

Christmas 1950 in America was much different from the year before. The sober hopes for a slowly improving world of stability and progress that had characterized the earlier holiday season were gone forever. So, pundits agreed almost unanimously, was the five-year-long cold war. "While they were being lived," the *New York Times* mused, the brief post-Hiroshima years "had seemed the most anxious of ages; in retrospect, they appeared almost as calm as a landscape by Corot. For in June, 1950, a fighting war was begun. In the months that followed, the world was gripped by the eerie fear that War 3, Armageddon, was impending. At the year's close, that sensation has subsided a little; but great dangers remain." A "fundamental debate" was now raging "over the whole Truman-Acheson concept of trying to contain the world push of Soviet communism." If letters to the editors around the country were an accurate barometer of public opinion, Herbert Hoover's call for a return to isolationism, to the defense of a "'Western Hemisphere Gibraltar,'" seemed to be gaining converts.[102]

Christmas was an anxious time for everyone. The weather over most of the nation had been abominable ever since Thanksgiving, when heavy rains caused flooding across much of the Far West and blizzards paralyzed the central and eastern sections of the country, followed by record low temperatures day after day. It seemed that nature was determined to give the country a taste of the kind of weather its soldiers were enduring thousands of miles away.

One more time, Luce sent his reporters to the heartland: to Kankakee, a town of twenty-five thousand, fifty-six miles south of Chicago's Loop on the rolling prairies of east-central Illinois. The crowds that jammed the stores along snow-packed Court Street seemed as carefree as ever while they went about their holiday shopping to the accompaniment of Christmas tunes by Bing Crosby and the Andrews Sisters. But beneath the surface unease and apprehension ran deep. The town "had been through five fat years" since the end of the war, "and now lean ones were coming." No one could believe that there would not be wartime shortages again, and no one knew how long they would last. Certainly the town's several large industrial plants would be reconverting to war production again; one had already received its first orders. But the changeover meant at least temporary layoffs as civilian demand inevitably declined before the defense orders began arriving.[103]

Above all, the visceral fears of the telephone call, the sudden appearance of the Western Union boy on the front porch, and the terrible empty feeling of loss, were returning. "Already 85 Kankakee boys have been called, the last group just in time to spend Christmas in the Army." Luce's cameramen were at the railroad station to record the sad farewells: tearful parents and siblings waving goodbye from the snowy train platform as the Illinois Central carted cherished sons and brothers off to basic training and then to God knew where. The draft was forcing all veterans to reexamine their status, "knowing that soon a lot of Kankakee is going to be in the Army and remembering what it was like when they themselves were raw recruits." [104]

A *Life* photographer posed the Mallaney family around its Christmas table, laden with Yuletide abundance. Like most Americans, the Mallaneys had been "touched by one war and the threat of another." A daughter was with her navy husband in Hawaii. Another was the wife of a naval reservist who was likely to be recalled. One of the sons was 4F. Another son, twenty-two, had been in the occupation army in Japan and awaited orders back to duty. The third son would probably go into the army in a few weeks. A son-in-law was a navy veteran "who expects to be called again"; a fourth son had been a navy pilot in the last war and hoped to be deferred from this one because he had a factory job and a farm. His young wife was the widow of an army pilot killed in 1944.[105]

What the future would bring, no one sitting uneasily around that table or anywhere else in the United States could begin to imagine. All they knew was that they were back at war and that it might last a very long time.

Epilogue

In 1950, the cold war finally came home to Main Street America, and the nation began to fully experience its awful pressures.

❖ ❖ ❖

The bomb instilled a quiet panic, especially among the young, who would come to maturity in the sixties and early seventies.[1] In a confusing spasm of compassion and concern, adult Americans tried to both warn and soothe their children about nuclear warfare. The effort failed dismally. In August of the midcentury year, school systems in such "target cities" as New York, Los Angeles, Chicago, Detroit, Milwaukee, Fort Worth, San Francisco, and Philadelphia made plans to implement a civil defense system and soon conducted "cover drills," during which teachers in the middle of a classroom discussion would suddenly yell "Drop!" The drills were harrowing to the children. Years later, novelist Mary Mackey remembered those terrifying moments as she and her classmates waited for the enemy A-bombs to fall: "Obediently we would fold our bodies into that attitude of prayer and supplication known only to the children of the fifties: legs folded, head between the knees, hands raised to protect the fragile, invisible nerve that floated somewhere in the blackness behind our eyes." To ensure that their students understood the seriousness of the exercise, "teachers passed out maps of cities upon which were superimposed ominous bulls-eyes showing the lethal reach of the bomb." Baby boomers, as they would soon be called, "never forgot the lesson that their world could someday end in a flash of light and heat while they were crouched helplessly in gyms and basements among heating ducts and spare blackboards."[2]

A handful of critics were appalled. A university professor complained that the press "abounds . . . in pictures of teachers standing grimly erect over children prostrate in cover-drill." Another observer said it was unnerving to see schoolchildren searching the skies for Soviet bombers. But such characterizations of "overwrought, anxious" teachers, students, and parents were rare, and the critics were almost reflexively reviled as subversives or worse, so the children continued to suffer horrifying rituals and dreams. "At night I would lie awake in my bed and count slowly to twenty-five as each plane passed over, afraid to miss the flash of light that would be my only warning." Another survivor of a fifties childhood later wrote that between the ages of ten and twenty he experienced "fairly regular nightmares about the destruction of the world with nuclear weapons. These dreams almost always began with a flash of dazzling light" and continued with a "murky series of episodes in which I stumbled through rubble" looking for friend or family "whom I could never find. Often I was chased by sinister figures, but my legs could hardly move."[3]

Misplaced zeal and sensitivity induced educational leaders and journalists to cloak the horrors of nuclear warfare in calmness and rationality. The National Parent-Teachers Association (PTA), following government guidelines and advice, was determined to "domesticate" the bomb, to remove its terror and make life with it livable, calm, even carefree. Parents were urged to develop a "positive mental health program" in response to their own and their children's atomic anxieties. Education journalists refused to discuss unpalatable realities of an atomic or thermonuclear blitz such as mass death, injuries, shock, blindness, burns, radiation sickness, and total social dislocation. At the beginning of the 1951 school year, soon after Truman announced the establishment of a Federal Civil Defense Administration, Los Angeles, New York, and other systems across the country handed out "dog tags" to schoolboys and identification necklaces to schoolgirls. The larger cities provided the tags and necklaces free of charge. In smaller urban areas, such as Seattle and Denver, either the PTA or the Board of Education found the money to make and distribute individual identification discs. Educators from across the country met at the Civil Defense Staff College in Maryland to consider other forms of identification in case of a nuclear or thermonuclear holocaust. Tatooing was considered but rejected because of its recent "associations" and its "impermanence in the case of severe burns."[4]

Historian JoAnne Brown concluded that for anxiety-ridden adults this mass exercise in denial apparently worked. The nation's children seemed to stop worrying and begin to accept, if not love, the bomb, and civil defense became "a way of life in the schools" and by extension in the country at large. But as the years passed, appearances proved to have been deceiving. "Anger, fear, and disillusionment" followed the school generation of the fifties into young adulthood with often devastating results for itself and the country.[5]

While the nation's educators and politicians tried to shield their young charges from the realities of nuclear war, some business people saw the issue as a means to big money. Before midcentury, communist plots and agents had vied with various exotic criminal elements as villains in comic books, which were a staple of young life before television. After 1950, comic book demons were almost invariably Commies out to destroy the American way of life through deceit, disloyalty, and violence. In 1951, the Bowman Gum Company of Philadelphia, which had been known for issuing an annual series of stylish baseball cards to America's youth, brought out a new set of more than seventy pasteboards titled "Children's Crusade against Communism." Several front covers depicted the leaders of communism in suitably devilish style. Others showed scenes of communist-inspired or -directed mayhem or, most chilling of all, of communist mayhem to come. Card number 21, for example, titled "Mined Harbor," pictured ships blowing up and spewing irradiated shrapnel all over frightened yard workers as they sought to escape. "We know that the Reds have the atom bomb," the text on the back of the card told the kids. "In a war with the Soviet Union we would have to watch the skies for atomic raiders. But that is not all. We would have to be equally alert at the waterfront" because a "leading scientist has warned us that tramp steamers could plant A-bombs in our harbors" and "just one atomic explosion could spread ruin through an entire port." Such things were not "sure to happen. We still hope for world peace." But the not too subtle message was that the hope was pretty forlorn. One way to retain peace was to make and keep the country not only strong but alert. The price of survival was eternal vigilance.[6]

If the bomb produced soul-wrenching terror, Korea produced a strange mixture of anguish and apathy. Early in 1951, pollster Samuel Lubell visited an elderly farm couple in central Ohio to learn their views on the state of the union. The swing to conservatism in the recent off-year elections intrigued Lubell. Did it represent a resurgence of traditional isolationism or something else? He learned that the Leon Hunters espoused neither isolationism nor internationalism but a "general mood of frustration which the Korean War produced, and which was apparent wherever I went."[7]

Mrs. Hunter first gave Lubell a piece of homemade cake and then a piece of her mind on what was wrong with the country. "Truman and Acheson are too soft with the Communists. Why doesn't Truman get rid of those Communists in the government? With our boys dying in Korea, he won't kick out the people who are fighting us—it makes me sick!" There was no chance of an agreement with the Soviets. But thermonuclear war was unthinkable. Yet the Hunters were not content "with the present nightmarish twilight of neither war nor peace." Mr. Hunter wanted to "show those Russians where they get off. . . . When Malik and Vishinsky say those things about us in the United Nations, someone ought to go up to them and slap their faces!" As Lubell got up to leave, Hunter struggled to sum up his feelings: "I guess what I've been trying to say is that it's time we got back to the American way of living."

It was a hope beyond realization. Washington and Main Street together had crossed a threshold in 1950; there was no way back. The war dragged on inconclusively, and the coffins containing the remains of last year's high school quarterback or the kid that used to fill the gas tank or serve the hamburgers came back to the train stations and graveyards of Middletown and Plainville. Division and distrust replaced the sense (however artificially contrived it had often been) of shared values and purpose that had defined the nation since Franklin Roosevelt's time. Shortly after the war finally ended, editor Herbert Agar recalled how quickly "this painful" conflict "came to seem so useless to so many . . . people." Agar believed the critics were "misled," that they did not understand that national greatness always required national sacrifice.[8] But only a small number could sustain the illusion that Korea was a crusade at all comparable to those in Europe and the Pacific just a few years before. The unhappy school and farm boys of village Ohio and the young urban workers of Manhattan who sullenly faced their draft boards reflected much of the country's mood.

In the summer of 1953, as the war was winding down, pollster Edward A. Suchman and his colleagues reported on public attitudes toward the conflict.[9] They had concentrated their attention on college students but emphasized that the youngsters' responses mirrored the beliefs of the country at large. Despite more than 100,000 American soldiers killed and wounded, "the united and wholehearted support of public opinion which characterized the last war is conspicuous by its absence in the Korean war. Instead of consensus we have partisanship—in place of conviction and faith, we have divided opinion and doubt." There was no "fanfare" for the young men sent to or returning from the battlefront. Nearly three thousand college students, when asked about the importance to them of the ideas and policies being fought for in the Korean War, responded tepidly. Only 20 percent replied that the ideas were "tremendously important." Another 41 percent replied that they meant "quite a bit." But 22 percent said they meant "not very much." Only 12 percent were "strongly in favor" of U.S. policy in Korea, another 36 percent were "in favor," 19 percent were neutral, 20 percent were against, and 13 percent were "strongly against." When asked whether it was "worthwhile" to fight an "all-out war" to stop communism, 26 percent replied that it was "very worthwhile" and 14 percent agreed that it was worthwhile. But 18 percent claimed it was hardly worthwhile, and 24 percent thought that it was not at all worthwhile.

Suchman stated that student opinion was sharply divided not only over the merits of the Korean conflict but also over "the effectiveness of the United Nations, American aid to Europe, and other current political matters." But his conclusions contradicted Agar's assertion that those who opposed the Korean venture were misled. Although the results he and his colleagues obtained could have been interpreted as demonstrations of a lack of faith, Suchman admitted, "the internal evidence indicates that they are less likely to indicate [public] 'confusion and doubt' than a realistic appraisal of the current world" and the "differences present" in American society at large.

As the war had settled into a bloody stalemate in 1951, a "raging political conflict" gripped the country. The major economic groups—farmers, labor, business—and their representatives in Congress fought to "shift the burdens of the cold war to someone else" through such "tricky stratagems" as rigging tax legislation to favor this or that interest, exempting one group from government controls while clamping down on others, and protecting and promoting one or another bloc "through technical formulas for guaranteeing higher profits, higher prices, or higher wages."[10] The federal establishment became everyone's antagonist; it seemed part of the problem rather than part of the solution.

"This inability to distribute the burden of rearmament equitably and without gutting the economy" through inflation, Lubell wrote, "points to the real governmental crisis tearing the country today." The crisis could not be overcome either by weakening the federal establishment, as the enemies of the New Deal demanded, or by advancing additional schemes of social engineering and improvement, as Truman's Fair Dealers wished. "The real need is to strengthen government—not to protect either business-as-usual or social-gains-as-usual, but to discipline both to the national interest."[11] But such a glittering generality as the national interest was now beyond the ability of a disillusioned country to articulate. Instead the nation continued to receive from its capital frightening doses of political paranoia and conspiracy-mongering that further polarized Manhattan and Main Street.

Joe McCarthy and his minions would rampage unchecked for four years beyond midcentury, sowing fear and loathing across the land. Clark Clifford, whose knowledge of Washington folkways and American politics over the past half-century is perhaps unmatched, has recently reminded us that McCarthy terrorized the Washington community and that, on the eve of his undoing during the army hearings of 1954, polls indicated that half the country more or less supported Wisconsin's junior senator.[12] William L. Shirer, one of CBS Radio News's most eminent foreign correspondents, came home in 1951 and was appalled at what the communist witch hunts had done to the spirit of the people. An "inexplicable atmosphere of intolerance, suspicion, fear, and even hysteria" pervaded the country.

> Everywhere I went a surprisingly large number of people seemed afraid. Of what, in God's name? Of becoming involved in controversy, they said, of getting into trouble by expressing an opinion that someone might not like.
>
> That WHO might not like?
>
> Well, they said, hesitantly and usually in a whisper (was I back in Germany under the snooping nose of the Gestapo, I wondered), the government, or the F.B.I., or some loyalty board, or the University Board of Trustees, or Senator McCarthy, or the un-American Committee, or the moguls in Hollywood, or the sponsor of a T.V. or radio program, or the local newspaper, or any one of a hundred groups of self-appointed vigilantes—even your boss at the office or your next-door neighbor. You will be destroyed if you don't watch out.[13]

Shirer believed that he had already been ruined by his beloved CBS Radio News. His unpopular opposition to the Truman doctrine may have led to his "reassignment" from a coveted daily news spot to one much less appealing. Shirer attributed his demotion to midcentury America's new spirit of intolerance, which centered around McCarthy, and he claimed that his boss, the ostensibly saintly, untouchable Edward R. Murrow, refused to stand up for him.[14] Virtually removed from the occupation he loved best, Shirer first expressed his bitterness in a rather transparent novel about his ordeal and then redeemed—and enhanced—his reputation by writing his monumental history of Nazi Germany.

McCarthy's triumph would turn long-standing American concerns about the possible dimensions of domestic communism into a raging crusade against the federal government, academia, the schools, and the communications industry. In the process he and his followers so traumatized the nation that it became obsessed with "subversives" and "disloyalty." In a 1946 poll 19 percent of those surveyed believed that "a good many" labor leaders were communists, a not irrational conclusion given what was known then and now about Red penetration of the labor movement. But only 6 percent mistrusted federal employees, 4 percent distrusted teachers, and 3 percent mistrusted journalists.[15] McCarthy and his followers convinced much of the country that nearly the entire federal establishment, along with broad segments of the entertainment community and the media, was disloyal, that the nation was being led by out-and-out traitors.

In 1951, popular journalists Jack Lait and Lee Mortimer expounded what would become the essential anticommunist catechism in a crude, coarse, bitter tome titled *Washington Confidential*, which focused on the vague tales from the late forties of communist spooks and then raised them to a much higher level of paranoia. The book sold almost a million copies within a year and may still be found nearly half a century later on the shelves of many used bookstores across the country.[16]

Washington, D.C., was a nest of vipers, the two men reported, "a cesspool of drunkenness, . . . whoring, homosexuality, municipal corruption and public apathy, protected crime . . . hooliganism, racketeering, pandering and plundering." The federal establishment was "still up to its neck in conspirators and collaborationists." The bureaucracy was recruited from skid row; the State Department was all pinko; the CIA was loaded with Commies at the lowest level, "with some seeping right up into the upper brackets." Suburban Georgetown's millionaire radicals gave "exotic, erotic parties" for gullible government girls and clerks. "Aphrodisiac get-togethers," complete with "rich oriental costumes" and "Arabian Nights music," were designed to lure these low-ranking, modestly paid federal workers into a life of treason.

The city was awash in drugs provided by Commie infiltrators. One could buy a reefer on almost any street corner. Something called the "Permanent

Central Opium Board" in Geneva had identified the Soviet Union as a major violator of international narcotics laws, but no one in Washington was interested in doing anything about it. The "Pervert Sections" of foreign embassies were working overtime to compromise the countless "homos" who were "snugly ensconced" throughout the federal bureaucracy, screened and protected "by the radicals in high places." Treacherous Jews and credulous Negroes in the District of Columbia wittingly and unwittingly advanced the Commie cause in a variety of ways.

The lowdown about the nation's capital was thus simple and frightening: "The Reds are not on the run in Washington." The various communist control laws and boards meant nothing because Truman's Fair Deal administration did not want them to function. There were some courageous men in the city. Styles Bridges and Harold Velde, to name only two, were sincere Redhunters, but they were repeatedly frustrated and repressed by the liberal big government crowd around the White House. J. Edgar Hoover was a great cop who had been fighting Nazi and Commie moles in America for years and would continue the fight. But like all cops he had to take orders; in the last analysis, despite all his crusading, he was hamstrung. A communist-ridden, conspiracy-riddled liberal federal government thus remained the primary repository of the country's moral sewage and a direct threat to the nation's integrity and existence. It could only be cleansed with a steady diet of vigilantism.

Such ideas pervaded the American community. On college campuses young men and women who aspired to careers in one of the most interesting and challenging segments of society now discovered that if they applied for federal service F.B.I. agents were on their heels, digging into their pasts for questionable affiliations. Shirer was outraged. Students were being harassed and their futures were jeopardized whenever they were identified as subscribing to an unpopular point of view: "Not to a Communist view, note, but to an *unpopular* point of view."[17]

The growing public obsession with disloyalty and its handmaidens—keeping one's mouth shut and one's ears closed—had begun to erode what had recently been a reasonably sophisticated, knowledgable electorate. Traveling across the country, Shirer no longer got the impression that people were well informed about world or domestic politics; "nor did we always grasp the very issues on which our existence depended." Shirer quoted the dean of American pollsters, George Gallup: "'Today for the first time I am concerned lest lack of information lead the American people to decisions which they will regret.'"[18] To bolster Gallup's point, Shirer cited several recent surveys, which demonstrated that an alarmingly large portion of the populace did not understand references to the thirty-eighth parallel or to the Atlantic Pact.

By the end of 1951, the strange, unhappy atmosphere of suspicion, fright, and silence had also begun to damage the creative life of the country. New York's premier drama critic, Brooks Atkinson, wrote that "something elusive and intangible seems to have drained the vitality out of the theatre and perhaps out of other American arts as well."

> No one knows the reason exactly. But could it be that the spiritual climate in which we are now living smothers art that is really creative, and that the emphasis on public expression of all kinds is toward meekness and conformity? . . . People are playing safe. They hesitate to say what they think. The intellectual and artistic life of the country has been flattened out. The ignorant heresy-hunting and the bigoted character-assassination that have acquired the generic title of McCarthyism are succeeding.[19]

In 1952, Whittaker Chambers published his own condemnation of the American establishment. If Chambers is remembered at all today, it is as a seedy, not particularly respectable informer. But nearly half a century ago much of Main Street considered him the nation's chief anticommunist philosopher, and indeed he possessed eloquence and a sense of drama. Chambers gave to the burgeoning crusade against the Red menace critical ingredients it had previously lacked: vision and purpose, a lofty rationale for repression, and above all an apparent dignity. Here was no mudslinger in the gutter like McCarthy, even though he in fact slung the same kind of mud—if of an ostensibly higher quality—as did the Wisconsin senator.[20] Chambers articulated in a new form for a new age the fundamental Christian belief that each soul was important because each was a battleground between good and evil, God and the devil. Without quite making the connection explicit, Chambers equated capitalism with Christianity while reiterating the theme that communism was the latest, "modern" incarnation of devilment.

Chambers submitted most of the manuscript for *Witness*, his eventual best-seller, to a national weekly for prepublication serialization. The venue he chose was significantly not one of the "highbrow" journals of the day such as *Harpers* or the *Atlantic Monthly*, either of which would have published his story solely because it was sellable. Instead he shrewdly chose one of the bibles of Middletown-Plainville opinion, the *Saturday Evening Post*.

"I Was the Witness" appeared in February 1952 and was written in the form of a letter to Chambers's two teenage children.[21] The *Post* editors introduced his essay with a brief, lyrical preface: "Here begins one of the great books of your lifetime . . . because it explains—for the first time—what communism really is, how it threatens you, why such able men as Hiss and Chambers gave their lives to it." Communism, Chambers began,

> remains the historical ordeal of the world in the twentieth century. For in this century, within the next decades, will be decided for generations whether all mankind is to become communist, whether the whole world is to become free, or whether, in the struggle, civilization as we know it, is to be completely destroyed or completely changed. It is our fate to live upon that turning point in history.

Communism was not simply a "vicious plot hatched by a few men in a cellar"; it was not just Marx or Lenin or dialectical materialism or the labor theory of value. It was not evil men sitting on a politburo somewhere. Communism was a conspircy of and for change, based on powerful visions and convictions and the willingness of dedicated men and women to act on those visions and convictions. Most of the rest of the world had lost its power to dream and to believe, but communists had not, and so the world was ripe for penetration by the dedicated agents of Red revolution.

But communism was much worse than a mere political or social threat, for it revived the never-ending battle between materialism and spirituality. Communists would exclude God from human life. Communism was "an intensely practical vision. The tools to turn it into reality are at hand—science and technology, whose traditional method, the rigorous exclusion of all supernatural factors in solving problems, has contributed to the intellectual climate in which the [communist] vision flourishes, just as they have contributed to the crisis in which Communism thrives." Communism "has posed in practical form the most revolutionary question in history: God or man? . . . It says to every man who joins it: the vision is a practical problem of history; the way to achieve it is a practical problem of politics, which is the present tense of history." Communism asked individuals to bear the moral burden of guilt for the crimes of history so that through those crimes "man at last may close his chronicle of age-old, senseless suffering, and replace it with purpose and plan." If people accepted this responsibility, they became communists; if they refused, they became "miscellaneous socialists, liberals, fellow travelers, unclassified progressives [or] men of good will" who shared communism's vision but were unwilling to accept the penalties of its faith.

Chambers's depiction of a sharply divided world clearly placed socialists, liberals, and progressives in the camp of communist fellow travelers. True communists, real believers in Marx and Lenin, had to be grudgingly respected for their fanaticism and their ruthless dedication, however warped and criminal, to a cause and a vision. Chambers thus sought personal absolution for a previous life of criminality. It was the essentially passive liberal and socialist adherents to collectivism who deserved the contempt and scorn of decent men and women, for they were the people who were capable of undermining rugged individualism and the American way of life without even possessing the courage of ultimate conviction that what they were doing represented the only course for humanity. Chambers's argument contained the not very subliminal message that *any* social planning or engineering, such as that so exuberantly undertaken by the New and Fair Deals, had to be not only communistic but atheistic, literally ungodly.

Above all, Chambers armed fundamentalist conservatives with a new conviction in their old values. Life really was an uncomplicated struggle throughout the world between good and evil, materialism and spirituality, individualism and collectivism, God and fallen man. Life was not gray but black and white; it was not fundamentally ambiguous but simple, and brave men and women needed to summon the courage to think and act simply. All individuals were soldiers in the global struggle against communism, and they had to unite with their fellows to harass and rout the implacable foe. Victory would come only to those who reinvigorated their own and the nation's faith in the power of traditional visions and beliefs and in the triumph of individualism, with its emphasis on personal effort, toughness, honest toil, initiative, sobriety, thrift, and God-fearing righteousness over collectivism, with its stress on social planning, mass prosperity, and entitlements.

The flagrant, paranoid Red-baiting of McCarthy, Lait, and Mortimer fueled a long-term if largely subliminal movement of right-wing vigilantism.[22] On the other hand, Chambers's vision of a righteous, militantly armed America going out into the world to battle the hosts of communism in order to save its own soul attracted a surprising number of the nation's increasingly dispirited writers and intellectuals, many of whom identified themselves on the left of the political spectrum. These individuals had become disgusted with the ineptitude and corruption of the second Truman administration, were instinctively alienated from the business culture and ethics of Eisenhower and his "modern" Republicans, and were badly frightened by McCarthy. They began to identify themselves as liberal anticommunists. Their critics on the far Left charged that the concept was oxymoronic because anticommunism demanded a profoundly illiberal willingness to surrender basic civil rights.

The chief expression of liberal anticommunism in the midfifties was Americans for Democratic Action, one of whose founders, Arthur Schlesinger, Jr., had asserted as early as 1949 the right of democratic government to deny employment if not expression to those it deemed disloyal. Many liberals, confused and unhappy with the complexities of contemporary life, became entranced with the fashionably exhausted, essentially antipolitical leadership of Adlai Stevenson and with young Schlesinger's concept of a "vital center" in American politics, which, without much energy or charisma, would nonetheless dutifully continue the crusade against international and domestic communism. A handful of liberals, to the shame of their colleagues, were even willing to share public platforms with Chambers. Adrift and unhappy, thousands of professors and pundits listlessly awaited a new call to action.[23]

The country, too, was numbed by the horrors and frustrations that Korea, McCarthy, and the bomb had unleashed. As the war passed into recent memory and McCarthy irretrievably corrupted himself on television, the American people turned to other preoccupations. They took refuge in the unprecedented cornucopia of goods and services provided by a white-hot cold war economy capable of producing both guns and butter. A bracing if seldom profound national dialogue began over the meaning and direction of the new society of affluence and the place of the individual in it. In the "mass society" being created by national television, Madison Avenue hucksters, and roaring prosperity, where could and should the lines be drawn between private conduct and public responsibility? Was it necessary to become a mindless, conforming "organization man" to get ahead and prosper? Why were increasingly well-paid workers still discontented in their jobs? Were Americans increasingly enslaved by "hidden persuaders" who manipulated what they thought and bought? Would a looming age of automation destroy meaningful work and the work ethic that had stimulated and shaped American society from the beginning? Popular sociologists Vance Packard and William H. Whyte argued that too many Americans impulsively accepted an economic and status hierarchy and their place in it, and Packard argued that the gates of opportunity might be closing for millions of Americans: Costs kept rising, wages were flattening, opportunities were narrowing for those without college degrees, and labor unions with their demands for rigid seniority systems were stifling individual initiative. Was it true that the nation was losing its soul, that critical, humane thought was finally being sacrificed to a mindless quest for money, goods, and security?[24]

As the country began debating these domestic issues, the Supreme Court suddenly reversed three centuries of race relations by insisting that separate education was inherently unequal education. And if separate was unequal in the classroom, was it not also unequal, unjust, and truly un-American in the workplace and the neighborhood—even in the bedroom? Was it not time for white America to finally confront what it had done to and what it owed black America?

Americans were torn between private preoccupations and public pressures. Agar grasped at least part of the temperament of the times and in 1957 quoted a remark by the bomb's father, J. Robert Oppenheimer: "This is a world in which each of us will have to cling to what is close to him, to what he knows, to what he can do, to his friends and his tradition and his life, lest he be dissolved in a universal confusion and know nothing and love nothing." It was, Agar concluded, sound advice.[25]

But even as Agar wrote, a substantial number of influential writers, journalists, statesmen, and pundits of both conservative and liberal persuasion were rousing themselves to renewed action. Sputnik and the apparently eternal communist menace required more of America than mindless materialism and thoughtless individualism. It was time, they concluded, to subordinate domestic preoccuptions to what they saw as the major issues confronting the nation: the cold war and foreign policy. From these interlocking perspectives the critics despaired over what they perceived as the nation's plunge into hedonism and personal obsessions under Ike's avuncular, uninspiring leadership.

One of the first Jeremiahs was James A. Michener, just beginning his remarkable career as a storyteller. In his celebrated 1953 novella, *The Bridges at Toko-ri*, Michener used the story of an embittered World War II carrier pilot, returned to duty in Korea against his will, to warn Americans that if they did not fight on distant battlefields now they might soon be fighting communists at home. Michener did not try to obscure or gloss over America's distaste for the war.

Young Nancy Brubaker, the doomed carrier pilot's wife, disgustedly tells her husband about taking the couple's two small daughters from their Denver home to Cheyenne to see the annual Frontier Days festival, where she "almost screamed with agony because everything was exactly the way it was in 1946. Nobody gave a damn about Korea. In all America nobody gives a damn." But wise old George Tarrant, the carrier task force commander, supplies a different, ostensibly wiser perspective. Any war is the wrong one, he tells Brubaker, but "all through history free men have had to fight the wrong war in the wrong place . . . that's the one they're stuck with." The burden of maintaining freedom always falls on a few, Tarrant adds. "Nobody ever knows why he gets the dirty job. But any society is held together by the efforts, . . . yes, and the sacrifices of only a few." The admiral tells his skeptical young pilot that one morning communist generals and commissars will meet to discuss the future of the war. "And a messenger will run in with news that the Americans have knocked out even the bridges at Toko-ri. And that little thing will convince the Reds that we'll never stop . . . never give in . . . never weaken in our purpose." Later, pacing his narrow carrier bridge above the stormy winter seas off Korea, Tarrant continues to brood about his country's unwillingness to understand the threats against it: "What would they have us abandon to the enemy? . . . Korea? Then Japan and the Philippines? Sooner or later Hawaii? . . . Maybe California. Colorado. Perhaps we'd stabilize at the Mississippi."[26]

Michener was reflecting conventional wisdom in Washington, where policymakers concluded that the country could not abandon either its explicit commitments or its implicit responsibilities to confront the Red menace on every front. MacArthur might be told that the Korean War was of limited importance and that the Far East remained secondary to Europe in American security calculations. But, in fact, the Truman and Eisenhower administrations advanced the national defense line from the offshore islands and archipelagoes of Asia (Japan, Formosa, the Philippines) to the mainland itself. Indeed, by the summer of 1952, Indochina was perceived as perhaps the key to Western global security. In justifying their actions, U.S. policymakers used almost the identical language first heard on Main Street in November and December of 1950, when knowledgeable citizens despaired that defeat in Korea would lead to the progressive loss of Southeast Asia, India, the Middle East, and Western Europe.

Top secret NSC Memorandum 124/2 ("United States Objectives and Courses of Action with Respect to Southeast Asia"), signed by Truman on June 25, 1952, stated as "general considerations" that

> the loss of any of the countries of Southeast Asia to Communist control as a consequence of overt or covert Chinese Communist aggression would have critical psychological, political and economic consequences. In the absence of effective and timely counteraction, the loss of any single country would probably lead to relatively swift submission to or an alignment with communism by the remaining countries of this group. Furthermore, an alignment with communism of the rest of Southeast Asia and India, and in the longer term, of the Middle East (with the probable exceptions of at least Pakistan and Turkey) would in all probability progressively follow. Such widespread alignment would endanger the stability and security of Europe.[27]

Eisenhower Republicans found no fault with the domino policy of their Democratic predecessors. Only six days after the new administration took office in January 1953, Secretary of State John Foster Dulles, in a nationwide radio and television address, used maps to emphasize the pivotal importance of Southeast Asia to the free world's defense network. "The Soviet Russians" were making a concerted drive to gain control of Japan, Dulles asserted. If the Kremlin and its Chinese allies conquered the peninsula that comprised Indochina, Siam (Thailand), Malaya, and Burma, they could command the Asian rice bowl on which Japan—and India—absolutely depended for subsistence.[28]

The next afternoon, a group of high-level officials, including Dulles, the Joint Chiefs of Staff, and Mutual Security Director Harold Stassen, met at the Pentagon to plan the next eight years of Republican foreign and national security policy. Stassen asked how bad it would really be if the free world lost Indochina but strengthened Japan. Omar Bradley, who remained JCS chairman, replied that "it would still be bad. It would lead to the loss of all Southeast Asia." Dulles added that if Southeast Asia were lost, Japan would inevitably fall to communism. "The situation of the Japanese is hard enough without China being Commie. You would not lose Japan immediately, but from there on out the Japs would be thinking on how to get to the other side." Two months later, as the administration settled comfortably into business, Eisenhower, Dulles, and the secretaries of defense and the treasury met at the White House to compare notes on the forthcoming visit of French Premier René Mayer and Foreign Minister Georges Bidault. The discussion soon turned to Indochina, and a general "recognition" was soon reached "that it probably had top priority in foreign policy, being in some ways more important than Korea because the consequences of loss there could not be localized, but would spread throughout Asia and Europe."[29]

Six weeks after the Korean armistice, Dulles issued a public policy statement, warning that the Korean War was not "an isolated affair." Instead, it formed "one part of the worldwide effort of communism to conquer freedom. More immediately it is part of that effort in Asia." Apparently seeking to extend Winston Churchill's Fulton, Missouri, clarion call about the cold war ("From Stettin on the Baltic to Trieste on the Adriatic, an Iron Curtain has descended across Europe") eastward to Asia, Dulles asserted that "a single Chinese-Communist aggressive front extends from Korea on the north to Indochina in the south. The armistice in Korea, even if it leads to a political settlement in Korea, does not end United States concern in the western Pacific area. . . . In Indochina a desperate struggle is in its eighth year. The outcome affects our own vital interests in the western Pacific."[30]

But the communist tide seemed unstoppable even by such obsessive anti-communists as Dulles.[31] The Soviet launch of Sputnik in 1957 added a further burden of apparently endless, limitless communist challenge. From cradle to grave, it seemed, Ivan and Ivana could do things that Johnnie and Jeannie could not. The communists seemed so purposeful; the Americans, awash in Eisenhower-era prosperity and its challenges, seemed so aimless and slothful.

By the end of the decade, influential opinion makers, from Stevenson to conservative guru Clinton Rossiter and evangelical fundamentalist Billy Graham, were close to despair. The country had gone soft, they concluded, had lost its way, and needed a regenerative crusade to restore its moral fiber and political health. Such a crusade would not involve a reconsideration of the cold war, only its intensification. The views of Stevenson, Rossiter, and Graham, along with those of a handful of other influential thinkers and doers, including Walter Lippmann, John W. Gardner, David Sarnoff, and Archibald MacLeish, were solicited by Henry Luce in 1959, first published in *Life* magazine, and then collected in a book appropriately titled *The National Purpose,* which reached stores just as John Kennedy and Richard Nixon began their epic 1960 battle for the White House. Although Chambers was not invited to contribute, his spirit pervaded every essay.[32]

"That something has gone wrong in America most of us know," poet and liberal bureaucrat MacLeish asserted.[33] The United States was richer than any nation in history. "We have more Things in our garages and kitchens and cellars than Louis Quatorze had in the whole of Versailles. We have come nearer to the suppression of grinding poverty than even the 19th Century Utopians thought seriously possible." Americans had wiped out many of the pests and scourges that afflicted humanity from the beginning. "We have lengthened men's lives and protected their infancy. We have advanced science to the edges of the inexplicable and hoisted our technology to the sun itself. We are in a state of growth and flux and change in which cities flow out into countryside and the countryside moves into cities," where amazing new industries were being born and obsolescent factories were dying, where the customs of generations were being overthrown and fathers spoke different languages than did their sons.

Despite these breathtaking advances in the private sphere, the country no longer felt right about itself. No one could blame domestic communists any longer.[34] The days had apparently passed when "all we needed to do to be saved was to close the State Department and keep the Communists out of motion pictures. It isn't just the Russians now: it's ourselves. It's the way we feel about ourselves as Americans. We feel that we've lost our way in the woods, that we don't know where we are going—if anywhere." Having defeated Hitler and the Japanese so magnificently, "we acted again as though freedom were an accomplished fact. We no longer thought of it as safe but . . . we thought of it as something that could be protected by building walls around it, by 'containing' its enemy." But freedom was never an accomplished fact. It had to be defended and fought for militantly every day. "The only way freedom can be defended is not by fencing it in but by enlarging it, exercising it." If the Soviet objective throughout the world was to seem more vigorous, pertinent, and compelling than the United States, "then we have indeed lost the 'battle for men's minds' of which we talk so much." America need not fashion a national purpose but merely exercise its historic mission, which was nothing less than "the liberation of humanity" to ensure "the freedom of man."

Conservative philosopher Rossiter echoed his liberal colleague.[35] He titled his essay "We Must Show the Way to Enduring Peace" and assigned an almost Darwinian nature to American history. The country had necessarily been born "lean and hungry, a people 'on the make,' and we generated a sense of mission almost instinctively in order to survive and move ahead. Now we are fat and complacent, a people that 'has it made,' and we find it hard to rouse to the trumpet of sacrifice—even if anyone in authority were to blow it." The "challenge of peace," Rossiter maintained, "calls upon us to deal not just with ourselves but with all mankind. . . . A sense of national purpose is at bottom a sense of international purpose." It had become the destiny of the United States "to lead the world prudently and pragmatically" toward a single world government, "having power to enforce peace." The country had to labor "in the world at large" to secure its dream. "A nation that has counted as a special force in history must strive to count again or reap the fruits of demoralization."

The liberal Gardner was not at all certain that Americans *could* answer Rossiter's call. "We lack leadership on the part of our leaders, and commitment on the part of every American." The only way Gardner could see out of the morass was to convince the country that "the greatness and strength of a free society" depended on developing and applying a sense of "excellence" to public and private affairs. But Gardner could not say precisely what he meant by excellence.[36]

Stevenson agreed that "mankind" was crying out for a "convincing working model of a free society"[37] and that America was failing to provide it. Instead the nation was drowning in a spirit of mass consumerism, which did not and could not translate into "spiritual growth." Private interest had replaced public responsibility. "Never before in my lifetime," Stevenson scolded,

> not even in the days of Harding and Coolidge—has the mystique of privacy seemed to me so pervasive. The face which we present to the world—especially through our mass circulation media—is the face of the individual or the family as a high consumption unit with minimal social links or responsibilities—father happily drinking his favorite beer, mother dreamily fondling soft garments newly rinsed in a marvel detergent, the children gaily calling from the new barbecue pit for a famous sauce for their steak. And, of course, a sleek new car is in the background.

The result of such radical privatism, as Lubell had discovered in 1951, was "a 'lobby' or 'pressure group' state in which each organized group jostles for its own interests, at the expense of the weak, the isolated or the unorganized." America was better and nobler than that. Stevenson argued that with inspiring leadership the American people "are prepared to face the cost, the rigors, the efforts and the challenge which are involved in recovering the public image" of a great nation.

The same year that *The National Purpose* appeared, the Special Studies Project of the Rockefeller Brothers Fund, organized in 1956, completed its four-year study of the prospects for America. The project had enlisted the views of more than one hundred prominent Americans, and its Planning Committee included such luminaries as young Henry Kissinger, well-known columnist Emmett John Hughes, and Nancy Hanks, who later served in several prominent executive posts in Washington. The Rockefeller panelists were probably somewhat more to the right politically than most of the contributors to Luce's project. Yet the tone of the Rockefeller reports was as assertive, if not more so, as that of the essays in *The National Purpose*. The thrust was summed up in a sentence: "We are required, then, to strengthen the conditions of freedom at home and to help build them everywhere in the world."[38]

From 1957 onward, John F. Kennedy would champion this vision. Although the Senate's Church Committee in 1975 revealed just how brutal a cold warrior Ike could be,[39] it was Kennedy and his New Frontiersmen, however, who publicly pledged the country to pay any price and bear any burden, support any friend, and oppose any foe to rid the world of the demons that Korea, McCarthy, and the bomb had let loose in the American psyche.

Kennedy was determined to "get the country moving again," and that meant a vigorous, incessant confrontation with Soviet power. However prudent they may have been in specific instances, Kennedy and his men projected a public image of joyous battle and incessant, zestful crisis management. In Camelot it was always the hour of maximum danger. Muscular liberals, sharing Chambers's apocalyptic anticommunism but determined to live down his contemptuous dismissal of their creed and their manhood through constant applications of "excellence," would fulfill Rossiter's image of an America once more "on the make." Kennedy and his men would not shrink from this burden—they would welcome it—and the president invited his fellow citizens to do the same. In ever larger numbers they responded.

Clark Clifford, an ardent admirer of the young president, admitted years later that Kennedy yearned above all to inspire the nation "with a heroic vison of the Presidency as the center of action in American life." Clifford found no fault with that aspiration, but he was deeply disturbed by many of those around the president, certainly young men of brilliance but generally dismissive of history and therefore arrogant. A decade after Camelot, Harvard economist John Kenneth Galbraith, Kennedy's ambassador to India and sometime Vietnam troubleshooter, who should have had a strong sense of the recent past, ruefully recalled: "This was a period in our history when reputations were being made in foreign policy. A goodly number of people were saying, now if I'm . . . I'm just associated with the right crisis at the right time, the right association with the Pentagon, the right approach to military force, I will be the great man that nobody but my wife ever suspected me of being before, and so there was an enthusiasm for crises."[40]

But Kennedy, his men, and much of the public that he won over so charmingly after the Bay of Pigs fiasco had forgotten the terrible lessons of midcentury. The cold war, with its thermonuclear balance of terror on the one hand and its frustrating, local, comparatively low-intensity conflicts on the other, was not susceptible to heroics or resolution through vague appeals to excellence. "Communism" had apparently been on the march throughout the fifties in the non-Western world. But free-world victories would always be costly and ambiguous (Korea proved that); defeats could be contained and overcome by wisdom and counterpressure. There were, perhaps, no places on earth worth the price of thousands of young American dead except the key areas that George Kennan had pointed out in 1946: Western Europe and Japan for certain, parts of the Middle East, and perhaps India as well. Successful prosecution of the cold war in the face of the enormous changes occurring in American life required prudence, not posturing; wisdom, not theatrics. Occasionally, as in one or two sentences in his inaugural address and in his memorable American University speech in the spring of 1963, Kennedy seemed to understand. But in Vietnam he did not.

Nor did the nation. Scarcely a decade after Fuchs's betrayal, McCarthy's alleged discovery of traitors honeycombing the State Department, and the terrible defeat of the Eighth Army and X Corps in North Korea, the country was ready to sacrifice again. The immediate triumph and ultimate tragedy of the Kennedy administration was to recreate the sober but confident mood of the late forties, when the United States thought itself capable of achieving any objective it set. In the Kennedy and early Johnson years, Americans forgot the lessons of 1950 and so were condemned to relive them in a growing catastrophe that soon became boundless and whose consequences we still have not escaped.

Notes

Introduction

1. Joseph Goulden, *The Best Years, 1945–1950* (New York: Atheneum, 1976), pp. 5–10 (Russell is quoted on p. 6); Studs Terkel, *"The Good War": An Oral History of World War II* (New York: Ballantine Books, 1985), p. 10.

2. Merle Miller, *Plain Speaking: An Oral Biography of Harry S. Truman* (New York: Berkley Books, 1974), p. 441.

3. Terkel, *"The Good War,"* p. 65.

4. Robert Kelley, "Ideology and Political Culture from Jefferson to Nixon," *American Historical Review* 82, no. 3 (June 1977):531.

5. Walter Lippmann, *The Cold War: A Study in U.S. Foreign Policy* (New York: Harper & Brothers, 1947).

6. The polling data from the late spring of 1946 are in Lisle A. Rose, *After Yalta* (New York: Charles Scribner's Sons, 1973), pp. 173–74n; subsequent data are from "The Quarter's Polls," *Public Opinion Quarterly* 11, nos. 1, 3 (Spring, Fall 1947):139, 489; 12, no. 4 (Winter 1948–49):766; 13, no. 4 (Winter 1949–50):728.

7. "The Quarter's Polls," *Public Opinion Quarterly* 13, no. 1 (Spring 1949):164.

8. George H. Hall, "The Sinister Alliance between McCarthy and Taft," *St. Louis Post-Dispatch*, 18 February 1951.

CHAPTER 1
Liberals

1. Robert Wallace, "Baby Shaw," *Life*, 2 January 1950, pp. 4–5, 8.

2. Robert E. Sherwood, *Roosevelt and Hopkins: An Intimate History* (New York: Harper & Brothers, 1948), pp. 20–21.

3. Allan Nevins, "The Audacious Americans," *Life*, 2 January 1950, p. 85 (Nevins's italics).

4. John Kenneth Galbraith, *American Capitalism: The Concept of Countervailing Power* (Boston: Houghton Mifflin, 1956), pp. 1–2.

5. Nevins, "Audacious Americans," p. 85; see also "America Takes Stock at Mid-Century," *Washington Post*, 4 January 1950.

6. "The State of the Union," *New Republic*, 16 January 1950, 7.

7. Athan G. Theoharis and John Stuart Cox, *The Boss: J. Edgar Hoover and the Great American Inquisition* (New York: Bantam ed., 1990), 304, 311n.

8. Bosley Crowther, "Best Films of 1949," *New York Times*, 25 December 1949; Theoharis and Cox, *The Boss*, pp. 238–39.

9. The best general account of the late forties is Joseph C. Goulden, *The Best Years, 1945–1950* (New York: Atheneum, 1976); see also Michael Barone, *Our Country: The Shaping of America from Roosevelt to Reagan* (New York: Free Press, 1990), pp. 197–203.

10. William Manchester, *The Glory and the Dream: A Narrative History of America*, 2 vols. (Boston: Little, Brown, 1973, 1974), 1:512.

11. Goulden, *The Best Years*, p. 430.

12. Editorial: "Death of Forrestal," *Washington Post*, 23 May 1949, in Papers of George M. Elsey, Box 91, Folder 1 (Papers of James Forrestal), Harry S. Truman Library, Independence, Mo. (hereafter cited as HSTL).

13. "Back to the Atom," *Economist*, 157 (1 October 1949):707; "The News of the Week in Review," *New York Times*, 25 December 1949; "The News of the Year in Review," ibid.; "*The Gallup Poll*: A Democratic Triumph by 2000," *Washington Post*, 1 January 1950.

14. U.S., Central Intelligence Agency, Document ORE 69-49: "Relative US Security Interest in the European-Mediterranean Area and the Far East," 12 September 1949, in Records of the Central Intelligence Agency, Estimates of the Office of Research Evaluation, 1946–1950, Record Group 263, National Archives, Washington, D.C.; idem, Document ORE 29-49: "Prospects for Soviet Control of a Communist China," 15 April 1949, republished in *CIA Cold War Records: The CIA under Harry Truman*, ed. Michael Warner (Washington, D.C.: CIA History Staff, 1994), p. 278.

15. "The News of the Week in Review," *New York Times*, 25 December 1949.

16. "Dollars Abroad in a Tourist Tide," *Newsweek*, 4 July 1949, 33.

17. Walter Isaacson and Evan Thomas, *The Wise Men: Six Friends and the World They Made* (London: Faber & Faber, 1986), pp. 513–18.

18. U.S., Central Intelligence Agency, "Review of the World Situation," CIA 10-49, 19 October 1949, in Harry S. Truman Papers, President's Security File, Box 206, HSTL.

CHAPTER 2
The Red Menace

1. Arthur Krock, "Kremlin Casts Shadow on Most U.S. Affairs," *New York Times*, 25 December 1949; Editorial: "Uneasy Peace," *Washington Post*, 1 January 1950.

2. Henry Steele Commager, "Five Great Problems of the New Half-Century," *New York Times Magazine*, 1 January 1950, p. 3.

3. Woodford McClellan, "Molotov Remembers," *Cold War International History Project Bulletin,* 1 (Spring 1992), p. 17 (hereafter cited as *CWIHPB*)

4. Milovan Djilas, *Conversations with Stalin,* trans. Michael B. Petrovich (New York: Harcourt, Brace & World, 1962), 106, 114–15; Michael Dobbs, "How Soviets Stole U.S. Atom Secrets," *Washington Post,* 4 October 1992. Stalin's comments to Molotov are quoted in Sergei N. Goncharov, John W. Lewis, and Xue Litai, *Uncertain Partners: Stalin, Mao, and the Korean War* (Stanford, Calif.: Stanford University Press, 1993), pp. 55–56, and also in McClellan, "Molotov Remembers," p. 19.

5. "Molotov Remembers," p. 19; see also pp. 18–20.

6. Ibid. On Soviet thermonuclear research, see David Holloway, "Sources for Stalin and the Bomb," *CWIHPB,* 4 (Fall 1994), p. 3.

7. Robert S. Lynd and Helen Merrell Lynd, *Middletown in Transition: A Study in Cultural Conflicts* (New York: Harcourt, Brace & World, 1937), pp. 431, 433.

8. "Congress and Un-American Activities," *Congressional Digest* 18, no. 11 (November 1939):260; *National Republic,* May 1935, back page advertisement.

9. Raymond G. Carroll, "Aliens in Subversive Activities," *Saturday Evening Post,* 22 February 1936, pp. 10–11, 84–90.

10. Eugene Lyons, *The Red Decade: The Stalinist Penetration of America* (Indianapolis: Bobbs-Merrill, 1941), p. 17.

11. Information on the Dies Committee can be found in Frank J. Donner, *The Un-Americans* (New York: Ballantine Books, 1961); D. A. Saunders, "The Dies Committee: First Phase," *Public Opinion Quarterly* 3, no. 2 (April 1939):223–38; "Congress and Un-American Activities," pp. 259–61. An excellent short summary is in William E. Leuchtenberg, *Franklin D. Roosevelt and the New Deal, 1932–1940* (New York: Harper & Row, 1963), pp. 280–81.

12. Alan Barth, *The Loyalty of Free Men* (New York: Pocket Books, 1951), p. 54n.

13. Martin Dies, *The Trojan Horse in America* (1940), quoted in Barth, *The Loyalty of Free Men,* pp. 55–56.

14. "Congress and Un-American Activities," p. 260.

15. John Huston, *An Open Book* (New York: Knopf, 1980), p. 129.

16. Barth, *The Loyalty of Free Men,* p. 103; Leuchtenberg, *Franklin D. Roosevelt and the New Deal,* 301. The Smith Act is quoted in David M. Oshinsky, *A Conspiracy So Immense: The World of Joe McCarthy* (New York: Free Press, 1983), p. 93.

17. Lyons, *The Red Decade,* pp. 9–327 passim (the quotations are from pp. 15, 16).

18. John Roy Carlson [Arthur Derounian], *Under Cover: My Four Years in the Nazi Underworld of America—The Amazing Revelations of How Axis Agents and Our Enemies within Are Now Plotting To Destroy the United States* (New York: Dutton, 1943), p. 24.

19. "I am going back to the world I left behind four and a half years ago," Carlson concluded, "to renew friendships and live in the sunshine again—if the countless 'friends' I met in the Nazi underworld permit me to live" (p. 519). The theme of private citizens risking everything by going underground to expose subversion would resurface a decade later at the height of the McCarthy hysteria in such accounts as Herbert Arthur Philbrick's *I Led 3 Lives: Citizen, "Communist," Counterspy* (New York: McGraw-Hill, 1952) and the popular radio serial "I Was a Communist for the F.B.I."

20. Carlson, *Under Cover*, dust jacket.

21. Lyons, *The Red Decade*, p. 401; Carlson, *Under Cover*, p. 9.

22. David McCullough, *Truman* (New York: Simon & Schuster, 1992), p. 332.

23. Speaking to the annual convention of the American Veterans of Foreign Wars (AMVETS) in April 1949, McGrath warned that communists infiltrated America in huge numbers. "They are everywhere—in factories, offices, butcher stores, on street corners, in private businesses. And each carries in himself the germ of death for society." Athan G. Theoharis and John Stuart Cox, *The Boss: J. Edgar Hoover and the Great American Inquisition* (New York: Bantam Books, 1990), p. 257.

24. David Caute, *The Great Fear: The Anti-Communist Purge under Truman and Eisenhower* (New York: Simon & Schuster, 1979), p. 54.

25. The following review of anticommunist propaganda, literature, films, advertisements, and programs is from Albert Kahn, *High Treason: The Plot against the People* (Croton-on-the-Hudson, N.Y.: Hour Publishers, 1950), pp. 330–32n; Robert Griffith, "American Politics and the Origins of McCarthyism," in *The Spectre: Original Essays on the Cold War and the Origins of McCarthyism*, ed. Robert Griffith and Athan Theoharis (New York: Franklin Watts, 1974), pp. 2–17; and Michael Barson, *"Better Dead Than Red": A Nostalgic Look at the Golden Years of Russiaphobia, Red-Baiting, and Other Commie Madness* (New York: Hyperion, 1992), passim.

26. Garry Wills, introduction to Lillian Hellman, *Scoundrel Time* (New York: Bantam books, 1976), p. 7.

27. Athan G. Theoharis and John Stuart Cox, *The Boss: J. Edgar Hoover and the Great American Inquisition* (New York: Bantam Books, 1990), p. 278; Christopher Andersen, "Nixon Derails Hoover's Plans," *The Seattle Times*, July 13, 1997.

28. James Bryant Conant, "Freedom and the University," *NEA Journal* 39, no. 8 (November 1950):581.

29. Editorial: "Strengthening American Democracy," *Educational Research Bulletin* 27, no. 5 (12 May 1948):136–37.

30. Thomas Woody, "Why Raise an Oath-Umbrella?" *School and Society* 74 (21 July 1951):37.

31. The NEA-AASA booklet is quoted in "American Education and International Tensions," *NEA Journal* 38, no. 6 (September 1949):457; see also Raleigh W. Holmstedt, "Problems in School Administration," *Bulletin of the School of Education Indiana University* 26, no. 1 (January 1950):34.

32. Woody, "Why Raise an Oath-Umbrella?" p. 37.

CHAPTER 3
Conservatives

1. Robert S. Lynd and Helen Merrell Lynd, *Middletown in Transition: A Study in Cultural Conflicts* (New York: Harcourt, Brace & World, 1937); James West, *Plainville, U.S.A.* (New York: Columbia University Press, 1945).

2. Vance Packard, *The Status Seekers: An Exploration of Class Behavior in America and the Hidden Barriers That Affect You, Your Community, Your Future* (New York: David McKay, 1959); Paul S. Lazarsfeld, Bernard Berelson, and Hazel Gaudet, *The People's Choice*, excerpt reprinted in *American Social Patterns: Studies of Race Relations, Popular Heroes, Voting, Union Democracy, and Government Bureaucracy*, ed. William Petersen (Garden City, N.Y.: Doubleday Anchor Books, 1956), pp. 119–70.

3. Daniel Bell, *The End of Ideology: On the Exhaustion of Political Ideas in the Fifties*, rev. ed. (New York: Collier Books, 1962), pp. 112–14; West, *Plainville, U.S.A.*, pp. 55–56.

4. William S. White, "Portrait of a Fundamentalist," *New York Times Magazine*, 15 January 1950, p. 22; Billy James Hargis, *Why I Fight for a Christian America* (Nashville, Tenn.: Thomas Nelson, 1974), p. 29.

5. R. H. Tawney, *Religion and the Rise of Capitalism* (New York: Mentor Books, 1948), p. 210; Max Weber, *The Protestant Ethic and the Spirit of Capitalism* (New York: Scribner's, 1958), pp. 176–77.

6. Michael Paul Rogin, *The Intellectuals and McCarthy: The Radical Specter* (Cambridge, Mass.: M.I.T. Press, 1967), pp. 52, 58.

7. Carnegie's most representative writings have been collected in E. C. Kirkland, ed., *Andrew Carnegie: The Gospel of Wealth and Other Timely Essays* (Cambridge, Mass.: Harvard University Press, 1962).

8. Lynd and Lynd, *Middletown in Transition*, pp. 403–21; West, *Plainville, U.S.A.*, 106–28; Sanford M. Jacoby, "Employees and the Welfare State: The Role of Marion B. Folsom," *Journal of American History* 80, no. 2 (September 1993):525–56.

9. Henry R. Seager and Charles A. Gulick, Jr., *Trust and Corporation Problems* (New York: Harper & Brothers, 1929), p. 665; see also Gabriel Kolko, *The Triumph of Conservatism: A Reinterpretation of American History, 1900–1916* (Chicago: Quadrangle Books, 1967; first published 1963).

10. *National Republic*, May 1934, inner cover.

11. Ibid.

12. William E. Leuchtenburg, *The Perils of Prosperity, 1914–32* (Chicago: University of Chicago Press, 1958), p. 208; see also p. 207.

13. Richard Hofstadter, *The Age of Reform: From Bryan to F.D.R.* (New York: Vintage Books, 1960), pp. 302–28, esp. pp. 323–24 n.7; Geoffrey Douglas, *Class: The Wreckage of an American Family* (New York: Warner Books, 1994), pp. 95–96. An excellent account of the shifting political values in early twentieth-century American life is in Otis L. Graham, Jr., *An Encore for Reform: The Old Progressives and the New Deal* (New York: Oxford University Press, 1967), esp. pp. 69–73.

14. David Brinkley, *Washington Goes to War* (New York: Ballantine Books, 1988), p. 125.

15. Ibid., pp. 125, 126.

16. President Franklin D. Roosevelt's Annual Message to Congress, 11 January 1944, reprinted in *The Roosevelt Reader: Selected Speeches, Messages, Press Conferences, and Letters of Franklin D. Roosevelt*, ed. Basil Rauch (New York: Holt, Rinehart & Winston, 1957), p. 348.

17. David M. Oshinsky, *A Conspiracy So Immense: The World of Joe McCarthy* (New York: Free Press, 1983), pp. 49–51.

18. William Manchester, *The Glory and the Dream: A Narrative History of America, 1932–1972*, 2 vols. (Boston, Little, Brown, 1974), 1:576.

19. Clinton L. Rossiter, "Wanted: An American Conservatism," *Fortune*, March 1950, pp. 95–112 (the quotation is on p. 95).

20. Walter Isaacson and Evan Thomas, *The Wise Men: Six Friends and the World They Made* (London: Faber & Faber, 1986), p. 510.

21. David McCullough, *Truman* (New York: Simon & Schuster, 1992), pp. 760–61.

22. Herbert Agar, *The Price of Power: America since 1945* (Chicago: University of Chicago Press, 1957), p. 49.

23. Quoted in Arthur H. Vandenberg, Jr., and Joe Alex Morris, eds., *Private Papers of Senator Vandenberg* (Boston: Houghton Mifflin, 1952), p. 166 (Vandenberg's italics).

24. Ibid., pp. 472–73.

25. Ibid., pp. xiii–xiv.

26. Mildred Strunk, "The Quarter's Polls," *Public Opinion Quarterly* 14, no. 3 (Fall 1950):598.

27. Stephen Ambrose, *Nixon: The Education of a Politician, 1913–1962* (New York: Simon & Schuster, 1987), p. 26.

28. Ibid., photos 3, 4, and 5 following p. 224.

29. "Dean Joins 'Watergate' To Combat 'Revisionists,'" *Seattle Times*, 7 August 1994.

30. Ambrose, *Nixon*, photo no. 7 following p. 224.

31. Ibid., p. 121.

32. Ibid., p. 143.

33. *The Journals of David E. Lilienthal*, 7 vols. (New York: Harper & Row, 1964–83), Vol. 2, *The Atomic Energy Years, 1945–1950*, p. 545.

34. Ibid., pp. 531, 538.

35. "Atomic Energy Commission Congress and the Scientists," *Bulletin of the Atomic Scientists* 5, no. 12 (December 1949):325, 326.

36. H. G. Nicholas, "Fear and the American Constitution," *Fortnightly*, n.s., no. 997 (January 1950), p. 37.

37. S. K. Ratcliffe, "The Tragedy of Alger Hiss," *Fortnightly*, n.s., no. 999 (March 1950), p. 170.

38. "Hiss Was Lying," *Newsweek*, 30 January 1950, p. 19.

39. Ibid.

40. "Is America Safe for Spies?" *Newsweek*, 20 December 1948, p. 17.

41. "News of the Week in Review," *New York Times*, 25 December 1949.

CHAPTER 4
The Bomb

1. "American Survey—Atomic Handicap Race," *Economist* 157 (8 October 1949):780. Accounts of the president's announcement are in Eric F. Goldman, *The Crucial Decade—and After: America, 1945–1960* (New York: Vintage Books, 1961), p. 99; and in "The Bomb: The Story Explodes around the World," *Newsweek*, 3 October 1949, p. 18.

2. "Truman Reveals Red A-Blast," *Washington Post*, 24 September 1949.

3. "Russ Got the Bomb?" *Seattle Times*, 24 September 1949; Editorial: "Hiroshima's Warning," ibid., 26 September 1949.

4. Walter Trohan, "Truman Tells Cabinet of Recent Explosion," *Chicago Tribune*, 24 September 1949; Editorial: "The Bomb," ibid.

5. "American Survey—Atomic Handicap Race," 780.

6. Bernard Brodie, "What Is the Outlook Now?" *Bulletin of the Atomic Scientists* 5, no. 10 (October 1949):268.

7. Raymond Aaron, "The Atomic Bomb and Europe," *Bulletin of the Atomic Scientists* 6, no. 4 (April 1950):111.

8. "Reds Say They Have A-Weapon," *Washington Post*, 25 September 1949.

9. "Scientists Give New Warning," *Bulletin of the Atomic Scientists* 5, no. 10 (October 1949):264.

10. Frederick Seitz, "The Danger Ahead," *Bulletin of the Atomic Scientists* 5, no. 10 (October 1949):266.

11. Eugene Rabinowitch, "Forewarned—But Not Forearmed," *Bulletin of the Atomic Scientists* 5, no. 10 (October 1949):273–75 (Rabinowitch's italics).

12. Leo Szilard, "Shall We Face the Facts?" *Bulletin of the Atomic Scientists* 5, no. 10 (October 1949):269–73.

13. Harold Urey, "Needed: Less Witch Hunting and More Work," *Bulletin of the Atomic Scientists* 5, no. 10 (October 1949):265.

14. "U.S. Held Unable To Protect Europe," *Washington Post*, 25 September 1949; "Red Rocket Bases Ring Western Europe," ibid., 26 September 1949; "U.S. 'Laxity' Aided by Reds, Velde Alleges," ibid. See also "Russ Dot East Europe with Bases for Rockets," *Seattle Times*, 26 September 1949.

15. Vyshinsky's proposal at the United Nations is quoted in "Back to the Atom," *Economist* 157 (1 October 1949):707.

16. Notes on the Sixth Meeting of the Sponsoring Powers, Lake Success, New York, 8 September 1949, in U.S., Department of State, *Foreign Relations of the United States, 1949*, 9 vols. (Washington, D.C.: U.S. Government Printing Office, 1974–76), 1:154–55 (hereafter cited as *FRUS, 1949*).

17. "Back to the Atom," p. 707.

18. "American Survey—Atomic Handicap Race," p. 780.

19. "U.S. 'Laxity' Aided Reds, Velde Alleges."

20. Ibid.

21. The following discussion of Soviet wartime espionage and its exploitation by the Russian scientific community is based on Canada, Royal Commission, *The Report of the Royal Commission Appointed Under Order in Council P.C. 411 of February 5, 1946, to Investigate the Facts Relating to and the Circumstances Surrounding the Communication, by Public Officials and Other Persons in Positions of Trust of Secret and Confidential Information to Agents of a Foreign Power, June 27, 1946* (Ottawa: Controller of Stationery, 1946) and on David Holloway, *Stalin and the Bomb: The Soviet Union and Atomic Energy, 1939–1956* (New Haven, CT: Yale University Press, 1994), pp. 60–61, 82–83, 173.

22. Holloway, *Stalin and the Bomb*, pp. 96–108.

23. Vladislav Zubok, "Atomic Espionage and Its Soviet 'Witnesses,'" *Cold War International History Project Bulletin*, Issue 4 (Fall 1994), p. 52.

24. "The Bomb: The Story Explodes around the World," *Newsweek*, 3 October 1949, pp. 17, 21.

25. Anne Wilson Marks, "Washington Notes," *Bulletin of the Atomic Scientists* 5, no. 12 (December 1949):327.

26. Hans J. Morgenthau, "The Conquest of the United States by Germany," *Bulletin of the Atomic Scientists* 6, no. 1 (January 1950):24.

27. Richard G. Hewlett and Francis Duncan, *Atomic Shield, 1947–1952* (Washington, D.C.: U.S. Atomic Energy Commission, 1972), pp. 383–84; Richard G. Hewlett and Oscar E. Anderson, Jr., *The New World, 1939/1946* (University Park, Pa.: The Pennsylvania State University Press, 1962), p. 104.

28. Memorandum for the President by the U.S. Atomic Energy Commission, 9 November 1949, in *FRUS, 1949*, 1:578.

29. Hans Thirring, "The Super Bomb," *Bulletin of the Atomic Scientists* 6, no. 3 (March 1950):69–70.

30. Norman Moss, *Men Who Play God: The Story of the H-Bomb and How the World Came to Live with It* (New York: Harper & Row, 1968), p. 71.

31. Lewis Strauss, *Men and Decisions* (Garden City, N.Y.: Doubleday, 1962), p. 217; his comment to his secretary is in Richard Pfau, *No Sacrifice Too Great: The Life of Lewis L. Strauss* (Charlottesville: University Press of Virginia, 1984), p. 112. Pfau (p. 113) states that Latimer, Lawrence, and Alvarez met on October 6.

32. Moss, *Men Who Play God*, pp. 26–27; Pfau, *No Sacrifice Too Great*, p. 114.

33. David Alan Rosenberg, "American Atomic Strategy and the Hydrogen Bomb Decision," *Journal of American History* 66, no. 1 (June 1979):64.

34. George W. Baer, *One Hundred Years of Sea Power: The U.S. Navy, 1890–1990* (Stanford, Calif.: Stanford University Press, 1994), pp. 279, 284–92.

35. Rosenberg, "American Atomic Strategy and the Hydrogen Bomb Decision," p. 68.

36. Ibid, p. 72.

37. Ibid., p. 69.

38. Ibid., p. 77.

39. Ibid., p. 75; Memorandum to Secretary Johnson from Symington, 8 November 1949, in Student Research File (Development of Atomic Weapons

Program), Box 2, Folder 16, Harry S. Truman Library, Independence, Mo. (hereafter cited as HSTL).

40. *The Journals of David E. Lilienthal*, 7 vols. (New York: Harper & Row, 1964–83), vol. 2, *The Atomic Energy Years, 1945–1950*, p. 549 (hereafter cited as *Lilienthal Journals*, 2).

41. Ibid., p. 577; Annex to Memorandum by the Executive Secretary of the NSC, 10 October 1949, in *FRUS, 1949*, 1:564.

42. Pfau, *No Sacrifice Too Great*, pp. 114–15.

43. John Newhouse, *War and Peace in the Nuclear Age* (New York: Knopf, 1989), p. 75.

44. Accounts of the 29–30 October meetings are in *Lilienthal Journals*, 2:580–81; Hewlett and Duncan, *Atomic Shield*, pp. 381–85; and Newhouse, *War and Peace in the Nuclear Age*, pp. 75–76.

45. Enclosure 1: Statement Appended to the Report of the GAC, 30 October 1949, in *FRUS, 1949*, 1:570–71.

46. Enclosure 2: Statement Appended to the Report of the GAC, 30 October 1949, ibid., pp. 572–73.

47. *Lilienthal Journals*, 2:582.

48. Richard Rhodes, *Dark Sun: The Making of the Hydrogen Bomb* (New York: Simon & Schuster, 1995), p. 404.

49. Pfau, *No Sacrifice Too Great*, p. 117.

50. Strauss's letter and accompanying memo to Truman are reprinted in *FRUS, 1949*, 1:596–99; and in Strauss, *Men and Decisions*, p. 219; see also ibid., p. 218.

51. Memorandum for the President by the U.S. Atomic Energy Commission, 9 November 1949, in *FRUS, 1949*, 1:582–84.

52. Ibid., pp. 578–79.

53. Moss, *Men Who Play God*, p. 31.

54. McMahon's November 21 letter, reprinted in *FRUS, 1949*, 1:588–595.

55. "The President Orders Exploration of the Super Bomb," *Bulletin of the Atomic Scientists* 6, no. 3 (March 1950):66.

56. Draft Memorandum from the Director of the Policy Planning Staff to the Secretary of State, 18 November 1949, in *FRUS, 1949*, 1:586.

57. R. Gordon Arneson, "The H-Bomb Decision," *Foreign Service Journal*, June 1969, p. 24. See also Robert Dennison, "Memorandum For the President," 18 November 1949, in Student Research File (Development of an Atomic Weapons Program), Box 1, Folder 5, HSTL.

58. Memorandum by the Joint Chiefs of Staff to the Secretary of Defense, 23 November 1949, in *FRUS, 1949*, 1:595.

59. Strauss's letter and memo to Truman are cited in note 46.

60. R. Gordon Arneson, Oral History Interview, pp. 62–63, HSTL.

61. Memorandum Circulated by the Defense Members of the Working Group of the Special Committee of the NSC, n.d., in *FRUS, 1949*, 2:604–10. (the quotations that follow are on pp. 606, 608, 608 n. 2).

62. Memorandum by the Deputy Director of the Policy Planning Staff, 19 December 1949, ibid., pp. 610–11.

63. "The President Orders Exploration of the Super Bomb," p. 66.

64. Acheson's memorandum, dated 20 December 1949, is in *FRUS, 1949,* 1:612–17 (the quotations that follow are on pp. 613, 615).

65. Marks, "Washington Notes," 327; see also p. 328.

66. Dean Acheson, *Present at the Creation: My Years in the State Department* (New York: Signet Books, 1970), p. 455; *Lilienthal Journals,* 2:613–14.

67. Arneson, "The H-Bomb Decision," p. 24; Memorandum by R. Gordon Arneson, Special Assistant to the Undersecretary of State, 29 December 1949, in U.S., Department of State, *Foreign Relations of the United States, 1950,* 7 vols. (Washington, D.C.: U.S. Government Printing Office, 1976–80), 1:2 (hereafter cited as *FRUS, 1950*).

68. See Editorial Note, n.d., in *FRUS, 1950,* 1:512; George F. Kennan, *Memoirs (1925–1950)* (New York: Bantam Books, 1969; first published 1967), pp. 495–500.

69. *Lilienthal Journals,* 2:615.

70. Ibid., p. 616.

71. Ibid., p. 617.

72. "The President Orders Exploration of the Super Bomb," p. 66.

73. Memorandum of Telephone Conversation, by the Secretary of State, 19 January 1950, in *FRUS, 1950,* 1:511.

74. Memorandum by the Joint Chiefs of Staff to the Secretary of Defense, 13 January 1950, ibid., pp. 503–11 (the quotations that follow are from pp. 504, 506–508).

75. "President to Say If U.S. Gets Weapon: Urey, Baruch and Others Urge Going Ahead on Fearful Hydrogen Explosive," *Washington Post,* 28 January 1950.

76. Connally and Byrd are quoted in "Manufacture of H-Bomb Is Advocated by Connally," *Washington Post,* 29 January 1950.

77. "H-Bomb Seen Meeting Topic," *Washington Post,* 27 January 1950; "Truman Alone to Decide on Super-Bomb," ibid., 28 January 1950.

78. Editorial: "The Ultimate Bomb," *Life,* 30 January 1950, p. 20.

79. "Men as Devil-Gods," *Christian Century,* 8 February 1950, pp. 167–69 (the quotation is on p. 169).

80. The most detailed accounts of the Special Committee meeting are in *Lilienthal Journals,* 2:623–32 (the quotation about Bradley is on p. 628); and Arneson, "The H-bomb Decision," pp. 26–27.

81. Arneson, "The H-bomb Decision," p. 27.

82. The report by the Special Committee of the NSC to the President, 31 January 1950, is printed in *FRUS, 1950,* 1:513–17 (the following quotations are on pp. 514, 516).

83. *Lilienthal Journals,* 2:632.

84. Newhouse, *War and Peace in the Nuclear Age,* 78.

85. *Lilienthal Journals,* 2:632.

86. "A Week of Shock and Decision," *Life,* 13 February 1950, pp. 36–37.

87. "Hydrogen Bomb Secret Feared Given Russians," *Washington Post*, 4 February 1950.

88. Ibid.

89. "Hydrogen Bomb Data Given Russia by Fuchs, Gen. Groves Declares," *Washington Post*, 5 February 1950; "A Week of Shock and Decision," p. 37.

90. "A Week of Shock and Decision," pp. 36, 37.

91. The round table discussion was reprinted in "Facts about the Hydrogen Bomb," *Bulletin of the Atomic Scientists* 6, no. 4 (April 1950):106–9.

92. See Hans A. Bethe, "The Hydrogen Bomb," *Bulletin of the Atomic Scientists* 6, no. 4 (April 1950):101; "The Hydrogen Bomb," *Life*, 30 January 1950, p. 23.

93. "Facts about the Hydrogen Bomb," p. 107.

94. Memorandum for the Preident by Sidney W. Souers, Executive Secretary, National Security Council, enclosing letter of Sumner T. Pike, December 7, 1949, in Student Research Files (Development of an Atomic Weapons Program), Box 1, Folder 5, HSTL.

95. "Facts about the Hydrogen Bomb," p. 107.

96. William L. Laurence, *The Hell Bomb* (New York: Knopf, 1951), pp. 54–55.

97. Quoted in "Mr. Lilienthal's Criticism," *Bulletin of the Atomic Scientists* 6, no. 4 (April 1950):109.

98. "Dr. Szilard's Reply," *Bulletin of the Atomic Scientists* 6, no. 4 (April 1950):109, 126.

99. "The Soul-Searchers Find No Answer," *Life*, 20 March 1950, p. 37.

100. Fred Seitz, "Impossibility of Compromise between the Two Ideals," *Bulletin of the Atomic Scientists* 6, no. 3 (March 1950):83–89 (the quotations are on p. 84).

101. *Men and Decisions*, pp. 225–26.

102. Mildred Strunk, ed., "The Quarter's Polls," *Public Opinion Quarterly* 14, no. 2 (Summer 1950):372.

103. "A Week of Shock and Decision," 36; quotation from the Denver man, ibid.

104. "Worry in Washington," *Newsweek*, 20 February 1950, p. 18.

105. Memorandum for the Secretary of State from the Executive Secretary of the National Security Council, 1 March 1950, enclosing Memorandum for the President from the Secretary of Defense, 27 February 1950, in Student Research File (Development of an Atomic Weapons Program) Box 2, Folder 11, HSTL.

106. "Watching and Waiting for Peace," *Newsweek*, 6 March 1950, p. 17.

107. Editorial: "The Elemental Fact of 1950," *Life*, 27 February 1950, p. 30.

108. "War Can Come: Will We Be Ready?" *Life*, 27 February 1950, p. 19.

109. "The Elemental Fact of 1950," 30.

110. "How Could Soviet Attack Come?" *Life*, 27 February 1950, p. 21.

111. Strunk, "The Quarter's Polls," pp. 372–73, 381.

112. "Hydrogen Age . . . Whither America?" *Newsweek*, 13 February 1950, p. 17.

113. Memorandum by the Executive Secretary of the NSC, with Annex, 1 March 1950, in *FRUS, 1950*, 1:538–39; Report by the Special Committee of the

NSC to the President, 9 March 1950, in ibid., pp. 541–42. Copies of these documents are also in Student Research File (Development of an Atomic Weapons Program), Box 2, Folder 11, HSTL.

114. Memorandum for the President from the Executive Secretary of the National Security Council, 2 October 1950, in Student Research File (Development of an Atomic Weapons Program), Box 1, Folder 2, HSTL.

115. "How Does One Feel?" *Grandview* (Washington) *Herald,* 2 March 1950.

116. "The Hydrogen Bomb," *New Republic,* 13 February 1950, pp. 5–6.

117. William S. White, "McMahon, Senator and Atomic Specialist," *New York Times Magazine,* 12 February 1950, p. 19.

118. Robert Chadwell Williams, *Klaus Fuchs, Atom Spy* (Cambridge, Mass.: Harvard University Press, 1987), pp. 166–67 (the headline is quoted on p. 167).

119. "Red Shadows on a Worried World," *Newsweek,* 20 February 1950, p. 17; "Watching and Waiting for Peace," p. 17.

CHAPTER 5
McCarthyism

1. "Acheson on the Spot," *Newsweek,* 6 February 1950, p. 17; see also Dean Acheson, *Present at the Creation: My Years in the State Department* (New York: Signet Books, 1970), pp. 469–70.

2. "Hiss Story Kept from Public by Administration, Nixon Says," *Washington Post,* 22 January 1950.

3. For reactions to Acheson's defense of Hiss, see "Acheson on the Spot," pp. 17–18; and David M. Oshinsky, *A Conspiracy So Immense: The World of Joe McCarthy* (New York: Free Press, 1983), pp. 104–5. J. Edgar Hoover's role in aiding Nixon's exposure of Hiss is in Theoharis and Cox, *The Boss,* pp. 275–76.

4. S. K. Ratcliffe, "The Tragedy of Alger Hiss," *Fortnightly,* n.s., no. 999 (March 1950):173.

5. Richard M. Nixon, *Six Crises* (Garden City, N.Y.: Doubleday, 1962), pp. 1–71; idem, *In the Arena: A Memoir of Victory, Defeat, and Renewal* (New York: Simon & Schuster, 1990), pp. 28–277 passim.

6. Athan Theoharis and John Stuart Cox uncovered the identity of McCarthy's ghost writers years later (*The Boss,* p. 310). Ernest K. Lindley, "McCarthy and Acheson," *Newsweek,* 27 March 1950, p. 24.

7. "McCarthy Bombshell," *Newsweek,* 6 March 1950, p. 19; and in Seymour Martin Lipset, "The Sources of the 'Radical Right,'" in *The Radical Right,* ed. Daniel Bell (Garden City, N.Y.: Doubleday Anchor Books, 1964), p. 361 (Lipset's italics).

8. "McCarthy Bombshell," p. 19.

9. McCarthy cable to Truman, 11 February 1950, in Student Research File (McCarthyism), Box 1, Folder 2, Harry S. Truman Library, Independence, Mo. (hereafter cited as HSTL).

10. Truman's unsent reply to McCarthy's cable is reprinted in Robert H. Fer-

rell, ed., *Off the Record: The Private Papers of Harry S. Truman* (New York: Harper & Row, 1980), p. 172.

11. "McCarthy's Great Red Scare," *New Republic,* 20 March 1950, p. 5.

12. "McCarthy Bombshell," p. 19.

13. Richard H. Rovere, *Senator Joe McCarthy* (Cleveland: Meridian Books, 1960), p. 7.

14. The earliest systematic efforts to understand McCarthyism can be found in a series of essays by such renowned historians and social scientists of the fifties and early sixties as Daniel Bell, Peter Viereck, Seymour Martin Lipset, Richard Hofstadter, and others. They emphasized the pluralistic structure of American society, which from the beginning had inevitably generated deep social and economic frustrations over status, expressed in a series of reactionary "reform movements." See Bell, *The Radical Right.* For opposing arguments, see Michael Paul Rogin, *The Intellectuals and McCarthy: The Radical Specter* (Cambridge, Mass.: M.I.T. Press, 1967). Rogin has argued that McCarthy emerged from and appealed to a group of profoundly frustrated postwar conservative Republicans. McCarthy's most sophisticated biographer, David Oshinsky, has emphasized McCarthy's own coarse and dynamic personality, which both attracted and repelled small-town Main Street America, to whom he deliberately appealed. See Oshinsky, *A Conspiracy So Immense,* p. 14. Richard Rovere, in his pioneering 1959 study *Senator Joe McCarthy,* argued that the media and a submissive Congress together helped promote McCarthy's myth of a communist conspiracy (see pp. 162–70).

15. Willmoore Kendall, "McCarthyism: The *Pons Asinorum* of American Conservatism," reprinted in *The Meaning of McCarthyism,* ed. Earl Latham (Boston: D. C. Heath, 1965), p. 41; David H. Bennett, *The Party of Fear: The American Far Right from Nativism to the Militia Movement,* rev. ed. (New York: Random House, 1995), pp. 314–15.

16. The following information on McCarthy's earliest supporters is from Alfred Friendly, "The Noble Crusade of Senator McCarthy," *Harper's Magazine,* August 1950, p. 42, and Theoharis and Cox, *The Boss,* p. 311.

17. Earl Latham, *The Communist Controversy in Washington: From the New Deal to McCarthy,* excerpt reprinted in *McCarthyism,* ed. Thomas C. Reeves (Huntington, N.Y.: Robert E. Kreiger, 1978), p. 91; William S. White, "Portrait of a Fundamentalist," *New York Times Magazine,* 15 January 1950, p. 14.

18. Graham Hutton, *Midwest at Noon* (Chicago: University of Chicago Press, 1946), p. 295.

19. John Gunther, *Inside U.S.A.* (New York: Harper & Brothers, 1947), pp. 359–69.

20. Ibid., pp. 359, 361–62.

21. Ibid., p. 362; Hutton, *Midwest at Noon,* pp. 308–15.

22. White, "Portrait of a Fundamentalist," pp. 14, 22, 24.

23. Paul F. Healy, "Big Noise from Nebraska," *Saturday Evening Post,* 5 August 1950, p. 23.

24. Ibid.

25. White, "Portrait of a Fundamentalist," p. 27 (italics in original); see also ibid., p. 22.

26. Ibid., p. 24.

27. Ibid., p. 14.

28. Billy James Hargis, *Why I Fight for a Christian America* (Nashville: Thomas Nelson, 1974), p. 25.

29. Ibid., p. 30.

30. Ibid., pp. 30, 31, 38.

31. Ibid., p. 34.

32. Ibid., p. 38.

33. Ibid., pp. 139, 151–52.

34. Ibid., p. 140.

35. Ibid., p. 41.

36. Arnold Forster and Benjamin R. Epstein, *Danger on the Right* (New York: Random House, 1964), pp. 50–51, 100.

37. Maureen Orth, "Arianna's Virtual Candidate," *Vanity Fair*, November 1994, p. 162.

38. Louis F. Budenz, *The Techniques of Communism* (Chicago: Henry Regnery, 1954), p. 309.

39. Eric F. Goldman, *The Crucial Decade—and After: America, 1945–1960* (New York: Vintage Books, 1961), p. 116.

40. The standard biography of Luce is W. A. Swanberg's *Luce and his Empire* (New York: Scribner's, 1972), which is hostile to its subject. Swanberg considered Luce an "ideologist-missionary-propagandist" (p. 193) who gloried in cozying up to power and to those who possessed it but was not above twisting the truth to serve his interests. The *Time, Life,* and *Fortune* circulation figures and the popularity of the *March of Time* are from Patricia Neali, *China Images in the Life and Times of Henry Luce* (Savage, Md.: Rowman & Littlefield, 1990), p. 7. A rich sample of Luce's writings may be found in John K. Jessup, ed., *The Ideas of Henry Luce* (New York: Atheneum, 1969). An excellent example of the excitable, anecdotal appeals of the old China hands to "save" that country is Daniel A. Poling, "Communism, the Superfoe," *Vital Speeches of the Day* 7, no. 8 (1 February 1951): 231–36.

41. Henry R. Luce, "China: To the Mountains," *Life*, 30 June 1941, p. 88.

42. "Petition in Bankruptcy," *Time*, 15 August 1949, pp. 11–13.

43. Eugene Lyons, *Assignment in Utopia* (New York: Harcourt, Brace, 1937), pp. 3–4.

44. Ibid., p. 591.

45. Budenz, *The Techniques of Communism*, p. v.

46. Jacob Spolansky, *The Communist Trail in America* (New York: Macmillan, 1951), p. 9.

47. Ibid., p. 14 (Spolansky's italics).

48. Spolansky, *The Communist Trail*, p. 14.

49. David Caute, *The Great Fear: The Anti-Communist Purge under Truman and Eisenhower* (New York: Simon & Schuster, 1978), pp. 505, 522–23.

50. Robert A. Taft, "How Much Government Can Free Enterprise Stand?" *Colliers*, 22 October 1949, pp. 16–17, 74, 76.

51. Robert A. Taft, "'Hang On' to Formosa: Hold until a Peace Treaty with Japan Is Signed," *Vital Speeches of the Day* 16, no. 8 (1 February 1950): 237.

52. Special Gang Dinner, 15 March 1950, Honoured Guest: Dean Acheson, in Papers of Dean Acheson, General Correspondence—Subject File (I-S), Box 58, Folder: "Scrapbook—Items Concerning Acheson Record as Secretary of State," HSTL.

53. The White House and Senator Tydings agonized over the issue for several days. Tydings asked Truman for terms and conditions under which State Department papers might be turned over to his Senate subcommittee. Attorney General J. Howard McGrath argued that the administration should withhold all documentation until McCarthy "has actually supplied all the information which he has to back up his charges." McGrath told the president that "as you know, there is no question as to your authority to withhold these files from the [Tydings] subcommittee." State, however, believed that delay was not enough. The president should issue a statement reaffirming and reexplaining existing loyalty and internal security procedures "as it will help Senator Tydings hold the line and prevent further public smear sessions." Others in the White House urged Truman to appoint a special assistant to manage the whole messy affair. See memorandum from Seth Dawson to Matt Connelly aboard U.S.S. *Williamsburg*, 16 March 1950, in Student Research File (McCarthyism), Box 1, Folder 4, HSTL; Memorandum for the President from the Attorney General, 17 March 1950, and Memorandum for Mr. Connelly from Robert Dennison, 17 March 1950, in Papers of Robert Dennison, Box 3, Folder: "White House Message Traffic 1950," HSTL.

54. "Critic: He May Score Yet with Wild Shots," *Newsweek*, 27 March 1950, p. 20; see also "Mr. Secretary and the Hot Seat," ibid., 20 March 1950, p. 22.

55. "Critic: He May Score Yet with Wild Shots," p. 20.

56. Ibid.

57. The following information is based on "Mr. Secretary and the Hot Seat," pp. 21–22; "Trap for McCarthy," *Newsweek*, 3 April 1950, pp. 19–21.

58. Irving Brant, "531 Secretaries of State," *New Republic*, 13 March 1950, p. 13.

59. "Mr. Secretary and the Hot Seat," p. 21.

60. Ibid., p. 20.

61. "Trap for McCarthy," p. 19.

62. Ibid., p. 20.

63. Ibid.

64. "McCarthy Still Pitching," *Newsweek*, 24 April 1950, p. 26.

65. Editorial: *Grandview* (Washington) *Herald*, 5 January 1950; "Is It a Trick?" ibid., 19 January 1950; Editorial: ibid., 23 February 1950; "We Know How They Feel," ibid., 16 March 1950.

66. "Spuds Are Spuds," *Grandview Herald,* 30 March 1950; "Turning against McCarthy," ibid., 6 April 1950.

67. "McCarthy and the Past," *Life,* 10 April 1950, p. 32 (italics in original); see also "The Boom Goes On," ibid., 24 April 1950, p. 38.

68. Oshinsky, *A Conspiracy So Immense,* p. 142.

69. Truman's letter to Mrs. Truman is reprinted in Robert H. Ferrell, ed., *Dear Bess: The Letters from Harry to Bess Truman, 1910–1959* (New York: Norton, 1983), p. 559. His note to his cousin Ralph is reprinted in Monte M. Poen, ed., *Letters Home by Harry Truman* (New York: Putnam's, 1984), p. 237.

70. The President's News Conference at Key West, 30 March 1950, is reprinted in *Public Papers of the Presidents of the United States: Harry S. Truman, January 1 to December 31, 1950* (Washington, D.C.: U.S. Government Printing Office, 1965), pp. 232–38.

71. "We Drift, We Dream, and We Brawl," *Newsweek,* 10 April 1950, p. 19 .

72. Ibid., p. 20.

73. On April 3, Truman, still in Key West, responded to a formal subpoena issued by Tydings, summoning Acheson, McGrath, and Civil Service Commission Chairman Harry B. Mitchell to appear before the Senate subcommittee. The president in effect sought to be more McCarthyist than McCarthy in pursuing an effective loyalty program. He reiterated a point made in an earlier letter to Tydings that disclosure of State Department files to any congressional committee or subcommittee "would seriously prejudice the future effectiveness and usefulness of the Federal Bureau of Investigation as an investigative agency; the embarrassment, and even danger, to those who have given confidential information cannot be over-emphasized." Letter from Charles S. Murphy, Special Counsel to the President to Harry B. Mitchell, 3 April 1950, with enclosure, in Student Research File (McCarthyism), Box 1, Folder 4, HSTL.

74. "We Drift, We Dream, and We Brawl," p. 20.

75. Ibid.

76. Memorandum for the President, 12 April 1950, in Student Research File (McCarthyism), Box 5, HSTL; italics in original.

77. "Lattimore's Inning," *Newsweek,* 17 April 1950, p. 29.

78. "Was Lattimore a Communist?" *Life,* 1 May 1950, p. 38.

79. Ibid.

80. The following quotations are from "The Conservative Revival," *Life,* 15 May 1950, p. 38 (italics in original).

81. Mildred Strunk, ed., "The Quarter's Polls," *Public Opinion Quarterly* 14, no. 3 (Fall 1950):596; "New Shocker," *Newsweek,* 29 May 1950, p. 18.

82. Rovere, *Senator Joe McCarthy,* p. 179.

83. Ken Hechler, *Working with Truman: A Personal Memoir of the White House Years* (New York: Putnam's, 1982), p. 142; Hechler oral history interview, pp. 144–45, HSTL.

84. "McCarthy's Needle," *Newsweek,* 5 June 1950, p. 19.

85. Oshinsky, *A Conspiracy So Immense,* pp. 182–84.

86. "Amerasia Odor," *Newsweek,* 12 June 1950, p. 21.

87. "New Shocker," p. 18.

88. Ibid.

89. Rovere, *Senator Joe McCarthy,* p. 65.

90. "Finally, many prominent liberals failed actively to oppose McCarthy. . . . The failure of the American elites to confront McCarthy immeasurably enhanced his power." Rogin, *The Intellectuals and McCarthy,* p. 256.

91. "The Red Hunt Goes On," *Newsweek,* 22 May 1950, p. 21; see also "War on McCarthy," ibid., 15 May 1950, pp. 24–25.

92. Memorandum for Mr. Dawson (unsigned), 8 May 1950, in Student Research File (McCarthyism), Box 1, Folder 4, HSTL.

93. Secretary's Press & Radio News Conference, 26 May 1950, in Papers of Dean Acheson, Box 82, Folder: "Press Conferences, Jan-Dec 1950," HSTL.

94. "McCarthy's Needle," p. 20.

95. "Sudden Death," *Newsweek,* 29 May 1950, p. 14.

96. "U.S. Town Stages a Communist Coup," *Life,* 15 May 1950, pp. 46–47 (including photo captions).

97. "Peace and the High Cost Thereof," *Newsweek,* 12 June 1950, pp. 19–21.

98. "The Sun Shines on Harry Again," *Newsweek,* 26 June 1950, p. 15.

99. Ferrell, *Dear Bess,* p. 561.

CHAPTER 6
The Guns of Summer

1. John J. Muccio Oral History Interview, p. 19, Harry S. Truman Library, Independence , Mo. (hereafter cited as HSTL).

2. Margaret Truman, *Harry S. Truman* (New York: Pocket Books, 1974), pp. 494–95.

3. John D. Hickerson Oral History Interview, pp. 88–93, HSTL.

4. U. Alexis Johnson Oral History Interview, pp. 35–42, HSTL; Harry S. Truman, *Memoirs,* 2 vols. (New York: Signet Books, 1956), Vol. 2, *Years of Trial and Hope,* pp. 378–79.

5. NSC 48/2 is printed in U.S. Department of State, *Foreign Relations of the United States, 1949,* 9 vols. (Washington, D.C.: U.S. Government Printing Office, 1974–76), 7:1215–20.

6. Minutes of the 171st Meeting of the Policy Planning Staff, 16 December 1949, ibid., 1:413–14; Central Intelligence Agency Document ORE 69-49, "Relative US Security Interest in the European-Mediterranean Area and the Far East," 12 September 1949, p. 1, in U.S., Central Intelligence Agency, Records of the Central Intelligence Agency, Record Group 263: Estimates of the Office of Research Evaluation, 1946–1950, National Archives, Washington, D.C. (hereafter cited as

CIA Records, RG 263); James F. Schnabel and Robert J. Watson, *The Korean War, Part I*, The History of the Joint Chiefs of Staff, vol. 3 (Washington, DC: Joint Chiefs of Staff, Joint Secretarial Historical Division, 1978), pp. 47–48.

7. Clay Blair, *The Forgotten War: America in Korea, 1950–1953* (New York: Times Books, 1987), pp. 4, 9, 31; Merle Miller, *Plain Speaking: An Oral Biography of Harry S. Truman* (New York: Berkley Publishing Corporation, 1974), pp. 435–36.

8. Blair, *The Forgotten War*, p. 8. The information on military force levels is from ibid., pp. 7–9; Roy E. Appleman, *South to the Naktong, North to the Yalu (June–November 1950)* (Washington, D.C.: Department of the Army, Office of the Chief of Military History, 1960), p. 49; and Schnabel and Watson, *The Korean War, Part I*, p. 46.

9. Blair, *The Forgotten War*, pp. 14–16, 25, 29. MacArthur biographer D. Clayton James placed the blame for American unpreparedness on Congress; see James, *The Years of MacArthur*, 3 vols. (Boston: Houghton Mifflin, 1970–85), vol. 3, *Triumph and Disaster, 1945–1964*, p. 402. A more balanced and sophisticated contemporary account is "Background for War: Why the U.S. Was Unprepared," *Time*, 2 October 1950, pp. 18–19. Frank Pace, who had been Truman's budget director before being appointed army secretary several months before the outbreak of the Korean War, later admitted that the U.S. defense establishment, especially the army, was in very poor shape by June 1950. See Frank Pace Oral History Interview, p. 64, HSTL.

10. See Pace Oral History Interview, pp. 64, 66.

11. NSC 68, in its development from a brief, tentative draft prepared as a general policy statement in early January 1950 to NSC 68/1 of November 10, 1950, is printed in U.S., Department of State, *Foreign Relations of the United States, 1950*, 7 vols. (Washington, D.C.: U.S. Government Printing Office, 1976–80), 1:126–492 (hereafter cited as *FRUS, 1950*); NSC 68, April 14, 1950, is on pp. 234–93.

12. Ibid., p. 236.

13. The conclusions of NSC 20/4 were reiterated at the end of NSC 68; see ibid., pp. 288–89.

14. Ibid., p. 241.

15. Ibid., pp. 256, 257.

16. Ibid., p. 265.

17. Ibid., p. 287.

18. K. Zilliacus, "Communism and Peace," *Fortnightly*, n.s., no. 1003 (July 1950), p. 13.

19. Acheson's frequently quoted speech was summarized in "Who Killed Cock Robin?," *Newsweek*, 23 January 1950, pp. 30–31.

20. Muccio Oral History Interview, p. 16 (italics in original).

21. CIA Document ORE 76-49, "Survival Potential of Residual Non-Communist Regimes in China," 19 October 1949, p. 1, in CIA Records, RG 263.

22. Record of Conversation Between Comrade I. V. [*sic*] Stalin and Chairman of the Central People's Government of the People's Republic of China Mao Zedong on December 16, 1949, reprinted in "Stalin's Conversations with Chi-

nese Leaders," *Cold War International History Project Bulletin*, issues 6–7 (Winter 1995/1996), pp. 5–6 (hereafter cited as *CWIHPB*).

23. Record of Conversation between Comrade I. V. Stalin and Chairman of the Central People's Government of the People's Republic of China Mao Zedong, 22 January 1950, ibid., p. 7.

24. Vladislav Zubok, "'To Hell with Yalta!'—Stalin Opts for a New Status Quo," in *CWIHPB*, issues 6–7 (Winter 1995/1996), p. 25 (Zubok's italics).

25. Record of Conversation between Stalin and Mao, 22 January 1950, *CWIHPB*, issues 6–7 (Winter 1995/1996), p. 9.

26. Central Intelligence Agency Research and Analysis Paper ORE 29-49, "Prospects for Soviet Control of a Communist China," 15 April 1949, in Michael Warner, ed., *CIA Cold War Records: The CIA under Harry Truman* (Washington, D.C.: CIA History Staff, 1994), pp. 278, 279.

27. Sergei N. Goncharov, John W. Lewis, and Xue Litai, *Uncertain Partners: Stalin, Mao, and the Korean War* (Stanford, Calif.: Stanford University Press, 1993), p. 151; see also Memorandum by John Foster Dulles, Consultant to the Secretary of State, 18 May 1950, in *FRUS, 1950*, 1:314.

28. Goncharov, Lewis, and Litai, *Uncertain Partners*, p. 55. Shtykov's cable to Stalin is reprinted in Kathryn Weathersby, "New Russian Documents on the Korean War," *CWIHPB*, issues 6–7 (Winter 1995/1996), p. 36.

29. Scholar Dieter Heinzig has argued that Stalin apparently did not tell Mao that as early as January 30 he had implicitly given Kim a "green light" to invade South Korea. In 1956, Mao complained to Soviet ambassador Pvel Yudin that he had not been consulted and that all that he and Stalin had discussed was the strengthening of North Korea. This complaint is of little moment, because there is abundant evidence that once Kim got the tacit go-ahead from Stalin for his scheme, he immediately approached Mao to obtain his concurrence as well. Thus, Mao's subsequent complaint that Korea represented "a serious miscalculation" on Stalin's part is self-serving at best. Dieter Heinzig, "Stalin, Mao, Kim and Korean War Origins, 1950: A Russian Documentary Discrepancy," *CWIHPB*, 8–9 (Winter 1996–1997), p. 240.

30. Goncharov, Lewis, and Litai, *Uncertain Partners*, p. 31; see also ibid., pp. 69–73, 148; and Kathryn Weathersby, "New Findings on the Korean War," *CWIHPB*, 3 (Fall 1993), p. 14.

31. Soviet Representative Aleksei Ignatieff in Pyongyang to [Soviet Foreign Minister Andrey] Vyshinsky, 10 April 1950, reprinted in Weathersby, "New Russian Documents on the Korean War," p. 38; Shtykov to Vyshinsky, 12 May 1950, reprinted, ibid., pp. 38–39.

32. Shtykov to Vyshinsky, 12 May 1950, p. 39.

33. Goncharov, Lewis, and Litai, *Uncertain Partners*, pp. 139–44; Weathersby, "New Findings on the Korean War," pp. 13–35; idem, "Korea, 1949–50: To Attack or Not to Attack? Stalin, Kim Il Sung, and the Prelude to War," *CWIHPB*, 5 (Spring 1995), pp. 1–2.

34. Goncharov, Lewis, and Litai, *Uncertain Partners*, pp. 148–49.

35. Sulzberger to MacArthur, 19 October 1949, MacArthur to Sulzberger, October 28, 1949, in Papers of General Douglas MacArthur, Record Group 5, Records of Headquarters, Supreme Commander for the Allied Powers (SCAP), 1946–1951, MacArthur Memorial, Norfolk, Va.

36. "A Dangerous Situation," *Time*, 3 July 1950, p. 17.

37. CIA Document ORE 32-48, "Communist Capabilities in South Korea," 21 February 1949, p. 1, in CIA Records, RG 263.

38. CIA Document ORE 44-48, "Prospects for Survival of the Republic of Korea," 28 October 1948, ibid.

39. Memorandum of Conversation, by the Officer in Charge of Korean Affairs (Bond), 3 April 1950, in *FRUS, 1950,* 7:42–43.

40. Ibid., p. 41; Memorandum of Conversation by the Chargé in Korea (Drumright), 9 May 1950, in *FRUS, 1950,* 7:77; Chargé in Korea to the Secretary of State, 11 May 1950, ibid., p. 83; "A Dangerous Situation," p. 17.

41. Secretary's Press & Radio News Conference, 3 May 1950, in Papers of Dean Acheson, Box 82, Folder: "Press Conferences, Jan–Dec 1950," HSTL.

42. Schnabel and Watson, *The Korean War, Part I,* p. 49.

43. "Brief Summary of Activities: 441st Counter Intelligence Corps Detachment During Korean War," pp. 1, 2, in U.S. Army, United Nations Command/Far East Command General Headquarters, Military Intelligence Section General Staff, Army-AG Command Reports, 1949–54, Staff Section Reports, 1 January–31 October 1950, Record Group 407, Washington Federal Records Center, Suitland, Md.

44. CIA document ORE 18-50, "Current Capabilities of the Northern Korean Regime," 19 June 1950, in CIA Records, RG 263.

45. Undated and unsigned memorandum in U.S., Joint Chiefs of Staff, Records of the U.S. Joint Chiefs of Staff, Chairman's File, General Bradley, 1949–53, Folder 91, Box 1, Record Group 218, National Archives, Military History Branch, Washington, D.C. (hereafter cited as JCS Records, RG 218).

46. Shtykov to Comrade Zakharov [head of Soviet mission to North Korea], 26 June 1950, in Weathersby, "New Russian Documents on the Korean War," p. 39; Appleman, *South to the Naktong, North to the Yalu,* pp. 19–20.

47. Bruce Cumings, *The Origins of the Korean War,* 2 vols. (Princeton: Princeton, N.J.: University Press, 1981, 1991), vol. 2, *The Roaring of the Cataract,* pp. 603–15.

48. Robert H. Ferrell, ed., *Dear Bess: The Letters from Harry to Bess Truman, 1910–1959* (New York: Norton, 1983), p. 562.

49. "Washington Wire," *New Republic,* 10 July 1950, p. 3.

50. Ibid.

51. The text of Governor Dewey's message and Truman's cordial reply are in Student Research File (Korean War: Response to North Korean Invasion), Box 1, Folder 2, HSTL. See also Editorial: "The Elections and Asia," *Life,* 20 November 1950, p. 38.

52. Editorial: "Korea Danger Spot," *Washington Post,* 26 June 1950; Joseph and Stewart Alsop, "Matter of Fact: Staying the Course in Korea," ibid., 29 June 1950. See also "North Korea's Attack Catches 'Hill' Committees by Surprise," ibid., 26

June 1950; Marshall Andrews, "Military Advantage Seen in North Korea," ibid.; Robert C. Albright, "Congress Eyes Chance of War; Keep Calm, Its Leaders Urge," ibid., 27 June 1950; idem, "Truman Gets Full Backing in Congress," ibid.; Walter Lippmann, Editorial: "Today and Tomorrow: The President's Decision," ibid., 29 June 1950.

53. Cabell Phillips, *The Truman Presidency: The History of a Triumphant Succession* (Baltimore: Penguin Books, 1969; first published 1966), p. 299.

54. A copy of Kirk's cable is in Student Research File (Korean War: Response to North Korea's Invasion), Box 1, Folder 1, HSTL; the State Department intelligence paper is printed in *FRUS, 1950, 7*:148–50; Pace's recollections are in Pace Oral History, pp. 77–78, HSTL (italics in original).

55. "A Dangerous Situation," p. 17; "U.S. Throws Forces into Korean War," *Newsweek*, 3 July 1950, p. 17; "Uncle Sam Takes Role as World Cop," ibid., 10 July 1950, p. 17; "Showdown in the Far East: Can America Hold the Line?" *U.S. News & World Report*, 7 July 1950, p. 11.

56. Walter Isaacson and Evan Thomas, *The Wise Men: Six Friends and the World They Made* (London: Faber & Faber, 1986), pp. 510, 517; see also "Test Case," *Economist*, 1 July 1950, p. 1; "Strength with Speed," ibid., 8 July 1950, p. 57.

57. Secretary's Press & Radio News Conference, 28 June 1950, in Papers of Dean Acheson, Box 82, Folder: "Press Conferences, Jan–Dec 1950," HSTL; "In the Cause of Peace," *Time*, 10 July 1950, p. 17.

58. Frank Pace remembered that he raised the issue of a joint congressional resolution backing the Korean decision later in the summer, but Truman brushed it aside: "Frank, it's not necessary. They are all with me." "Yes, Mr. President," Pace replied, "but we can't be sure that they'll be with you over any period of time." Pace Oral History, pp. 78–79, HSTL.

59. "Washington Wire," p. 5.

60. George Gallup, "Survey Finds 8 of 10 Voters Approve U.S. Help to Korea," *Washington Post*, 2 July 1950. Gallup's conclusion is supported by a mass of public opinion documentation compiled by George Elsey and other White House staffers in late July, 1950 in response to Truman's first radio fireside chat on the war. See Student Research File, "Korean War: Response to North Korea's Invasion," Box 1, folders 6, 7, 10.

61. "Sycamore Backs the President," *Life*, 10 July 1950, pp. 30, 32.

62. Muccio Oral History Interview, p. 32, HSTL.

63. Ibid., pp. 57–59.

64. Stalin to Shtykov, 1 July 1950, in Weathersby, "New Russian Documents on the Korean War," p. 40; Shtykov to Stalin, 1 July 1950 and 4 July 1950, ibid., p. 42; Stalin to Zhou Enlai, 5 July 1950, ibid., p. 43; Stalin to the Soviet Ambassador N. V. Roshchin in Beijing, 8 July 1950, ibid., p. 44; Chen Jian, "China's Road to the Korean War," *CWIHPB*, 6–7 (Winter 1995/1996), p. 41.

65. Goncharov, Lewis, and Litai, *Uncertain Partners*, p. 157.

66. Walter Karig, Malcolm W. Cagle, and Frank A. Manson, *The War in Korea*, Battle Report Series, vol. 6 (New York: Rinehart, 1952), p. 18.

67. "Green Men under Fire," *Newsweek,* 17 July 1950, p. 16.

68. David Lawrence, "Bloodshed the Penalty for Lack of Foresight," *Seattle Times,* 16 July 1950; Joseph and Stewart Alsop, "Our Suicidal Approach to the War in Korea," ibid., 17 July 1950.

69. Memorandum by the Secretary of the Army (Pace), the Secretary of the Navy (Matthews), and the Secretary of the Air Force (Finletter) to the Secretary of Defense (Johnson), 1 August 1950, in *FRUS, 1950,* 1:353.

70. Dean Acheson, *Present at the Creation: My Years in the State Department* (New York: Signet Books, 1970), pp. 546–47.

71. See "Gears Grinding toward Mobilization," *Newsweek,* 17 July 1950, p. 20; Blair, *The Forgotten War,* pp. 126–27; Memorandum for the Secretary of Defense from the Chairman of the Joint Chiefs of Staff, penciled notation "8-23-50," Memorandum by the Chief of Naval Operations, 23 July 1950, and related documents, in Geographic File, 1948–50, Box 22, Folder CCS 381: Far East S.3, JCS Records, RG 218.

72. James L. Matray, "Truman's Plan for Victory: National Self-Determination and the Thirty-Eighth Parallel Decision in Korea," *Journal of American History* 66, no. 2 (September 1979):321.

73. "Manpower Goals Up," *New York Times,* 2 September 1950.

74. General of the Army Douglas MacArthur, Tokyo, to the president, 19 July 1950, copy in Student Research File (Korean War: Dismissal of General Douglas MacArthur), Box 1, Folder 1, HSTL.

75. Stalin to Kim Il Sung via Shtykov, 28 August 1950, in Weathersby, "New Russian Documents on the Korean War," p. 45; Shtykov to Stalin, 31 August 1950, transmitting letter from Kim to Stalin, ibid., p. 46.

76. Stalin to Zhou Enlai or Mao Zedong via Roshchin, 13 July 1950, ibid., p. 4.

77. Acheson, *Present at the Creation,* p. 541.

78. George F. Kennan, *Memoirs (1925–1950)* (New York: Bantam Books, 1969; first published 1967), p. 514; Matray, "Truman's Plan for Victory," p. 318.

79. Acheson, *Present at the Creation,* p. 543.

80. S. L. A. Marshall, *The River and the Gauntlet: Defeat of the Eighth Army by the Chinese Communist Forces, November, 1950, in the Battle of the Chongchon River, Korea* (New York: Time, 1962; first published 1953), pp. 2–5.

81. Secretary Press & Radio Conferences, 5 July 1950, 30 August 1950, in Papers of Dean Acheson, Box 82, Folder: "Press Conferences Jan–Dec 1950," HSTL.

82. Goncharov, Lewis, and Litai, *Uncertain Partners,* p. 159.

83. See, for example, Hanson W. Baldwin, "The Outlook in Korea," *New York Times,* 30 August 1950; "Significance: Will the Chinese Reds Move?" *Newsweek,* 17 July 1950, p. 17; "Key to Conflict," ibid., 11 September 1950, p. 25.

84. George M. Elsey to James Lay, 12 July 1950, in Student Research File (Korean War: Response to N. Korea's Invasion), Box 1, Folder 5, HSTL.

85. Allison to Rusk, July 1, 1950, *FRUS, 1950;* 7:272.

86. Kennan, *Memoirs,* p. 515; see also pp. 522–23.

87. Matray, "Truman's Plan for Victory," pp. 324, 325.

88. Kennan, *Memoirs*, p. 516. Matray, "Truman's Plan for Victory," pp. 319, 325.

89. Kennan, *Memoirs*, pp. 518–19.

90. Ibid., p. 520.

91. Ibid.

92. Ibid., pp. 520–21; Nitze's views are summarized in Matray, "Truman's Plan for Victory," p. 323.

93. Kennan, *Memoirs*, p. 522.

CHAPTER 7
The Politics of Hysteria

1. George M. Fredrickson, *The Inner Civil War: Northern Intellectuals and the Crisis of the Union* (New York: Harper & Row, 1965), p. 136; Arthur S. Link, *Woodrow Wilson and the Progressive Era* (New York: Harper Torchbooks, 1963), p. 277.

2. The best discussion of the influence of gossip in shaping twentieth-century American culture is Neal Gabler, *Winchell: Gossip, Power and the Cult of Celebrity* (New York: Knopf, 1994).

3. David Brinkley, *Washington Goes to War* (New York: Ballantine Books, 1988), p. 187.

4. Eleanor Lattimore, "What It Was Like," *Harper's Magazine*, August 1950, pp. 43–52, September 1950, pp. 79–87; Alfred Friendly, "The Noble Crusade of Senator McCarthy," ibid., August 1950, pp. 34–42; Robert H. Jackson, "The Communists in America," ibid., September 1950, pp. 21–27 (*Harper's* indicated that Jackson's opinion had previously been published in the *New York Times Magazine* "and elsewhere.")

5. Joseph and Stewart Alsop, "Why Has Washington Gone Crazy?" *Saturday Evening Post*, 29 July 1950, pp. 20–21.

6. Ibid., pp. 21, 59.

7. Ibid., pp. 20, 59.

8. Ibid., pp. 60, 61.

9. Ibid., p. 60.

10. Ibid., p. 61.

11. Ibid., p. 21.

12. Ibid., pp. 60, 61.

13. Ibid., p. 60; see also p. 61.

14. "Propaganda: Whose Voice Is Best?" *Newsweek*, 17 July 1950, p. 23; "Point Four Snafu: How Red Tape Scrambled a Formosa Project," ibid., p. 28.

15. "GOP Hammers at Far Eastern Policy," *Newsweek*, 28 August 1950, pp. 28–29.

16. "Drifting toward War with China," *New Republic*, 21 August 1950, p. 7.

17. William Manchester, *American Caesar* (New York: Dell Books, 1978), p. 676.

18. "An Unsinkable Aircraft Carrier," *Time*, 4 September 1950, p. 10. Truman's contemporary, handwritten account of his firing of Johnson is in the President's Secretary's File, Box 333, Longhand Notes, 1945–1952, Folder: "1950," Harry S. Truman Library, Independence, Mo.

19. "President Acts 'to Avoid Confusion' on Formosa Policy," *Seattle Times*, 28 August 1950.

20. "The Presidency: The Face in the Lamplight," *Time*, 25 September 1950, p. 20.

21. "News of the Week in Review: Congress v Communists," *New York Times*, 3 September 1950.

22. The following descriptions and criticisms of the Nixon legislation are from "Bill for Rigid Curbs on Reds as Passed by House 354 to 20," *New York Times*, 30 August 1950; and "Personal Freedom in Wartime," *New Republic*, 4 September 1950, pp. 3–7.

23. "The Heat's On," *Time*, 4 September 1950, p. 13; "Early Sedition Laws Hardly an Issue Now," *Seattle Times*, 27 August 1950.

24. "The Heat's On," p. 13.

25. Ibid.; John Huston, *An Open Book* (New York: Knopf, 1980), p. 135.

26. "Anti-Communist Feeling Rising in West," *New York Times*, 10 September 1950.

27. A good, if brief, portrait of McCarran is Alfred Steinberg, "McCarran: Lone Wolf of the Senate," *Harper's Magazine*, November 1950, pp. 89–95.

28. "Congress: 'There Is a Danger . . . ,' " *Time*, 25 September 1950, p. 21; see also "Hogtied, Constitutionally," *Newsweek*, 25 September 1950, p. 34.

29. "Hogtied, Constitutionally," p. 34.

30. "The Anti-Communist Bill," *Time*, 25 September 1950, p. 22.

31. "Be Tougher with Communists in the U.S.," *Seattle Times*, 29 August 1950.

32. "Public Not to Blame for U.S. Weakness," *Seattle Times*, 27 August 1950.

33. "Hogtied, Constitutionally," p. 35; "The Congress: There Is a Danger," p. 21.

CHAPTER 8
Hubris

1. Clay Blair, *The Forgotten War: America in Korea, 1950–1953* (New York: Times Books, 1987), pp. 184, 187.

2. Sergei N. Goncharov, John W. Lewis, and Zue Litai, *Uncertain Partners: Stalin, Mao, and the Korean War* (Stanford, Calif.: Stanford University Press, 1993), pp. 171–72.

3. J. Lawton Collins, *War in Peacetime: The History and Lessons of Korea* (Boston: Houghton Mifflin, 1969), pp. 125–26; David Rees, *Korea: The Limited War* (Baltimore: Penguin Books, 1970), p. 83.

4. Douglas MacArthur, *Reminiscences* (New York: McGraw Hill, 1964), p. 97.

5. Collins, *War in Peacetime*, p. 115.

6. Robert Debs Heinl, Jr., *Victory at High Tide: The Inchon-Seoul Campaign* (Philadelphia: Lippincott, 1968), pp. 262–63.

7. T. R. Fehrenbach, *This Kind of War: A Study in Unpreparedness* (New York: Pocket Books, 1964), p. 289.

8. Alexander Kendrick, *Prime Time: The Life of Edward R. Murrow* (New York: Avon Books, 1970), p. 371; see also "Drifting toward War with China," *New Republic*, 21 August 1950, p. 7.

9. "Clear the Track," *Time*, 25 September 1950, p. 19; "Now It's Put Up or Shut Up for Reds," *Newsweek*, 25 September 1950, p. 21; "Victory Looms—So Does 38th Parallel," ibid., 2 October 1950, p. 19; White House Press Release, 29 September 1950, copy in Student Research File (Korean War: Dismissal of General Douglas MacArthur), Box 1, Folder 1, Harry S. Truman Library, Independence, Mo. (hereafter cited as HSTL).

10. "News of the Week in Review: We Close In," *New York Times*, 24 September 1950; *New York Times Magazine*, 1 October, 1950; ibid., 15 October 1950; "Korea's Future," *New Republic*, 30 October 1950, p. 6.

11. Editorial: "How about Joe?" *Portland Oregonian*, 22 September 1950.

12. James L. Matray, "Truman's Plan for Victory: National Self-Determination and the Thirty-Eighth Parallel Decision in Korea," *Journal of American History* 66, no. 2 (September 1979): 327; see also ibid., p. 329.

13. Unsigned document dated 2 September 1950, in Papers of Dean Acheson, Box 82, Folder: "Press Conferences Jan–Dec 1950," HSTL.

14. Acting Secretary of State to the Embassy in India, 16 September 1950, in U.S., Department of State, *Foreign Relations of the United States, 1950*, 7 vols. (Washington, D.C.: U.S. Government Printing Office, 1950), 7:733 (hereafter cited as *FRUS, 1950*).

15. Statement issued by Foreign Ministry of the People's Republic of China, 10 October 1950, quoted in Editorial Note, n.d., in *FRUS*, p. 914; "Fight for the Consolidation and Development of the Chinese People's Victory," *China Monthly Review*, November 1950, p. 104, reprinted in Goncharov, Lewis, and Litai, *Uncertain Partners*, p. 274.

16. Goncharov, Lewis, and Litai, *Uncertain Partners*, pp. 168, 171, 172–73.

17. Ibid., p. 173; Allen S. Whiting, *China Crosses the Yalu: The Decision to Enter the Korean War* (Stanford, Calif.: Stanford University Press, 1960), p. 158.

18. Alexandre Y. Mansourov, "Stalin, Mao, Kim, and China's Decision to Enter the Korean War, September 16–October 15, 1950: New Evidence from the Russian Archives," *Cold War International History Project Bulletin*, 6–7 (Winter 1995/1996), pp. 95–96 (hereafter cited as *CWIHPB*).

19. Goncharov, Lewis, and Litai, *Uncertain Partners*, p. 174; see also Stalin to Mao Zedong and Zhou Enlai, 1 October 1950, in Mansourov, "Stalin, Mao, Kim, and China's Decision," p. 114.

20. Mansourov, "Stalin, Mao, Kim, and China's Decision," p. 95; see also Soviet Defense Minister A. M. Vasilevsky to Stalin, 21 September 1950, ibid., p. 108.

21. Stalin to General M. V. Zakharov and Ambassador Shtykov, 27 September 1950, in Mansourov, "Stalin, Mao, Kim, and China's Decision," p. 109.

22. Ibid.

23. Zakharov to Stalin, 26 September 1950, in Mansourov, "Stalin, Mao, Kim, and China's Decision," p. 110; Shtykov to [Soviet] Deputy Foreign Minister Andrei Gromyko and Stalin, 29 September 1950, ibid., pp. 110–11.

24. Kim Il Sung and South Korean Communist leader Pak Hon-Yong to Stalin, 29 September 1950, ibid., pp. 111–12; Stalin to Mao Zedong and Zhou Enlai, 1 October, 1950, ibid, p. 114.

25. Ambassador Roshchin in Beijing [Peking] to Stalin, 3 October 1950, conveying 2 October 1950 message from Mao to Stalin, ibid., pp. 114–15. Apparently Mao had personally drafted a sharply different cable to Stalin on October 2, pledging to send troops to Korea immediately. However, this message was never sent. Chinese historian and archivist SHEN Zhihua states that the cable announcing immediate intervention reflected Mao's true state of mind, but he had yet to convince his apprehensive politburo and he also hoped that by emphasizing China's current military weakness, he could obtain necessary concessions from Stalin, especially a pledge of air support over the battlefield. Therefore, instead of replying directly to Stalin's request with a pledge of immediate intervention, Mao replied through Ambassador Roshchin with a calculated message of delay and concern. SHEN Zhihua, "The Discrepancy Between the Russin and Chinese Versions of Mao's 2 October 1950 message to Stalin on Chinese Entry into the Korean War: A Chinese Scholar's Reply. *CWIHPB*, 8–9 (Winter 1996/1997), pp. 237–41.

26. Letter from Stalin to Kim Il Sung (via Shtykov), 8 October 1950, in Mansourov, "Stalin, Mao, Kim, and China's Decision To Enter the Korean War," p. 116.

27. Ibid.

28. Ibid; SHEN Zhihua, "The Discrepancy Between The Russian and Chinese Versions of Mao's 2 October 1950 Message to Stalin on Chinese Entry into the Korean War," p. 241.

29. John M. Allison to Paul Nitze, 24 July 1950, in *FRUS, 1950*, 7:458–61; Memorandum of Conversation by John M. Allison of the U.S. Delegation to the UN General Assembly, 18 September 1950, ibid., p. 735; Position Paper Prepared for the U.S. Delegation to the UN General Assembly, 19 September 1950, ibid., p. 736. The UN Commission and Trygve Lie are quoted in "Peace Aims for Korea," *New Republic*, 25 September 1950, p. 5.

30. Consul General at Hong Kong to the Secretary of State, 22 September 1950, *FRUS, 1950*, 7:765; Ambassador in India to the Secretary of State, 27 September 1950, ibid., p. 790; Memorandum by the Director of the Office of Chinese Affairs to the Assistant Secretary of State for Far Eastern Affairs, 27 September 1950, ibid., p. 795.

31. Memorandum for the President from the Acting Secretary of State, 27 September 1950, in Student Research File (Korean War: Dismissal of General Douglas MacArthur), Box 1, Folder 1, HSTL.

32. Secretary of State to the Acting Secretary of State, 28 September 1950, in

FRUS, 1950, 7:817–18. For Truman's reticence, see Matray, "Truman's Plan for Victory," pp. 329–30.

33. The text of the JCS Directive to MacArthur was first conveyed in an information cable: Acting Secretary of State to the U.S. Mission to the United Nations, 26 September 1950, in *FRUS, 1950,* pp. 781–82; see also Secretary of Defense to the President, 27 September 1950, ibid., p. 793 n. 2.

34. Acting Secretary of State to U.S. Mission, 26 September 1950, p. 782; Secretary of Defense to the Commander in Chief, Far East, 29 September 1950, in *FRUS, 1950,* 7:826.

35. Anthony Farrar-Hockley, *The British Part in the Korean War,* vol. 1, *A Distant Obligation* (London: Her Majesty's Stationery Office, 1990), p. 217.

36. Ibid., pp. 217, 218 (italics in original).

37. Editorial Note, n.d., in *FRUS, 1950,* 7:734; "United Nations: Exhibit A," *Time,* 2 October 1950, p. 20.

38. Goncharov, Lewis, and Litai, *Uncertain Partners,* p. 175.

39. Mao Telegram to Stalin re the Decision to Send Troops to Korea, 2 October 1950, reprinted, ibid., pp. 275–76. In view of more recent documentary evidence from Soviet archives, it seems that this cable was either deliberately or inadvertently misdated. It was probably the October 7 cable to which Stalin alluded in his October 8 message to Kim.

40. Zhou Enlai Talk with Indian Ambassador K. M. Panikkar, 3 October 1950, ibid., p. 277.

41. Ibid., pp. 277–78.

42. Ambassador in India to Secretary of State, 6 October 1950, in *FRUS, 1950,* 7:892; Annex 4 to Memorandum of Conversation by the Assistant Secretary of State for Far Eastern Affairs, 6 October 1950, ibid., pp. 896–97.

43. UN Resolution 376 (V), ibid., pp. 904–6.

44. Joint Chiefs of Staff to the Commander in Chief, Far East, 9 October 1950, ibid., p. 915.

45. Editorial Note, n.d., ibid., p. 914.

46. Mildred Strunk, ed., "The Quarter's Polls," *Public Opinion Quarterly* 15, no. 1 (Spring 1951):170.

47. Goncharov, Lewis, and Litai, *Uncertain Partners,* p. 184; see also Mao Telegram to Kim Il Sung re China's Entry in the War, 8 October 1950, ibid., p. 279.

48. Memorandum of Conversation, by the Ambassador at Large, with Annex, 12 October 1950, in *FRUS, 1950,* 7:930–32.

49. George M. Elsey Oral History, pp. 275–78, HSTL; Harry S. Truman, *Memoirs,* 2 vols. (New York: Signet Books, 1965; first published 1955–56), vol. 2, *Years of Trial and Hope, 1946–1952,* p. 414.

50. Blair, *The Forgotten War,* pp. 188–89; "The Sad Case of Harold Stassen," *New Republic,* 6 November 1950, p. 12.

51. Elsey Oral History, p. 277; Notes on the Wake Conference, in Student Research File (Korean War: Response to North Korea's Invasion), Box 1, Folder 9; Truman, *Years of Trial and Hope,* pp. 413–14.

52. Statement by the President, 10 October 1950, in Student Research File (Korean War: Dismissal of General Douglas MacArthur), Box 1, Folder 1.

53. Alonzo L. Hamby, *Man of the People: A Life of Harry S. Truman* (New York: Oxford University Press, 1995), p. 486.

54. A copy is in U.S., Central Intelligence Agency, Records of the Central Intelligence Agency, Estimates of the Office of Research Evaluation, 1946–1950, Record Group 263, National Archives, Washington, D.C. (the quotations that follow are on pp. 3, 4); it is also published in *FRUS, 1950*, 7:933–38.

55. The CIA's assessment of the possibility of Soviet intervention was equally ambiguous and disturbing. Soviet forces currently in the Far East could intervene in Korea at any time with devastating effect. But they would suffer heavy losses, and the Kremlin would have to be prepared for a full-scale world war. Under the circumstances it was "estimated" that Stalin would send troops to Korea only after he had concluded that a global nuclear war was somehow in his interest. See "Critical Situations in the Far East," p. 13.

56. "The Presidency: The General Rose at Dawn," *Time*, 23 October 1950, p. 19.

57. Robert Smith, *MacArthur in Korea* (New York: Simon & Schuster, 1982), p. 93; D. Clayton James, *The Years of MacArthur*, 3 vols. (Boston: Houghton Mifflin, 1970–85), vol. 3, *Triumph and Disaster, 1945–1964*, p. 503.

58. "The European Recovery Program and Truman and MacArthur: Interview with W. Averell Harriman," p. 10, in Averell Harriman Oral History File, HSTL.

59. James, *Triumph and Disaster*, p. 503.

60. Five weeks later, as the debacle in Korea began to materialize, former haberdasher Truman wrote a lengthy note on White House stationery titled "Wake Island," in which he complained that MacArthur met the presidential party "at the Airport with his shirt unbuttoned, wearing a greasy ham and eggs cap that evidently had been in use for twenty years." Truman personal note, 25 November 1950, in Student Research File (Korean War: Dismissal of General Douglas MacArthur), Box 1, Folder 1.

61. Truman, *Years of Trial and Hope*, p. 416, which is based in large part on his handwritten note of November 25, 1950 cited in footnote 60 above. James, *Triumph and Disaster*, pp. 504–5; "The Presidency: The General Rose at Dawn," p. 19.

62. According to Truman and others, Jessup's secretary, Vernice Anderson, took notes of the conference on her own initiative from "next door," and Bradley later compiled them into an account that can be found under the title "Substance of Statements Made at Wake Island Conference on 15 October 1950," in U.S., Joint Chiefs of Staff, Records of the U.S. Joint Chiefs of Staff, Chairman's File, General Bradley, 1949–53, Box 2, folder "Wake Island," Record Group 218, National Archives, Washington, D.C. (hereafter cited as JCS Records, RG 218). This document is also published in *FRUS, 1950*, 7:948–60, which states that the "main portions" of the Bradley document were issued jointly by the Senate Armed Forces and Foreign Relations Committees in 1951 (see p. 948 n. 1); the quotations that follow are on pp. 949, 953–955, 959, 960.

President Truman made use of the Bradley document for his extensive account in Truman, *Years of Trial and Hope*, pp. 417–18; see also James, *Triumph and Disaster*, p. 505.

63. "European Recovery Program and Truman and MacArthur," Harriman Oral History File, p. 10.

64. J. V. Fitzgerald, White House, to Charles G. Ross, Presidential Party, n.d., Papers of Harry S. Truman: President's Secretary's Files, Box 244, Wake Island Conference, Folder: "Korea—Wake Island, General," HSTL.

65. Truman quoted extensively from this speech in *Years of Trial and Hope*, pp. 419–22; MacArthur's message to Truman is in Memorandum to Brigadier General George I. Back, 18 October 1950, in Papers of General Douglas MacArthur, Record Group 5: Records of Headquarters, Supreme Commander for the Allied Powers (SCAP), 1946–1951, MacArthur Memorial, Norfolk, Va.

66. Goncharov, Lewis, and Litai, *Uncertain Partners*, p. 188.

67. Ibid., p. 189.

68. Ibid., pp. 189–191; Khrushchev's account of Stalin's reaction to the Zhou mission is in Jerrold L. Schecter and Vyacheslav V. Luchkov, trans. and eds., *Khrushchev Remembers: The Glasnost Tapes* (Boston: Little, Brown, 1990), p. 147.

69. Goncharov, Lewis, and Litai, *Uncertain Partners*, p. 193.

70. Ibid., pp. 193–94.

71. Ibid., p. 195.

72. Blair, *The Forgotten War*, p. 186.

73. Ibid., pp. 196, 197.

74. An interesting contemporary observation that did not address specific combat weaknesses in the U.S. ground forces but did advocate "a light Army" to counteract Korean-type wars that the Kremlin would wage in the future is in Eric Larrabee, "Korea: The Military Lesson," *Harper's Magazine*, November 1950, pp. 51–57.

75. Larry Keighley, "The Wives Wait Out the War," *Saturday Evening Post*, 30 September 1950, pp. 29, 116; "Border Byplay," *Newsweek*, 6 November 1950, photo caption p. 29.

76. "U.S. War Casualties," *Time*, 23 October 1950, p. 19; James, *Triumph and Disaster*, p. 496.

77. James, *Triumph and Disaster*, p. 496; and in Rees, *Korea: The Limited War*, p. 123.

78. Matthew B. Ridgway, *The Korean War* (New York: Popular Library, 1967), p. 57; "Korea Summary: G-2 Estimate of the Situation," 14–15 October 1950, p. 1-a, in U.S. Army, United Nations Command/Far East Command General Headquarters, Military Intelligence Section General Staff, Army-AG Command Reports, 1949–54, Record Group 407, Washington Federal Records Center, Suitland, Md. (hereafter cited as Army-AG Command Reports, RG 407).

79. James, *Triumph and Disaster*, p. 497; Memorandum by the Chief of Naval Operations, 25 October 1950, in Geographic File, 1948–50, Box 22, Folder "CCS

381 Far East S.4," JCS Records, RG 218; Roy E. Appleman, *South to the Naktong, North to the Yalu (June–November 1950)* (Washington, D.C.: Department of the Army, Office of the Chief of Military History, 1960), p. 669.

80. "Wonsan Welcome," *Newsweek,* 6 November 1950, p. 30; see also James, *Triumph and Disaster,* p. 497.

81. "Border Byplay," p. 26; "Battle of Korea," *Time,* 23 October 1950, p. 27.

82. James, *Triumph and Disaster,* pp. 498–99; see also Editorial Note, n.d., in *FRUS, 1950,* 7:995–96.

83. "Command Report, November 1950," Staff Section Reports, Annexes 1–3, p. 1, in Army-AG Command Reports, RG 407.

84. James, *Triumph and Disaster,* p. 499; see also Editorial Note, n.d., in *FRUS, 1950,* 7:995–96.

85. James F. Schnabel and Robert J. Watson, *The Korean War, Part I,* The History of the Joint Chiefs of Staff, vol. 3 (Washington, D.C.: Joint Chiefs of Staff, Joint Secretariat Historical Division, 1978), p. 263.

86. James, *Triumph and Disaster,* p. 498.

87. "Border Byplay," p. 26.

CHAPTER 9
Disaster

1. Ira Peck, "A Night at Local Draft Board No. 14," *New York Times Magazine,* 29 October 1950, pp. 15, 47–49.

2. Frederick Fox, "Report from Wauseon—Fall, 1950," *New York Times Magazine,* 5 November 1950, pp. 12–13.

3. Max Hastings, *The Korean War* (New York: Simon & Schuster, 1987), p. 44.

4. Dean Acheson, *The Korean War* (New York: Norton, 1971), p. 64. Certainly some people in Washington remained blissfullly wedded to the vision of irresistible American force days after events in Korea should have warned them otherwise. As late as November 14, Paul Nitze, the director of State's Policy Planning Staff, sent Acheson the latest copy of NSC 68/1, which the staff had just finished drafting. The introduction contained a rhapsodic statement of U.S. cold war objectives, which Nitze claimed had been taken from NSC 68 the previous spring. "A peaceful resolution of the world crisis" required from the United States and its allies political and economic measures by which the West could frustrate Kremlin designs through "the steady development of the moral and material strength of the free world *and its projection into the Soviet world in such a way as to bring about an internal change in the Soviet system.*" Memorandum by the Director of the Policy Planning Staff (Nitze) to the Secretary of State, 14 November 1950, in U.S. Department of State, *Foreign Relations of the United States, 1950,* 7 vols. (Washington, D.C.: U.S. Government Printing Office, 1976–80), 1:405 (hereafter cited as *FRUS, 1950*); italics added.

5. Consul General at Hong Kong to the Secretary of State, 27 October 1950,

in *FRUS, 1950,* 7:1003–4. Acheson's directive to MacArthur is contained in a cable from the Secretary of State to the Embassy in Korea, 28 October 1950, ibid., pp. 1007–10.

6. Memorandum by the Director of the CIA to the President, 1 November 1950, ibid., pp. 1025–26.

7. Memorandum by the Director of the Office of Chinese Affairs to the Assistant Secretary of State for Far Eastern Affairs, 1 November 1950, ibid., pp. 1023–24; Consul General at Hong Kong to the Secretary of State, 3 November 1950, ibid., pp. 1034–35.

8. The most important passages of the MacArthur communiqué are reprinted in Secretary of State to the Embassy in the United Kingdom, 6 November 1950, ibid., p. 1051 n. 3.

9. MacArthur's draft report was transmitted to New York on November 5. See Secretary of State to the U.S. Mission at the United Nations, 5 November 1950, ibid., pp. 1046–48.

10. Harry S. Truman, *Memoirs,* 2 vols. (New York: Signet Books, 1965; first published 1955–56), Vol. 2, *Years of Trial and Hope,* p. 425.

11. *Chicago Tribune,* 3 November 1950, 4 November 1950, 5 November 1950; *Portland Oregonian,* 5 November 1950.

12. "Yanks Suffer Worst Defeat," *Portland Oregonian,* 3 November 1950.

13. Secretary of State to the Embassy in the United Kingdom, 6 November 1950, p. 1051; Memorandum by John P. Davies of the Policy Planning Staff, 7 November 1950, in *FRUS, 1950,* 7:1081.

14. MacArthur's messages of November 6 and 7 are reprinted in Truman, *Years of Trial and Hope,* pp. 427, 430; Acheson's account of the affair is in Memorandum of Conversations, 6 November 1950, in *FRUS, 1950,* 7:1055–56.

15. Joint Chiefs of Staff to the Commander in Chief, Far East, 6 November 1950, in *FRUS, 1950,* 7:1057.

16. Memorandum by the Director of the Policy Planning Staff, 4 November 1950, ibid., pp. 1041–42; Memorandum by the Planning Adviser, Bureau of Far Eastern Affairs, to the Assistant Secretary of State for Far Eastern Affairs, 8 November 1950, ibid., pp. 1098–1100.

17. Truman, *Years of Trial and Hope,* p. 428; Secretary Acheson to Secretary Marshall, 16 November 1950, in U.S., Joint Chiefs of Staff, Records of the U.S. Joint Chiefs of Staff, Geographic File, 1948–50, Box 21, "CCS 062 Far East, Sec 1," Record Group 218, National Archives, Washington, D.C. (hereafter cited as JCS Records, RG 218).

18. Korea [Intelligence] Summary, No. 2981, 7 November [1950], IV. G-2 Estimate of the Situation, in U.S., Army, United Nations Command/Far East Command General Headquarters, Military Intelligence Section General Staff, Army-AG Command Reports, 1949–54, Staff Section Reports 1–10, November 1950, Record Group 407, Washington Federal Records Center, Suitland, MD (hereafter cited as Army-AG Command Reports, RG 407); Memorandum by Major General Doyle O. Hickey with enclosure titled "Order of Battle Information,

Chinese Communist Regular Ground Forces, Fourth Field Army," 7 November 1950, in ibid; NIE-3, "Soviet Capabilities and Intentions," n.d. [a statement on the title page reads: "This paper is based on information available on 11 November 1950], p. 2, in U.S., Central Intelligence Agency, Records of the Central Intelligence Agency, National Intelligence Estimates Concerning the Soviet Union, 1950–1961, Box 1, Record Group 263, National Archives, Washington, D.C. (hereafter cited as CIA Records, RG 263).

19. Joint Chiefs of Staff to the Commander in Chief, Far East, 8 November 1950, in *FRUS, 1950,* 7:1097–98; Commander in Chief, Far East, to the Joint Chiefs of Staff, 9 November 1950, ibid., pp. 1107–9.

20. T. R. Fehrenbach, *This Kind of War: A Study in Unpreparedness* (New York: Pocket Books, 1964), p. 299; see also Command Report, November 1950, p. 2, in Army-AG Command Reports, RG 407; D. Clayton James, *The Years of MacArthur,* 3 vols. (Boston: Houghton Mifflin, 1970–85), vol. 3, *Triumph and Disaster, 1945–1964,* p. 519.

21. "War in Korea," *New Republic,* 27 November 1950, p. 7.

22. Carl A. Spaatz, "Enter the Chinese Communists," *Newsweek,* 13 November 1950, p. 35.

23. Ibid.

24. "Fresh War with a Fresh Red Army," *Newsweek,* 13 November 1950, p. 30; Hastings, *The Korean War,* p. 137.

25. Hastings, *The Korean War,* p. 138.

26. Memorandum by the Joint Chiefs of Staff to the Secretary of Defense, 8 November 1950, in *FRUS, 1950,* 7:1121.

27. The following account of the NSC meeting is from Truman, *Years of Trial and Hope,* pp. 431–33; and Richard E. Neustadt, *Presidential Power: The Politics of Leadership* (New York: Signet Books, 1964), p. 136.

28. A copy of the pamphlet is in the George M. Elsey Papers, Subject File, Box 91, Folder: "Politics, 1950 (1)," Harry S. Truman Library, Independence, Mo. (hereafter cited as HSTL).

29. "Bipus Warns Democratic Vote Would Peril Freedom," *Chicago Tribune,* 1 November 1950.

30. "Backer of Red Fronts 'Sells' Helen Douglas," *Chicago Tribune,* 3 November 1950; "Give U.S. Facts on China Reds, Truman Told," ibid., 4 November 1950; "East Raps Lucas for Deceit," ibid.

31. "Where Is Peace, Dirksen Asks; Cites Big Draft," *Chicago Tribune,* 4 November 1950.

32. Editorial: "Another Acheson Betrayal," *Chicago Tribune,* 4 November 1950.

33. "Stassen Lays New Slaughter at Truman's Door," *Chicago Tribune,* 5 November 1950; Fox, "Report from Wauseon," p. 12.

34. "McCarthy in Maryland," *New Republic,* 13 November 1950, p. 8; see also "McCarthy Wins," ibid., 20 November 1950, p. 7.

35. "The Losing Candidate," *Chicago Tribune,* 8 November 1950; "Washing-

ton Wire," *New Republic*, 20 November 1950, p. 3; "Truman on the Strait and Narrow," *Newsweek*, 20 November 1950, p. 26.

36. "Mr. Republican," *New Republic*, 20 November 1950, p. 8; see also "Douglas Defeated," ibid.; "Kick-in-the-Teeth Vote," *Newsweek*, 20 November 1950, p. 25; Samuel Lubell, *The Future of American Politics*, 2d ed. rev. (Garden City, N.Y.: Doubleday Anchor Books, 1956), p. 107.

37. "Washington Wire," p. 4; see also "Anti-Truman Line-up," *Newsweek*, 20 November 1950, p. 23; "Democrats on the Ropes," ibid., p. 24; "Finger on Acheson," ibid., p. 25.

38. Lubell, *The Future of American Politics*, pp. 106–15 (the handbill is reproduced on p. 109); Harold L. Ickes, "Fear Rides Hard," *New Republic*, 20 November 1950, p. 17. For further information on the 1950 elections, see "New York Stands Pat," ibid.; "Illinois Shuns Bossism," ibid., pp. 8–9; "Cost of the Elections," ibid., p. 9; "Democratic Gains," ibid., pp. 9–10; "The Periscope," *Newsweek*, 20 November 1950, p. 19; "The House: Closeness and Upset," ibid., p. 24; "Headaches in the Senate," ibid., p. 26; "Only an Idiot . . . ," *Time*, 20 November 1950, p. 19; "Is It True . . . ?" ibid., pp. 19–20; "Man in a New Hat," ibid., p. 20; "Not for Publication," ibid.; "The Election: What Happened?" ibid., pp. 20–21; "American Notes," *Economist* 159 (11 November 1950):743–44; Editorial, "Has G.O.P. Played Rough Enough to Win an Election?" *Saturday Evening Post*, 4 November 1950, p. 10; "Dirksen, Bobb Big Winners, Taft Victory Foe Concedes," *Chicago Tribune*, 8 November 1950; Editorial: "The Voice of the Voters," *New York Times*, 9 November 1950.

39. Daily Report No. 2986, 12 November 1950, in Staff Section Reports, 11–20 November 1950, Army-AG Command Reports, RG 407.

40. Daily Reports Nos. 2995 and 2997, 21 November 1950, 23 November 1950, 21–30 November 1950, ibid.

41. Roshchin to Stalin, 14 October 1950, in Alexandre Y. Mansourov, "Stalin, Mao, Kim, and China's Decision To Enter the Korean War, September 16–October 15, 1950: New Evidence from the Soviet Archives," *Cold War International History Project Bulletin*, 6–7 (Winter 1995/1996), pp. 118–19 (hereafter cited as *CWIHPB*).

42. Soviet Military Representative in Beijing, S. E. Zakharov, to Stalin, 2 November 1950, in Kathryn Weathersby, "New Russian Documents on the Korean War," *CWIHPB*, 6–7 (Winter 1995/1996), p. 48; Mao Zedong to Stalin, 15 November 1950, ibid., p. 49; Jerry Scutts, *Air War over Korea* (London: Arms and Armour Press, 1982), p. 28.

43. Daily Report No. 2997, 23 November 1950.

44. "The Bitter Cold of Korea," *Newsweek*, 4 December 1950, p. 22.

45. Ibid.

46. "A Small Task Force Fights and Freezes on Far North Front," *Life*, 11 December 1950, pp. 34–37.

47. Ibid., pp. 34, 35.

48. Hugh Moffett, "The Situation in Korea: 'Bug Out,'" *Life*, 18 December 1950, p. 24.

49. "A Face to the World," *Time*, 27 November 1950, p. 15; the casualty figures are from "U.S. War Casualties," ibid.

50. "A Face to the World," p. 15.

51. "Aggressive China Becomes a Menace," *Life*, 20 November 1950, p. 31; "Spectre of World War," *New Republic*, 27 November 1950, p. 6.

52. MacArthur's day in Korea is reported in "Battle of Korea: 'Massive Envelopment,'" *Time*, 4 December 1950, p. 22; see also Command Report, November 1950, p. 3.

53. MacArthur is quoted in "Battle of Korea: 'Massive Envelopment,'" p. 22. The remark by Gen. Leven Allen relating the success of the offensive to MacArthur's presence is in Roy E. Appleman, *South to the Naktong, North to the Yalu (June–December, 1950)* (Washington, D.C.: Department of the Army, Office of the Chief of Military History, 1960), p. 776.

54. "Battle of Korea: After the Breakthrough," *Time*, 11 December 1950, p. 27.

55. William Manchester, *American Caesar* (New York: Dell Books, 1978), p. 726.

56. Hastings, *The Korean War*, pp. 166–67.

57. Ibid., p. 166.

58. Ibid., p. 167; the scorched earth admission is in "Escape from the Chinese Trap," *Newsweek*, 18 December 1950, photo caption p. 25.

59. "Escape from the Chinese Trap," pp. 25–26.

60. Ibid., pp. 25–26.

61. Pat Frank, *Hold Back the Night* (Philadelphia: Lippincott, 1952).

62. "The Face of Mars," *Time*, 11 December 1950, pp. 17–18.

63. "Tense Nation," *Newsweek*, 18 December 1950, p. 18.

64. "How Our Victory Turned to Defeat," *Newsweek*, 11 December 1950, p. 29.

65. A typescript copy of MacArthur's press conference is in Student Research File (Korean War: Dismissal of General Douglas MacArthur), Box 1, Folder 1, HSTL.

66. "Yardstick from Tokyo," *Life*, 4 December 1950, p. 42.

67. Douglas MacArthur to Hugh Baillie, 1 December 1950, in MacArthur Papers, Record Group 5, OMS Correspondence, Box 57, Folder: "United Press Associates," MacArthur Memorial, Norfolk, Va. (hereafter cited as MacArthur Papers, RG 5). A typed notation on the last page reads: "The foregoing was handed to Mr. Hoberecht, United Press Manager for Japan, on December 1st, 1950 for his disposition."

68. Roy Howard to Douglas MacArthur, 5 December 1950, ibid., Box 28: "Howard."

69. MacArthur to Roy Howard, 20 December 1950, ibid.

70. Commander-in-Chief, UN Command, Tokyo to DA Washington, D.C., 8 December 1950, in Records of Headquarters, Supreme Commander for the Allied Powers (SCAP), 1946–1951, MacArthur Papers, RG 5.

71. Moffett, "The Situation in Korea," p. 25; "The Great Retreat Continues,"

Life, 18 December 1950, p. 23; "There Was a Christmas," ibid., 25 December 1950, pp. 9–14.

72. David McCullough, *Truman* (New York: Simon & Schuster, 1992), p. 821.

73. "Once More 'We Got a Hell of a Beating,'" *Life,* 11 December 1950, p. 33; Editorial, "The Prospect Is War," ibid., p. 46.

74. "Peace without Appeasement," *New Republic,* 18 December 1950, p. 2.

75. "The Life Story of a Dead Marine," *Life,* 18 December 1950, p. 31; see also "The Face of Mars," p. 18.

76. "The Congress: 'I Never Felt Worse,'" *Time,* 18 December 1950, p. 20.

77. Boykin to Souers, 5 December 1950, in Truman Papers, Official File, Box 471, Folder 471-B: "Korean Emergency (Dec 1950–Mar 1951)," HSTL.

78. A drastically abridged account written by Philip Jessup is in *FRUS, 1950,* 7:1242–49. To obtain the full flavor of the meeting one should consult the twenty-two-page minutes in the Student Research File "Korean War: Response to Communist China's Intervention," Box 1, Folder 2, HSTL (hereafter cited as NSC Minutes, 28 November 1950). See also the account in Undersecretary of the Navy Dan A. Kimball Memorandum, 28 November 1950, in Dan A. Kimball Papers, Box 2, Folder: "Diary Notes," HSTL.

79. NSC Minutes, 28 November 1950, pp. 4–5.

80. Ibid., p. 9.

81. Ibid., p. 9.

82. Ibid., pp. 12, 15.

83. Ibid., pp. 16–17.

84. Minutes of the Cabinet Meeting, 4:00 P.M., 28 November 1950, in Student Research File (Korean War: Response to Communist China's Intervention), Box 1, Folder 2.

85. Rosemary Foot, *The Wrong War: American Policy and the Dimensions of the Korean Conflict, 1950–1953* (Ithaca, NY: Cornell University Press, 1985), pp. 115, 117.

86. "The People: The Great Debate," *Time,* 18 December 1950, p. 21; see also "The Face of Mars," p. 18.

87. The quotations that follow are from "Sycamore Revisited," *Life,* 18 December 1950, pp. 28–29.

88. "World without Friends," *Time,* 25 December 1950, p. 9.

89. Lewis Bergman, "The Year in Review: Outstanding Trends in a Critical Period," *New York Times,* 31 December 1950.

90. "Agreeing To Disagree," *Time,* 18 December 1950, pp. 15–16.

91. Memorandum for General Bradley, Chairman of the Joint Chiefs of Staff, signed by Marshall, 29 November 1950, in Chairman's File, General Bradley, 1949–53, Box 1, Folder 091, Korea 1950, JCS Records, RG 218.

92. NIE-11, "Soviet Intentions in the Current Situation," 5 December 1950, p. 1, in National Intelligence Estimates Concerning the Soviet Union, 1950–61, CIA Records, RG 263.

93. NIE-15, "Probable Soviet Moves To Exploit the Present Situation," 11 December 1950, ibid. (the quotations that follow are on p. 1).

94. NIE-18, "The Probability of Soviet Employment of BW and CW [bacteriological and chemical warfare] in the Event of Attacks upon the U.S.," 10 January 1951, ibid.

95. Truman, *Years of Trial and Hope*, p. 476. Meeting of the President with Congressional Leaders in the Cabinet Room, 10:00 A.M., 13 December 1950, in Student Research File (Korean War: Response to Communist China's Intervention), Box 1, Folder 1, HSTL.

96. Radio and Television Report to the American People on the National Emergency, 15 December 1950, printed in *Public Papers of the Presidents of the United States: Harry S. Truman, January 1 to December 31, 1950* (Washington, D.C.: U.S. Government Printing Office, 1965), pp. 741–46; Proclamation 2914: Proclaiming the Existence of a National Emergency, 16 December 1950, ibid., pp. 746–47.

97. Memo from Presidential Naval Aide Robert Dennison to Presidential Press Secretary Matthew Connelly, 24 December 1950, in Dennison Papers, Box 3, Folder: "White House Message Traffic, 1950," HSTL.

98. "From JCS Personal for MacArthur," 29 December 1950, pp. 1, 2, in Geographic File, 1951–53, Box 14, Folder "CCS 381 Far East S.1," JCS Records, RG 218.

99. Ibid., pp. 3–4. Acheson's comment is in Memorandum of Conversation, by Mr. Lucius D. Battle, Special Assistant to the Secretary of State, 27 December 1950, in *FRUS, 1950*, 7:1601.

100. Clay Blair, *The Forgotten War: America in Korea, 1950–1953* (New York: Times Books, 1987), pp. 590–91.

101. By the end of 1950 Dean Rusk and perhaps others intuitively grasped the limited nature of the Korean War on *both* sides. If the U.S.–UN forces were to be limited in their actions, the Communist enemy had already demonstrated restraint. During a meeting on December 27 between Acheson, Jessup, Matthews, and Rusk, the assistant secretary for Far Eastern affairs said that the Chinese-Soviet air forces along the Manchurian border "could have dealt us a heavy blow by air attack during the [Hungnam] evacuation and that they did not do so." Rusk added that "the [Communist air] blow could have destroyed any possibility we had of defending Japan." Memorandum of Conversation, by Mr. Lucius D. Battle, 27 December 1950, in *FRUS, 1950*, 7:1603.

102. Bergman, "Outstanding Trends in a Critical Period"; "Survey Shows Letters to Editors Divide on Meeting Red Aggression," *New York Times*, 31 December 1950.

103. "Kankakee Knows What's Coming," *Life*, 1 January 1951, pp. 10–11.

104. Ibid., p. 10

105. Ibid.

Epilogue

1. Two excellent discussions of the bomb's effect on the children of the fifties are JoAnne Brown, "'*A* Is for Atom, *B* Is for Bomb': Civil Defense in American

Public Education, 1948–1963," *Journal of American History* 75, no. 1 (June 1988): 68–90; and Landon Y. Jones, *Great Expectations: America and the Baby Boom Generation* (New York: Ballantine Books, 1980), pp. 59–60.

2. Brown, "'*A* Is for Atom, *B* Is for Bomb,'" p. 80; Jones, *Great Expectations*, p. 59.

3. "'*A* Is for Atom, *B* Is for Bomb,'" p. 75; Jones, *Great Expectations*, p. 60.

4. "'*A* Is for Atom, *B* Is for Bomb,'" pp. 76, 83.

5. Ibid., p. 90.

6. Michael Barson, *"Better Dead Than Red!": A Nostalgic Look at the Golden Years of Russiaphobia, Red Baiting, and Other Commie Madness* (New York: Hyperion, 1992), n.p.

7. The views of the Hunters are discussed and quoted in Samuel Lubell, *The Future of American Politics*, 2d ed. rev. (Garden City, N.Y.: Doubleday Anchor Books, 1956), p. 166.

8. Herbert Agar, *The Price of Power: America since 1945* (Chicago: University of Chicago Press, 1957), p. 122.

9. Edward A. Suchman, Rose K. Goldsen, and Robin M. Williams, Jr., "Attitudes toward the Korean War," *Public Opinion Quarterly* 17, no. 2 (Summer 1953): 171–84 (the statistics are on pp. 173, 174; the quotations are on pp. 171, 183–84).

10. Lubell, *The Future of American Politics*, p. 261.

11. Ibid., p. 262.

12. Clark Clifford and Richard Holbrooke, *Counsel to the President: A Memoir* (New York: Random House, 1991), p. 290.

13. William L. Shirer, *Midcentury Journey: The Western World through Its Years of Conflict* (New York: Farrar, Straus & Young, 1952), pp. 271, 275–76.

14. Alexander Kendrick, *Prime Time: The Life of Edward R. Murrow* (New York: Avon Books, 1970), pp. 333–35.

15. Richard M. Fried, *Nightmare in Red: The McCarthy Era in Perspective* (New York: Oxford University Press, 1990), p. 60.

16. Jack Lait and Lee Mortimer, *Washington Confidential* (New York: Crown Publishers, 1951), pp. ix, 99–109. For indications of the book's popularity and sales, see "The Confidential Men," *Newsweek*, 23 June 1952, pp. 60–61. I have recently found copies in a dozen or more used bookstores from Seattle to Tucson to the East Coast.

17. Shirer, *Midcentury Journey*, p. 285 (Shirer's italics).

18. Ibid., p. 287.

19. Ibid., p. 296.

20. Chambers's dormant reputation has recently been revived, at least in intellectual circles, in a splendid new study by Sam Tanenhaus, *Whittaker Chambers: A Biography* (New York: Random House, 1997).

21. Whittaker Chambers, "I Was the Witness," *Saturday Evening Post*, 9 February 1952, pp. 17–19, 60, 62–63, 66, 68 (the quotations that follow are on pp. 17, 19, 60, 62).

22. McCarthy died in 1957 of a broken heart and a liver turned to sawdust

from a lifetime of steady boozing. But his followers never wavered in either their affection for the senator or their belief in his crusade. During the 1952 senatorial campaign, a *New York Times* reporter wrote that "many people in Wisconsin frankly say that they thought they were voting for Joe McCarthy against Joe Stalin—and they picked McCarthy." (See John B. Oakes, "Report on McCarthy and McCarthyism," *New York Times Magazine*, 2 November 1952, p. 26.) In 1958, soon after McCarthy's death, reporter Richard Rovere wrote a critical article about him for *Esquire* magazine. "Then the furies descended. I have half a file drawer full of suggestions that I walk into the Atlantic Ocean until my hat floats, that I ask God's forgiveness for my acts of desecration, that I buck for the next Stalin Prize, and so forth. . . . What impressed me was the volume of letters from terribly anguished men and women who would not stand idly by while McCarthy's name was dishonored. The letters were ugly, threatening, in many cases vile. Yet they bespoke a love for the man which, though it was doubtless a form of self-love, was not entirely without a power to be affecting." Richard H. Rovere, *Senator Joe McCarthy* (Cleveland: Meridian Books, 1960), pp. 236–37.

Just months after McCarthy's death, candy executive Robert Welch, "a man completely preoccupied with the Communist conspiracy he sees everywhere," founded the John Birch Society. According to Welch, the United States was already "50%–70% Communist-controlled." By 1964, the Anti-Defamation League had identified nearly a score of influential right-wing religious and political groups, lobbyists, and publicists who had joined Welch in saving the nation from falling to communists or their fellow travelers. Despite its diligent research, the League failed to extend its inquiries into such burgeoning anticommunist paramilitary groups as the Minutemen ("a gun-toting band of super patriots who make the John Birch Society look like a Cub Scout troop"), the Paul Revere Yeomen, and the Counter-Insurgency Council of Illinois. It also ignored the continuing influence of Billy James Hargis and a growing band of right-wing preachers who had joined him on the nation's airways. These crusaders for a Christian anticommunist America would provide Ronald Reagan with a critical measure of support in 1980.

The Anti-Defamation League findings were published in Arnold Forster and Benjamin R. Epstein, *Danger on the Right* (New York: Random House, 1964); the quotations about Welch are on pp. 12, 15. Further important supplementary information and evaluation of the mainstream radical Right groups was gathered in Daniel Bell, ed., *The Radical Right* (Garden City, N.Y.: Doubleday Anchor Books, 1964). The paramilitary groups were identified and discussed in James Ridgeway, "Don't Wait, Buy a Gun Now!" *New Republic* 150, no. 23 (6 June 1964):9–10; and in an unsigned article, "Waiting for Armaggedon," *Newsweek*, 26 April 1965, pp. 33–34. For Hargis's continuing influence as late as 1970, see Peter Schrag, "America's Other Radicals," *Harper's Magazine*, August 1970, reprinted in Robert Paul Wolff, ed., *Styles of Political Action in America* (New York: Random House, 1972), pp. 135–47. The essential role played by "thousands of conservative Christian ministers," including Pat Robertson, Jerry Falwell, and James Robison, in the 1980 campaign was emphasized by Reagan's chief ideologue in Richard A. Viguerie, *The New Right: We're Ready To Lead* (Falls Church, Va.: Viguerie Company, 1981), p. 6. Viguerie observed that together these thousand-odd ministers reached an estimated radio-TV audience of twenty-seven million daily.

23. Irving Howe, "Stevenson and the Intellectuals," *Dissent* 1, no. 1 (Winter 1954):12–21; idem, "The Problem of U.S. Power," ibid. 1, no. 3 (Summer 1954):211–20; Arthur M. Schlesinger, Jr., *The Vital Center: The Politics of Freedom* (Boston: Houghton Mifflin, Sentry Books, 1962; first published 1949), p. 213; H. Stuart Hughes, "Why We Had No Dreyfus Case," *American Scholar* 30, no. 4 (Autumn 1961):473–80.

24. Five representative books of the fifties are William H. Whyte, Jr., *The Organization Man* (Garden City, N.Y.: Doubleday Anchor Books, 1957); Vance Packard, *The Hidden Persuaders* (New York: David McKay, 1955); idem, *The Status Seekers: An Exploration of Class Behavior in America and the Hidden Barriers That Affect You, Your Community, Your Future* (New York: David McKay, 1959); Sloan Wilson, *The Man in the Gray Flannel Suit* (New York: Simon & Schuster, 1955); and Daniel Bell, *The End of Ideology: On the Exhaustion of Political Ideas in the Fifties*, rev. ed. (New York: Collier Books, 1962).

25. Agar, *The Price of Power*, p. 9.

26. James A. Michener, *The Bridges at Toko-ri* (New York: Bantam Books, 1954), pp. 28, 30, 33, 55.

27. U.S., Department of State, *Foreign Relations of the United States, 1952–1954*, 16 vols. (Washington, D.C.: U.S. Government Printing Office, 1979–87), 12:127.

28. Editorial Note, n.d., ibid., 13:360.

29. Pentagon and White House discussions of January 28, 1953, and March 24, 1953, ibid., pp. 361–63, 419–20.

30. Dulles's statement is reprinted in *America in Vietnam: A Documentary History*, ed. William Appleman Williams et al. (Garden City, N.Y.: Doubleday Anchor Books, 1985), p. 150.

31. Dulles's hatred of communism and communists literally consumed him at the end. Foreign Service Officer Cecil Lyon, who worked closely with Dulles in his last years, once told me that when the secretary was dying from cancer in 1959 he refused to enter the hospital but instead went off to Paris to battle the Reds a final time. At night Dulles would try to ease his terrible pains by lying on the cold bathroom floor of his hotel room for hours. But the next morning, spruce as always in his dark three-piece suit, he would be at the green baize table, body rigidly erect, characteristically whittling away with a pocket knife, and arguing with and baiting his antagonists.

32. John K. Jessup et al., *The National Purpose* (New York: Holt, Rinehart & Winston, 1960).

33. Quotations from MacLeish's essay, ibid., pp. 37–38, 45, 46, 48.

34. John F. Kennedy, that prudent, knowledgeable politician, knew otherwise. As the New Frontier began in 1961, two of the new president's ardent admirers

wrote that "loyalty procedures will remain approximately as they were" under Truman and Eisenhower. "No legislation will be repealed. Kennedy is not out to break lances in the interests of the lost causes of liberties. Most people branded in the past by unfair procedures will not be rehabilitated today by government security agencies. However, [current] government employees can feel reassured that they will be fairly treated and unreasonable use will not be made of security procedures. Careful screening will protect Kennedy from vulnerability on loyalty questions." James Tracy Crown and George P. Penty, *Kennedy in Power* (New York: Ballantine Books, 1961), p. 46.

35. Jessup et al., *The National Purpose*, pp. 83, 91, 92, 93.

36. Ibid., pp. 75, 78.

37. Ibid., pp. 24, 26–27, 34.

38. Rockefeller Brothers Fund, *Prospect for America: The Rockefeller Panel Reports* (Garden City, N.Y.: Doubleday, 1961), p. xxi.

39. U.S. Congress, Senate, Select Committee to Study Governmental Operations with Respect to Intelligence Activities, *Alleged Assassination Plots Involving Foreign Leaders: An Interim Report*, 94th Cong., 1st Sess., 1975.

40. Clifford, *Counsel to the President*, pp. 334, 379; National Broadcasting Corporation, "An NBC News White Paper: Vietnam Hindsight," 2 parts, broadcast 21–22 December 1971 (transcript provided by NBC News), pt. 1, sect. 2, pp. 10–11.

Bibliography

Manuscript Collections

Federal Records Center, Suitland, Md.
  U.S. Army. United Nations Command/Far East Command General Head-
  quarters, Military Intelligence Section General Staff. Army-AG Command
  Reports, 1949–54. Staff Section Reports, January–November 1950. Record
  Group 407.
MacArthur Memorial, Norfolk, Va.
  Papers of General Douglas MacArthur, Record Group 5. Records of Head-
  quarters, Supreme Commander for the Allied Powers (SCAP), 1946–1951.
OMS Correspondence.
National Archives, Washington, D.C.
  U.S. Central Intelligence Agency. Records of the Central Intelligence Agency.
  Estimates of the Office of Research Evaluation, 1946–1950. Record Group
  263.
  _____. Records of the Central Intelligence Agency. National Intelligence Esti-
  mates Concerning the Soviet Union, 1950–1961. Record Group 263.
National Archives, Military History Branch, Washington, D.C.
  U.S. Joint Chiefs of Staff. Records of the U.S. Joint Chiefs of Staff. Record
  Group 218.
Harry S. Truman Library, Independence, Mo.
  Papers of Dean Acheson
  Papers of Clark Clifford
  Papers of Robert L. Dennison
  Papers of George M. Elsey
  Papers of Dan A. Kimbal
  Papers of Felix Larkin
  Papers of Francis P. Matthews
  Papers of Frank Pace, Jr.
  Papers of George J. Richards
  Papers of John L. Sullivan
  Papers of Harry S. Truman
    Naval Aide File

Official File
President's Secretary's Files
Selected Records Relating to the Korean War, Defense Department
Selected Records Relating to the Korean War, State Department
SMOF: Matthew Connelly Files
Papers of James E. Webb
Student Research File (B File)

Oral History Collections

Harry S. Truman Library, Independence, Mo.
Dean Acheson
R. Gordon Arneson
Clark Clifford
George M. Elsey
Thomas K. Finletter
Averell Harriman
Kenneth Hechler
John Hickerson
U. Alexis Johnson
Walter Judd
Livingston Merchant
John Muccio
Frank Pace, Jr.
Harold Stassen
Stuart Symington

Published Materials

Acheson, Dean. *Present at the Creation: My Years in the State Department.* New York: Signet Books, 1970.
_____. *The Korean War.* New York: Norton, 1971.
Agar, Herbert. *The Price of Power: America since 1945.* Chicago: University of Chicago Press, 1957.
Alperovitz, Gar. *Atomic Diplomacy, Hiroshima and Potsdam: The Use of the Atomic Bomb and the American Confrontation with Soviet Power.* New York: Vintage Books, 1967.
Ambrose, Stephen E. *Rise to Globalism: American Foreign Policy since 1938.* Baltimore: Penguin Books, 1971.
_____. *Nixon: The Education of a Politician, 1913–1962.* New York: Simon and Schuster, 1987.

"American Education and International Tensions." *NEA Journal* 38, no. 6 (September 1949):457.

Anderson, Orvil A. "Air Warfare and Morality." *Air University Quarterly Review* 3, no. 3 (Winter 1949), unpaginated typescript reprint in Harry S. Truman Library, Independence, Mo.

Appleman, Roy E. *South to the Naktong, North to the Yalu (June–November 1950).* Washington, D.C.: Department of the Army, Office of the Chief of Military History, 1960.

Arneson, R. Gordon. "The H-Bomb Decision." *Foreign Service Journal,* June 1969, pp. 24–27, 43.

Barone, Michael. *Our Country: The Shaping of America from Roosevelt to Reagan.* New York: Free Press, 1990.

Barson, Michael. *"Better Dead Than Red": A Nostalgic Look at the Golden Years of Russiaphobia, Red-Baiting, and Other Commie Madness.* New York: Hyperion, 1992.

Barth, Alan. *The Loyalty of Free Men.* New York: Pocket Books, 1951.

Bell, Daniel. *The End of Ideology: On the Exhaustion of Political Ideas in the Fifties.* Rev. ed. New York: Collier Books, 1962.

_____, ed. *The Radical Right.* Garden City, N.Y.: Doubleday Anchor Books, 1964.

Bennett, David H. *The Party of Fear: The American Far Right from Nativism to the Militia Movement.* Rev. ed. New York: Random House, 1995.

Bernstein, Barton J. "The Quest for Security: American Foreign Policy and International Control of Atomic Energy, 1942–1946." *Journal of American History* 60, no. 4 (March 1974): 1003–44.

_____, ed. *Towards a New Past: Dissenting Essays in American History.* New York: Vintage Books, 1969.

Bernstein, Barton J., and Allen J. Matusow, eds. *The Truman Administration: A Documentary History.* New York: Harper & Row, 1966.

Birnbaum, Jeffrey H. "The Pat Solution." *Time,* 6 November 1995, pp. 24–30.

Blackett, P. M. S. *Atomic Weapons and East-West Relations.* Cambridge, England: Cambridge University Press, 1956.

Blair, Clay. *The Forgotten War: America in Korea, 1950–1953.* New York: Times Books, 1987.

Bodard, Lucien. *The Quicksand War: Prelude to Vietnam.* Translated by Patrick O'Brian. Boston: Little, Brown, 1965.

Bohlen, Charles E. *Witness to History, 1929–1969.* New York: Norton, 1973.

Boyer, Paul. *By the Bomb's Early Light.* New York: Pantheon Books, 1985.

Brinkley, Alan. "A Swaggering Tradition." *Newsweek,* 4 March 1996, pp. 28–29.

Brinkley, David. *Washington Goes to War.* New York: Ballantine Books, 1988.

Brown, JoAnne. "'A Is for *Atom,* B Is for *Bomb*': Civil Defense in American Public Education, 1948–1963." *Journal of American History* 75, no. 1 (June 1988):68–90.

Buchanan, Pat. "The Election Is about Who We Are." *Vital Speeches of the Day* 58, no. 23 (15 September 1992):712–15.

Buckley, William F., Jr., and Brent Bozell. *McCarthy and His Enemies: The Record and Its Meaning.* Chicago: Henry Regnery, 1954.

Budenz, Louis F. *The Techniques of Communism.* Chicago: Henry Regnery, 1954.

Bulletin of the Atomic Scientists. Vols. 5–6 (August 1949–December 1950).

Buzzanco, Robert. "Prologue to Tragedy: U.S. Military Opposition to Intervention in Vietnam, 1950–1954." *Diplomatic History* 17, no. 2 (Spring 1993):201–22.

Canada. Royal Commission. *The Report of the Royal Commission Appointed under Order in Council P.C. 411 of February 5, 1946, To Investigate the Facts Relating to and the Circumstances Surrounding the Communication, by Public Officials and Other Persons in Positions of Trust of Secret and Confidential Information to Agents of a Foreign Power, June 27, 1946.* Ottawa: Controller of Stationery, 1946.

Carlson, John Roy [Arthur Derounian]. *Under Cover: My Four Years in the Nazi Underworld of America—The Amazing Revelations of How Axis Agents and Our Enemies Within Are Now Plotting To Destroy the United States.* New York: Dutton, 1943.

Carroll, Raymond G. "Aliens in Subversive Activities." *Saturday Evening Post,* 22 February 1936, pp. 10–11, 84–90.

Caute, David. *The Great Fear: The Anti-Communist Purge under Truman and Eisenhower.* New York: Simon and Schuster, 1978.

Chambers, Whittaker. "I Was the Witness." *Saturday Evening Post,* 9 February 1952, pp. 17–19, 60, 62–63, 66, 68.

Chester, Lewis, Godfrey Hodgson, and Bruce Page. *An American Melodrama: The Presidential Campaign of 1968.* New York: Dell Books, 1969.

Chicago Tribune. September 1949—December 1950.

"The Christmas Covenant." *U.S. News and World Report,* 19 December 1994, pp. 62–71.

Clifford, Clark, and Richard Holbrooke. *Counsel to the President: A Memoir.* New York: Random House, 1991.

Cohen, Warren I. *America's Response to China.* 3d ed. New York: Columbia University Press, 1990.

Cold War International History Project Bulletin. Issues 1–7 (Spring 1992–Winter 1995/1996).

Colliers. January 1949–December 1950.

Collins, J. Lawton. *War in Peacetime: The History and Lessons of Korea.* Boston: Houghton Mifflin, 1969.

Conant, James Bryant. "Freedom and the University." *NEA Journal* 39, no. 8 (November 1950):581–82.

"The Confidential Men." *Newsweek,* 23 June 1952, pp. 60–61.

"Congress and Un-American Activities," *Congressional Digest* 18, no. 11 (November 1939):259–61.

Corn, David. "Playing with Fire." *Nation* 260, no. 19 (15 May 1995):657–58.

Crosette, Barbara. "Study Says Soviets Held 125 Lost by U.S. in Korea." *New York Times,* 24 June 1992.

Crown, James Tracy, and George P. Penty. *Kennedy in Power*. New York: Ballantine Books, 1961.

Cumings, Bruce. *The Origins of the Korean War*. 2 vols. Princeton, N.J.: Princeton University Press, 1981, 1991.

_____, ed. *Child of Conflict: The Korean-American Relationship, 1943–1953*. Seattle: University of Washington Press, 1983.

Dionne, E. J., Jr. *Why Americans Hate Politics*. New York: Simon & Schuster, 1992.

Djilas, Milovan. *Conversations with Stalin*. Translated by Michael B. Petrovich. New York: Harcourt, Brace & World, 1962.

Dobbs, Michael. "How Soviets Stole U.S. Atom Secrets." *Washington Post*, 4 October 1992.

Donner, Frank J. *The Un-Americans*. New York: Ballantine Books, 1961.

Donovan, Robert J. *Eisenhower: The Inside Story*. New York: Harper & Brothers, 1956.

Douglas, Geoffrey. *Class: The Wreckage of an American Family*. New York: Warner Books, 1994.

Duiker, William J. *The Communist Road to Power in Vietnam*. Boulder, Colo.: Westview Press, 1981.

Economist. October 1949–December 1950.

Editorial, "Strengthening American Democracy." *Educational Research Bulletin* 27, no. 5 (12 May 1948):136–37, 140.

Eisenhower, Dwight D. *The White House Years*. 2 vols. Vol. 1: *Mandate for Change, 1953–1956*. New York: Signet Books, 1965.

Fairlie, Henry. *The Kennedy Promise: The Politics of Expectation*. New York: Dell Publishing, 1974.

Farley, Christopher John. "Patriot Games." *Time*, 19 December 1994, pp. 48–49.

Farrar-Hockley, Anthony. *The British Part in the Korean War*. Vol. 1, *A Distant Obligation*. London: Her Majesty's Stationery Office, 1990.

Fehrenbach, T. R. *This Kind of War: A Study in Unpreparedness*. New York: Pocket Books, 1964.

Ferrell, Robert H. *Harry S. Truman and the Modern American Presidency*. Boston: Little, Brown, 1983.

_____, ed. *Dear Bess: The Letters from Harry to Bess Truman, 1910–1959*. New York: Norton, 1983.

Flynn, Kevin, and Gary Gerhardt. *The Silent Brotherhood: The Chilling Inside Story of America's Violent Anti-Government Militia Movement*. New York: Signet Books, 1995; first published 1990.

Foot, Rosemary. *The Wrong War: American Policy and the Dimensions of the Korean Conflict, 1950–1953*. Ithaca, N.Y.: Cornell University Press, 1985.

_____. "Anglo-American Relations in the Korean Crisis: The British Effort to Avert an Expanded War, December 1950–January 1951." *Diplomatic History* 10, no. 1 (Winter 1986): 43–58.

_____. *A Substitute for Victory: The Politics of Peacemaking at the Korean Armistice Talks*. Ithaca, N.Y.: Cornell University Press, 1992.

Forster, Arnold, and Benjamin R. Epstein. *Danger on the Right.* New York: Random House, 1964.

Fortnightly. September 1949–December 1950.

Fortune. January–December 1950.

Frank, Pat. *Hold Back the Night.* Philadelphia: Lippincott, 1952.

Fredrickson, George M. *The Inner Civil War: Northern Intellectuals and the Crisis of the Union.* New York: Harper & Row, 1965.

Freeland, Richard M. *The Truman Doctrine and the Origins of McCarthyism: Foreign Policy, Domestic Politics, and Internal Security, 1946–1948.* New York: Knopf, 1972.

Fried, Richard M. *Nightmare in Red: The McCarthy Era in Perspective.* New York: Oxford University Press, 1990.

Fülöp-Miller, René. *Leaders, Dreamers, and Rebels: An Account of the Great Mass-Movements of History and of the Wish-Dreams That Inspired Them.* Translated by Eden Paul and Cedar Paul. New York: Viking Press, 1935.

Gabler, Neal. *Winchell: Gossip, Power and the Cult of Celebrity.* New York: Knopf, 1994.

Gaddis, John Lewis. "Presidential Address: The Tragedy of Cold War History." *Diplomatic History* 17, no. 1 (Winter 1993):1–16.

Galbraith, John Kenneth. *American Capitalism: The Concept of Countervailing Power.* Boston: Houghton Mifflin, 1956.

Gardner, Lloyd C. *Architects of Illusion: Men and Ideas in American Foreign Policy, 1941–1949.* Chicago: Quadrangle Books, 1970.

Garrett, Garet. *The People's Pottage.* Boston: Western Islands, 1965.

Garrow, David J. *The FBI and Martin Luther King, Jr.* New York: Penguin Books, 1983.

Garver, John W. "Little Chance: Revolutions and Ideologies." *Diplomatic History* 21, no. 1 (Winter 1997):87–94.

Goldman, Eric F. *Rendezvous with Destiny: A History of Modern American Reform.* New York: Vintage Books, 1958.

_____. *The Crucial Decade—and After: America, 1945–1960.* New York: Vintage Books, 1961.

Goldwater, Barry M. *The Conscience of a Conservative.* New York: McFadden Books, 1961.

Goncharov, Sergei N., John W. Lewis, and Xue Litai. *Uncertain Partners: Stalin, Mao, and the Korean War.* Stanford, Calif.: Stanford University Press, 1993.

Goodwin, Richard N. *Remembering America: A Voice from the Sixties.* Boston: Little, Brown, 1988.

Goulden, Joseph C. *The Best Years, 1945–1950.* New York: Atheneum, 1976.

Graham, Otis L., Jr. *An Encore for Reform: The Old Progressives and the New Deal.* New York: Oxford University Press, 1967.

Grandview (Washington) *Herald.* January–December 1950.

Griffith, Robert, and Athan Theoharis, eds. *The Spectre: Original Essays on the Cold War and the Origins of McCarthyism.* New York: Franklin Watts, 1974.

Gunther, John. *Inside U.S.A.* New York: Harper & Brothers, 1947.

Haldeman, H. R. *The Haldeman Diaries: Inside the Nixon White House.* New York: Berkley Books, 1995.

Hall, George H. "The Sinister Alliance between McCarthy and Taft." *St. Louis Post-Dispatch,* 18 February 1951.

Hamby, Alonzo L. *Man of the People: A Life of Harry S. Truman.* New York: Oxford University Press, 1995.

Hargis, Billy James. *Why I Fight for a Christian America.* Nashville, Tenn.: Thomas Nelson, 1974.

Harper's Magazine. January–December 1950.

Hastings, Max. *The Korean War.* New York: Simon & Schuster, 1987.

Hechler, Ken. *Working with Truman: A Personal Memoir of the White House Years.* New York: Putnam's, 1982.

Heinl, Robert Debs, Jr. *Victory at High Tide: The Inchon-Seoul Campaign.* Philadelphia: Lippincott, 1968.

Hellman, Lillian. *Scoundrel Time.* New York: Bantam Books, 1977.

Herken, Gregg. *Counsels of War.* Rev. ed. New York: Oxford University Press, 1987.

Hewlett, Richard G., and Oscar E. Anderson, Jr. *The New World, 1939/1946.* University Park, Pa.: Pennsylvania State University Press, 1962.

Hewlett, Richard G., and Francis Duncan. *Atomic Shield, 1947– 1952.* Washington, D.C.: U.S. Atomic Energy Commission, 1972.

Hofstadter, Richard. *The Age of Reform: From Bryan to F.D.R.* New York: Vintage Books, 1960.

_____. *The Paranoid Style in American Politics and Other Essays.* New York: Vintage Books, 1967.

Holloway, David. *Stalin and the Bomb: The Soviet Union and Atomic Energy, 1939–1956.* New Haven, Conn.: Yale University Press, 1994.

Holmes, Stephen A. "Hearings Opened on Korean M.I.A.'s." *New York Times,* 11 November 1992.

Holmstedt, Raleigh W. "Problems in School Administration." *Bulletin of the School of Education Indiana University* 26, no. 1 (January 1950):1–63.

Horowitz, David. *The Free World Colossus: A Critique of American Foreign Policy in the Cold War.* New York: Hill & Wang, 1965.

Howe, Irving. "Stevenson and the Intellectuals." *Dissent* 1, no. 1 (Winter 1954):12–21.

_____. "The Problem of U.S. Power," *Dissent* 1, no. 3 (Summer 1954):211–20.

Hughes, H. Stuart. "Why We Had No Dreyfus Case." *American Scholar* 30, no. 4 (Fall 1961):473–80.

Huston, John. *An Open Book.* New York: Knopf, 1980.

Hutton, Graham. *Midwest at Noon.* Chicago: University of Chicago Press, 1946.

Isaacson, Walter, and Evan Thomas. *The Wise Men: Six Friends and the World They Made.* London: Faber & Faber, 1986.

Jacoby, Sanford M. "Employees and the Welfare State: The Role of Marion B. Folsom." *Journal of American History* 80, no. 2 (September 1993):525–56.

James, D. Clayton. *The Years of MacArthur.* 3 vols. Boston: Houghton Mifflin, 1970–85. Vol. 3, *Triumph and Disaster, 1945–1964.*

Jervis, Robert. *The Meaning of the Nuclear Revolution: Statecraft and the Prospect of Armageddon.* Ithaca, N.Y.: Cornell University Press, 1989.

Jessup, John K., Adlai Stevenson, Archibald MacLeish, David Sarnoff, Billy Graham, John W. Gardner, Clinton Rossiter, Albert Wohlstetter, James Reston, and Walter Lippmann. *The National Purpose.* New York: Holt, Rinehart and Winston, 1960.

Jessup, John K., ed. *The Ideas of Henry Luce.* New York: Atheneum, 1969.

Jian, Chen. "The Myth of America's 'Lost Chance' in China: A Chinese Perspective in Light of New Evidence." *Diplomatic History* 21, no. 1 (Winter 1997):77–86.

Johnson, Paul. *Modern Times: The World from the Twenties to the Eighties.* New York: Harper Colophon Books, 1983.

Jones, Landon Y. *Great Expectations: America and the Baby Boom Generation.* New York: Ballantine Books, 1980.

Joravsky, David. "Communism in Historical Perspective." *American Historical Review* 99, no. 3 (June 1994):837–57.

The Journals of David E. Lilienthal. 7 vols. New York: Harper & Row, 1964–83. Vol. 2, *The Atomic Energy Years, 1945–1950.*

Kahn, Albert. *High Treason: The Plot against the People.* Croton-on-the-Hudson, N.Y.: Hour Publishers, 1950.

Karig, Walter; Malcolm W. Cagle, and Frank A. Manson. *The War in Korea.* Battle Report Series, vol. 6. New York: Rinehart, 1952.

Kelley, Robert. "Ideology and Political Culture from Jefferson to Nixon." *American Historical Review* 82, no. 3 (June 1977):531–62.

Kendrick, Alexander. *Prime Time: The Life of Edward R. Murrow.* New York: Avon Books, 1970.

Kennan, George F. *American Diplomacy, 1900–1950.* New York: Mentor Books, 1952.

––––––. *Memoirs (1925–1950).* New York: Bantam Books, 1969; first published 1967.

Kirkland, E. C., ed. *Andrew Carnegie: The Gospel of Wealth and Other Timely Essays.* Cambridge, Mass.: Harvard University Press, 1962.

Kitchell, Mark, director and producer. *Berkeley in the Sixties.* 16 mm, 152 min. Documentary film, 1990.

Kolko, Gabriel. *The Triumph of Conservatism: A Reinterpretation of American History, 1900–1916.* Chicago: Quadrangle Books, 1967; first published 1963.

––––––. *The Politics of War: The World and United States Foreign Policy, 1943–1945.* New York: Harper & Row, 1968.

Kolko, Joyce, and Gabriel Kolko. *The Limits of Power: The World and United States Foreign Policy, 1945–1954.* New York: Harper & Row, 1972.

Lacey, Michael J., ed. *The Truman Presidency.* Cambridge: Cambridge University Press, 1989.

LaFeber, Walter. *America, Russia and the Cold War, 1945–1971.* New York: Wiley, 1972.

_____. *Inevitable Revolutions: The United States and Central America.* New York: Norton, 1984.

Lait, Jack, and Lee Mortimer. *Washington Confidential.* New York: Crown Publishers, 1951.

Landis, Mark. *Joseph McCarthy: The Politics of Chaos.* Selingrove, Pa.: Susquehanna University Press, 1987.

Lasch, Christopher. *The Agony of the American Left.* New York: Vintage Books, 1969.

Lashmar, Paul. *Spy Flights of the Cold War.* Annapolis, Md.: Naval Institute Press, 1996.

Latham, Earl, ed. *The Meaning of McCarthyism.* Boston: D. C. Heath, 1965.

Laurence, William L. *The Hell Bomb.* New York: Knopf, 1951.

Lears, T. J. Jackson. "The Concept of Cultural Hegemony: Problems and Possibilities." *American Historical Review* 90, no. 3 (June 1985):567–93.

Leffler, Melvyn P. "The American Conception of National Security and the Beginnings of the Cold War." *American Historical Review* 89, no. 2 (April 1984):346–81.

_____. *A Preponderance of Power: National Security, the Truman Administration and the Cold War.* Stanford, Calif.: Stanford University Press, 1992.

_____. "Presidential Address: New Approaches, Old Interpretations, and Prospective Reconfigurations." *Diplomatic History* 19, no. 2 (Spring 1995):173–96.

Leuchtenburg, William E. *The Perils of Prosperity.* Chicago: University of Chicago Press, 1958.

_____. *Franklin D. Roosevelt and the New Deal, 1932–1940.* New York: Harper & Row, 1963.

Levin, Murray B. *Political Hysteria in America: The Democratic Capacity for Repression.* New York: Basic Books, 1971.

Life. October 1948–January 1951.

Lifton, Robert Jay. *History and Human Survival: Essays on the Young and Old, Survivors and the Dead, Peace and War, and on Contemporary Psychohistory.* New York: Vintage Books, 1971.

Limbaugh, Rush H., III. *The Way Things Ought to Be.* New York: Pocket Books, 1992.

_____. *See, I Told You So.* Thorndike, Me.: G. K. Hall, 1994.

Linnington, Elizabeth. *Come to Think of It.* Boston: Western Islands, 1965.

Lippmann, Walter. *The Cold War: A Study in U.S. Foreign Policy.* New York: Harper & Brothers, 1947.

Lipset, Seymour Martin. *Political Man: The Social Bases of Politics.* Garden City, N.Y.: Doubleday Anchor Books, 1963.

Long, Huey P. *Every Man a King: The Autobiography of Huey P. Long.* Chicago: Quadrangle Books, 1964.

Lubell, Samuel. *The Future of American Politics.* 2d ed. rev. Garden City, N.Y.: Doubleday Anchor Books, 1956.

_____. *The Future of American Politics.* 3d ed. rev. New York: Harper & Row, 1965.

Luce, Henry R. "China: To the Mountains." *Life,* 30 June 1941, pp. 82–96.

Lynd, Robert S., and Lynd, Helen Merrell. *Middletown in Transition: A Study in Cultural Conflicts.* New York: Harcourt, Brace and World, 1937.

Lyons, Eugene. *Assignment in Utopia.* New York: Harcourt, Brace, 1937.

_____. *The Red Decade: The Stalinist Penetration of America.* Indianapolis: Bobbs-Merrill, 1941.

McCarthy, Joseph. *America's Retreat from Victory: The Story of George Catlett Marshall.* Boston: Western Islands, 1965; first published 1951.

McCullough, David. *Truman.* New York: Simon & Schuster, 1992.

McLean, David. "American Nationalism: The China Myth and the Truman Doctrine: The Question of Accommodation with Peking." *Diplomatic History* 10, no. 1 (Winter 1986):25–42.

McNamara, Robert S., with Brian VanDeMark. *In Retrospect: The Tragedy and Lessons of Vietnam.* New York: Vintage Books, 1996.

Manchester, William. *The Glory and the Dream: A Narrative History of America, 1932–1972.* 2 vols. Boston: Little, Brown, 1973, 1974.

_____. *American Caesar.* New York: Dell Books, 1978.

Marshall, S. L. A. *The River and the Gauntlet: Defeat of the Eighth Army by the Chinese Communist Forces, November, 1950, in the Battle of the Chongchon River, Korea.* New York: Time, 1962; first published 1953.

Matray, James I. "Truman's Plan for Victory: National Self-Determination and the Thirty-Eighth Parallel Decision in Korea." *Journal of American History* 66, no. 2 (September 1979):314–33.

May, Elaine Tyler. *Homeward Bound: American Families in the Cold War Era.* New York: Basic Books, 1988.

_____. "Commentary: Ideology and Foreign Policy: Culture and Gender in Diplomatic History." *Diplomatic History* 18, no. 1 (Winter 1994):71–78.

Mearsheimer, John J. "Why We Will Soon Miss the Cold War." *Atlantic,* August 1990, pp. 35–50.

Melby, John F. "Vietnam—1950." *Diplomatic History* 6, no. 1 (Winter 1982):97–109.

"Men as Devil-Gods." *Christian Century,* 8 February 1950, pp. 167–69.

Meyers, Marvin. *The Jacksonian Persuasion: Politics & Belief.* New York: Vintage Books, 1960.

Michener, James A. *The Bridges at Toko-ri.* New York: Bantam Books, 1954.

Miller, John C. *Crisis in Freedom: The Alien and Sedition Acts.* Boston: Little, Brown, 1951.

Miller, Merle. *Plain Speaking: An Oral Biography of Harry S. Truman.* New York: Berkley Books, 1974.

Milligan, Robert H. *The Jungle Folk of Africa.* New York: Fleming H. Revell Company, 1908.

Mills, C. Wright. *The Power Elite*. New York: Oxford University Press, 1956.

Morrow, Lance. "Pat's School Days with 'the Pope's Marines.'" *Time*, 26 February 1996, p. 35.

Moss, Norman. *Men Who Play God: The Story of the H-Bomb and How the World Came To Live with It*. New York: Harper & Row, 1968.

Mufson, Steven. "Gingrich Tells China: 'We'd Defend Taiwan.'" *International Herald Tribune* (Hong Kong edition), 31 March 1997.

Murray, Robert K. *Red Scare: A Study of National Hysteria, 1919– 1920*. New York: McGraw-Hill, 1964; first published 1955.

National Broadcasting Corporation. "An NBC News White Paper: Vietnam Hindsight." 2 parts. Broadcast 21–22 December 1971. Transcript provided by NBC News.

National Republic. 1925–37.

National Review. 1955–63.

Neali, Patricia. *China Images in the Life and Times of Henry Luce*. Savage, Md.: Rowman & Littlefield, 1990.

Neustadt, Richard E. *Presidential Power: The Politics of Leadership*. New York: Signet Books, 1964.

Newhouse, John. *War and Peace in the Nuclear Age*. New York: Knopf, 1989.

New Republic. January–December 1950.

Newsweek. November 1948–December 1950.

New York Times. September 1949–December 1950.

New York Times Magazine. January–December 1950.

Nichols, Roy Franklin. *The Disruption of American Democracy*. New York: Macmillan, 1948.

Nixon, Richard. *Six Crises*. Garden City, N.Y.: Doubleday, 1962.

_____. *In the Arena: A Memoir of Victory, Defeat, and Renewal*. New York: Simon & Schuster, 1990.

Noonan, Peggy. *What I Saw at the Revolution: A Political Life in the Reagan Era*. New York: Random House, 1990.

Oakes, John B. "Report on McCarthy and McCarthyism." *New York Times Magazine*, 2 November 1952, pp. 12, 26, 28, 30.

O'Brien, Michael. *McCarthyism in Wisconsin*. Columbia: University of Missouri Press, 1980.

O'Keefe, Sean. "A World Lit by Lightning." *Naval Institute Proceedings* 121, no. 1 (January 1995):28–31.

Orth, Maureen. "Arianna's Virtual Candidate." *Vanity Fair*, November 1994, pp. 160–64, 194–200.

Oshinsky, David M. *A Conspiracy So Immense: The World of Joe McCarthy*. New York: Free Press, 1983.

Packard, Vance. *The Hidden Persuaders*. New York: David McKay, 1955.

_____. *The Status Seekers: An Exploration of Class Behavior in America and the Hidden Barriers That Affect You, Your Community, Your Future*. New York: David McKay, 1959.

Paige, Glenn D. *The Korean Decision, June 24–30, 1950.* New York: Free Press, 1968.

Parmet, Herbert S. *JFK: The Presidency of John F. Kennedy.* New York: Dial Press, 1983.

Paterson, Thomas G. *Soviet-American Confrontation: Postwar Reconstruction and the Origins of the Cold War.* Baltimore: Johns Hopkins Press, 1973.

———. Introduction to "A Round Table: Explaining the History of American Foreign Relations." *Journal of American History* 77, no. 1 (June 1990):93–180.

Patterson, James T. *Grand Expectations: The United States, 1945–1974.* New York: Oxford University Press, 1996.

Petersen, William, ed. *American Social Patterns: Studies of Race Relations, Popular Heroes, Voting, Union Democracy, and Government Bureaucracy.* Garden City, N.Y.: Doubleday Anchor Books, 1956.

Pfau, Richard. *No Sacrifice Too Great: The Life of Lewis Strauss.* Charlottesville: University Press of Virginia, 1984.

Phillips, Cabell. *The Truman Presidency: The History of a Triumphant Succession.* Baltimore: Pelican Books, 1969; first published 1966.

Poen, Monte M., ed. *Letters Home by Harry Truman.* New York: Putnam's, 1984.

Pollack, Norman, ed. *The Populist Mind.* Indianapolis: Bobbs-Merrill, 1967.

Portland Oregonian. January–December 1950.

Powers, Richard Gid. *Secrecy and Power: The Life of J. Edgar Hoover.* New York: Free Press, 1987.

———. *Not Without Honor: The History of American Anticommunism.* New York: Free Press, 1995.

Powers, Thomas. *Diana: The Making of a Terrorist.* New York: Bantam Books, 1971.

Preston, William, Jr. *Aliens and Dissenters: Federal Suppression of Radicals, 1903–1933.* New York: Harper Torchbooks, 1966.

Public Opinion Quarterly. 1939, 1946–53.

Public Papers of the Presidents of the United States: Harry S. Truman, January 1 to December 31, 1950. Washington, D.C.: U.S. Government Printing Office, 1965.

"Radicals: Waiting for Armageddon." *Newsweek,* 26 April 1965, pp. 33–34.

Rauch, Basil, ed. *The Roosevelt Reader: Selected Speeches, Messages, Press Conferences, and Letters of Franklin D. Roosevelt.* New York: Holt, Rinehart & Winston, 1957.

Rees, David. *Korea: The Limited War.* Baltimore: Penguin Books, 1970.

Reeves, Richard. "1954." *American Heritage,* December 1994, pp. 30–41.

Reeves, Thomas C., ed. *McCarthyism.* Huntington, N.Y.: Robert E. Kreiger, 1978.

Rhodes, Richard. *Dark Sun: The Making of the Hydrogen Bomb.* New York: Simon & Schuster, 1995.

Ridgeway, James. "Don't Wait, Buy a Gun Now!" *New Republic,* 6 June 1964, pp. 9–10.

Ridgway, Matthew B. *The Korean War.* New York: Popular Library, 1967.

Robertson, Pat. *The New World Order.* N.p.: Successful Living Edition, 1991.

Rockefeller Brothers Fund. *Prospect for America: The Rockefeller Panel Reports.* Garden City, N.Y.: Doubleday, 1961.

Rogin, Michael Paul. *The Intellectuals and McCarthy: The Radical Specter.* Cambridge, Mass.: M.I.T. Press, 1967.

Rose, Lisle A. *After Yalta: America and the Origins of the Cold War.* New York: Scribner's, 1973.

Rosenberg, David Alan. "American Atomic Strategy and the Hydrogen Bomb Decision." *Journal of American History* 66, no. 1 (June 1979):62–87.

Rosenberg, Emily S. *Spreading the American Dream: American Economic and Cultural Expansion, 1890–1945.* New York: Hill & Wang, 1982.

Rosenberg, Ron. "Kim Philby and the Age of Paranoia." *New York Times Magazine,* 10 July 1994, pp. 29–37, 50, 53–54.

Rovere, Richard H. *Senator Joe McCarthy.* Cleveland: Meridian Books, 1960.

Samuelson, Robert. "The American Dream Unraveled." *Newsweek,* 21 March 1992, pp. 32–35.

Saturday Evening Post. January–December 1950.

Schaller, Michael. "Securing the Great Crescent: Occupied Japan and the Origins of Containment in Southeast Asia." *Journal of American History* 69, no. 2 (September 1982):392–414.

Schecter, Jerrold L., and Vyacheslav V. Luchkov, trans. and eds. *Khrushchev Remembers: The Glasnost Tapes.* Boston: Little, Brown, 1990.

Schlafly, Phyllis, and Chester Ward. *The Gravediggers.* Alton, Ill.: Pere Marquette Press, 1964.

_____. *Strike from Space: A Megadeath Mystery.* Alton, Ill.: Pere Marquette Press, 1965.

Schlesinger, Arthur M., Jr. *The Vital Center: The Politics of Freedom.* Boston: Houghton Mifflin, Sentry Books, 1962; first published 1949.

Schnabel, James F., and Watson, Robert J. *The Korean War, Part I.* The History of the Joint Chiefs of Staff, vol. 3. Washington, D.C.: Joint Chiefs of Staff, Joint Secretariat Historical Division, 1978.

Schwartz, Fred. *You Can Trust the Communists (To Be Communists).* Englewood Cliffs, N.J.: Prentice-Hall, 1960.

Scutts, Jerry. *Air War over Korea.* London: Arms & Armour Press, 1982.

Seager, Henry R., and Charles A. Gulick, Jr. *Trust and Corporation Problems.* New York: Harper & Brothers, 1929.

Seattle Post-Intelligencer. September 1993–August 1996.

Seattle Times. September 1949–December 1950, August 1994–May 1995.

Shaw, Irwin, screenwriter. *I Want You.* Hollywood, Calif.: Samuel Goldwyn Company, 1951.

Sheehan, Neil, Hedrick Smith, E. W. Kenworthy, and Fox Butterfield. *The Pentagon Papers as Published by the New York Times.* New York: Bantam Books, 1971.

Sherwood, Robert E. *Roosevelt and Hopkins: An Intimate History.* New York: Harper & Brothers, 1948.

Sheymov, Victor. *Tower of Secrets.* Annapolis, Md.: Naval Institute Press, 1993.

Shirer, William L. *Midcentury Journey: The Western World through Its Years of Conflict.* New York: Farrar, Straus and Young, 1952.

Smith, Geoffrey S. "Commentary: Security, Gender, and the Historical Process." *Diplomatic History* 18, no. 1 (Winter 1994):79–90.

Smith, Robert. *MacArthur in Korea*. New York: Simon & Schuster, 1982.

Smoot, Dan. *The Business End of Government*. Boston: Western Islands, 1973.

Spolansky, Jacob. *The Communist Trail in America*. New York: Macmillan, 1951.

Stone, I. F. *The Hidden History of the Korean War*. New York: Monthly Review Press, 1952.

Strauss, Lewis. *Men and Decisions*. Garden City, N.Y.: Doubleday, 1962.

Stueck, William. *The Korean War: An International History*. Princeton, N.J.: Princeton University Press, 1995.

Swanberg, W. A. *Luce and His Empire*. New York: Scribner's, 1972.

Tanenhaus, Sam. *Whittaker Chambers: A Biography*. New York: Random House, 1997.

Tawney, R. H. *Religion and the Rise of Capitalism*. New York: Mentor Books, 1948.

Terkel, Studs. *"The Good War": An Oral History of World War II*. New York: Ballantine Books, 1985.

Thelen, David, ed. "A Round Table: What Has Changed and Not Changed in American Historical Practice." *Journal of American History* 76, no. 2 (September 1989): 393–487.

Theoharis, Athan G., and John Stuart Cox. *The Boss: J. Edgar Hoover and the Great American Inquisition*. New York: Bantam Books, 1990.

Thompson, Hunter S. *Fear and Loathing: On the Campaign Trail, '72*. New York: Popular Library, 1973.

Time. January 1949–December 1950.

Toledano, Ralph de. *Spies, Dupes and Diplomats*. New Rochelle, N.Y.: Arlington House, 1967.

Truman, Harry S. *Memoirs*. 2 vols. New York: Signet Books, 1965; first published 1955–56. Vol. 2, *Years of Trial and Hope, 1946–1952*.

Truman, Margaret. *Harry S. Truman*. New York: Pocket Books, 1974.

Tuchman, Barbara W. *Stilwell and the American Experience in China*. New York: Bantam Books, 1971.

_____. *Notes from China*. New York: Collier Books, 1972.

Unger, Irwin. "The 'New Left' and American History: Some Recent Trends in United States Historiography." *American Historical Review* 97, no. 3 (July 1972):1237–63.

U.S. Congress. Senate. Committee on Foreign Relations. *Military Situation in the Far East, May 3–31, 1951*. 82d Cong., 1st Sess. Vol. 2, *15–31 May 1951*.

_____. *Executive Sessions of the Senate Foreign Relations Committee (Historical Series)*. Vol. 13, pt. 1, pt. 2. 87th Cong., 1st Sess., 1961 (made public 1984).

U.S. Congress. Senate. Select Committee to Study Governmental Operations with Respect to Intelligence Activities. *Alleged Assassination Plots Involving Foreign Leaders: An Interim Report*. 94th Cong., 1st Sess., 1975.

U.S. Department of State. *Postwar Foreign Policy Preparation, 1939–1945*. Washington, D.C.: U.S. Department of State, Office of Public Affairs, 1949.

_____. *The China White Paper, August 1949: Originally Issued as United States Rela-*

tions with China with Special Reference to the Period 1944–1949. 2 vols. Stanford, Calif.: Stanford University Press, 1967.

_____. *Foreign Relations of the United States, 1948.* 9 vols. Washington, D.C.: U.S. Government Printing Office, 1972–76.

_____. *Foreign Relations of the United States, 1949.* 9 vols. Washington, D.C.: U.S. Government Printing Office, 1974–76.

_____. *Foreign Relations of the United States, 1950.* 7 vols. Washington, D.C.: U.S. Government Printing Office, 1976–80.

_____. *Foreign Relations of the United States, 1952–1954.* 16 vols. Washington, D.C.: U.S. Government Printing Office, 1979–87.

U.S. News & World Report. January–December 1950.

U.S. Peace Corps. "Africa Region Integrated Planning & Budget System, FY95–97: Strategy Statement and Individual Goal Report." Typescript provided by Peace Corps, Washington, D.C., n.d.

Vandenberg, Arthur H., Jr., and Joe Alex Morris, eds., *The Private Papers of Senator Vandenberg.* Boston: Houghton Mifflin, 1952.

Viguerie, Richard A. *The New Right: We're Ready to Lead.* Falls Church, Va.: Viguerie Company, 1981.

Vital Speeches of the Day. January 1950–December 1951.

Warner, Michael, ed. *CIA Cold War Records: The CIA under Harry Truman.* Washington, D.C.: CIA History Staff, 1994.

Washington Post. September 1949–December 1950.

Weart, Spencer R. *Nuclear Fear: A History of Images.* Cambridge, Mass.: Harvard University Press, 1988.

Weber, Max. *The Protestant Ethic and the Spirit of Capitalism.* New York: Scribner's, 1958.

Weiss, Philip. "A Hoplophobe among the Gunnies." *New York Times Magazine,* 11 September 1994, pp. 64–71, 84–86, 100.

_____. "Outcasts Digging in for the Apocalypse." *Time,* 1 May 1995, pp. 48–49.

West, James. *Plainville, U.S.A.* New York: Columbia University Press, 1945.

"Where Does Goldwater Stand?" *U.S. News and World Report,* 2 September 1963, pp. 34–39.

White, Theodore H. *The Making of the President 1960.* New York: Pocket Books, 1961.

_____. *The Making of the President 1964.* New York: Atheneum, 1965.

_____. *In Search of History: A Personal Adventure.* New York: Warner Books, 1978.

_____. *America in Search of Itself: The Making of the President, 1956–1980.* New York: Harper & Row, 1982.

Whiting, Allen S. *China Crosses the Yalu: The Decision to Enter the Korean War.* Stanford, Calif.: Stanford University Press, 1960.

Whyte, William H., Jr. *The Organization Man.* Garden City, N.Y.: Doubleday Anchor Books, 1957.

Williams, Robert Chadwell. *Klaus Fuchs, Atom Spy.* Cambridge, Mass.: Harvard University Press, 1987.

Williams, T. Harry. *Huey Long.* New York: Bantam Books, 1970.

Williams, William Appleman. *The Tragedy of American Diplomacy.* New York: Delta Books, 1962.

―――. *The Contours of American History.* New York: Franklin Watts, 1972.

Williams, William Appleman, Thomas McCormick, Lloyd Gardner, and Walter LaFeber, eds. *America in Vietnam: A Documentary History.* Garden City, N.Y.: Anchor Books, 1985.

Wills, Garry. *Reagan's America: Innocents at Home.* Garden City, N.Y.: Doubleday, 1987.

Wilmot, Chester. *The Struggle for Europe.* London: Collins Clear-Type Press, 1952.

Wilson, Sloan. *The Man in the Gray Flannel Suit.* New York: Simon & Schuster, 1955.

Wolff, Robert Paul, ed. *Styles of Political Action in America.* New York: Random House, 1972.

Woodward, C. Vann. *The Strange Career of Jim Crow.* 2d rev. ed. New York: Oxford University Press, 1966.

Woody, Thomas. "Why Raise an Oath-Umbrella?" *School and Society* 74 (21 July 1951):33–38.

Yergin, Daniel. *Shattered Peace: The Origins of the Cold War and the National Security State.* Boston: Houghton Mifflin, 1977.

Young, Marilyn B. "Sights of an Unseen War." *Diplomatic History* 17, no. 3 (Summer 1993):495–502.

Index

❖ ❖ ❖ ❖ ❖ ❖ ❖